To the Jew First
or to the Jew at Last?

To the Jew First
or to the Jew at Last?

Romans 1:16c and Jewish Missional Priority
in Dialogue with Jews for Jesus

ANTOINE X. J. FRITZ

☙PICKWICK *Publications* · Eugene, Oregon

TO THE JEW FIRST OR TO THE JEW AT LAST?
Romans 1:16c and Jewish Missional Priority in Dialogue with Jews for Jesus

Copyright © 2013 Antoine X. J. Fritz. All rights reserved. Except for brief quotations in critical publications or reviews, no part of this book may be reproduced in any manner without prior written permission from the publisher. Write: Permissions, Wipf and Stock Publishers, 199 W. 8th Ave., Suite 3, Eugene, OR 97401.

New Revised Standard Version Bible, copyright 1989, Division of Christian Education of the National Council of the Churches of Christ in the United states of America. Used by permission. All rights reserved.

Pickwick Publications
An Imprint of Wipf and Stock Publishers
199 W. 8th Ave., Suite 3
Eugene, OR 97401

www.wipfandstock.com

ISBN 13: 978-1-62032-825-5

Cataloguing-in-Publication data:

Fritz, Antoine X. J.

    To the Jew first or to the Jew at last? : Romans 1:16c and Jewish missional priority in dialogue with Jews for Jesus / Antoine X. J. Fritz, with a foreword by Henri A. G. Blocher.

    xl + 238 pp. ; 23 cm. Includes bibliographical references and index.

    ISBN 13: 978-1-62032-825-5

    1. Bible. Romans—Criticism, interpretation. 2. Jews in the New Testament. 3. Missions to Jews. 4. Jews for Jesus. I. Blocher, Henri. II. Title.

BV2620 F748 2013

Manufactured in the U.S.A.

To my wife Stéphanie and my three daughters, Évane, Lou, and Rose

Οὕτως ἔσονται οἱ ἔσχατοι πρῶτοι καὶ οἱ πρῶτοι ἔσχατοι.
(MATTHEW 20:16)

Contents

Foreword | ix
Acknowledgments | xiii
Abbreviations and Acronyms | xv
Introduction | xxi

I   *Wirkungsgeschichte* | 1
II *Status Quaestionis* | 44
III *Propositio* | 98
IV *Heilsgeschichte* | 147

Conclusion | 186
Bibliography | 199
Author Index | 219
Biblical Reference Index | 227
Subject Index | 235

Foreword

EDWARD GIBBON DERIDED THE zeal of the ancient church theologians who were ready to split Christianity open for one small Greek letter, one *iota*: the *iota* by which the two words used for Jesus Christ's relationship to God the Father differ, *homoousios*, "of the same substance," and *homoiousios*, "of a similar substance." The sarcastic historian did not realize that this *iota* represented the distance of which the greater cannot be conceived, the distance between Creator and mere creature.

Antoine Fritz focussed his Master's dissertation (Maîtrise en théologie) not on one but on three Greek letters: on the second *nyn*, "now," which the prestigious *Sinaiticus* and *Vaticanus* manuscripts of the New Testament (but not most others) include in Romans 11:31: Israelites now refuse to obey the faith, while Gentiles believe in the gospel, in order that they, the Israelites, may receive mercy *now*! The small word may significantly influence the interpretation of the whole chapter, and one's vision of Israel's future. Does the Apostle only envision, under the figure of the grafting back of cut off branches into the Olive-Tree (the Israel of God), *only* the coming to faith in Jesus/*Yēšûa'* of individual Jews in every generation, or also a *massive* turning to the Messiah and Lord, a final *těšûvâ* of the people before the glorious Advent? If original (Antoine Fritz concluded the other way), the *nyn* rather favours the former reading . . .

His doctoral research has led Antoine Fritz to scrutinize again a single word in the Epistle to the Romans, a six-letter word in Romans 1:16 (twice as long as the previous one, what a progress!). The word *prōton*, "first," confers a priority to Jews, compared to Greeks (representing Gentiles): the gospel is the power of salvation to the Jew *first*. What does the inspired Apostle to the Gentiles mean? What is the import of the statement? Antoine Fritz attentively surveys the history of its interpretation and gathers exegetical considerations with manifest scholarly competence, as may be expected from a good doctoral dissertation (I admired the way it was supervised).

Foreword

The burden of his work, however, which falls into the province of "missiology," is the critical examination of the *missional* interpretation of the *prōton*. Antoine Fritz thus labels an interpretation and use of the phrase "to the Jew first" that surfaced in 1809, when the London Society for Promoting Christianity Amongst the Jews was founded (he did not find an earlier occurrence in available records). His typology distinguishes three main views. The first understanding of the phrase is trite, merely *historical*: the Jews heard the gospel first. The second one, which Antoine Fritz calls *historico-covenantal*, adds theological sense and value to the factual and chronological sequence: the Jews were heirs to the promises, they were the "natural" branches of the Olive-Tree, it was *fitting* that they should be evangelized first. The *missional* one draws consequences for mission even today. In every age of the church, in ours too, the witness of the gospel should target Jews *first*. The strategy is not left to human devising: God decided on it, and reveals it in Romans 1:16.

Stakes are not negligible. Though much ambiguity remains (must all evangelists start with Jews? When are they allowed to turn to Gentiles? What of countries where there are practically no Jews?), the missional understanding of the priority has been used as a goad to awaken and arouse interest in various forms of testimony to the Jewish people, as a lever to raise support for mission agencies, as a proposed criterion in the allocation of funds, of manpower, of prayer energy. The dynamic mission *Jews for Jesus*, with which Antoine Fritz happily ministered for several years in Paris, has given it front-line visibility. And one may give thanks for evident fruits.

I did not perceive the shadow of prejudice. Antoine Fritz welcomes, and sifts, and weighs, the arguments in favor of the "missional" interpretation. He generously quotes from representative spokesmen of Jews for Jesus, who also encouraged him in his research project, whose orientation was not hidden to their eyes. In the end, however, he must draw from the evidence a rather negative conclusion: he cannot retain, at least as far as Romans 1:16 is concerned, the rule of a priority imposed on the present church's evangelistic practice (and no other serious argument is found elsewhere).

What strikes me most is the combination: Antoine Fritz' love for the mission among Jews, his affectionate solidarity with the missionaries of Jews for Jesus, and, *yet*, his choice and defence of an interpretation that will not (I presume!) please his friends. This teaches us all a fine lesson: honor God's Word first! The priority of priorities! It has been a temptation of evangelical biblicism to let pragmatic considerations unduly bend the reading of Scripture! Antoine Fritz' concentration on a single word of the God-breathed text, and his effort to discern exactly its meaning, is a fine confession that we are not called to "please men," even well-intentioned, zealous, brothers

Foreword

and sisters. Our ardent desire for a new wave of blessing does not excuse sloppy exegesis—the kind of "help" Uzzah thought he should give to the Lord's sacred ark (2 Sam 6:6–7)! Thank you, Antoine, for this model attitude towards God's Word.

It is not only a matter of obedience, but of *faith* (one cannot separate). In the long run honoring the truth better serves the cause one cherishes. God's Word wields the greater efficacy. The historico-covenantal understanding of the Romans 1:16 *prōton* opens the way for a remarkable development, which Antoine Fritz sketches before our eyes. Using the parabolic material of the Gospels (and this is rather new to me), he relates to his theme the Lord's saying: "The first shall be last." The priority of the Jews may be linked, in the symmetry of God's design, to the great revival among them, *at last*. That perspective quickens our hope that those who were first, and were (partially) hardened, will be the last to join in numbers, as numberless multitudes, the Body of the Messiah, just before he comes! Let this hope, with the signs that it may *soon* happen, energise our witness, both to Jews and Gentiles, now!

Henri A. G. Blocher
Doyen honoraire de la Faculté Libre de Théologie Évangélique de Vaux-sur-Seine (France) and formerly Gunther Knoedler Professor of Theology, Wheaton College Graduate School of Biblical and Theological Studies.

Acknowledgments

THIS BOOK WOULD NOT have been possible without the sacrifice of my wife and my two older daughters who moved with me from France to the UK, four years ago, to allow me to undertake this study at the London School of Theology and then work on its publication. My gratitude goes toward them, as well as my parents for their faithful support, and all those who sponsored me and encouraged me with this project. In particular, among them, Dr Richard Harvey, Professor Henri Blocher, Dr David L. Johnston, and my brothers and sisters from the Evangelical Baptist Church of Paris-centre and Hillingdon Park Baptist Church—London (a particular thank you to John Pearson who proofread my doctoral thesis).

The practical support of the London School of Theology has been much appreciated through its Research Guthrie Centre and its outstanding staff: in particular, Dr Steve Motyer, my supervisor, who was always available to give me constructive comments helping to develop my theological rigor during this study; Alan Linfield, the librarian, for being the best book and article researcher I have ever met; Dr. Annette Glaw for her meticulous proofreading and her patient theological German teaching. I also thank my friends from Training Leaders International—Minneapolis who encouraged me during this process of publication and proofread the final manuscript, the remaining mistakes being obviously mine.

This project would not have been undertaken without the cooperation of Jews for Jesus via its French director Joshua Turnil, its international director David Brickner, as well as its European Board members, who encouraged me in these studies, despite the risk incurred that I may reach different conclusions from theirs. I extend my thanks also to Dr Rich Robinson, who has been my dialogue partner with the mission. And of course, this book would not exist without the support of the staff of Wipf and Stock Publisher, in particular through Robin Parry, editor at Pickwick Publications.

Acknowledgments

Finally, I would like to express my gratitude to the one who enabled me "to will and to work," hopefully "for his good pleasure" (Phil 2:13), our God revealed in Christ Jesus.

Abbreviations and Acronyms

ABMJ	American Board of Missions to the Jews
ALNT	Analytical Lexicon of the New Testament
ANTC	Abingdon New Testament Commentaries
ASL	Abbott-Smith Lexicon
AUU	Acta Universitatis Upsaliensis
BBJE	Biblical Basis on Jewish Evangelism
BDAG	Bauer-Danker-Arndt-Gingrich Greek-English Lexicon
BECNT	Baker Exegetical Commentary on the New Testament
BFER	The British and Foreign Evangelical Review
BiblSac	Bibliotheca Sacra
BibZeit	Bible Zeitschrift
BJRL	Bulletin of the John Rylands University Library of Manchester
BL	The British Library
BNTC	Black's N. T. Commentaries
BSPGAJ	The British Society for the Proclamation of the Gospel Among the Jews
BST	The Bible Speaks Today
CBG	Crossway Bible Guide
CBQMS	Catholic Biblical Quarterly Monograph Series
CBSC	The Cambridge Bible for Schools and Colleges

Abbreviations and Acronyms

CEB	Commentaire Évangélique de la Bible
CEPRJ	Comité Épiscopal Pour les Relations avec le Judaïsme
CF	Cogitatio Fidei
CFS	Cistercian Fathers Series
CIM	China Inland Mission
CMJ	The Church's Ministry Among Jewish People
CMS	Church Mission Society
CohNT	Commentaar op het Nieuwe Testament
CollegevilleBC	Collegeville Bible Commentary
COQG	Christian Origins and the Question of God
CornBC	Cornerstone Biblical Commentary
COWE	The Consultation On World Evangelization
CPM	Chosen People Ministries
CRJ	Christian Research Journal
CSNT	Commentaires sur le Nouveau Testament
CT	Christianity Today
CTJ	Calvin Theological Journal
DLT	Darton, Longman & Todd
DNI	Den Norske Israelsmisjon
DOTB	A Dictionary of the Bible
EBC	Everyman's Bible Commentary
EDNT	Exegetical Dictionary of the New Testament
EDT	Evangelical Dictionary of Theology
EGNT	The Expositor's Greek New Testament
EKKNT	Evangelisch Katholischer *Kommentar* zum Neuen Testament
EMQ	Evangelical Missionary Quarterly
EOWB	Expository Outlines on the Whole Bible
ERT	Evangelical Review of Theology

EspVie	Esprit et Vie
EvTh	Evangelische Theologie
FB	Forschung zur Bibel
FV	Foi et Vie
FLTE	Faculté Libre de Théologie Évangélique
GBS	Grove Biblical Series
GELNTBSD	Greek-English Lexicon of the New Testament Based on Semantic Domains
GRS	Grove Renewal Series
HBCCN	The Holy Bible with a Commentary and Critical Notes
HC	The Hebrew Catholic
HCP	Historico-Covenantal Priority
HervormdeTS	Hervormde Theologise Studies
HGMC	Holy Ghost Missionary College
HP	Historical Priority
HTKNT	Herders theologischer Kommentar zum Neuen Testament
IBCTP	Interpretation: A Bible Commentary for Teaching and Preaching
IBG	Institut Biblique de Genève
ICC	International Critical Commentary
IJFM	International Journal of Frontier Missions
IVPNTC	InterVarsity Press New Testament Commentary
JBL	Journal of Biblical Literature
JCD	Jewish-Christian Dialogue
JFJ	Jews for Jesus
JFJNL	Jews for Jesus Newsletter
JSNT	Journal of Studies of the New Testament
JSNTS	Journal of Studies of the New Testament Supplement series

Abbreviations and Acronyms

JSOT	Journal of Studies of the Old Testament
JSOTS	Journal of Studies of the Old Testament Supplement series
KEK	Kritisch-exegetischer Kommentar
KJV	King James Version
LBC	The Layman's Bible Commentary
LBH	London Borough of Hillingdon
LCC	The Library of Christian Classics
LCFNE	Lives of the Chief Fathers of New England
LCJE	Lausanne Consultation on Jewish Evangelism
LCWE	Lausanne Committee for World Evangelization
LdV	Livre de Vie
LJS	The London Jews Society
LMS	London Missionary Society
LNTS	Library of the New Testament Studies (former JSNTS)
LOP	Lausanne Occasional Paper
LSL	Liddell & Scott Lexicon
LSPCAJ	London Society for Promoting Christianity Amongst the Jews
LuThK	Lutherische Theologie und Kirche
LW	Luther's Works
MHP	Miscellanea Historiae Pontificiae
MLW	Martin Luthers Werke
MP	Missional Priority
MR	The Maria Regina Series
MTP	Metropolitan Tabernacle Pulpit
NA27	Novum Testamentum Graece n°27
NAC	New American Commentary
NASB	New American Standard Bible

Abbreviations and Acronyms

NASV	New American Standard Version
NIB	The New Interpreter's Bible
NIBC	New International Biblical Commentary
NICNT	New International Commentary on the New Testament
NIDCC	The New International Dictionary of the Christian Church
NRSV	New Revised Standard Version
NAC	New American Commentary
NT	New Testament
NTD	Das Neue Testament Deutsch
OMF	Overseas Missionary Fellowship
ÖRK	Ökumenischer Rat der Kirchen
OT	Old Testament
PBM	Paternoster Biblical Monograph
PCE	Presbyter of the Church of England
PCNT	Paideia Commentaries on the New Testament
PelicanNTC	Pelican New Testament Commentaries
PillarNTC	Pillar New Testament Commentary
PJM	Pentecostal Jewish Mission
RJ	Reform Judaism
RNT	Regensburger Neues Testament
RTHC	Romans Through History and Cultures Series
SBT	Studies in Biblical Theology
SI	Studies in Israel
SLNPNFCC	A Select Library of the Nicene and Post-Nicene Fathers of the Christian Church
SMJT	Studies in Messianic Jewish Theology
SNTSMS	Society for New Testament Studies Monograph Series
SNTW	Studies of the New Testament and its World

Abbreviations and Acronyms

SouthwesternJT	Southwestern Journal of Theology
TynBul	Tyndale Bulletin
TCB	The Century Bible
TCC	The Communicator's Commentary
TE	The Ecumenist
TEBC	The Expositor's Bible Commentary
TEF	Theological Educational Fund
TGELNT	Thayer's Greek-English Lexicon of the New Testament
ThKNT	Theologischer Kommentar zum Neuen Testament
TLM	The Lausanne Movement
TNT	The Treasury of the New Testament
TNTC	Tyndale New Testament Commentaries
TPINTC	Trinity Press International New Testament Commentaries
USCWM	U.S. Center for World Mission
VE	Vox Evangelica
VGT	The Vocabulary of the Greek Testament (Moulton and Milligan)
WCC	World Council of Churches
WdF	Wege der Forschung
WdW	Wege des Wortes
WEA	World Evangelical Alliance
WKJ	Westminster John Knox

Introduction

THE ORIGIN OF THE STUDY

SINCE MY ADOLESCENCE, I have been fascinated by the Jewish people. Their very long history, covering many astounding events, often makes me think of a people with an extraordinary fate, struggling with a life lived between blessings and curses. It was therefore a natural consequence to devote part of my research to the study of this people in the present day, in the light of the biblical texts. During my Master's studies in Theology, I attempted to discover whether the second "now" (*nyn*) in Romans 11:31—whose presence is contested and whose absence is used as the basis for an eschatological exposition of the text—was originally present in the verse. What was at stake was the understanding that "Israel according to the flesh" (Rom 9:3) was to be especially subject to the mercy of God during the time of the Apostle Paul or at any time since.[1] I discovered using textual, exegetical, and structural proofs that this second *nyn* was not likely to have been present in the original text. While working on this thesis I came across questions that I hoped Messianic Jews could answer. In this context I was introduced to the organization Jews for Jesus (JFJ) in November 2000, by whom I was then employed three years later.

From September 2003 to July 2009, I worked as the office manager of the Paris branch of JFJ. Taking advantage of my stay in Paris and encouraged by the Director of the Branch, I decided to pursue my theological study with a post-graduate diploma requested before undertaking a PhD. My subject was then inspired by my work with the mission.[2] Indeed, at the beginning of my employment, I learned that Romans 1:16 was a key verse for the

---

1. Cf. Fritz, "Le poids d'un mot."
2. Cf. Fritz, "L'expression 'Au Juif premièrement.'"

Introduction

ministry: "For I am not ashamed of the gospel; it is the power of God for salvation to everyone who has faith, to the Jew *first* and also to the Greek."[3]

The late Dr Moishe Rosen, founder of JFJ, offered a rather radical interpretation of this verse: Jewish people must be evangelized first. For him, Romans 1:16 was the key to the evangelization of the whole world:

> God has a formula for world evangelization, which, if we follow it, will have the gospel going forth in power until there will not be a segment of any society that remains unaffected. . . . My thesis is that if we plan a strategy to reach Jews, we will have a strategy to reach anyone. . . . By not following God's program for world evangelization, that is, beginning at Jerusalem or to the Jews first, we not only develop a bad theology, we also develop poor missiology.[4]

I did not pay much attention to that issue, one of the reasons being that I myself was not a missionary; but then, with time, this began to haunt me. If many Christians already have difficulties with the evangelization of the Jewish people in general, what will their opinion be regarding the priority of Jewish evangelism?[5] Do churches have to give priority to missions among the Jewish people and preach first the gospel to Jewish people of their city, and then to the non-Jews? Will this method exponentially increase the harvest?

My postgraduate research paper, concentrating on the way in which Romans 1:16c was understood by the church fathers until Constantine, did not really yield me answers, apart from the idea that the church fathers usually understood the expression "to the Jew first and also to the Greek" in historical terms. In this preliminary research paper, I found no indication that they would understand the phrase as expressing an order to evangelize the Jewish people in priority over the non-Jews, an order the church would otherwise still have to obey today.

My aim then became to continue studies on this issue at PhD level in order to:

1. Define how the Christian church understood Romans 1:16 throughout history;

---

3. Unless specified, the Bible quotations are taken from *The Holy Bible: New Revised Standard Version*. Italics mine.

4. Rosen, "Jewish Evangelism," 380–83. Cf. also Rosen, "Why First?," 2.

5. Cf., for instance, Hinson, "Jew First," 8. The statement of the *Norwegian Mission to Israel* (in Norwegian *Den Norske Israelsmisjon*) gathers other objections such as the fear of the assimilation and dissolution of the Jewish people or the abhorrence of the Christian creed tainted by Hellenism, in DNI, "Jew First," 54–55.

Introduction

2. Evaluate the arguments of those who think that the evangelization of the Jewish people should have priority today;

3. Undertake an exegesis of Romans 1:16;

4. Explore the eschatological implications drawn from salvation history (Rom 9–11).

The book you have before you is mainly the results of this work which first appeared as a PhD thesis.[6]

METHODOLOGY

This study is *missiological* with missiology as its disciplinary "home." As Christopher Wright expresses it, "Missiology is the study of mission. It includes biblical, theological, historical, contemporary, and practical reflexion and research."[7] Writing in the field of missiology constrains both the way I frame my questions and the way I handle the construction of my argument in response to the questions. A missiological study is essentially an *interdisciplinary* work, and therefore all the individual areas cannot receive the detailed engagement with secondary sources that they would require if each one of them was studied in their particular field.

Hence, if New Testament expertise will be employed in chapter 3 regarding the exegesis of Romans 1:16c, and on a lesser scale in chapter 4, I will approach Scripture and the various documents not as a New Testament scholar but as a missiologist, for whom Scripture is vitally important but for whom the arena of discussion lies not *within* the New Testament text but outside of it in the deliberations of contemporary theologians and missiologists regarding mission today.

I am aware that I am dealing with a very sensitive subject. Since the Second World War and the catastrophic Shoah,[8] debating Jewish issues when one is not Jewish is very delicate. The most awful jokes that I have been told regarding the concentration camps were by Jewish people. If I had made the big mistake to tell the joke myself, I would have been punished for it! At the same time, having worked for six years with JFJ made me feel to some extent like a Jew. I have been insulted like a Jew while on the phone, in the shop, or the van of JFJ. For six years, Jewish people talked to me and

---

6. Fritz, "Jew First or Jew at Last?."

7. Wright, *Mission of God*, 25.

8. I prefer the term "Shoah" ("storm", "tempest" in Hebrew) to refer to the "Holocaust." This later word indeed designates, in the Jewish mind, the animal sacrifice completely consumed by fire (cf. for example, Gen 22:2).

Introduction

treated me as if I was a *messianic Jew*—had I been a Jew they would not have considered me (as) a real Jew anyway! A Jew told me I had a Jewish nose, another one that I may be more *Ashkenazi* than *Sephardic*. Moreover, some of my relatives are Jewish by birth.

Nonetheless, the subject is still sensitive. Reading Bertold Klappert in particular helped me to apprehend the sensitive issues connected to Jewish evangelism, especially from a German point of view.[9] While dialoguing with my PhD supervisor Steve Motyer, I realized how the Shoah was shaping his understanding of Jewish mission: for him, because of these awful events, Jewish mission should be handled by Jewish people and should be given special care: "I believe that Christian mission amongst the Jews should receive priority on the list of Christian concerns."[10] For him, history changed Jewish-Christian relationships and shapes the way we have to read Romans: "any Israel theology which does not start from a deep grief at the Jews' unbelief, and proceed to an intense longing that they should turn to their Messiah, cannot claim to be Pauline."[11] For him, Paul would certainly exhort us to evangelize courageously the Jewish people today by emphasizing the witness the Gentile church will give just by being filled with the Spirit and bringing forth those fruits.

While very conscious of the atrocities perpetrated towards the Jewish people, my purpose in this study is not to be guided by emotions. Romans 1:16 needs to be explored in its context and its teaching is to be put into practice in our twenty-first-century world. Does it teach us that we have to preach the gospel first to the Jewish people and then to the Gentiles? The church has then to put this lesson into practice and put the mission to the Jewish people at the top of its list. Does it teach us that the Jewish people were the first to be the recipients and benefactors of the gospel? If so, we then have to reach all the peoples of the earth that have not yet heard of Jesus, without forgetting the Jewish people, but doing this according to a strategy that aims to apply the "Great Commission"[12] in the wisest way possible.

Romans 1:16 is the main biblical verse examined in this study. I chose to study it because it contains the whole issue of what I came to call the *Jewish Missional Priority* (*MP*) in a nutshell, but also because it appears to be its strongest argument. This is the reason why I first decided to explore how it had been interpreted throughout history. I chose to examine all the

9. Cf. Klappert, "Dialog mit Israel," 407–30.

10. Motyer, *Israel*, 169.

11. Ibid., 33.

12. To use the common phrase, whose origine is uncertain, referring especially to Matt 28:18–20. Cf. Carey, *Enquiry*, Section I, 9–12: "An Enquiry whether the Commission given by our Lord to his Disciples be not still binding on us."

Introduction

arguments of the *MP* in order to understand the different connections with Romans 1:16. As a matter of fact, this examination demonstrated that Romans 1:16 is also—together with Romans 2:9–10 and chapters 9–11—at the heart of the debate and does not only function as a motto for the *MP*. The way these passages are exegetically interpreted will influence the way the mission to the Jewish people is handled. Studying Romans 9–11 led me to view the issue from the angle of salvation history, but not in the way I suspected. Indeed, while working on the issue of the *MP*, I have become haunted by the idea of priority: all the biblical passages where the adverb "first" (*prōton* / πρῶτον) was employed, where an idea of priority was expressed, drew my attention. This was the case not only in Romans but throughout the Bible, in particular with regard to Jesus' gospel sayings "the first will be the last and the last will be the first." At the same time, the use of these passages has not been—I believe—an excuse. Having examined them closely, in their context, I decided to put some of them on the side, while keeping those that were entering into the debate. Indeed, the theologians and authors I read throughout the process also helped me to tie the whole thing together in a logical way.

THE MAIN INTERPRETATIONS

Surveying how Romans 1:16 was understood throughout history (see chapter 1), one needs to imitate an entomologist dissecting the texts of all these commentators, churchmen, and thinkers, and classifying them according to the different interpretations that were applied. One of the difficulties of this task is to understand the meaning of the words used by the commentators in their respective time regarding the interpretation of those texts speaking about the evangelization of the Jewish people. Indeed, it is usually the aim of a commentary to explain Paul's statements in their first-century setting rather than to apply his words to a modern context.[13] However, after much reflection and struggle, I decided to distinguish three interpretations, all building upon each other: *Historical Priority (HP)*, *Historico-covenantal*

---

13. To give a modern example: Martin Pakula, in his missiological lecture on the subject, declares: "Two excellent modern commentaries on Romans are the ones by C. E. B. Cranfield and Douglas Moo. In their comments on the meaning of the phrase: 'first for the Jew', they assert that this phrase cannot be merely an historical assertion: that the gospel went first to the Jew (which is true enough), but that the gospel is first for the Jew in a sense that must still be relevant today." However, do these well-known commentators mean that a priority to Jewish evangelism should be advocated today or are they simply explaining the verse in its first-century context? Cf. Pakula, *First for Jews*, 3.

Introduction

Priority (HCP), and *Missional Priority (MP)*.[14] I need to describe them in some depth.

Historical Priority

This interpretation contains two steps: the first step considers the priority expressed by *prōton* in Romans 1:16 to be a historical fact—in the history of the early church, the gospel first went to the Jewish people through Jesus' mission—and a second one describes the pattern employed by the disciples in Acts. I estimate that they can be classed in the same category. The *HP* is the basis for the other interpretations: I can state that the word *prōton* of Romans 1:16 could, at the very least, indicate this priority.

Historical Fact

I did not find anyone who contested the fact that the gospel, the good news of Jesus Christ, came to the Jewish people first. Charles H. Dodd, for example, explains it in this way: Paul "will admit that the Jews have a certain priority: it is for the Jew first. That is in the first instance a simple matter of historical fact. The gospel had been offered to the Jews by Jesus."[15]

This historical fact, recounted in the gospels, can be summed up by the declaration of Jesus: "I was sent only to the lost sheep of the house of Israel" (Matt 15:24) and the order given to his disciples: "Go nowhere among the Gentiles, and enter no town of the Samaritans, but go rather to the lost sheep of the house of Israel" (Matt 10:5–6). Of course, the time will come when Jesus will order them to preach the gospel to the Gentiles, but only after the cross: "Go therefore and make disciples of all nations, baptizing them in the name of the Father and of the Son and of the Holy Spirit" (Matt 28:19).[16]

---

14. As we will see, this presentation is not very original. With some light variations, it is also chosen by Glaser, *BBJE*, II.A. However, the former JFJ missionary Stuart Dauermann distinguishes (rather unconvincingly) five different ways to view this priority (*descriptive position, paradigmatic position, restrictive position*, and *prescriptive position*, before giving his *prophetic-progressive position*). See Dauermann, "Jew of Course," 3–6. He also did not convince two other members of the conference who gave him a response: Sibley, "Response," 1–2, and Goldsmith, "Jew of Course," 1–2. For these papers, cf. LCJE website. Online: http://www.lcje.net/Papers%20of%20the%20conference%20 High%20Leigh.html, accessed March 2012.

15. Dodd, *Romans*, 9.

16. Cf. Jeremias, *Jesus' Promise*, 84.

Introduction

Historical Pattern

Following the final call from Jesus to be his "witnesses in Jerusalem, in all Judea and Samaria, and to the ends of the earth" (Acts 1:8), his disciples went on mission. The twelve, under Peter, were more dedicated to the Jewish people, while Paul was called to be the Apostle to the Gentiles (cf. Gal 2:7–8). It is Paul who seems to incarnate best the "Historical Pattern" practice, going first to the Jewish people, and then to the Gentiles. It can be summed up by the words of Acts 13:46: "Then both Paul and Barnabas spoke out boldly, saying, 'It was necessary that the word of God should be spoken first to you. Since you reject it and judge yourselves to be unworthy of eternal life, we are now turning to the Gentiles.'"

Dodd, again, expresses this pattern as follows: "According to the Acts of the Apostles, it was his [Paul's] own normal practice, on opening work at a fresh place, to approach the Jews first of all, wherever it was possible. But it was for the Greek as well."[17] Having said that, some questions remain: was this pattern unique to the early church and followed for practical, strategic, or theological reasons? The two other interpretations that I am going to consider now differ: for the second interpretation, this pattern is reserved for the beginning of the church and is part of a *Covenantal Priority*, for the third, this pattern was not only reserved for this period but is still valid, i.e., it is a *Missional Priority*.

Covenantal Priority

The second interpretation explains the historical fact and pattern. If the gospel went first to the Jewish people, it was because of their status as chosen people. As God chose Abraham and his descendants through Isaac and Jacob as his people, it was natural that the promise of salvation would come to them first. To continue with Dodd, he resumes this interpretation as follows: "And that, Paul thought, indicated that it was the will of God that they should have the first chance of accepting it (cf. xv.9 [sic])."[18] This interpretation gains status as we go through history. Usually, the proponents of this interpretation will believe that "the lost sheep of the house of Israel" enjoyed this privilege during the apostolic time. The supporters of the third interpretation claim its ongoing validity.

---

17. Dodd, *Romans*, 9.

18. Ibid. Rom 15:8 is to be preferred: "For I tell you that Christ has become a servant of the circumcised on behalf of the truth of God in order that he might confirm the promises given to the patriarchs."

Introduction

Missional Priority

The supporters of the *Missional Priority* interpretation (*MP*) together consider that, historically, the Jewish people received the gospel first because of the covenant and that, because of their election, they *still* have the right to receive the gospel before the Gentiles (see chapter 2). The biblical proof claimed for this is that Jesus and his twelve disciples preached the gospel first to the lost sheep of Israel and that Paul, the "Apostle to the Gentiles," went first to the Jewish people before going to the Gentiles, and that there is no reason why this priority should not be valid today. Meanwhile, the *MP* proponents also assume—as the supporters of the first two interpretations do—that the gospel is for Jewish people and Gentiles alike.

The *MP* interpretation is put into practice—for instance by Jews for Jesus—by focusing every missionary effort on the Jewish population. JFJ campaigns are conducted in Jewish cities all around the world. Advertising is expressed in a Jewish way.[19] The songs interpreted by its evangelistic band, called The Liberated Wailing Wall, are composed using traditional Jewish chords. This does not mean that Gentiles are not evangelized—as a matter of fact, JFJ usually reaches four times more Gentiles than Jewish people[20]—but they are not the priority. If a Gentile is interested in the Christian faith, he is counseled by pastors of local churches. If a Jew is interested, he is automatically followed up by the mission. JFJ is a "one issue mission" as well as a devotee of "direct evangelism," which prefers direct methods:[21] "Direct Jewish Evangelism as our priority" is the first core value of the mission.[22] Even if the phrase "to the Jew first" does not occur in the Jews for Jesus mission statement—"We exist to make the messiahship of Jesus an unavoidable issue to our Jewish people worldwide"[23]—it is regularly used in the publications of the mission.[24]

The very aim of this book is to study this third interpretation, in dialogue with Jews for Jesus (JFJ). My work will not deal with the fact that JFJ, as a "one issue mission," is targeting the Jewish people—as the Christian Union targets students or Arab World Ministries Arabs. It will be focused

---

19. A famous tract gives this slogan: "Be more Jewish, believe in Jesus." A slogan that can only be understood by the Jewish Community.

20. E.g., these statistics from 1955 to 1965: "265 New Jewish Believers for 1100 New Gentile Believers." In Rosen and Proctor, *Jews for Jesus*, 48.

21. Ibid., 87–88.

22. Cf. JFJ website. Online: http://www.jewsforjesus.org/about/corevalues/#direct, accessed July 2010.

23. Cf. JFJ website. Online: http://www.jewsforjesus.org/about, accessed August 2010.

24. Cf. for instance Brickner, "First and Also," 1–2, and my chapter 2.

on its teaching of the *Jewish Missional Priority* (see a more detailed definition further on). When JFJ is using the phrase "To the Jew first," it is not as part of its "one issue mission" ministry among the Jewish people, but as an important statement the church should follow. I will try to discern the *raison d'être* of JFJ in the history of missions (story, identity, practice) and its main arguments regarding our issue (theological basis, interpretations, eschatological schemes), in order to evaluate the *Missional Priority*. This dialogue will take place in particular through the publications of the mission as well as through my personal involvement within it.

THE PLAN OF THE STUDY

It appears that the major focus of research done on this subject has been within biblical studies, rather than systematic theology. However, in order to answer the question, one should not only consider three specific verses (Rom 1:16; 2:9–10) and Paul's usual practice of evangelization in Acts, but rather take a wider theological view. Of course, this would include subjects such as "the story of the people of Israel" or "the place of Romans 1:16–17 in the structure of the Epistle." But the thematic development of the covenant of God with Israel or the eschatological plan of God for humanity should also be considered, as well as the historical and theological development of mission among the Jewish people during twenty centuries of Christianity.

At the same time, interpreters are influenced by their tradition, by their geographical or ethnic background, in which they were raised, and by their socio-cultural feelings expressed through their understanding of the political issues in the Middle East or by their memory of the Shoah's atrocities. We need to be careful not to distort issues of the first century through our modern hermeneutic: we need to understand what Paul meant when he wrote his Epistle to the Romans in the first century. Hopefully, some missiological conclusions will then be able to be drawn.

The aim of this study is to engage with this issue by following the four points stated above (cf. end of "Origin of this study"). Basically, these four points define the four chapters of this work: a *wirkungsgeschichte* (*history of effect*) to understand how Romans 1:16 was understood and applied throughout history, a *status quaestionis* (*state of the question*) to gather and critique all the claims of the proponents of the interpretation in question, a *propositio* (*proposition*) emerging from the exegesis of Romans 1:16–17, and a *heilsgeschichte* to consider *salvation history* from the angle of this study. Finally, in the *Conclusion*, a useful scheme for today's missions will emerged hopefully, Jewish mission in particular. I believe this work, which has never

Introduction

been done in such an extensive way, will shine an important light on this issue.

Wirkungsgeschichte (History of Effect)

The first chapter is a historical one. Its aim is to present a survey of the interpretation of Romans 1:16 throughout history. A *wirkungsgeschichte* or *history of effect*[25] is undertaken here to try to find how the text was understood in the historical context of the thinker, a thinker who is, whether he likes it or not, influenced by his tradition and epoch. This survey deals concurrently with the different interpretations of the verse by our predecessors (theory), the different ways in which the Jewish people were evangelized in the last 2,000 years (practice), and the influence of the relations between Jewish people and Gentiles on the whole issue (context). It demonstrates the background of Jews for Jesus' perspective.

Status Quaestionis (State of the Question)

The second chapter is literary in nature. Quite a few books and articles have been written to defend the *MP* interpretation. I attempted to gather them as extensively as possible, which is part of my originality.[26] They are usually the work of pastors and missionaries—some of them are sermons or tracts—although a few scholarly books and articles were written to promote the thesis. A recent book edited by Darell L. Bock and Mitch Glaser, compiling fourteen articles written by some of the most well-known proponents of the interpretation, is entitled *To the Jew First: The Case for Jewish Evangelism in Scripture and History* and indicates that the issue is very topical.[27] The phrase "To the Jew first" has been increasingly used as a slogan to encourage Jewish evangelism, which means that, while using the slogan, some of these books are not really a proper study of Romans 1:16.[28] As far as I am aware, and rather surprisingly, no specific work on the subject has been

---

25. See chapter 1 for a definition.

26. We were for instance unable to access Heward, *Jew First* and we are still waiting to receive from a library a copy of Mussen, *Jew First*.

27. Bock and Glaser, *Jew First*. Among the writers: Walter C. Kaiser, Darell L. Bock, Arnold G. Fruchtenbaum, Mitch Glaser, and Arthur F. Glasser.

28. The best example is the book of Wilson and Wilson, *The Tabernacle: To the Jew First and Also to the Greek*, which does not deal at all with Romans 1:16! Cf. also Bietz, *Jew First*, which is more a testimony; MacLachlan, *Unfulfilled Prophecies: To the Jew First*, which deals with the promise of the land.

Introduction

published countering this thesis. Of course, some commentators chose to counter it while writing their comments on Romans 1:16, but no scholar has written a monograph to that purpose. However, the 295 page study of John H. Stek commissioned by the General Home Missions Committee of the Christian Reformed Church (USA) in 1966 needs a special mention.[29] His first chapter was published in the *Calvin Theological Journal*, but the others, though announced, have never been really made available publicly.[30] At the end of his unpublished work, Stek shows that he is not in favor of the *MP* interpretation.

My *State of Question* gathers all these works in order to extract the arguments for the missional interpretation in a methodical as well as a critical way. Thereby I am familiarizing myself with their thought so that I can evaluate it in a proper manner and continue my study particularly focused on its understanding by Jews for Jesus.

Propositio (Proposition)

My third chapter is an exegetical one. The aim of this chapter is to understand the place of Romans 1:16 in the Epistle and in the New Testament. As an evangelical researcher, I am particularly interested—as Jews for Jesus—in Paul's original meaning. For that purpose, I will use the historico-grammatical method[31] and attempt, as much as possible, to approach the texts in an empathic manner.[32] Even though I will draw upon New Testament studies, I will not engage with the secondary literature to the extent it would be necessary, if this was a monograph on New Testament studies.

Heilsgeschichte (Salvation History)

The fourth chapter is systematic in nature since the whole issue raised by Romans 1:16 is grounded in the *heilsgeschichte* or *salvation history*, in connection with chapters 9–11. The aim of the chapter is to define how the

---

29. Stek, *Jew First: Exegetical Examination*.

30. Stek, "Jew First," 15–52. I heard of the unpublished thesis of Stek via *Googlebooks*, which refers to it as a thesis of 590 pages, because it counts the blank versos or the work as a whole. Holwerda, *Jesus & Israel*, 174 (note 34) quotes it regarding Rom 11. In 2010, it was available in eight different libraries in the USA and, thanks to Meredith M. Kline of Gordon-Conwell Theological Seminary, I was able to get it in December 2010.

31. As defined, for instance, by Bruce, "Interpretation of the Bible," 565–66.

32. Cf. the "Critical-realist reading" and "hermeneutic of love" as defined in Wright, *New Testament*, 61–67.

Introduction

sense of priority I have discovered can be understood in our twenty-first century context.

Conclusion

This concluding chapter will be the place for a summary of the study, a self-critique, as well as a missiological introduction. What are the issues that were not taken into account in this study and which should be undertaken in the future? How should the mission to the Jewish people be advocated among other missions? What are the consequences of the use of the *MP interpretation* in mission today or what would be the consequences if it is given up?

DEFINITIONS

A few terms or notions directly connected to the study need to be defined here to avoid any misunderstanding or misrepresentation.

"Jew" and "Israel according to the Flesh"

Defining Jewishness is without doubt a difficult task, for the Jew as well as the non-Jew. David Brickner agrees with that:

> Jewishness is defined broadly within the Jewish community. It is a fact of birth, a product of social development, education and identification, and lastly, a matter of religious affiliation. Yet when it comes to the specifics of Jewish identity, even the leaders of the community disagree. In fact, the question of who is a Jew is one of the most hotly contested issues in the State of Israel today.[33]

For Jean-Paul Sartre, "the Israelite is one whom other men consider an Israelite."[34] *The Oxford Dictionary of the Jewish Religion* informs us that "[i]n the 1980s, the Reform movement agreed to regard someone either of whose parents were Jewish as a Jew by birth. . . . For religious Jews, the question of Jewish identity continues to be decided by *halakhah*,"[35] *halakhah* which "defines a Jew as a person born of a Jewish mother or one who has converted

---

33. Brickner, "Jewish Resistance," I.C.
34. Sartre et al., "Jewish Question," 42.
35. Hertzberg, "Jewish Identity," 371.

to Judaism."³⁶ It is certain that for me, as well as for JFJ which employs only Jewish missionaries or spouses of Jewish people,³⁷ the definition of the Jew is closer to the Reform than the Orthodox tradition; however, I need to add that being a Jew is not simply to be defined genetically, but also culturally and socially. Moreover, I believe that a "Messianic Jew" or a "Jewish believer in Jesus" remains a Jew.³⁸ In 2009, the worldwide Jewish population was 13,421,000.³⁹

Defining Jewishness according to the New Testament is easier but not without difficulties. Even if the word "Jew" (*Ioudaios*)⁴⁰ is related etymologically to the territory and to the people of Judah (*Ioudas*), one of the twelve tribes born of Jacob, the Jewish people are recognized in the first century and today as being all the descendants of Jacob/Israel, son of Isaac, son of Abraham: they are Israelites or "Israel."⁴¹ Israel, the "people" (*'ām*; *laos*), is generally opposed to the "nations" (*gôyim*; *ethnē*), which I will not use "in the more restricted sense of 'nation state' that developed in post-Reformation Europe,"⁴² but rather as the different peoples of the earth. As for the one converted to Judaism, he is a "proselyte" and in its full expression he is the one who "converts out of love of Judaism and accepts all its laws and ceremonies."⁴³ He is not to be confused with the "God-fearers," which refers "to non-Jews in ancient times who observed some of the precepts of the Torah without fully converting to Judaism."⁴⁴

As Dan Cohn-Sherbok expresses it,

> Paul's reference to Israel according to the flesh (1 Cor. 10.18) implies that there is a different Israel "according to the spirit."

---

36. Anonymous, "Jew," 369.

37. Susan Perlman, Director of Communication for JFJ, answered my question "Who is a Jew according to JFJ?" by email on the 14th March 2012 by writing that "the standard of Jewishness for missionaries is determined according to ethnic descent as the first consideration. That qualifying ethnic decent is established through the applicant having one or both parents who have two Jewish parents. So more specifically Jewishness can be established from two fully Jewish parents or Jewishness from parents that were a Jewish-Gentile couple (A fully Jewish parent + a Gentile parent)."

38. See Brickner, "Jewish Resistance," I.C.

39. According to the Israeli Central Bureau of Statistics website. Online: http://www.cbs.gov.il/reader/shnaton/templ_shnaton_e.html?num_tab=st02_27&CYear=2010, accessed March 2012.

40. Cf. Esth 2:5.

41. Cf. Dunn, *Romans 9–16*, 526.

42. Wright, *Mission of God*, 456 n.3.

43. Anonymous, "Proselyte," 550.

44. Bohak, "God Fearers," 279. A God-fearer is hence not circumcised.

> Such a distinction is based on the conviction that the Christian community constitutes a new Israel that is due to inherit the privileges of ancient Israel.[45]

While I would agree that the church, composed of Jewish people and Gentiles who have believed and believe in Jesus, is the new Israel (Gal 6:16),[46] I also argue that "Israel according to the flesh" still has a special destiny in the plan of God. Moreover, non-Christian Jews today "would be 'non-Jews' by the standards of Revelation 2:9; 3:9; Romans 2:28."[47] As for modern Judaism, this note of Henri Blocher is also helpful:

> Judaism [today] should not be confused with Second Temple Judaism, much less Old Testament religion. Judaism was born, through the work and debates of several generations, of the victory of one party over the others (basically the Pharisaic party) in the radically changed situation created by the ruin of the Temple.[48]

Evangelism, Jewish Evangelism, Jewish Missional Priority

According to the Lausanne Movement,

> To evangelize is to spread the good news that Jesus Christ died for our sins and was raised from the dead according to the Scriptures, and that as the reigning Lord he now offers the forgiveness of sins and the liberating gifts of the Spirit to all who repent and believe.[49]

Jewish evangelism is evangelism of the Jewish people.[50] *Jewish Missional Priority* is a phrase I have coined to express the idea that the priority for the church today in mission should be the mission to the Jewish people.[51] Glaser considers that "the most lucid explanation of the Present Prior-

---

45. Cohn-Sherbok, "Israel," 79.
46. The *kai* in this verse can be epexegetical. Cf. Martyn, *Galatians*, 567.
47. Blocher, "Two Covenant Theology," 201.
48. Ibid., 201.
49. LCWE, "Lausanne Covenant," 9.
50. See Robinson, "Jewish Mission," 190–92.
51. Throughout this book, I will rather use the short version: *Missional Priority* (*MP*). For the use of "missional" instead of "missiological," see Wright, *Mission of God*, 24–25: "*Missional* is simply an adjective denoting something that is related to or characterized by mission, or has the qualities, attributes or dynamics of mission. Accordingly, I will normally use *missiological* when . . . a theological or reflective aspect is

Introduction

ity view of Romans 1:16 [*MP*] can be found in the statement of the *Lausanne Committee for Jewish Evangelism* in the *Occasional Papers #7*":⁵²

> There is, therefore, a great responsibility laid upon the church to share Christ with the Jewish people. This is not to imply that Jewish evangelism is more important in the sight of God, or that those involved in Jewish evangelism have a higher calling. We observe that the practical application of the scriptural priority is difficult to understand and apply. We do not suggest that there should be a radical application of "to the Jew first" in calling on all the evangelists, missionaries, and Christians to seek out the Jews within their sphere of witness before speaking to non-Jews! Yet we do call the church to restore ministry among this covenanted people of God to its biblical place in its strategy of world evangelization.⁵³

Stewart Dauermann—President of *Hashivenu* and former JFJ missionary—gave a paper on our issue at the LCJE International Conference held at High Leigh Conference Centre in Hoddesdon (Hertforshire, UK) in August 2011.⁵⁴ Here, he expresses the priority using the image of the *foundation* to highlight the importance of this doctrine and to prevent the shaking of the foundation of the house:

> No one enjoys going underneath the house to examine the foundation, and no one welcomes the added expense and inconvenience of repairing foundations in need of work. But only a fool would simply paint over cracked foundations with the whitewash of civility.⁵⁵

The Oxford English Dictionary defines "priority" as "[t]he condition or quality of being earlier or previous in time, or of preceding something else" or "Precedence in order, rank, or dignity."⁵⁶ Christopher J. H. Wright, while talking about the priority of mission, declares:

---

intended." Since choosing the phrase, I came across it in the 2011 paper of Stuart Dauermann: "The *restrictive position* holds that because the Jews are singled out in the New Testament as a missional priority, the church can only be said to truly be doing mission when its mission includes outreach to the Jews." Dauermann, "Jew of Course," 3.

52. Glaser, *BBJE*, II.B.4. Same argument in Wilks Jr, "Jew First," third point.
53. COWE, "Christian Witness," 5.
54. Dauermann, "Jew of Course," 1–15, a paper that has not been published in the following *LCJE Bulletin*, despite a few allusions, for instance in Downey, "Theological Impressions," 16–17. At the time of writing, it is the most recent paper advocating the *MP*.
55. Dauermann, "Jew of Course," 4–5.
56. Murray et al., *Oxford English Dictionary*, 2305.

Introduction

> First, the language of "priority" implies that all else is "secondary" at best. . . . In other words, the language of priority and primacy quickly tends to imply singularity and exclusion. Evangelism is the *only* real mission. . . . The word *priority* suggests something that has to be your starting point. A priority is whatever is most important or urgent. It is the thing that must get done first before anything else.[57]

Applied to Jewish evangelism, this last definition might appear extreme. It is, however, the definition I think we should keep in mind throughout my work. It may explain that Jewish Missional Priority is in fact rarely applied in such an extreme way, as we will see in my second chapter.

Regarding Jewish evangelism, and Jewish Missional Priority in particular,[58] we must be aware of the influence of JFJ in the Lausanne Movement, and especially in the Lausanne Consultation on Jewish Evangelism (*LCJE*).[59] Since the first Lausanne Congress on World Evangelism in 1974, Moishe Rosen and Susan Perlman labored hard to create the *LCJE* during the Consultation on World Evangelization (*LCWE*) held in Pattaya (Thailand) in 1980, as Susan Perlman recalls in "A Tribute to Moishe Rosen."[60] Since Pattaya, JFJ members have always been part of the *LCJE*. The *Lausanne Occasional Paper No. 60*, written during the *LCWE* in Pattaya in 2004 and which in a way expands the *Occasional Paper No. 7*, presents its seven-member team as composed of: Tuvya Zaretsky (JFJ; Editor), Kai Kjær-Hansen (Convener), Ole Chr. Kvarme (Theological Consultant), Bodil F. Skjøtt (Facilitator), Richard Harvey (JFJ), Theresa Newell and Susan Perlman (JFJ). The same applies to the Willowbank and the Berlin Declarations

---

57. Wright, *Mission of God*, 317.

58. Dauermann, in Dauermann, "Jew of Course," 1, is bold enough to say that: "Although not officially sanctioned, 'to the Jew first' is the only viable candidate for the Lausanne Consultation on Jewish Evangelism (LCJE) motto." At the same time, he adds: "However, anyone who looks or listens in closely will discover widespread disagreement in the LCJE on how to interpret 'to the Jew first' for Paul's context and ours."

59. For more information, go to Lausanne Movement website. Online: www.lausanne.org, accessed March 2011. Also the LCJE website. Online: www.lcje.net, accessed March 2011.

60. Cf. Perlman, "A Tribute to Moishe Rosen,". In June 1980, the Pattaya participants were Betty Baruch (Australia), Menehem Benhayim (Israel), Rev. David Harley (England; International co-ordinator), Dr. G. D. James (Australia), Kai Kjær-Hansen (Denmark), Rev. Ole Chr Kvarme (Israel), Tony Lewin (South Africa), Rev. Murdo MacLeod (England), Rev. Rodney Mechanic (South Africa), Jh'an (Alan) Moskowitz (JFJ - U.S.A.), Susan Perlman (JFJ-U.S.A.), Rev. J. S. Uhrinak (U.S.A.) and Brian Wells (New Zealand) and the consultants Dr. Gerald Anderson, (U.S.A.), Dr. Richard R. de Ridder (U.S.A.), Dr. Louis Goldberg (U.S.A.), Dr. Erwin J. Kolb (U.S.A.; consultant chairman) and Moishe Rosen (JFJ-U.S.A.).

produced in 1989 and 2008 respectively by the World Evangelical Alliance and the Lausanne Movement, but in very close collaboration with Jews for Jesus.[61] David Parker, while introducing the different papers given during the International Consultation on "The Uniqueness of Jesus and Jewish Evangelism," organized by The Theological Commission of the World Evangelical Alliance (*WEA*) at Woltersdorf, near Berlin, in August 2008, states:

> Indeed, Christianity has been charged with the responsibility of sharing the gospel with all people, irrespective of who they are or of any other actions of service that may be carried out in the name of Christ. This mandate [Jewish evangelism] is considered even more urgent in this case because of the biblical pattern, "to the Jew first."[62]

Finally, in the 2011 LCJE International Conference, this statement was made:

> We are dismayed by any reluctance among Christians to share the gospel with Jewish people, since "it is the power of God for salvation to everyone who believes." . . . We rejoice in the power of the gospel that enables Messianic Jews and Arab believers in Jesus to find reconciliation in Christ. Therefore, we encourage the whole church always and everywhere to take the gospel "to the Jew first" and to all the nations. It is vital that all who are concerned for the spiritual welfare of the Jewish people join us in the cause of Jewish evangelism. We call upon the whole church to take the whole gospel to Jewish people always and everywhere.[63]

Church, Christendom, Christianity

In the present book, the word "church" will be used in its universal sense, i.e., "The Christian community collectively," as referring to "Christianity" or

---

61. Via Tuvya Zaretsky, Susan Perlman, and Richard Harvey. For the full text of the Willowbank Declaration, see the WEA website. Online: http://www.worldevangelicals.org/commissions/list/index.php?com=tc&id=52, accessed April 2012. For the Berlin Declaration, see WEA, "Berlin Declaration on the Uniqueness of Christ," 4–5. For information, the foreword writer of the present book has participated to the drafting of both declarations.

62. Parker, *Jesus, Salvation & Jewish People*, 5.

63. LCJE, "To all concerned," 5.

Introduction

"Christendom," "The whole body of Christians,"[64] including the Evangelical Church as defined, for instance, by the World Evangelical Alliance.[65]

Covenant(s)

Paul, in Romans 9:4, uses the plural when he refers to the "covenants" that belong to the Jewish people. As Paul R. Williamson recalls, "[t]here is no consensus over the precise number of divine covenants in Scripture."[66] In his article, Williamson refers to nine covenants, among which are the following: the Noahic, Abrahamic, Mosaic, priestly, Davidic, and new covenant; the Abrahamic and Mosaic are instituted in different stages.[67] For the purpose of the study and for a global understanding of God's plan of salvation, I will focus on the Abrahamic covenant as the one representing all the others, except for the Noahic.

LIMITATIONS

A few areas, commonly found in theology, will not be tackled in this work, mainly for reasons of irrelevance:

Firstly, I will not deal with the intertestamental literature, because my aim is to concentrate on the mission of the church toward the Jewish people and hence is mainly governed by the literature after the coming of Jesus.

Secondly, even if I have learned a great deal from the discussion between the so-called *old* and *new perspectives on Paul*, I will not enter into this debate in this study.[68]

Thirdly, if I use the *rhetorical* features in Romans, *Speech-Act Theory* will not be considered in this study: no commentary consulted makes reference to it and I came to the conclusion that only the verb *epaischynomai* ("to be ashamed of") in Romans 1:16 might be investigated using this system;

---

64. Onions et al., *Shorter Oxford*, 308, 311.

65. Cf. WEA website. Online: http://www.worldevangelicals.org/aboutwea/, accessed March 2012.

66. Williamson, "Covenant," 420b.

67. Ibid., 419–29.

68. Cf. for instance Dunn, *New Perspective*; Stuhlmacher, *Revisiting Paul's Doctrine*; Carson et al., *Variegated Nomism I* and Carson et al., *Variegated Nomism II*.

Introduction

however, "shame" or "boasting" are not really the point of my focus.[69] As for *speech-in-character*, I discuss it with Stanley Kent Stowers.[70]

Fourthly, on account of the time of research on this present study, only works published before 2012 have been considered.

Fifthly and finally, when the following issues are mentioned and defined in my work, I will not go into the whole debate surrounding them: The legitimacy of Jewish evangelism by Christians in the post-Holocaust world, universalism, and two-covenant theology. My interest is clearly in relation to Romans 1:16 and Jews for Jesus.

PRESUPPOSITIONS

It is important to consider the role of presuppositions, in mathematics as well as in theology,[71] here are my own ones. As evangelical, I hold the confession of faith of the World Evangelical Alliance, which views "the Holy Scriptures as originally given by God, divinely inspired, infallible, entirely trustworthy; and the supreme authority in all matters of faith and conduct."[72] Of course, we do not possess the original biblical texts and my study will use textual criticism, but I mean that any theological argument that would not assume the biblical text or the biblical writer divinely inspired will be treated very cautiously.

Moreover, I recognize that my own evangelical and theological education has an impact on the way I handle my reflection. I cannot dismiss completely where I come from and what I have become. However, I have sought in this study to engage each issue with theological professionalism, ready to reform my mind as every evangelical, son of the Reformation, should be able to do (*semper reformanda*)! Actually, when I started this study, I was sincerely unable to answer this question: Must the church today prioritize evangelizing Jews over Gentiles as Jews for Jesus advocates on the basis of Romans 1:16? I believe I now have the answer. I hope to convince you, for the global spread of the gospel and for the glory of our Lord.

---

69. See Austin, *Things with Words*, 12, for a definition of Speech-Act Theory: "to say something, at least in all cases worth considering, i.e., all cases considered, is always and simply to *state* something."

70. Stowers, *Rereading*, 11–15.

71. See Poythress, "A Biblical View of Mathematics," 159–88.

72. Cf. WEA website [formerly World Evangelical Fellowship]. Online: http://www.worldevangelicals.org/aboutwea/statementoffaith.htm, accessed March 2012. Statement written originally in 1951, under the presidency of Sir Arthur Smith; cf. *Billy Graham Center* archives on the Wheaton College website. Online: http://www2.wheaton.edu/bgc/archives/GUIDES/338.htm, accessed August 2012.

1

Wirkungsgeschichte
A Brief Look at the Interpretation and Impact of the Expression "To the Jew First" (Romans 1:16c) throughout Christian History until the Founding of Jews for Jesus

IN THE MARCH 2008 edition of *Christianity Today*, Stan Guthrie, Editor at Large of the magazine, certainly did not know he would provoke an argument when he wrote in his column *Foolish Things* "Why Evangelize the Jews? God's Chosen People Need Jesus as Much as We Do": "Good news is no news at all if it is not communicated. And it must be shared *first* with the Jews (Rom. 1:16)."[1] He was, however, not the first to write about this subject in the magazine: Richard Mouw, president at Fuller Theological Seminary in Pasadena (California) wrote in his time an editorial on the subject: "To the Jew First: Witnessing to the Jews is Nonnegotiable."[2] But the difference was that Guthrie's article was read by Rabbi Yehiel E. Poupko, Judaic Scholar at the Jewish Federation of Metropolitan Chicago. For Poupko, Guthrie's column was outright anti-Semitic:

> First for the gospel, and because of that, first for persecution and suffering. That is what "to the Jew first" has meant for 2,000 years. . . . Can Guthrie explain why he is so sure that he and

1. Guthrie, "Jew First," 76.
2. Mouw, "Jew First," 12–13. Cf. also Hinson, "Jew First," 18.

> his fellow evangelicals will be the first Christians in 2,000 years, who when they say and practice "to the Jews first," will bring no harm to the Jewish people? . . . Continue your work with atheists, and all types of other religious groups. Give us a break for a few centuries. When you have succeeded with the others, come back to us; perhaps we'll talk then.[3]

Guthrie sounded embarrassed when he replied:

> I believe that the gospel of Jesus Christ is Good News for Jewish people, too. When we say (quoting Paul, a Hebrew of Hebrews) that the gospel is "first for the Jew," we mean it as an honor to Jewish people, who, after all, were the first followers of Jesus. . . . The Jewish people are not lowest in God's economy; I see them as special, chosen people, worthy of honor and precious to God. As Paul said, you are the "natural branches."[4]

This evangelical reply did not calm the Rabbi who reacted even more strongly:

> There is much scholarship on the meaning of that surely famous verse and phrase "to the Jews first." Not only is there much Roman Catholic theology written on the meaning of this verse, there is evangelical scholarship on this verse as well. And not all such scholarship holds that the meaning of this verse is that the first obligation of preaching the "Good News" is to preach the "Good News" to the Jews first.[5]

This "exchange of views" went on and will certainly never stop until the coming of the Messiah! It is a good example of how each one can interpret a verse according to his religious background. In this chapter, my attention will be focused on one point: how has Romans 1:16 been interpreted and put into practice throughout Christian history?

In order to gain a sense of the ways in which these interpretations have influenced Jewish-Christian relationships, I undertake a survey of the *Wirkungsgeschichte* of the text through all the varied contexts of Christian history. The concept of *Wirkungsgeschichte* or "history of effect" was first used by Hans Georg Gadamer in his book *Truth and Method*.[6] It is "the

---

3. Poupko and Guthrie, "Jew First," Poupko's first response.
4. Ibid., Guthrie's Reply.
5. Ibid., Poupko's Second Response.
6. Gadamer, *Truth*. We will use *Wirkungsgeschichte* in a wider sense and apply a *Rezeptionsgeschichte* as developed by Hans Robert Jauss. For differences between these fields, see Knight, "Wirkungsgeschichte, Reception History, Reception Theory," 137–46.

Wirkungsgeschichte

operative force of a tradition over those that belong to it, so that even in rejecting or reacting to it they remain conditioned by it":[7]

> The real meaning of a text, as it speaks to the interpreter, does not depend on the contingencies of the author and whom he originally wrote for. It certainly is not identical with them, for it is always partly determined also by the historical situation of the interpreter and hence by the totality of the objective course of history.[8]

Across the centuries, hundreds of theologians have been influenced by their own background when reading the Bible: every interpretation is made in a geographical, historical, sociological, and ethnic context. Even though I have considered more than a hundred commentaries or theological witnesses—mostly, in French, German and English—I am conscious that there are many more, including those written by non-Western theologians. My aim was to sift through these works and consider those theologians who have had the biggest influence on this question. However, as the question is reflected on in dialogue with Jews for Jesus, a Western evangelical mission, my selection does not appear illegitimate.[9] Commentaries are of particular interest, since they deal with the biblical verses as well as having an influence on mission.

For this preliminary study, two themes are of particular interest: the relationship between Jewish people and Gentiles, and the issues of philo-Semitism or anti-Semitism throughout history.[10] Following the "partings of the ways," Christian history includes events—most of them tragic—from the charges of "Deicide" to the Crusades, from the Shoah to Zionism, which need to be considered alongside my theological study. Moreover, it seems essential to include a history of missions among the Jewish people in this survey.

---

7. Warnke, *Gadamer: Hermeneutics, Tradition and Reason*, 80.

8. Gadamer, *Truth*, 263.

9. The Catholic Church seems to have traditionally adopted a historico-covenantal priority. Cf., however, e.g., Küng, *The Church*, 142, according to Hicks, "Romans 1:16," 10–11.

10. In my work, "Semitism" will refer to the Jewish people as a group, since this is how the word is commonly used today, and despite the fact that it should refer to a cognate group of languages (including Hebrew, Aramaic, Arabic, Babylonian, Assyrian and Ethiopian). Cf. Keith, *Hatred*, 2–4.

To the Jew First or to the Jew at Last?

ANTIQUITY (UNTIL AD 476)

Because of its proximity to the birth of the church, this part of the history is obviously particularly worthy of interest. One comment must be made at the outset: the important word *prōton*, "first," of the debated phrase is a problematic issue in itself according to textual criticism. This problem will be discussed in chapter 3 where I reach the following conclusion: its omission from Marcion of Sinope can be easily understood and it is very likely that it did influence a few other manuscripts. This textual issue shows us at once that *prōton* was able to disturb the first readers of the Letter of St Paul to the Romans.

After considering briefly a few significant texts in the New Testament, which will sum up the situation, I will focus my attention on the important theme of the partings of the ways, to finally deal with the church fathers' understanding of Romans 1:16.

The New Testament (before AD 70)

Three steps can be distinguished at this stage that describe how the gospel was first spread and that raise the question of method and strategy, which will be discussed in more detail in chapters 2 and 3.[11]

Firstly, Jesus limited his ministry (and at the beginning the ministry of his disciples) to "the lost sheep of the house of Israel":

> [Jesus] answered, "I was sent only to the lost sheep of the house of Israel" (Matt 15:24). He said to her, "Let the children be fed *first [prōton]*, for it is not fair to take the children's food and throw it to the dogs." (Mark 7:27; italics mine)
>
> These twelve Jesus sent out with the following instructions: "Go nowhere among the Gentiles, and enter no town of the Samaritans, but go rather to the lost sheep of the house of Israel." (Matt 10:5–6)

Secondly, after the death of Jesus, the gospel was offered to the Gentiles:

> "Go therefore and make disciples of all nations, baptizing them in the name of the Father and of the Son and of the Holy Spirit, and teaching them to obey everything that I have commanded you. And remember, I am with you always, to the end of the age." (Matt 28:19–20)

---

11. See Neill, *History*, 18–23.

> Then both Paul and Barnabas spoke out boldly, saying, "It was necessary that the word of God should be spoken *first* [*prōton*] to you. Since you reject it and judge yourselves to be unworthy of eternal life, we are now turning to the Gentiles." (Acts 13:46; italics mine)

Thirdly, the ministry of the Apostles went on, trying to reach both Jewish people and Gentiles, planting, building, and encouraging many churches in obedience to Jesus' commission.

Thus, Romans 1:16 and the phrase "to the Jew first, and also to the Greek" did not just appear from nowhere. As John Stek expresses it:

> No one can read the New Testament without discovering among its dominant themes that one which is epitomized by the Pauline phrase, "to the Jew first." This theme is pervasive in the Gospels as a fact of history and a constitutive element in the Divine purpose.... In the book of Acts this theme also appears as a fact of history. Beginning at Pentecost the apostles proclaimed the risen Lord first of all to the Jews.[12]

At this stage, I also admit that, as the work of Rosemary Ruether shows, most anti-Semitism—or at least anti-Judaism—can find its roots in a certain understanding of verses of the New Testament itself. The proper interpretation of those verses is another huge debate I cannot enter into in my present work.[13]

The Partings of the Ways (AD 70–135)

Dating the exact moment when Judaism and Christianity went their separate ways is highly debated. For James Dunn, the "Partings of the Ways" can be considered according to the four pillars of Judaism: Temple, Law, Monotheism, and Election of Israel:[14]

> The Parting of the Ways came about because the new movement which stemmed from Jesus found it increasingly necessary to question and redefine each of these four axioms in greater or

---

12. Stek, "Jew First," 15–16.

13. Cf. Ruether, *Faith*. The most notorious verse, Matthew 27:25, is a sufficient example: "Then the people as a whole answered, 'His blood be on us and on our children!'"

14. "'Christianity' was initially defined by way of contrast or antithesis to 'Judaism.'" Dunn, *Partings*, xvii.

less [sic] degree—at any rate, to a degree unacceptable to mainstream Judaism.[15]

There were many opportunities for the first century Jew to react against the new sect. John 9:22 shows clearly that it began early:[16] "His parents said this because they were afraid of the Jews; for the Jews had already agreed that anyone who confessed Jesus to be the Messiah would be put out of the synagogue."

However, assuming that the beginning of the parting started from the persecution of Stephen,[17] and ended with Constantine and the Christian Empire (AD 313),[18] three events seem to seal the outcome.

The Destruction of Jerusalem and its Temple in AD 70 was, in this part of the world, the first major event. This episode was a sign of judgment for the generation who had known Jesus and at the same time the sign of the end of the Old Covenant. This disaster has certainly had a great impact on the way Jewish people would be seen henceforth by Christians. While the church was expanding following the apostolic succession, many of the early interpretations of Romans 1:16c need to be read with this disaster in mind. This disaster also led to the demise of the Essenes (AD 68), the Sadducees (AD 70), and the Zealots (AD 73–74 in Masada).[19]

The second event was a decision taken by the "Council of Javneh" in a Judean city on the Mediterranean coast, where the Pharisees obtained the right to restart a school under Yohanan ben Zakkai. There, a revision of the Jewish prayer *Birkat ha-minim* took place—probably in the mid-80s—under Gamaliel II, confirming the fact that *the minim*—sectarians, which Christians were likely to have been part of—were not welcomed in the synagogues.[20] It was a time of rebuilding the nation around Torah and redefining Judaism. "From being heterodox, Christianity became heretical."[21]

The Revolt of Bar-Kochba (132–35), which seems to have been initiated by the desire of the Emperor Hadrian to build a Temple to Jupiter on the former site of the Jewish Temple, was finally the third event. Bar-Kochba managed to bring independence to the Province of Judea, and he was considered by Rabbi Akiba to be the true Messiah. Hence, the Jewish Christians

---

15. Ibid., 47–48.
16. See also John 12:42 or 16:2.
17. See Wright, *New Testament*, 451–52.
18. Cf. Dunn, *Partings*, xxiii–xxiv.
19. Ibid., 302–3.
20. Cf. Simon, *Verus Israel*, 196–201; 254–64.
21. Dunn, *Partings*, 313. The Christians are the *Minim* or "heretics."

Wirkungsgeschichte

"had to choose between Jesus and bar-Kohba."[22] In 135, Jerusalem was destroyed again, leaving the place to Aelia Capitolina.

My first witness, *The Epistle of Barnabas*,[23] gives us an early insight. According to Michael W. Holmes, it could have been written out of the "anxiety that a rebuilt temple in Jerusalem might result in a Jewish renaissance, or competition from a vibrant Jewish messianic movement." With a great use of allegory, the author of the epistle deals with the covenant Israel has lost through her idolatry, disobedience, and ignorance. In chapter 4, it is interesting to note an allusion to Romans 2:6–10:

> 4:12 The Lord will judge [*krinei*; *apodōsei* in Rom] the world, playing no favorites [*aprosōpolēmptōs*; *prosōpolēmpsia* in Rom]. Each will receive according to what he has done [*epoiēsen*; *ta erga autou* in Rom]. If he is good [*agathos*; *to agathon* in Rom], his righteousness [*hē dikaiosunē*; *dikaioi* in Rom] will precede [*proēgēsetai*] him; if evil [*ponēros*; *to kakon* in Rom], the reward for his wickedness [*tēs ponērias*] will be before [*emprosthen*] him. 13 As those who are called we must never lie down and lose consciousness of our sins, allowing the evil ruler to receive the authority against us and force us out of the Lord's kingdom. 14 And still, my brothers, consider: when you observe that Israel was abandoned even after such signs and wonders had occurred in it, we too should pay close attention, lest, as it is written, "many of us were found called, but few chosen."[24]

At first glance, and because of the different vocabulary, it seems that there is not a clear parallel with Romans 2:9–10 regarding the idea of priority. There is no use of the word *prōton*,[25] even though two words indicate a kind of priority: *proēgēsetai* and *emprosthen*. The righteousness will precede the righteous, and the wickedness will be before the wicked. But Barnabas 4:14 also indicates that for the author the judgment had indeed fallen on Israel—since she was abandoned because of her deeds—ahead of "us" (the Greeks) who need to be aware of the fact that it can fall on us (them) too.

Definitively, these three verses of *The Epistle of Barnabas* give us an idea of how Israel was seen by the early church. If we cannot detect any anti-Semitism, we can, however, at least detect anti-Judaism. If priority was

---

22. Ibid., 317–18.

23. Anonymous. This very early text was placed just after *Revelation* and before *The Shepherd of Hermas* in the Vaticanus Manuscript. It was dated in accordance with the two major events of this period: the destruction of Jerusalem and the end of the Revolt of Bar-Kochba (cf. Barn. 16:4). See Holmes, *Apostolic Fathers*, 175.

24. Ehrman, *Apostolic Fathers*, 25.

25. Marcion himself kept the word in these two verses.

given to the Jew, it was a *historical priority*, in his reception of the Law as well as his judgment.

Moreover, when in chapter 13 the author of the epistle is considering "whether it is this people or the first one [*ho prōtos*; the Jewish people] that receives the inheritance, and whether the covenant is for us [the Christians] or them,"[26] he does an allegorical exegesis of the history of Jacob blessing Ephraim and Manasseh in the presence of Joseph, the younger blessed before the older, and concludes: "You see about whom he has decreed, that this people will be the first [*prōton*], and the heir of the covenant."[27] Here, it is clearly stated that if Israel is the older brother regarding the history of the covenant, it is her younger brother who is blessed and the real heir of the covenant.

The Church Fathers until the End of the Roman Empire (135–476)

A general understanding seems to have been in the minds of theologians at the beginning of the Christian era: the principle idea being that the church is the real Israel, the expression of God's ultimate thought.[28] Even though the gospel came to the Jewish people first, because of the covenant made by God with them (*historico-covenantal priority*), it is *also* for the Gentiles. Even if Christianity, historically speaking, comes after Judaism, the younger brother has been blessed in preference to the older. As a result, polemical literature developed over time. Besides evoking some of these dialogues between Jewish people and Gentiles, I will consider the main works written on The Epistle to the Romans during this time. What were the church fathers thinking about the priority inherent in the sixteenth verse of its first chapter?

Origen (185–254): Commentary on Romans

As a great commentator of Romans, Origen's views are important. His commentary on Romans 1:17 shows us that he seems to put more weight on the fact that the gospel is *also* to the Gentile, and *not only* to the Jew:

> The righteousness of God is revealed in the gospel in that no one is excluded from salvation, whether he be a Jew, a Greek or a barbarian. For the Savior says to everyone equally: *Come to me, all who labor and are heavy laden* [Matt 11:28]. Concerning *through*

---

26. *Barn.* 13:1, Ehrman, *Apostolic Fathers*, 61.
27. *Barn.* 13:6, Ibid., 63.
28. Cf. Simon, *Verus Israel*, 91–97.

> *faith for faith,* we have already said that first people were in the faith, because they believed God and Moses his servant, from which faith they have now gone over to the faith of the gospel.[29]

By insisting that the gospel is also for Gentiles this text demonstrates the fear that existed at the beginning of the church, viz. that the Jewish people were the only beneficiaries of salvation. On account of the covenant, by believing God and Moses, Israel was saved first by faith. Now believing in Jesus, she is still saved by faith. But the Gentiles need to know that the gospel is addressed to them too. We will see later that this interpretation won a lot of approval throughout the centuries. Eusebius Pamphili (c. 265–340) expresses the same idea in his *Proof of the Gospel*.[30] For Mark Reasoner, Associate Professor of Biblical and Theological Studies at Bethel University (St Paul, MN), "Origen, perhaps inspired by Romans 3:2 and 9:4, says that Paul is right to place the Jews first, since they were the first people to live under laws, laws in their divine origin better than Greek laws."[31] This statement expresses a clear *historical priority (HP)*.

Ambrosiaster (~375): Commentary on Romans[32]

In the commentary of Ambrosiaster on Romans 1:16 and 2:9, there is a reference to the ancestors of the Jewish people, expressing a *historico-covenantal priority*: "Therefore, although Paul puts the Jews first because of their ancestors, nevertheless he says that they must also accept the gift of the gospel in the same way as the Gentiles."[33] Regarding Romans 2:9-10, he states:

> Paul always puts the Jew first, whether he is to be praised or blamed, because of the privileged ancestry. If he believes he will be all the more honored because of Abraham, but if he doubts he will be treated all the worse, because he has rejected the gift promised to his forefathers.[34]

---

29. Bray, *Ancient Christian Commentary*, 30-31.

30. "But further by His own Presence also He shared Righteousness with all men, shewing by His works that God is not only the God of the Jews, but also of the Gentiles." In Eusebius, *The Proof of the Gospel*, 121.

31. Reasoner, *Romans*, 2.

32. *Ambrosiastri qui dicitur Commentarius in Epistulas Paulinas*. "The most intriguing suggestion [as regards his identity, is] . . . that he may have been a monk known as Isaac the Jew, who was a converted Jew in Rome." In Bray, *Ancient Christian Commentary*, xxiii.

33. Ibid., 29.

34. Ibid., 61.

To the Jew First or to the Jew at Last?

The heretical bishop Apollinaris of Laodicea (c. 300-391), in his *Pauline Commentary from the Greek Church*, has the same understanding regarding 2:9: "Paul is right to put the Jew first here and then the Greek. For those who are closer to the Lord and to his rebukes are honored above others, and they enjoy their rewards more than others."[35] If the Jewish people are honored because of Abraham, no opportunity is taken to affirm that the church first needs to proclaim the salvation in Jesus to them. But, rather, they need to receive the gospel in the same way as the Gentiles. The honor lies in the fact that they were the first to be served.

John Chrysostom (347-407): *Homilies on Romans*

The commentary by this famous preacher on Romans 1:16 shows a clear *HP*: "the 'first' is an honor in order of time only. For he has no such advantage as that of receiving greater righteousness, but is only honored in respect of his receiving it first."[36] Regarding Romans 2:9, he understands that the Jew will be judged "first" because of the instruction he did receive. In his mind, it concerns the situation "before Christ's coming":[37]

> Having shown the extreme seriousness of the disease . . . Paul goes on to give the Jew the greater burden in the tribulation. For the Jew has enjoyed a larger share of instruction and so also deserves to suffer a larger share of the punishment if he does wrong. The wiser or mightier we are, the more we will be punished if we sin [See Luke 12:48].[38]

We know that Chrysostom had to deal with a crisis in a congregation at Antioch regarding "Judaizing" behavior (desire to celebrate Easter at Passover, fast on the Jewish fast days, for example).[39] This crisis may have hardened his thoughts about the Jewish people and influenced his view to the extent that he abandoned the idea that they could be converted.[40]

Pelagius (350-420), in his *Commentary on Romans*, follows the same argument. While he does not mention the phrase "to the Jew first and also

---

35. Ibid., 62.
36. Schaff, *Chrysostom*, 349.
37. Ibid., 363.
38. Bray, *Ancient Christian Commentary*, 61.
39. Cf. Harkins, *Chrysostom*, xxvi-xxvii.
40. "Certainly, it is the time for me to show that demons dwell in the synagogue, not only in the place itself but also in the souls of the Jews." Ibid., 24.

to the Greek" in Romans 1:16 and 2:9,[41] he states as regards 2:10: "The word *first* is emphatic and means *indeed*, because God does not play favorites. Or it may mean first in time but not in honor."[42]

Augustine (354–430): Commentaries on Romans and Psalms

Reasoner notices that Augustine does not deal with Romans 1:16–17 in his *Commentary on Statements in the Letter to the Romans* and his *Unfinished Commentary on the Letter to the Romans*: "The omission of any comment especially in the former work fits with the general impression that in the patristic period these verses were not viewed as the thesis of the letter in the way they are often assumed to be now."[43] Augustine's note on Romans 9:24 indicates, however, that he follows in the wake of the general thought previously examined:

> "We whom he has called not only from the Jews but also from the Gentiles," . . . the Jews should not glory on account of their works, who, when they had received the Gospel, thinking that this should be attributed to their own merit, did not want it to be given to the Gentiles.[44]

Clearly, Augustine recognizes that the Jewish people do not deserve any preferential treatment; his interpretation could certainly be seen as supporting the HP. In his *Enarrationes in Psalmos,* he offers an allegorical exegesis of Psalm 58:11 (MT 59:11) and identifies the enemies of David as the Jewish people at the time of Jesus and at his own time: David asks God not to kill them but to scatter them. Augustine states as a fact that "through all nations there have been scattered abroad the Jews, are witnesses of their own iniquity and witnesses of our truth."[45] For him, the Jewish people have a position to fill and a role to play: they have been scattered throughout all nations and are witnesses to their iniquity as well as to the Christian truth. The Jewish people need to survive in order to make the number of Christians

---

41. De Bruyn, *Pelagius's Commentary*, 63; 71.
42. Bray, *Ancient Christian Commentary*, 63.
43. Reasoner, *Romans*, 3.
44. Augustine, *Propositions on Romans*, 37 (#64).
45. Augustine, *Psalms*, 241. Cf. Augustini, *Psalmos*, Sermon I. 22, 705, with a reference to Romans 11: "per omnes gentes dispersi sunt Judaei, testes iniquitatis suae et veritatis nostrae." See also Blaise Pascal in his *Pensées*: "If the Jews had all been converted by Jesus-Christ, we should have none but questionable witnesses. And if they had been entirely destroyed, we should have no witnesses at all." In Pascal and Eliot, *Pensées*, 225 (#749).

increase ("'Slay not them, lest sometime they forgot Thy law:' [Ps 59:12], in order that the nation of Jews might remain, and by it remaining the number of Christians might increase."),[46] until they themselves are saved: "for how they were found together in iniquity, come together in such a way to salvation. 'Not only to the Jews,' says the Apostle, 'but also even to Gentiles.'"[47] As Marcel Simon points out:

> So then, at the same time as it encouraged both official and popular anti-Jewish attitudes, the Church did have an eye to the survival of Judaism and the Jews. Hatred must no be pushed to the point at which the Jews were exterminated. The law takes account of this theological necessity. . . . The Church held it to be a duty to pray for the Jews, and the fathers frequently recall the fact. Israel had prepared the way for the Church and the Church owed its existence to her.[48]

Here we see an extremely interesting concept, which we do not find amongst the preceding church fathers: a theological necessity.[49] This theological necessity of the survival of Israel will be fully realized when Israel, according to Romans 9–11, is saved at the end of time. A somewhat paradoxical idea thus develops: Israel has been stripped of her place and has only herself to blame, but at the same time, her presence is indispensable for the existence of the church. It is interesting to note that there is no incentive to proclaim the gospel to the Jewish people, let alone to give Jewish evangelism priority. Later in history, the interpretation will be pushed further: in order to see Israel saved the gospel first needs to be preached to the Gentiles, until their number is complete.

Conclusion

If the sources at my disposal by the first theologians seem clearly to present a historical interpretation of the expression "To the Jew first" (with some reference to the Jewish ancestors), I have on the other hand no evidence for a *missional priority (MP)*, a permanent priority in evangelism given to the Jewish people that would still be valid today, for instance, according to the

---

46. Augustine, *Psalms*, 241.

47. Ibid., 243, with a surprising reference to Rom 2:10 (cf. note 5) instead of Rom 9:24 as in Augustini, *Psalmos*, 711: "quomodo enim pariter inventi sunt in iniquitate; ita pariter pervenient ad salutem. *Non solum ex Judaeis*; inquit Apostolus, *verum etiam ex Gentibus* (Rom. IX, 24)."

48. Simon, *Verus Israel*, 229–31.

49. Cf. Fritz, "L'expression 'Au Juif premièrement,'" 22.

understanding of Jews for Jesus. The conviction of a conversion of the Jewish people at the end of time, if it exists, falls under the sovereignty of God.

As Jewish-Christian relations were progressing little by little towards a clear-cut separation—due to an anti-Judaism tinged with anti-Semitism—the destiny of Israel according to the flesh was settled. She was a fallen people and, in the end, a witness of God's intervention in human history, destined to be a sign for the world until the end of time.

THE MIDDLE AGES (476–1492)

For my purposes the medieval period can be divided into two major phases separated by the memorandum against the Talmud, submitted to Pope Gregory IX in 1236. In Europe, the church was well settled, well structured, and had great authority in spiritual, social and political affairs. It was also a time when persecution of the Jewish people took place continuously until a strong attempt was made to convert the Jewish people.

From the End of the Roman Empire to the Memorandum against the Talmud

In the first part of the Middle Ages, relationships between the Jewish people and the church were, *grosso modo*, relatively good.[50] It was even a time of some prosperity for the Jewish people. Augustine's understanding of the Jewish people as "witnesses of their own iniquity and witnesses of our truth" seems to have been the view of the papacy, introduced first by Gregory the Great (590–604)[51] and lasting until Pope Innocent III (1160–1216).[52]

At the same time, in order to fight against the Turkish Muslim power and free the holy city of Jerusalem, a first crusade was announced in 1095 by Pope Urban II during the Council of Clermont. This holy campaign was

---

50. Cf. Keith, *Hatred*, 117.

51. Gregory the Great wrote: "Just as one ought not to grant any freedom to the Jews in their synagogues beyond that is permitted by law, so should the Jews in no way suffer in those things already conceded to them." In Marcus and Saperstein, *Jew in Medieval World*, 126.

52. In a letter to the Count of Nevers, he wrote: "Thus the Jews, against whom the blood of Jesus Christ calls out, although they ought not be killed, lest the Christian people forget the Divine Law, yet as wanderers ought they to remain upon the earth, until their countenance be filled with shame and they seek the name of Jesus Christ, the Lord." In Grayzel, *Church & Jews*, 127.

not directed at the extermination of the Jewish people.[53] However, due to its popularity and a lack of clear directives given by the papacy to the populace, the crusades became a Jewish issue. Some crusaders clearly chose to give the Jewish people the alternative between baptism and death, and others took advantage to enrich themselves at Jewish expense. Others satisfied their hatred towards this people, while some others had millenarian expectations of the situation.[54] Accusations against the Jewish people emerged during the beginning of the twelfth century: e.g., the first charge of a child ritual murder in England in 1144, cannibalism and stealing of hosts to torture Christ, first caricature of Jewish people drawn as fiends.[55]

Finally, after the memorandum against the Talmud, the Inquisition—which was at first not directed against the Jewish people but against heresies among Christians like the Cathars—was directed against them.[56] At the beginning of the thirteenth century, Jewish people were less and less the living witnesses to Christian truth, to restate Augustine's words.

Peter Abelard (1079–1142)

Abelard, scholastic philosopher and theologian, wrote a *Commentary on the Epistle to the Romans* where, according to Reasoner, he "gives no evidence of the latter fixation of these verses as the thesis statement of Romans"[57] and interprets *prōton* in historical terms:

> For *first* the apostles were converted from the Jews, through whom the preaching of the Gospel penetrated to the Greeks thereafter, and finally to the Latins. And so that passage, which says *first*, with regard to the Romans or other Gentiles, can refer at the same time to the Jews and the Greeks; or let us say that

---

53. Cf. Keith, *Hatred*, 127–28.

54. According to Keith (ibid., 128–29), the idea that some of the crusaders would have been influenced by millenarian expectations, which led them to suppose the end of the world was at hand and the conversion of the Jewish people was imminent, has no evidence, but Edwards states that "[i]t seems that the mighty spiritual upsurge which followed Pope Urban II's famous call to crusade at Clermont in late 1095 contained a significant element of such [a millenarian] sentiment, related to the approaching century 1100, and stimulated by the chance, suddenly offered, to be physically present in the Holy City, Jerusalem, where both Jews and Christians believed the events of the end of time would begin" (Edwards, *The Jews*, 18–19).

55. See Keith, *Hatred*, 131–34.

56. Ibid., 134–35.

57. Reasoner, *Romans*, 3.

in the time of the Apostle Paul they were converted *first*, that is, especially, from the other peoples.[58]

Guibert of Nogent (1095): Appeal of Urban II at the Council of Clermont

I have consulted six different appeals of Urban II at the Council of Clermont, the council that announced the first crusade. The one reported by Guibert, Abbot of Nogent, is worthy of interest:

> Behold, the Gospel cries out, "Jerusalem shall be trodden down by the Gentiles until the times of the Gentiles be fulfilled." ... Or, again, *"the times of the Gentiles" are the fulness of time for those Gentiles who shall have entered secretly before Israel shall be saved.* These times, most beloved brothers, will now, forsooth, be fulfilled, provided the might of the pagans be repulsed through You, with the cooperation of God. With the end of the world already near, even though the Gentiles fail to be converted to the Lord (since according to the apostle there must be a withdrawal from the faith), *it is first necessary, according to their prophecy, that the Christian sway be renewed in those regions either through you, or others,* whom it shall please God to send before the coming of Antichrist, so that the head of all evil, who is to occupy there the throne of the kingdom, shall find some support of the faith to fight against him.[59]

In this text, the millenarian expectation clearly gave more priority to the conversion of the Gentiles, who, in that part of the world, were not exposed to any Christian witness, than to the salvation of the Jewish people, which will follow that of the Gentiles.

William of St Thierry (1075–1148): Exposition on Romans

> The witness of the Abbot of St Thierry is interesting for this period of history. Regarding our phrase he wrote in his commentary on Romans: First to Jew and then to Greek, that is, to the Gentiles, "for salvation is of Jews." The Greeks first gave the human race two names, saying that every man was either a Greek or a barbarian, so that whoever was not a Greek was

---

58. Abelard, *Romans*, 111.
59. Krey, *First Crusade*, 36–40. Italics mine.

a barbarian. But Paul makes a much truer distinction, placing Jews first, then Greeks and finally barbarians. Since the Greeks preferred themselves to others because they used laws, the Apostle rightly sets the Jews before the Greeks, because they had previously received all their laws from God.[60]

St Thierry, in his interpretation, stated that the Jewish people previously received their laws from God, laws which then came to the Greeks (through the gospel), and in this way the "salvation is from Jews." No opportunity is taken to propose an *MP*. His interpretation is clearly based upon the *HP* argument.

From the Memorandum of 1236 to the Expulsion of the Jewish People from Spain

As I have already mentioned, if the Inquisition was not at first directed toward Judaism, the memorandum against the Talmud, submitted to Pope Gregory IX in 1236 by a French Jewish convert, Nicholas Donin, puts a new light on the issue. According to Donin and his acolyte Pablo Christiani, "The book of Judaism" was contradicting or even replacing the Bible, claiming for example that Jesus was a bastard.[61] Jewish converts should be regarded as insincere, as they might be influenced by other Jewish people to renounce their Christian faith, especially if they had been baptized forcibly.[62] Thus began hard times for the Jewish people: however important their social position, they were condemned to become money-lenders, with limited legal rights.[63]

At the same time, as tons of Jewish literature were destroyed, a great missionary effort to convert the Jewish people began in order to protect Christians from Jewish teaching. There is no indication that this happened as a response to an order from Romans 1:16c, understood as an *MP*. The interpretation of Augustine could not be sustained: instead of being witnesses, they were enemies of the Christian truth! The Dominican and Franciscan orders were given the task by Pope Nicholas III (1277–1280) to organize the mission among the Jewish people. Ramon Lull, Franciscan tertiary, was a typical representative of the monastic order and was described as being "the first to develop a theory of missions."[64] He studied Islam and Judaism alike,

60. Of Saint Thierry, *Romans*, 31.
61. Krey, *First Crusade*, 33–36.
62. Keith, *Hatred*, 134–35.
63. Ibid., 118–19.
64. Neill, *History*, 134.

wrote some 280 books and treatises, and preferred the reasoned argument to coercion. With the permission of King James II of Aragon, he used to enter the synagogues on the Sabbath to preach. He established a college for Jewish people to learn Latin and philosophy in order to win them for the gospel. Facing rejection from them, he stood in the tradition of Nicholas Donin and of the friars: Jewish people were guilty of serious blasphemy. As Edwards states:

> The friars were active preachers, especially the Dominicans who existed for this sole purpose, and there is no doubt that they saw conversion of the Jews as one of their main tasks. ... The starting point of this process was the assumption that, up to Jesus's birth on earth, the Jews had had a valid place in the divine plan for mankind. Up to that point, the Jews were indeed the Chosen People, as they themselves still claimed and their Law, or Torah, was divinely sanctioned. However, in Jesus, God had replaced the Torah with a new "law of grace," embodied in the Saviour himself.[65]

It was with the arrival of the Black Death (1348–1350), supposed to have been spread by Jewish people poisoning the wells, that anti-Semitism took a new turn.[66] Jewish Communities were expelled from many European countries, most significantly from Spain in 1492.[67] For the "conversos," life was hard. While some, like Paul of Burgos and his son Alonso de Cartagena, were respected because they engaged with the church, many had their faith called into question. The Spanish Inquisition was lying in wait.

Saint Thomas Aquinas: Lectures on the Letter to the Romans

Saint Thomas Aquinas was very prolific, and addressed our issue in his *Lectures on the Letter to the Romans*. He wrote some very useful, relevant, and lucid comments. Even if the word "covenant" is not employed in Aquinas' statement, a *historico-covenantal priority (HCP)* is expressed:

---

65. Edwards, *The Jews*, 19–20.
66. Keith, *Hatred*, 121–22.
67. The more well-known in reason of the shock lived by this massive expulsed population which had flourished in the thirteenth century. Others took place in Europe: "[W]hatever may be done to reduce the high tradition estimates of Jewish emigration from Spain, there is no doubt that a major movement of population took place, involving well over 100,000 people, in the four months of the official expulsion period and afterwards," while at least 300,000 conversos stayed in the country. See Edwards, *The Jews*, 34.

> 101. The third thing to be considered is the people for whom the Gospel works salvation, namely, both the Jews and the Gentiles. For God is God not of the Jews only, but also of the Gentiles, as he says below in 3(:19); hence he adds *to the Jews first and also to the Greeks*. . . . But since he says below (10:12) *There is no distinction between Jew and Greek*, why does he say here that the Jew is first? The answer is that there is no distinction as far as the goal of salvation to be obtained is concerned, for both obtain an equal reward, just as in the vineyard the early and the late workers received one coin in Matt 20(:10). But in the order of salvation the Jews are first, because the promises were made to them, as is said below in chapter 3(:2), whereas the Gentiles were included in their grace like a branch grafted into a cultivated olive tree, as is said in chapter 11(:24). Also, our savior was born from the Jews: "Salvation is from the Jews" (Jn 4:22).[68]

Development of the Mission to the Jewish People

In the late Middle Ages, the friars tried to develop resources to understand Hebrew, Aramaic, and Jewish theology and gave assistance to proving the fulfillment of the messianic prophecies, and to contradicting the Talmud. As Michael Rydelnick argues correctly, we are witnesses of a real effort to evangelize the Jewish people but with no indication of an *MP*. One thing is clear: the gospel was *also for the Jewish people* at that time.[69]

Conclusion

Thus, through the Middle Ages, the theological conviction of Augustine, that the Jewish people were "witnesses of their own iniquity and witnesses of our truth," was set aside. If it was at first the view of the papacy to handle the relationships between the church and the Jewish people cautiously, the memorandum against the Talmud submitted to Gregory IX by Nicholas Donin in 1236 changed this policy. As the Jewish people "had promoted the Talmud in preference to these [their own] Scriptures,"[70] they were no longer the witnesses to their truths,[71] and they became the enemies. With

---

68. Aquinas, *Romans*, 57.

69. See Rydelnik, "Ongoing Importance,", 261–91. Admittedly Rydelnik's purpose is not to argue for the *MP*. However, as it is part of a book dedicated to the "Jew first," it is interesting to note that no historical texts are given in support of the motto.

70. Keith, *Hatred*, 126.

71. Cf. ibid., 125–26.

a lack of clear directives given by the papacy regarding the first crusade, aided by anti-Semitism, the Jewish people were the object of hatred and forced conversion. The great effort by the friars to build a mission among the Jewish people was established more forcefully than sympathetically and was very ineffective. The expulsion of the Jewish people—seen as stubborn people who tried to kill Christians through the Black Death—from almost all the countries of Europe was a completion of anti-Semitism. In this context, we will understand that an *MP* was not on the agenda of the church, and there is apparently no indication of an understanding of Romans 1:16 in that sense. If the gospel was "to the Jew first" it was understood in the sense that "salvation was from the Jews" (*HCP*), but if there was any priority—seen especially during the crusades—it was to preach first the gospel to the Gentiles of the Middle East. These were oppressed by the power of the Muslim infidels, and this mission was energized by the belief it would speed up the fulfillment of the Gentile number, inaugurating the salvation of Israel and the return of Christ.

THE REFORMATION

The verses of Romans 1:16–17 have a very special place in the history and theological development of Martin Luther. But how, in general, did the Reformers understand the expression "to the Jew first"?

Erasmus (1466?–1536): *Paraphrases on Romans*

The Catholic priest Desiderius Erasmus Roterodamus, precursor of the Reformation, commented on Romans 1:16, though again understanding it in a historical way:

> Although this power is equally effective for all, nevertheless, as the Lord commanded, it was offered first to the Jews for the sake of honour; soon, through preachers of the gospel, to be spread among the Greeks and all the nations of the world, so that all equally might acknowledge their own righteousness and seek the righteousness of God, whether they be Scythians or Britons.[72]

---

72. Erasmus, *Paraphrases on Romans*, 17. Regarding the funny allusion to the "Britons," a note (13 on p. 141) specifies: "The 1517 edition reads: 'It has been propagated first among Jews and Greeks.' The change was made in 1532."

To the Jew First or to the Jew at Last?

Luther (1483–1546): *Lectures on Romans* and Other Writings

According to Johannes Ficker, the editor of the lectures in the Weimar Edition, Luther's lectures were delivered in 1515:[73]

> 1:16. *For I am not ashamed of the Gospel*, in spite of 1 Cor. 1:23: "A stumbling block to Jews and folly to Gentiles," *for it is the power*, that is, the strength, *of God for salvation to everyone*, both Gentile and Jew, *who has faith*, and on the other hand, for damnation to him who does not have faith, *to the Jew first*, because the Jews alone have the Promise, and *also to the Greek*, that is, the Gentiles.[74]

> 2:9–11. 9. *There will be tribulation and distress*, by which a man is held tight so that he cannot escape, *for every soul of man who does evil*, but he does evil who is outside of faith, as is revealed below, no matter how great his work may be, *the Jew first*, because to them everything was told first, *and also the Greek*, that is, the Gentiles. 10. *But glory*, praise, as explained above, *and honor*, reverence, *and peace*, both inwardly and outwardly, *for everyone who does good*, but no good work is done except in faith, *the Jew first, and also the Greek*. The Jew, I say, and also the Greek because: 11. *For there is no respect of persons with God*, namely, for punishing or rewarding both Jews and Gentiles less or more.[75]

Two observations can be drawn from these two short—but balanced—commentaries. First, the explanation provided by Luther concerning the "first issue" is that "the Jews alone have the Promise" and that is why "to them everything was told first." Even if this explanation will be the object of the third chapter, this interpretation can already be classed under the *HCP*. Secondly, Luther insists on the fact that Gentiles are not sidelined. It is also interesting to note that, in his commentary of Romans 2:10, Luther dissolves the second *prōton* into a strong "both inwardly and outwardly,"[76] leading into an assertion of "no respect of persons" in 2:11. Apparently for Luther, the phrase "*te prōton kai*" seems to mean an emphatic "both . . . and"! As for his understanding of Romans 11, he thinks that it does not talk about a conversion of a great number, but, despite the obscurity of the text, recognizes, however, "that the Jews who are now fallen shall return and be saved."[77]

---

73. Cf. Luther, *Lectures on Romans: Glosses and Scholia*, x.
74. Ibid., 8–9.
75. Ibid., 18.
76. Ibid., 18.
77. He expresses this view with the help of Luke 21:23–24; Deut 4:30–31; Hos

What about the anti-Semitism of the elderly Luther? According to Hillerbrand, his attitude could be explained by his political agenda, his apocalyptic views and his conviction of the imminence of the end of the world, as well as his health, and his late and mature understanding of the Jewish as a chosen people who have rejected the Messiah and whose influence therefore needed to be restricted. He expressed disappointment at the fact that, despite the gospel now being available to all, he did not see the Jewish people being converted.[78] Whatever the reason for this late anti-Semitism, I must recognize, however, that although Luther encouraged the evangelization of the Jewish people in his early life, it was not according to an *MP* coming from Romans 1:16c.[79] Luther was not the only Reformer to have anti-Jewish views. Martin Bucer opened the way, though in a less extreme way. At the same time, some other theologians can be quoted as having a positive approach to Jewry, for instance, Andreas Osiander who, in 1529, exonerated the Jewish people of the blood-libel charge.[80]

Zwingli (1484–1531): Early Writings

In his *A Friendly Request and Exhortation of Some Priests of the Confederates that the Preaching of the Holy Gospel be not Hindered, and also that no Offence be Taken if to Avoid Scandal the Preachers were Given Permission to Marry*, written in 1522, Ulrich Zwingli declares: "Now the Gospel is, as Paul writes to the Romans, I., 16, nothing but the power of God for the good or welfare of each who believes, be he Jew or heathen, although from the beginning of the world it was first revealed to the Jews."[81] This sentence shows us that, like Luther, Zwingli wants to insist that the gospel, if it was first revealed to the Jewish people, is also for the heathen: *historical priority*. Here Zwingli explicitly mentions that the "first" refers to the first preaching of the gospel in the first century and so, consequently, is not linked to the preaching of the gospel today.

3:4–5; 5:12, 15; Matt 23:38–39 and the figure of Joseph in Gen 37. Cf. Luther, *Lectures on Romans: Glosses and Scholia*, 429–30.

78. Cf. Hillerbrand, "Luther & Jews," 132–34.

79. Melanchthon, disciple of Luther, did not unfortunately comment on the expression "To the Jew first" in his commentary of 1540. See Melanchthon, *Romans*, 65–71.

80. Cf. Stern, *Josel of Rosheim*, 181–83, in Keith, *Hatred*, 177.

81. Zwingli, *Early Writings*, 167.

To the Jew First or to the Jew at Last?

Tyndale (1525): *The Pistle of. S. Paul to the Romayns*

It is interesting to look at Tyndale's translation of Romans, which has touched so many through its use in the King James version,[82] all the more since Tyndale did not literally translate the word *prōton* with "first," but with "namely," removing at the same time all idea of priority, as Pelagius had done: "For I am nott ashamed of the gospell of Christ, because it is the power of God unto salvacion to all that beleve, namely to the iewe, and also to the gentyle."[83] From this revealing error, I infer that, for Tyndale, Jewish people should not have any priority other than the one they had in history. I have no indication of any anti-Semitism by Tyndale and no note to explain this choice of translation to confirm my conclusion.

Calvin (1539): Commentary on Romans

Of course, the second great figure in the Reformation is Jehan Cauvin, alias John Calvin. If he seems silent on the Jewish question, his careful exegesis of Scripture tends to imply a more positive view of the Jewish people. His successors had the tendency to consider the Jewish people favorably, all the more so since they were likewise living in the Diaspora.[84] At the time that Calvinists were busy building the new Protestant Credo they did not really pay attention to the chosen people until they began to consider their unaccomplished future.[85]

As with Luther, the promise (and the calling) is the key to Calvin's interpretation of the adverb *prōton*. After discussing Paul's use of the doublet "Jews and Greeks" to summarize "all mankind," Calvin writes:

> By a figure of speech he therefore unites the Gentiles with the Jews in the participation of the Gospel, without depriving the Jews of their eminence and rank, *since they were the first in the promise and call.* Paul, therefore, maintains for the Jews their

---

82. Cf. Daniell, *Tyndales's New Testament*, vii.

83. Cooper and Daniell, *New Testament by Tyndale*, 321. The same word "namely" is used in the version of 1534: "For I am not ashamed of the gospel of Christ, because it is the power of God unto salvation to all that believe, namely to the Jew, and also to the gentile" (Cf. Daniell, *Tyndales's New Testament*, 225). Strangely, he keeps "first" in Rom 2:9–10. Nevertheless, The King James Version, issued in 1611, does not keep this mistake in its translation.

84. Keith, *Hatred*, 178.

85. Ibid.

Wirkungsgeschichte

prerogative, but he immediately adds the Gentiles as being sharers with them of the Gospel, though in a lesser degree.[86]

Calvin, who is not noted for his anti-Semitism, concedes that the Jewish people, because of the covenant, have the first rank and order in the plan of God. Hence they had the prerogative in regard of the gospel, as the older children. If Calvin mentions nothing about the issue of *MP*, he clearly appears to be a proponent of the *historico-covenantal priority*.

Conclusion

Although the Reformers initially tried to revive a positive consideration of Jewry, and while anti-Semitism and expulsions of Jewish people from countries in Europe were continuing until the 1570s, the words of Bucer and of the elderly Luther will leave a black mark in history. Although there was no clear exposition about a missional priority, the Reformation refocused the historical understanding of the priority on the covenant.[87]

MODERNITY: THE TURNING POINT

The period of "modernity" includes some very important historical occurrences regarding our discussion: Puritanism, Pietism, Modern Missions, dispensationalism, the Tübingen School, Modern Zionism, and the Shoah. This period is characterized by a better attitude toward Jewish people and Judaism with the desire to know more about them. As Jocz states:

> Instead of maintaining, as the old Church did, that the Jewish people is utterly rejected by God, it was now [in our modern age] recognized that Israel had still a great future. This change was to a large extent effected by the revival of eschatological interest . . .[88]

---

86. Calvin, *Romans & Thessalonians*, 27. Italics mine.

87. Also during that Reformation time, Emanuel Tremellius, a Jewish Christian, published *Catechism for Enquiring Jews* in 1554, reprinted by *The London Jews Society* in 1820, whose "catechetical technique of question and answer has a continuing place in evangelism today." See Harvey, "World Jewish Mission," 25.

88. Jocz, *Jewish People & Jesus Christ*, 221. However, anti-Semitic thoughts—and even anti-Judaic ones—were obviously expressed by such people as Johann Andreas Eisenmenger, Voltaire, Napoleon and Hitler (See Keith, *Hatred*, 195–241).

To the Jew First or to the Jew at Last?

Puritanism (c. 1560–1892)[89]

After the persecution of the Protestants by Mary Tudor, the accession of Elizabeth I of England in 1559 allowed the Marian Exiles and some Protestants who had stayed in the country to found the movement of Puritanism. The *Geneva Bible*, which included extensive marginal notes, took over from Tyndale's translation after its appearance in 1560.[90] In Calvin's own time in Geneva a new interest was emerging in a future mass conversion of Jewish people. Indeed, in its 1557 and 1560 editions, the *Geneva Bible* contained this note on Romans 11:26: "He sheweth that the time shall come that the whole nation of the Jews, though not every one particularly, shall be joined to the church of Christ."[91]

Due to the popularity of this Bible, the idea of a future large-scale conversion of Jewish people became widespread and influenced the Puritans who developed a vigorous interest in unfulfilled prophecies. Peter Martyr's *Commentary upon Romans*, published in London in 1568, was particularly influential, to such an extent that Hugh Broughton (1549–1612), one of his students at Cambridge, "had the distinction of being the first Englishman to propose going as a missionary to the Jewish people in the Near East, and also first to propose the idea of translating the New Testament into Hebrew for the sake of the Jews."[92] Several other thinkers taught on this massive conversion of Jewish people.[93]

It is interesting to note that this massive conversion could be understood in the same way as Augustine had done, i.e., a conversion of the Jewish people at the end of times, after the *plērōma* of the Gentiles had come in. Keith quotes an interesting critique by the Jewish historian Barbara Tuchman of "the leader of a nineteenth century English society":[94]

> To him, as to all the Israel-for-prophecy's-sake school, the Jews were simply the instrument through which biblical prophecy could be fulfilled. They were not a people but a mass error that must be brought to a belief in Christ in order that the whole

---

89. C. H. Spurgeon's death (31 January 1892) is regarded as the end of Puritan influence according to Murray, *Puritan Hope*, 185.

90. 140 editions of this Bible were issued until 1644. See ibid., 3–35.

91. Ibid., 41.

92. Ibid., 42

93. For example Johann Heinrich Alsted and Joseph Mede. Cf. Clouse, "Rebirth of Millenarianism," 42–65.

94. It is not specified who.

chain reaction leading to the Second Coming and the redemption of the mankind might be set in motion.⁹⁵

However, some divergences of views regarding these unfulfilled prophecies appeared likewise around 1670. Should one wait for a great conversion of the Jewish people or, in fact, of the nations? The question was focusing on the interpretation of the word *plērōma* ("fullness," "full number," etc.) in Romans 11:12, 25. To sum up, on the one hand, some were seeing the conversion of the Jewish people only as a way to bring a great blessing to the Gentiles, on the other hand, others were thinking of a double-conversion of the Gentiles, the first before the conversion of the Jewish people (Romans 11:25), the second after it (Romans 11:12):⁹⁶ "By *fullness* here, (as in ver. 12,) understand a great number or multitude of Gentiles, greater, by far, than was in the apostles' days."⁹⁷ Or:

> [T]he Scripture Speaks of a *double conversion* of the Gentiles, the first before the conversion of the *Jewes*, they being *Branches wilde by nature* grafted into the *True Olive Tree* instead of the *naturall Branches* which are broken off. This fulness of the *Gentiles* shall come in before the conversion of the *Jewes*, and till then *blindness* hath happened unto Israel, Rom. 11.25. The second, after the conversion of the Jewes . . .⁹⁸

Between 1627 and 1640, many ministers escaping from the Puritan persecution emigrated to New England and saw their responsibility to preach the gospel to the Heathen, the most well-known being John Elliot.⁹⁹ Considering the understanding of our phrase, it is interesting to look at the interpretation of Romans 1:16 by the same Matthew Poole quoted above: "*To the Jew first, and also to the Greek*; the gospel was first to be published to the Jewish people, and then to the Gentiles, whom he here calls Greeks:

---

95. Tuchman, *Bible & Sword*, 178, quoted by Keith, *Hatred*, 186–87. Tuchman expresses anti-Semitism in this quest of unfulfilled prophesies, but Keith notices at the same time that "[t]here is evidence from both England and the Netherlands of improved and more positive attitudes toward the Jews."

96. See Murray, *Puritan Hope*, 69–72. In that case, the *plērōma* of Rom 11:12 is understood in the same way as in 11:25. The Jewish people will live a *plērōma* which will bring the *plērōma* to the Gentiles (see chapter 4).

97. Poole, *Commentary on Holy Bible*, 519.

98. Corporation for Promoting the Gospel among the Indians in New England and Whitefield, *Strength out of Weakness*, no page, quoted by Murray, *Puritan Hope*, 72.

99. In 1649 the *Society for Propagation of the Gospel in New England* was created.

see Luke xxiv. 47; Acts i. 8. This order the apostles accordingly kept and observed, Acts xiii. 46."[100]

Here, Poole adopts an *HCP* and describes how this priority was observed according to Acts. He presumably thought that this priority lapsed after the period of Acts. As a representative Puritan thinker, the sermon on Romans 1:16 by John Owen on the 19th May 1670 is also worth quoting: "The word 'first' there, respects the order of dispensation, and not a priority of efficacy or excellence. The word was first to be preached to the Jews, as you know, in many places, and that for many ends not now to be insisted on."[101]

It is interesting to notice that a big movement of prayer in favor of the Jewish people followed this rediscovery of Romans 11:25–26, in order to hasten their conversion, even if there is no indication of an *MP*. Thomas Boston expresses it this way:

> Are you longing for a revival to the churches, now lying like dry bones, would you fain have the Spirit of life enter into them? Then pray for the Jews. "For if the casting away of them be the reconciling of the world; what shall the receiving of them be, but life from the dead."[102]

Pietism (from c. 1675)

Concurrently, Philipp Jacob Spener (1635–1705) awoke Lutheranism in Germany and called for an evangelical piety, not dissimilar to that of the Puritans, and mission. It is fascinating to read his understanding of the mystery of Romans 11:25–26 in the second part of his *Pia Desideria* (1675), which deals with "The Possibility of Better Conditions in the Church":

> If we consult the Holy Scriptures we can have no doubt that God promised his church here on earth a better state than this.
>
> In the first place, we have the glorious prophecy of St. Paul and the mystery revealed by him in Romans 11: 25–26, that after the full number of the Gentiles comes in, all Israel will be saved. So if not all, at least a perceptibly large number of Jews who have hitherto hardened their hearts will be converted to the Lord. . . . In order for the Jews to be converted, the true church must be in a holier state than now if its holy life is to be a means for that conversion, or at least the impediments to such conversion (which, as we have seen above, have

---

100. Poole, *Commentary on Holy Bible*, 480.
101. Goold, *John Owen*, 220.
102. Boston, *Whole Works* 3, 359.

hitherto consisted of offenses) are to be removed. On the other hand, if the Jews are converted by God's power in a manner which it is impossible for us to foresee, it is unthinkable that the example of this newly converted people (who would undoubtedly have a zeal like that of the early heathen who were converted to Christianity) would not be followed by a remarkable change and improvement in our church.[103]

Spener links the prosperity of the church with the conversion of a great number of Jewish people at the end of the world, and "[i]n order for the Jews to be converted, the true church must be in a holier state than now if its holy life is to be a means for that conversion."[104] Hence, he sees the evangelization of Jewish people based more on the attempt to "provoke their jealousy" (Rom 11:14) than on the preaching of the gospel by words. It is also interesting to see the link he makes with Romans 1:16 through the phrase "God's power [of salvation]." Having said that, can one argue on behalf of an *MP*? I have to admit, once again, that the idea is still not present. One of his disciples, Johann Albrecht Bengel, whose understanding of *plērōma* was similar to that of the Puritans', can write in 1740:

> [T]he age of missions to the heathen and to the Jews is not fully arrived.... But though it is too early for the *general* conversion of Jews and Gentiles, it appears a sin of omission on the part of Protestant churches, that they have not begun long ago to send missions to both.[105]

If Johann Heinrich Callenberg (1694–1760) "has become through his pietism the real father of the mission to the Jews,"[106] the great revival in British missionary societies occurred in the 1790s: The Baptist Missionary Society was founded in 1792, The Missionary Society (later renamed The London Missionary Society, or LMS) in 1795, The Church Missionary Society in 1799, etc. Until 1834, ten other societies saw the light of day, including The London Society for Promoting Christianity Amongst the Jews (LSPCAJ) in 1809.[107] "The results of their work is [*sic*] shown by the fact that at least a quarter of a million Jews were won for Christ during this century."[108]

---

103. Spener, *Pia Desideria*, 76–77.

104. Ibid., 77.

105. Burk, *John Albert Bengel*, 323, quoted in Murray, *Puritan Hope*, 132.

106. My translation. See De Le Roi, *Die evangelische Christenheit 1*, 253: "Er ist durch seinen Pietismus in Wahrheit der Vater der evangelischen Judenmission geworden."

107. And the nineteenth century saw the creation of a hundred of missions among the Jews! Cf. Thompson, *Century of Jewish Missions*.

108. Schonfield, *History*, 154.

To the Jew First or to the Jew at Last?

The London Society for Promoting Christianity Amongst the Jews (1809)

As I have already said, throughout the eighteenth century the idea of the conversion of the Jewish people gained greater credence. But it is only after the founding of the LSPCAJ, or simply called The London Jews Society (LJS), that the expression "to the Jew first" was used *for the first time* as an *MP* interpretation of Romans 1:16c.[109]

In its report dated May 23, 1809, its secretary Legh Richmond reports:

> On this ground, in conformity to our Lord and Master's last commandment, we feel it to be our indispensable duty to preach his gospel to every creature. In doing this, so far as *you* are concerned, we are additionally supported by the firm persuasion that this very gospel is the power of God unto salvation to everyone that believeth; to the Jew *first*, and also to the Gentile.[110]

According to the website of this mission, known since 1995 as the Church's Ministry among the Jewish People (CMJ),[111] everything began as follows, with a clear influence of Pietism:

> Providentially, in 1795, a young Jewish man, Joseph Levi, from Maynstocheim in a province of Franconia in Germany had a divine appointment with a pietist Christian and heard clearly about the promise of a new covenant with the house of Israel (Jeremiah 31). A few short years later in 1798, he came to faith in Jesus (Yeshua) as Messiah and was given a new name, Joseph Samuel Christian Frederick Frey, a well-known name in CMJ history.[112]

---

109. So Martin Pakula, Lecturer in missiology at Melbourne School of Theology, who is the only one among the proponents of a *missional priority* to recognize this fact. Cf. Pakula, *First for Jews*, 14: "The call of the gospel to go first to the Jew was taken up at last again in the early nineteenth century. In 1809 the London Society for Promoting Christianity among the Jews was formed." Hugh J. Schonfield comes close to this interpretation when he says: "The Church was awakening to the Gentile need of Christ in far off lands, but the Apostolic order 'To the Jew first,' had so far touched few Christian consciences. . . . It had to wait for Jewish Christians to plead the cause of their brethren before any real active work was started. Joseph Samuel Frey (1711–1837 [*sic*, 1771–1850 are to be preferred]) and Ridley Herschell (1807–1864) were the inspirers of the London Society and the British Society, respectively, for Promoting Christianity among the Jews." Cf. Schonfield, *History*, 154.

110. Richmond, *Report Of The Committee*, 50.

111. Cf. CMJ website. Online: www.cmj.org.uk, accessed April 2012.

112. CMJ website. Online: http://www.cmj.org.uk/about/ourhistory, accessed April 2012.

Wirkungsgeschichte

As for Kelvin Crombie, he recalls in his book, *For the Love of Zion*, that:

> For many years the LJS was the most popular of the many gospel societies of the time. Its motto "To the Jew First" alluded to the claim of the Apostles that the Jews were to be proselytized prior to the members of other faiths, because "the world should be evangelized through the Jews."[113]

Indeed, among the four statements of the founding of the LJS are:

1. declaring the Messiahship of Jesus to the Jew first and also to the non-Jew;
2. endeavouring to teach the church its Jewish roots;
3. encouraging the physical restoration of the Jewish people to Eretz Israel—the Land of Israel;
4. encouraging the Hebrew Christian/Messianic Jewish movement.[114]

In his article dealing with the first decade of the *LJS*, John Yeats explains the importance of the booklet *Obligations of Christians to Attempt the Conversion of the Jews* written by the anonymous "Presbyter of the Church of England." This promotes the prioritization of evangelism to the Jewish people as a pre-cursor to world mission.[115]

> The Jews are every where dispersed; they are the mediums of commercial communication, and the brokers of the world; they are trained up in the knowledge of the languages, habits, and manners of the nations amongst whom they dwell; and are thereby prepared with one of the essential qualifications of missionaries, whenever the Lord shall take the veil from their hearts.[116]

Within a world population of 800 million, among which many Gentiles were converted, the London Missionary Society judged it better to invest money in the evangelization of Gentiles rather than Jewish people. Conversely, the main committee of the *LJS* judged that "if the task of Jewish conversion could not be accomplished, the mission to the heathen engaged by the LMS, The Church Mission Society (*CMS*), and other organizations

---

113. Crombie, *Love of Zion*, 3. A link can be made between Spener's idea that the Jewish people "would undoubtedly have a zeal like that of the early heathen who were converted to Christianity" (see above) and the LJS's to see the world evangelized through the Jewish people.

114. Ibid., 3.

115. Yeats, "Jew First," 207–23, esp. 214–15.

116. PCE, *Obligations*, 26–27, quoted by Yeats, "Jew First," 215.

would ultimately fail."[117] Here we find again the idea expressed by Moishe Rosen in the *Evangelical Missionary Quarterly*.[118]

One main task of the *LJS* was to establish a church in Palestine in order to fulfill its goals. "Christ Church," a combination of an orthodox Anglican church and a synagogue, was built in 1849 and was protected by the British Consulate in Jerusalem.[119] Alexander McCaul was one of the famous leaders of the enterprise.[120]

For the *LJS*, part of the plan was to see the physical restoration of the Jewish people to Eretz Israel, a sign of the ultimate restoration ("restorationism"). At the same time the Society leased a church in London called "The Episcopal Jews Chapel" dedicated to the Jewish believers. This church was at the center of the Hebrew-Christian or Messianic Jewish movement, and its adherents got involved in all kinds of social work among the Jewish community, particularly under the auspices of the Church of England. As a result of this social aspect of *LJS*, a *Philo-Judaean Society* was founded in 1827, with a stronger focus on evangelization. In 1839, a four man "Mission of Inquiry into the state of the Jews" was sent from the Church of Scotland to Palestine. Among them was Robert Murray M'Cheyne.[121]

The commentary on *The Epistle to the Romans* by Robert Haldane in 1816 can be considered as a transition between the *HCP* and the Missional one:

> *To the Jew first.*—From the days of Abraham, their great progenitor, the Jews had been highly distinguished from all the rest of the world by their many and great privileges. . . . The preaching of the Gospel was to be addressed to them first, and, at the beginning, to them alone; . . . Thus, while Jews and Gentiles were united in the participation of the Gospel, the Jews were not deprived of their rank, since they were the first called.
>
> The preaching of the Gospel to the Jews *first*, served various important ends. It fulfilled Old Testament prophecies, as Isa. ii. 3. It manifested the compassion of the Lord Jesus for those who shed His blood, to whom, after His resurrection, He commanded His Gospel to be first proclaimed. It showed that it

---

117. Cf. Yeats, "Jew First," 213–16.

118. See Introduction.

119. It even had the first Anglican/Protestant bishop of Jewish birth since the Bar Kochba revolt: Michael Solomon Alexander, a former rabbi, in 1841. Cf. Crombie, *Love of Zion*, 8.

120. In fact, Dr McCaul's daughter Elisabeth became the wife of the British consul. Cf. ibid., 16.

121. See his influence on the proponents of the *MP* in chapter 2.

> was to be preached to the chief of sinners, and proved the sovereign efficacy of His atonement in expatiating the guilt even of His murderers. It was fit, too, that the Gospel should be begun to be preached where the great transactions took place on which it was founded and established; and this furnished an example of the way in which it is the will of the Lord that His Gospel should be propagated by His disciples, beginning in their own houses and their own country.[122]

In my view this commentary is a step towards an *MP* and reflects the views of the time, but I cannot say that Haldane was clearly in favor of an *MP*. In 1835, the very influential Charles Hodge, despite his belief in the future restoration of the Jewish people,[123] expresses, at least in his commentary, a historical understanding of Romans 1:16, certainly within a covenantal feature if we consider his reference to John 4:22:

> First, therefore, must refer to time: "To the Jew in the first instance, and then to the Gentile." Salvation, as our Saviour to the woman of Samaria, is from the Jews. From them the Messiah came, to them the Gospel was first preached, and through them it was preached to the Gentiles.[124]

Dispensationalism (from the 1820s)

The rise of dispensationalism at that time influenced fundamentalist thought and by extension the mission among the Jewish people, and continues to this day. The preacher Edward Irving especially promoted the idea of the pre-millennial advent of Christ during the May anniversary of the London Missionary Society in 1824. He was influenced by Hatley Frere and the Jesuit priest Manuel Lacunza.[125] But John Nelson Darby was the one who structured, promoted, and gave it very original features.[126] The evangelist D. L. Moody was very influenced by his ideas and promoted it even more.[127]

---

122. Haldane, *Romans*, 47–48.
123. See Sims, *Jew First*, 57.
124. Hodge, *Romans*, 29.
125. Cf. Murray, *Puritan Hope*, 188.
126. Interestingly, Mal Couch, President of *Scofield Ministries*, links the development of Darby's thesis with the Jewish expectation among the rabbis of the coming of the Messiah in 1840. See Couch, *Jew First*, 50–51.
127. In 1934, Hoffman Cohn writes that there are "[n]o colleges for Jewish Christians, the nearest we have is the Jewish Missions Course of the Moody Bible Institute of Chicago, and what a hard time even that department has to get its support!" In

To the Jew First or to the Jew at Last?

Darby's prophetic beliefs were spread all over the English-speaking world due to the popularity of the *Scofield Reference Bible*.

For Darby, who saw a "Church in ruins," only God could intervene to save his world. The hope of a gospel spreading over the whole earth "during the actual dispensation" was out of the question.[128] His pre-millennial thesis was the new hope given to Evangelical Christendom.[129] At the same time, Darby preached the restoration of Israel in her land.[130] In fact, in his thesis, he claims that for God, Israel is his terrestrial people and the church his spiritual. This is the reason why the Dispensationalist "concludes that when the Church was introduced God did not abrogate His promises to Israel nor enmesh them into the Church."[131]

In his commentary on Romans 1:16–17 Darby does not seem to express the idea that the Jew should be evangelized as a priority:

> This is the force of the expression which is translated "from faith to faith"—on the principle of faith unto faith. Now the importance of this principle is evident there. It admits every believing Gentile on the same footing as *the Jew, who has no other right to entrance than he*.[132]

According to dispensationalism, God will sovereignly intervene through the tribulation, ending the dispensation of the church and then pouring out the blessing on Israel. At the end of the seventieth week according to Daniel 9:27, Jesus will come back to establish his millennial kingdom and realize, in this way, all the unfulfilled prophecies regarding Israel according to the flesh.[133] Prophecies were not to be fulfilled through the church anymore but through the personal reign of Christ. Therefore, premillennialist missionaries tended to focus on the conversion of individual souls over establishing churches.

Three commentaries of that time can be quoted to express the variety of understandings regarding the priority of Romans 1:16.

Hoffman Cohn, *Beginning*, 90–91. David Brickner, actual director of Jews for Jesus went to Moody Bible Institute in Chicago, where the pre-millennial dispensationalism is still taught. Cf. Brickner, "Jesus' Return," 261–71.

128. Darby, "Progress of Evil on the Earth," 483.
129. Cf. Reese, *Advent of Christ*, 316.
130. Cf. Darby, "Lecture 4: Romans 11," 265–78.
131. Ryrie, *Dispensationalism*, 96.
132. Darby, *Synopsis Acts–Philippians*, 120. Italics mine.
133. Cf. Murray, *Puritan Hope*, 201.

Adam Clarke, in 1857, believes that "[n]ot only the Jews have the *first* offer of this gospel, but they have the *greatest* need of it; being so *deeply fallen*, and having sinned against such *glorious privileges*."[134]

Strangely enough, Charles Haddon Spurgeon (1834–92) does not remark on the expression.[135] Sims is quoting him as a supporter of the "Jew First Principle": "a greater prominence should be given to prophecies in teaching the Jews than among any other people."[136] It is true that Spurgeon believed in the political restoration and the resurrection of the people of Israel, and also in Jewish evangelism, but Sims omits the words preceding this quote. Spurgeon was of the opinion that prophecies should be preached *particularly* among the Jewish people, which is very different from an *MP*: "I would not commend, as some do, the everlasting preaching of prophesy in every congregation. But a greater prominence should be given to prophecies in teaching the Jews than among any other people."[137]

As for Frédéric Louis Godet, in 1879,

> It would be false to say that salvation is intended for the Jews *in preference* to the Greeks. Paul has in view the right of *priority in time* which belonged to Israel as the result of its whole history. . . . It was for Jewish believers to convert the world. For this end they must needs be the first to be evangelized.[138]

The Tübingen School (from 1826)

Ferdinand Christian Baur (1792–1860), founder of the *Tübingen School*, is a key figure in the development of Protestant Liberalism and is especially important regarding our topic. Using the wording of Karl Barth, Baur's *thesis* of the Gentile-Christian-Pauline Party (*Galatians*) and his *antithesis* of the Jewish-Christian-Petrene one (*Corinthians*) finds its synthesis in Primitive Christianity (*Romans*).[139] Baur's distinction of Jesus the Jew and Paul the founder of Christianity is still vigorous today and, even if he himself wrote

---

134. Clarke, *Romans*, notes on Rom 1:16.
135. Spurgeon, *St. Luke XV. 8 to Romans III. 25*, 883–88.
136. Sims, *Jew First*, 56.
137. Spurgeon, *Restoration & Conversion*, 10:426.
138. Godet, *Romans I*, 153.
139. See Harris, *Tübingen School*, xiii. Regarding our issue, Barth thinks: "The Jew, the religious and ecclesiastical man, is, it is true, FIRST summoned to make the choice; this is because he stand quite normally on the frontier of this world and at the point where the line of intersection by the new dimensional plane (i. 4) must be veritably seen (ii. 17–20; iii. I, 2; ix. 4, 5; x. 14, 15). But the advantage of the Jew provides him with no precedence." See Barth, *Romans*, 40.

no commentary on Romans, his thoughts shaped many scholars.[140] Even though I cannot prove that Baur was an anti-Semite, his thesis fueled anti-Semitic thought.[141]

From that date, commentaries dealt with the synthesis suggested by Baur in different ways. For example, Godet explains that

> Volkmar holds that Paul might ascribe a priority to the Jews in relation to *judgment*, as he does ii. 9, but not in connection with *salvation*; the πρῶτον of ii. 10 he therefore holds to be an interpolation from ii. 9, and that of our ver. 16, a second interpolation from ii. 10. An ingenious combination, intended to make the apostle the relentless enemy of Judaism, agreeably to Baur's system, but belied by the missionary practice of Paul, which is perfectly in keeping with our *first* and with that of ii. 10.[142]

As for W. Sanday & A. C. Headlam's commentary (1895), after referring to all the privileges of the Jewish people, it suggests:

> For the precedence assigned to the Jew comp. Rom. iii. 1, ix. 1ff., xi. 16 ff., xv. 9; also Matt. xv 24; Jo. iv. 22; Acts xiii. 46. The point is important in view of Baur and his followers who exaggerate the opposition of St. Paul to the Jews. He defends himself and his converts from their attacks; but he fully concedes the priority of their claim and he is most anxious to conciliate them.[143]

This last commentary recognizes that the Jewish people had the right to receive the gospel first, but nothing is said of an ongoing priority. At the same time, Modern Zionism was emerging.

Modern Zionism (beginning 1897)[144]

The movement established by Theodor Hertzel, which has seen thousands of Jewish people coming back to Palestine until this present day, has led to

---

140. Through J. B. Lightfoot, A. Ritschl, A. von Harnack, J. Weiss, W. Wrede, R. Bultmann to quote a few. See Dunn, *Partings*, 1–11.

141. "[I]t is Paul who has provided the theoretical structure for Christian anti-Judaism, from Marcion through Luther and F. C. Baur down to Bultmann . . ." in Gager, *Anti-Semitism*, 11.

142. Godet, *Romans I*, 153.

143. Sanday and Headlam, *Romans*, 24.

144. Date of the first General Zionist Congress. As for the book of Theodor Hertzel, *Judenstaat: Versuch einer modernen Lösung der Judenfrage*, it was published in 1896. The old Zionism is as old as the history of Israel (See Sokolow and Hertzberg, *Zionism*).

the success of dispensationalism and has delighted many Christians. Modern Zionism, despite its political overtones and despite being encouraged by an English-Christian coalition, has been the inheritor of the Puritan vision. Despite its potential influence on the theological views of that period, it was still the historical approach that met with universal approval among the commentators.[145]

We have already seen that the famous Charles H. Dodd believed an *MP* was limited to the beginning of the church (see Introduction). Paul Althaus had the same understanding; it was a priority in the *Heilsgeschichte*:

> therefore Paul emphasizes nevertheless in the "first" (see also 2:9) the special position of the Jews, which Israel has as the people of God regarding the history of Salvation: to her salvation is first promised (cf. 3:1 ff further, Chap 9–11). That is in accordance to the attitude of Jesus, see Mark 7:27; Matt 22:1 ff et al. That is why Paul also brings the gospel first to the Jews (see Acts 13:5 and often).[146]

R. C. H. Lenski did not believe that the "first" applies only to the "Jews," but also to the "Greeks." Neither had priority over the other in historical terms. His quite original views have never been explored further![147]

C. R. Erdman clearly expressed in 1925 an *HCP*: "Salvation is proclaimed for the Jew 'first' not only in time, but by way of eminence. The Scriptures are his, the promises are his, the Christ is his 'according to the flesh.'"[148]

As for A. Schlatter, the priority lay in the election of Israel:

> Paul first brings Jesus' call to the Jew; God's grace is seeking the Jew out first, not because the Jew is especially guilty on account of the conflict with the law (2:9), for the work of God is not based solely on the human need but is built upon God's previous work. The divine word that Jesus spoke does not disavow the divine word spoken previously but confirms it instead (1:2). For this reason

---

145. For Lietzmann, "prōton is a factually worthless (see 3:1ff) concession to the 'chosen people of God.'" My translation. See Lietzmann, *Römer*, 30, note on verse 16: "πρῶτον ist eine faktisch wertlose (vgl. 3 1 ff.) Konzession an das 'auserwählte Volk Gottes.'" As for Brunner, he says nothing (cf. Brunner, Romans, 15)."

146. My translation. See Althaus, *Römer*, 12–13: "so betont Paulus doch in dem 'zuerst' bei dem Juden (s. auch 2,9) die besondere Stellung, die Israel als das heilsgeschichtliche Gottesvolk hat: ihm zuerst ist das Heil verheißen (vgl. weiter 3,1 ff.; Kap. 9–11). Das entspricht der Haltung Jesu, vgl. Mk.7,27; Mt. 22,1 ff. u.a. Daher geht auch Paulus mit dem Evangelium zuerst zu den Juden (vgl. in der Apg. 13,5 und oft)."

147. Cf. Lenski, *Romans*, 76–77.

148. Erdman, *Romans*, 27.

> he is calling the Jew first because the Jew is blessed more than the Greek, on account of his share in God's elect community.[149]

Conclusion

Thus, it is clear that, following the impulse given by Puritanism and Pietism, the view that Jewish people should be given priority when evangelizing emerged at the beginning of the nineteenth century and was adopted by the constitution of The London Society for Promoting Christianity Amongst the Jews in 1809. A combination of factors, such as a huge missional effort toward Israel, dispensationalism, and Modern Zionism confirmed growing interest in the role of the Jewish people in eschatology (Romans 9–11 and Revelation 20 being the major texts). The nineteenth century saw the creation of one hundred missions among the Jewish people, and, although many disintegrated in the storm of the wars and other revolutions in Europe,[150] the beginning of the twentieth saw a great number of Jewish people become believers in Jesus, especially between the two wars.[151] But then came the Shoah . . .

SHOAH, ITS AFTERMATH, AND JEWS FOR JESUS

I cannot add to the many things that have already been written on the human disaster of the Shoah. This event, which led to the creation of the new State of Israel, marked a turning point in Jewish-Christian relationships. I do need to mention, however, as John Edwards perfectly states, that:

> It is important for the non-Jewish reader to remember, at all times, that any consideration by Jews of the Jewish role in European history in earlier periods is likely today to be, to a greater or a lesser extent, consciously or unconsciously, governed by

---

149. Schlatter, *Romans*, 19.

150. Cf. Glaser, "Lessons," 222: "Dozens of missions to the Jews, in fact, existed by the turn of the twentieth century, with more than five hundred missionaries to the Jewish people serving throughout the world. The vast majority are, of course, no longer functioning."

151. Sir Leon Levison (see ibid., 229) evaluates at 230,000 Jewish people become Christian believers during the first third of the century (more than the 224,000 Jews become believers in Jesus during the whole nineteenth century according to De Le Roi, *Judentaufen im 19*, 49! As Tucker, *Not Ashamed*, 62, reports by quoting *The Universal Jewish Encyclopedia*, "These [De Le Roi's] figures are manifestly too low. . . . Actually the number of converts during this period must have been considerably higher."

Wirkungsgeschichte

the experience, either personal or vicarious, of the Shoah or Holocaust.[152]

Shoah (1939–1945) and Its Aftermath

The Shoah has indeed deeply changed the way Christians see the Jewish People. The horrors of the genocide have transformed the general mindset of Christianity. How was such a terrible catastrophe able to occur in our educated and Christian European world? Since the Shoah, many books have been written to find the reason for this incredible event grounded in a supposedly Christian country.[153] Since the Shoah, mission among the Jewish people has been deeply challenged. Rosemary Ruether expresses this idea when she remarks:

> Missionary theology is itself in crisis, and the dogma that all men must be Christian to be saved is being rethought on the missionary front. Missionaries now seek to provide only human solidarity and service, rather than conversion, and even here it is often hard to separate "service" from Western acculturation. Christianity, having lost its own political establishment in the West, also has all but lost, except for fundamentalists, the notion that all men should become Christians. Today, for the first time, Christianity must come to terms with itself as a particularism among other particularisms, one language among other languages. This forces a rethinking of Christian universalism and its historic negation of the ongoing validity of Jewish particularism.[154]

Gregory Baum, German Catholic Jew, though he himself was convinced that the church needs to preach the gospel to the Jewish people, recognized in 1961 that the mission among the Jewish people needed to be rethought:

> It is not surprising then that many Christians of our day hesitate to use the term "mission" in regard to Israel. Some writers as a matter of fact go so far as to claim that, quite apart from the question of terminology, the Church of Christ has no mission at

---

152. Edwards, *The Jews*, 5.

153. See for example Rubenstein and Roth, *Approaches to Auschwitz: The Legacy of the Holocaust*. More recently, Landau, *Studying Holocaust* or Rittner et al., *Holocaust*. From a more Jewish point of view: Katz et al., *Wrestling with God* or Cohn-Sherbok, *Understanding Holocaust*.

154. Ruether, *Faith*, 235.

all to the Jewish people, that Christians are not sent to announce Christ to the Jews and that Jews are not meant to accept him now as their saviour. The Church, according to these writers, has a mission to the Gentile nations, not to Israel. . . . I conclude then that the Church has a mission in regard to the Jewish people and that individual conversions of Jews are part of the divine plan for the Church even in this age. I am, nevertheless, of the opinion that words such as "Jewish mission" have become unpleasant and almost offensive by reason of the memories they evoke, and that in our century proselytism and convert-making spread an atmosphere of tactlessness.[155]

As we have seen with Rabbi Poupko, the link between Shoah and Christianity appears to be so apparent for the Jewish people that, even until today, missions to the Jewish people are often accused of anti-Semitism.[156] On the other hand, for evangelicals, not to preach the gospel to the Jewish people—i.e., to let Jewish people go to hell—can appear to be as much anti-Semitic, as the *Manila Manifesto* declares: "We affirm, that they [the Jewish people] need Him [Jesus Christ] as much as anyone else, that it would be a form of anti-Semitism, as well as being disloyal to Christ, to depart from the New Testament pattern of taking the Gospel to 'the Jew first . . .'"[157]

The creation of the new State of Israel, initiated by the United Nations declaration of 1947 brought eschatological hope in many Christian minds, especially the ones convinced of dispensationalism and its various forms. "This event . . . gave credence to the dispensationalist integration of Old Testament predictions concerning a return of the Jews to possess their ancestral homeland."[158] However, as Mitch Glaser points out: "By the 1950s, missions to the Jews, although filled with enthusiasm over the establishment of Israel, was [sic] in a post-Holocaust decline, which would not be reversed until the turning to the Messiah of young, Jewish people during the 'Jesus movement.'"[159]

---

155. Baum, *Jew & Gospel*, 246–49.
156. Cf. Poupko and Guthrie, "Jew First," first response.
157. LCWE, "Manila Manifesto," no page.
158. Grenz, *Millennial Maze*, 92.

159. Glaser, "Lessons," 231. In 1993, Richard Harvey counted fifty-eight missions among the Jewish people, mainly stationed in the USA and nearly half of them founded after 1960, with 835 missionaries, of which 119 are Jewish believers. Cf. Harvey, "World Jewish Mission," 28–31. This shows the revival; obviously, many other missions among the Jewish people were created since then. As far as I know, no survey has been done since.

Wirkungsgeschichte

In this particular atmosphere, we will not be too surprised to discover that in the post-Holocaust period until post-modernity the historic understanding of the priority still, by and large, predominated.[160] Anders Nygren, in 1944, wondered: "Does this after all mean that the Jew has *special preference in salvation? That cannot be what Paul means.* The word may refer to Israel's special history. In that case their priority is now abolished with the coming of Christ."[161] The supporters of this HCP acknowledged the primacy of Israel due to her election, as, for instance, C. K. Barrett stated: "That the Jews were the first to hear the Gospel is to Paul more than a fact of history; it was due to God's election."[162] They were not keen to answer the question of priority directly and insisted on the fact that the gospel is for whoever believes, whether he be Jew or Greek.[163] H. W. Schmidt thought that *prōton* was signifying a greater need of the Jewish people (because of their religious advantage) just as well of the Greeks (because of their cultural advantage): "The concluding words of the sentence *Ioudaiō te prōton kai hellēni* do not give a description of the *panti* (*all*, i.e., both Jews and Non-Jews), but say that the gospel is especially needed most by those who think they do not need it."[164]

However, John Murray, though a Reformed theologian,[165] can be quoted as a representative of an *MP*. Even if the claim is ambiguous, he did clearly state that Christianity was still firstly for the Jewish people:

> it was the divine economy that the gospel should have been preached first of all to the Jew (*cf.* Luke 24:49; Acts 1:4, 8; 13:46). It does not appear sufficient to regard this priority as that merely of time. . . . The lines of preparation for the full revelation of the gospel were laid in Israel and for that reason the gospel is pre-eminently the gospel for the Jew. How totally contrary to

---

160. Some simply avoid the issue, as Barclay, *Romans*, 18-23, Foreman, *Romans*, 15, Steel and Thomas, *Romans*, 14-15, or even Bruce, *Romans*, 78-79 (see, however, Bruce, *The Hard Sayings of Jesus*, 106, which tends more toward a historical interpretation).

161. Nygren, *Romans*, 72-74. Italics mine.

162. Barrett, *Romans*, 29.

163. As for Leenhardt, *Romans*, 48-49, or Kuss, *Römerbrief*, 21-22.

164. My translation. See Schmidt, *Römer*, 27: "Die Schluβworte des Satzes Ἰουδαίῳ τε πρῶτον καὶ Ἕλληνι geben keine Umschreibung des παντὶ (*alle*, nämlich sowohl Juden wie Nichtjuden), sondern sagen, daβ das Evangelium gerade denen, die es nicht nötig zu haben meinen, am nötigsten ist."

165. For another plea for a *MP* from a Reformed angle, see Pratt Jr, "Jew First," 168-88. On page 168, he admits: "The Calvinistic tradition has without doubt many things to learn in this area, and perhaps a few things to contribute to an interdenominational discussion."

the *current* attitude of Jewry that Christianity is for the Gentile but not for the Jew.[166]

Vatican II (1962–65) put an emphasis upon dialogue instead of mission on the part of the churches regarding the Jewish people and, a fact worthy of note, issued an official declaration stating that the Jewish people were exempted from any accusation of deicide.[167] As for the Six-Days War of 1967, it allowed some evangelicals to think that Jerusalem was no more governed by Gentiles: the times of the Gentiles was fulfilled, according to Luke 21:24.[168] But it was the Jesus Movement (1968–80) that marked another turning point regarding our topic. It produced a flourishing or revival of many missions to the Jewish people, among them, Jews for Jesus.

Jesus Movement, Jews for Jesus, and American Zionism.

Although Jews for Jesus (JFJ) was officially founded in 1973, its roots can be situated ten years before. In fact, JFJ emerged from a combination of factors, namely a revival among the Jewish people in the Jesus Movement that began in the late 60s and the influence of Moishe Rosen (1932–2010).[169]

Rosen, who became a Christian in 1953, was a Baptist Minister before becoming a street evangelist with the American Board of Missions to the Jews (ABMJ), of which he became the director of recruiting and training in 1965. At the same time, Jewish Hippies were meeting in a Ranch in Oregon. Rosen, following a talk with Bob Berk, was concerned for the Hippies and their need for the gospel.[170] These events led in 1970 to the birth of a ministry in the "heart of the counterculture," San Francisco.[171] The merging finally took place after the parting of Rosen from the ABMJ and the creation of Hineni Ministries in 1973,[172] which soon became JFJ.

As already mentioned, Rosen understood Romans 1:16 as expressing an *MP*:

---

166. Murray, *Romans*, 28. Italics mine.

167. For this last part, see Cottier and Henry, *Nostra Aetate*.

168. Cf. Horner, *Future Israel: Why Christian Anti-Judaism must be challenged*, 81. Crombie recalls us that it is only "[o]n 30 July 1980 [that] the Israeli Knesset passed the Jerusalem Law, which declared that *all* of Jerusalem was to become the undivided and eternal capital of Israel." In Crombie, *Love of Zion*, 256.

169. Martin Meyer Rosen: Moishe is his Hebrew name. See Rosen and Proctor, *Jews for Jesus*, 15.

170. Ibid., 59.

171. Ibid., 64.

172. Ibid., 125–26.

Wirkungsgeschichte

> From the beginning, my desire to spread the gospel among the Jews was reinforced by what the Apostle Paul said in Romans 1:16.... I identify with that statement completely. It is a battle cry that echoed inside me from the earliest days of my Christian experience.[173]

JFJ is not the biggest mission currently among the Jewish people but it is the most well-known one. What was initially used as a slogan on the streets became and still is the nickname for numerous Messianic Jews in the world. The mission employs more than 200 Jewish missionaries in ten countries. It is a very creative mission that uses not only tracts but also music, media, and any other tools which can serve its purposes.

This revival among the American Jews has to be put alongside Evangelical Fundamentalism and American Christian Zionism. After the creation of the new State of Israel, a new fervor for Israel has been born among the evangelicals in America and, through its influence, all over the Western world. This fervor includes

> the promise of God's blessing for those who bless the Jews; gratitude to Jews for establishing the foundations of Christianity; remorse for the Church's past anti-Semitism; fear that God will judge the nations based on how they treated the Jewish people; and reliance on Israel as the West's firewall against Islamist terrorism.[174]

Today, it is mainly evangelicals (especially premillennian dispensationalist) who support JFJ spiritually and financially. At the same time, these same evangelicals often support Zionism and think that the return of the Jewish people to their land is the necessary and sufficient condition for their conversion before the Second Coming of Christ.[175]

Conclusion

Thus, if the first part of the post-Holocaust period saw the mission among the Jewish people called into question, post-modernity saw, in the midst of the evangelical world, the revival of a new Christian hope toward the Jewish people. Encouraged by the establishment of the State of Israel, and especially the Jewish control of Jerusalem in 1967,[176] and by new Jewish-

---

173. Ibid., 34
174. Spector, *Evangelicals & Israel*, inside cover.
175. Cf. Grenz, *Millennial Maze*, 96–97.
176. Jerusalem being no more "trampled on by the Gentiles." Cf. Luke 21:24.

Christian relations, this period provided good soil for the birth of many missions among the Jewish people and a new understanding of the *MP*.

CONCLUSION

In conclusion of this *Wirkungsgeschichte*, I can note that the idea of evangelizing the Jewish people first by referring to Romans 1:16c was only introduced in 1809, the date of the creation of the London Jews Society. It is therefore apparent that Rabbi Poupko was wrong when he was saying: "First for the gospel, and because of that, first for persecution and suffering. That is what 'to the Jew first' has meant for 2,000 years."[177]

Indeed, until 1809, it appears that the only reading of this verse was that the salvation of God—expressed either in the Old or in the New Testament—had been first proclaimed to the Jewish people because of the privilege inherent in the covenant of God with Abraham. After the descendants of the Patriarchs rejected it, the gospel of the New Covenant was then proclaimed to the Gentiles. It was a *historico-covenantal priority* (HCP). Actually, before 1809, the focus was to evangelize the Gentiles first, according to Romans 11:25–26, "A hardening has come upon part of Israel, until the full number of the Gentiles has come in. And so all Israel will be saved." The number of the Gentiles needing to be full, the effort should be concentrated on them, so that a massive conversion of Jewish people would precede the second coming of Christ. In this way, the Jewish people were rather witnesses of their iniquity and witnesses of our [Christian] truth, "testes iniquitatis suae et veritatis nostrae," to quote the famous words of Augustine.

Throughout history, the mission among the Jewish people evolved according to Jewish-Christian relations; the parting of the ways, anti-Semitism, occasional dialogues, and various interpretations of Romans 9–11. The chosen people became, alternately, a fallen one, a witness of God's intervention in human history, a threat to Christianity, a scapegoat and, finally, the hope of the second coming of Christ.

As a matter of fact, all the interpretations of Romans 1:16c can be categorized under one of these two interpretations, a *historico-covenantal priority* or a *missional priority*, whereas the latter also includes the former. The fact that Romans 1:16c was not interpreted in a missional way until 1809 does not invalidate it, even if it is not in its favor. Being heir of the Reformation, I am well aware of its spiritual revolution, and we are still reforming our minds. New insights into Scripture emerge because of the dialogue between the text and the conditions of the interpreter; we are all influenced by our age and

---

177. Poupko and Guthrie, "Jew First," Poupko's first response.

tradition and it is not surprising that the *missional priority* emerged with the birth of the modern missionary movement as well as in a time where love for Israel was newly awakened. I now need to outline the detailed arguments of the proponents of the *missional priority* and evaluate them.

II

Status Quaestionis
The State of the Question: A Critical Survey of the Arguments of the Proponents for the Missional Priority (MP) Interpretation

AT THE TIME OF writing of this chapter, the 2011 January American *Jews for Jesus Newsletter* was received in the mailbox of about 115,000 American Christians, mostly evangelical. Its main article, written by the Executive Director David Brickner, is entitled: "First and Also."[1] In it, Brickner notes that when Romans 1:16 is quoted, "the last nine words of this strong biblical admonition: 'for the Jew first and also for the Greek [Gentiles]'" are usually forgotten. In this January 2011 edition, Brickner's aim is clear: "As we begin this new year, I want to underscore those often omitted words from Romans 1:16, because I believe they *illuminate God's ongoing plan for evangelism.*"[2]

Commenting on his recent attendance at the third Lausanne Congress on World Evangelism,[3] Brickner regrets that even there, as this verse was quoted twice, the nine words were still missing, implying a certain interpretation of Scriptures: "Most likely, this interpretation reflects the discomfort

---

1. Brickner, "First and Also," 1–2.

2. Ibid., 1. Italics mine. The same aim is present in the "Congregational First Things" column of the January 2005 Newsletter. Cf. Brickner, "First Things," 2.

3. 4,000 Christian leaders from 198 countries met in Cape Town (South Africa) from the 15th to the 25th of October 2010, in order to talk about the global challenges facing the church's mission to evangelize in the twenty-first century.

many people would feel if the priority 'to the Jew first' was still in effect today."[4] For him, this priority does not refer to the fact that the Jewish people are "a kind of ethnic preference by God," or that the Gentiles are "some kind of an afterthought in God's plan," but to the fact that the Jewish people are God's chosen ones: "God's priority 'to the Jew first' remains intact because His faithfulness doesn't waver. He keeps His promises despite the failings of those to whom He makes those promises."[5]

As the caption of the "All Nations" Flag on the front page of the newsletter describes, *"God's intention (and His priority [sic]) was to bring the good news to all the nations."* God chose Abraham in order that all the families of the earth shall be blessed in him (Gen 12:3). Brickner concludes, "You see, God's priorities in saving people are never either/or, they are always both/and; or as the Apostle Paul put it: 'for the Jew first and also for the Gentile.'"[6]

The presence of the theme of the Jewish priority in evangelism—what I call *Jewish missional priority (MP)*—is not excessively mentioned in the JFJ *Newsletter*. Usually the theme is advocated about once a year.[7] However, it is present in every Sunday or weekly evening meeting where a missionary talks about the mission,[8] in the mind of those who hand out tracts in the street during weekly "sorties"[9] or the annual campaign,[10] in the written testimonies which end with the quotation of the verse,[11] or, more rarely, in articles published in the quarterly booklet *Issues*,[12] in the electronic mail *Realtime*[13] or in the *blog*[14] launched more recently. The book written by Ruth

4. Brickner, "First and Also," 1.

5. Ibid., 2.

6. Ibid.

7. Cf. besides the one already mentioned, for instance: Rosen, "Holocaust," 1; Rosen, "Why first?," 1–2; Glasser, "Nothing?," 7; Rosen, "You Asked," 6; Brickner, "Gospel Shout," 1; Brickner, "Russia," 1–2; Brickner, "Expect?," 12; Brickner, "What," 1; Brickner, "Jews Proclaim," 12; Brickner, "Power?," 1; Rosen, "Nuclear Christianity," 7.

8. There is a designated message on the priority of Jewish evangelism. Cf. Brickner, "Chosen for What," no page. However, the verse is easily referred to while preaching on another topic. Cf. also the conference of Brickner in Brickner, "Jewish Resistance," I.A.

9. This "military term" is used to describe the distribution of tracts and one-to-one talks in the streets.

10. Usually, there is at least one annual campaign in every country where the mission is based, besides the local campaign in the American branches and a traditional New York campaign.

11. Cf. Meyer, "Testimony,"; Cohen, "Testimony," and Tafjord, "Testimony," no page.

12. *Issues: A Messianic Jewish Perspective* is a booklet intended for Messianic Jews who want to reflect on their spirituality. Cf. Snyder, *Paul Founder* and Leventhal, "Christian Anti-Semitism?," 1–4.

13. Grady, "Stumbling Block," no page.

14. Brickner, "One Day in Wasilla," no page.

To the Jew First or to the Jew at Last?

Tucker and designed to tell the story of JFJ alludes already to Romans 1:16 in its title: "Not Ashamed: The Story of Jews for Jesus."[15] In the foreword, J. I. Packer writes:

> Paul's "to the Jew first" (Romans 1:16) remains a pointer to a permanent priority in Christian evangelism. For many centuries the church lost sight of it, and some moderns have argued that Jews need not be evangelized at all, but Jews for Jesus is what it sounds like—Jewish Christians sharing their faith with other Jews—and we should thank God that they are there doing that.[16]

The development of the *MP* in JFJ can be traced back to its founder, Moishe Rosen (1932–2010).[17] As we have seen in my first chapter, Rosen is not the inventor of the interpretation but a follower. However, the theme has been largely owned and promoted. Besides Rosen's one academic article published on the subject, whose substance has already been shared in the Introduction,[18] two unpublished documents are worthy of interest in my dialogue with JFJ. The first is the lesson on the *Biblical Basis for* (or *of*) *Jewish Evangelism* (*BBJE*) taught to every training missionary or Campaign volunteer,[19] the second is the message on Romans 1:16 delivered in churches and adapted by each preacher.[20] As Richard Robinson, Senior Researcher with JFJ in San Francisco and the staff member who was my dialogue partner for this research, sent me the *BBJE*, one of his comments struck me: "With the exception of the document *What Christians should know about Jews for Jesus*,[21] we don't seem to have that much that officially cites Romans 1:16—and even that document does not mention that verse again in order

---

15. Tucker, *Not Ashamed*.

16. Ibid., 7. This text is taken, for its most part, from a letter addressed to JFJ in 1993. Cf. Packer, "Letter from J. I. Packer," no page.

17. Moishe Rosen died on the 19th of May 2010, while we were doing this research. On his headstone, Romans 1:16 is quoted after the words "Loving husband, father and grandfather—Founder of Jews for Jesus—." See attached photo to the 6th July 2011 *Realtime* note of Brickner, "Under Construction," no page.

18. Rosen, "Jewish evangelism," 380–84.

19. Barron, *BBJE*. Andrew Barron, current Director of *Jews for Jesus* in Canada, has been responsible for the training at *Moody Bible Institute* for the New York Summer Witnessing Campaign for several years; his lesson *Biblical Basis for Jewish Evangelism* is based on, but quite different from, Mitch Glaser's one: *Biblical Basis of Jewish Evangelism*. Mitch Glaser, current director of *Chosen People Ministries*, is a former missionary with JFJ.

20. Wertheim, *Romans 1:16* and Brickner, "Chosen for What," no page; Steve Wertheim is the current personal assistant of David Brickner. The second document is audio.

21. JFJ, *About Jews for Jesus*. The leaflet indeed quotes part of Romans 1:16 on its cover: "I am not ashamed of the gospel, it is the power of God unto salvation, to the Jew first . . ."

to explicate it. Why that is, is an interesting question. *It is implicit rather than explicit* in our statements."²²

As I have already said in the Introduction, quite a few books and articles have been written to defend the *MP* interpretation in addition to the publications of JFJ. Many websites have also sprouted as www.tothejewsfirst. org (tothejewfirst.net or .com).²³ It turns out that the *MP* is, fundamentally, an Anglo-Saxon Protestant evangelical issue. Besides the commentaries, only a few articles have been written in German on this particular subject— and nothing in French—and only one sustains the *MP*.²⁴ As already said, the Catholic Church seems to have traditionally adopted a historico-covenantal view as demonstrated by the major work written by the Messianic Jewish Catholic scholar Roy H. Schoeman, *"Salvation is from the Jews."*²⁵ As a matter of fact, they have enough work to do to reaffirm a clear position in favor of Jewish evangelism; a Jewish *MP* would be a step too far for them.²⁶

I will now display in detail the arguments used by the proponents of the *MP* to claim that the evangelization of the Jewish people should be given priority over that of the Gentiles. Starting with the basis of JFJ's arguments, I will then build on those of other proponents of the *MP*. The whole will be presented in a critical manner: I will point out the relevant features while evaluating them. Some of the issues will be critically studied on the way while others will be postponed until a later chapter.

---

22. Email from the 14th of February 2011, revised in January 2013. Italics mine.

23. It is interesting to notice the Jews on First! website which has a different purpose. Online: www.jewsonfirst.org, accessed January 2011, which is "The Jewish Response to attacks on the First Amendment by the Religious Right," an amendment which is, according to the website, eroded by "fundamentalist Christians" who are "imposing their religious values through legislation, executive power, and intimidation."

24. For instance, among the Germans: Haacker, "Juden zuerst!," 87–93; Stolle, "Die Juden zuerst: Das Anliegen des Römerbriefs," 154–65; Lohse, "Juden zuerst," 201–12; Käser, "Den Juden zuerst, aber auch den Heiden: 'Mission' im Markusevangelium. Beobachtungen einer kompositionellen Lesung von Mk 4,35—8,26," 69–80 or Wengst, "Juden zuerst," which do not deal with the *MP*. Herwig Nadge, a member of the Messianic Jewish congregation *Beit Schomer Israel* in Berlin, is the only German writer we found who sustains the *MP* interpretation; he wrote a sixty-three page booklet after the Protestant church of Germany decided in 2000 against any mission among the Jewish people. Cf. Nadge, *Juden zuerst!*.

25. Schoeman, *Salvation*, esp. 51–53. In his article on Romans 1:16, the Catholic theologian Gregory Tatum does not even mention the *MP* interpretation: cf. Tatum, "To the Jew first," 275–86.

26. See Kessler, *Jewish-Christian Relations*, 183: "Since 1945, the place of mission has been a significant item on the agenda of the Protestant churches, particularly in terms of interfaith issues, but a rather lower priority for the Roman Catholic Church and the Orthodox Church."

To the Jew First or to the Jew at Last?

I will engage with varied texts—and one audio sermon—authored by thinkers that are remotely connected to JFJ (current and former staff, pastors, and theologians who are friends of JFJ and sometimes members of their different boards). Some of these written documents represent the official voice of the ministry, such as the "Statement of faith," "Mission Statement" or the "Cores values" as presented by the Jews for Jesus website.[27] Others are expression of ideas that can be shared by many in the mission but are not official statements by the mission (especially regarding eschatology). Each time I will mention the identity of the author in order to convey to the reader to what extent the opinion of the author is representative of the mission and thereby avoid undue generalization. A book or an article by David Brickner, current International Director of JFJ, will obviously have more weight than an article written, for instance, by Pastor Lon Solomon, although he is a member of the board of Directors of JFJ. However, if what Brickner says or writes can be taken by many to represent *the* voice of JFJ, I have to remind the reader that, although it is an important voice and at times an official voice of JFJ, it remains *one* voice. The words of Brickner in a national JFJ *Newsletter* can be taken to be quite official; however, his book *Future Hope*[28] that deals with eschatology is his personal voice. It is interesting to hear from some former missionaries of JFJ who stepped back from the mission, especially if I quote texts that they wrote while still part of JFJ—such as Mitch Glaser's lecture on the *Biblical Basis of Jewish Evangelism*.[29] However, we have to be aware that they have since left the mission so as not to identify JFJ thoughts with those of people who have moved on to other ministries. One example is Stuart Dauermann, who gave a paper recently at the *LCJE International Conference*.[30] At the same time, I have extended my study to include other witnesses dealing with the *MP* to enhance the debate and to allow us to grasp the extent of the issue under discussion and the possible interactions with and influences on JFJ.

Moreover, as already said in the Introduction, I recognize that my own evangelical and theological education has an impact on the way I carry out my reflection. For instance, I believe the church to be the continuation of the assembly of Israel,[31] composed of all the Jews and Gentiles who have

---

27. Cf. JFJ website. Online: http://www.jewsforjesus.org/about, accessed August 2012.
28. Cf. Brickner, *Future Hope*.
29. Cf. Glaser, *BBJE*.
30. Cf. Dauermann, "Jew of Course," 1–15.
31. Cf. the use by Stephen of the term *ekklēsia* (*qāhāl*) for the people of Israel in the desert (Acts 7:38).

believed in Jesus. In this sense, the church is the new Israel,[32] the people God always had in mind when he chose Abraham and his descendants to be a blessing to all the nations,[33] the people of the new covenant in Jesus.[34] The present study did not change my view in this regard and as we will see, this does not mean that God is not dealing with the Jewish people anymore. This point can be considered as an important issue as Dauermann notices: "Our passion for a particularist evangelistic mandate to the Jews is in conflict with trends and documents in the Lausanne Movement chastening Israel and reducing her to the status of being simply a nation like all others."[35] I might be accused of *supersessionism*. However, supersessionism is an ambiguous term, which, as defined for instance by R. Kendall Soulen, I do not endorse.[36] Actually, I have yet to meet a scholar who agrees to be labeled as "supercessionist." I do not think that the church has replaced Israel, but rather that the church is the continuation of Israel. Therefore, God is still dealing with Israel today allowing many Jewish people to believe in Jesus their Messiah. Moreover, Israel is so special in the eyes of God that I expect a majestic revival among the Jewish people before the coming of Christ. For me, the key text is the olive tree image of Romans 11, which clearly shows that the roots and the trunk of the tree stand for the believing Israel and the grafted branches for the believing Gentiles. My eschatological system has also been strengthened during this research: it considers the millennium of Revelation 21 to be a symbolic one that began at the death of Jesus when Satan was overcome[37] and is supposed to finish at his second coming.[38] I understand that this eschatological system may affect how the topic is approached.

---

32. Cf. Gal 6:16.
33. Cf. Gen 12:1–3.
34. Cf. Jer 31:31 and Luke 22:20.
35. Dauermann, "Jew of Course," 5.
36. Soulen is an authority in this field. However, I cannot align myself with Soulen's "economic supercessionism" because I do not believe that *"carnal Israel is obsolete"* (Cf. Soulen, *God of Israel*, 29), nor with his "punitive supercessionism" because I do not believe that "God abrogates God's covenant with Israel" (cf. ibid., 30), nor with his "structural supercessionism" because I do not believe that the Hebrew Scriptures are *"largely indecisive for shaping conclusions about how God's purposes engage creation in universal and enduring ways"* (cf. ibid., 31).
37. Cf. John 12:31; 16:11; Rev 20:2–3.
38. Cf. Rev 20:10.

To the Jew First or to the Jew at Last?

THE JEWISH NEED FOR THE GOSPEL

Dealing with the question of the priority of Jewish evangelism over Gentile evangelism requires that I, even if briefly, face the question of whether or not the Jewish people ought to be evangelized. As Steve Wertheim, personal assistant of David Brickner, expresses it:

> If we decline to preach the gospel to the Jews, it must be either because we consider our gospel unworthy of the Jews or the Jews unworthy of the gospel. In this first instance, we would be failing to exalt the Lord Jesus Christ as Lord and the only Savior of the world. And in the second instance, we would be guilty of the most subtle form of anti-Semitism.[39]

This bold affirmation is certainly the foundational truth of the ministry of JFJ, a biblical truth that convinced me to be part of this ministry a few years ago.[40] This question of the legitimacy of Jewish evangelism is tackled by Andrew Barron in his lecture on *BBJE*. Beginning with the "Great Commission"[41] of Matthew 28:19–20 and recognizing that the disciples were called to witness to "all the nations," he insists on the importance of the mission to the Jewish people for at least three reasons:

1. As individuals our Jewish people need Jesus, and like the Apostle Paul, our heart's desire is that Israel would be saved;
2. As a nation, Israel is God's elect to bring the Gospel to the world (nations)—but Israel can't *bring* the Gospel if Israel doesn't *possess* the Gospel; and

---

39. Wertheim, *Romans 1:16*, quoting Rosen. At the same time, Alfred Burchartz, founder of *Evangeliumsdienst für Israel* (*EDI*), reports Moishe Rosen's statement that "the present philo-Semitism in the churches intends the same as anti-Semitism: a church free of Jews." in Burchartz, "Heart of Our Mission," 17. Nadge goes further: "What are the 6 million Jews killed physically in contrast to the current 'remnant' of Jewish souls killed because mission to the millions of Jews is being resisted?" My translation. See Nadge, *Juden zuerst!*, 41: "Was sind die sechs Millionen am Leibe gemorderter Juden gegenüber dem heutigen 'Rest' getöteter jüdischer Seelen, weil Mission an Millionen von Juden verweigert wird?" Regarding Rom 2:14–16, Nadge considers on the same page that the Gentiles who have never heard of the gospel are not lost because God will judge their consciousness.

40. See the publication of the *Consultation On World Evangelization*: COWE, "Christian Witness," 4–6.

41. Jewish Messianic missionaries love saying that the mission among the Jewish people is the "Great Omission" of the church. For instance, Mitch Glaser in Bock and Glaser, *Jew First*, 17.

3. When we preach the Gospel as Jews, we also challenge the church to be all that God has called her to be in reaching out to Jewish people.[42]

If the issues of Israel as "light of the Nations" and the call of the church will be tackled during the study, I can say that I am in agreement on the first affirmation. "My heart's desire [*ē men eudokia tēs emēs kardias*]" (Rom 10:1) should be to see Israel saved. It is particularly understandable to be moved by the rejection of the people for whom the Messiah came first. If a people should know Jesus, it is the Jewish people (cf. Rom 9:4–5)! It is the reason why we must evangelize them today. This point could appear as a strong argument in favor of a *Jewish Missional Priority*, if we were not reminded that the desire of God was always to save the *whole* world: "For since, in the wisdom of God, the world did not know God through wisdom, God decided [*eudokēsen*, lit. "God desired"], through the foolishness of our proclamation, to save those who believe" (1 Cor 1:21). Our heart's desire should be to see all the nations saved. I can understand if someone is particularly eager to see his own people saved, but our overall desire should be to see all the nations believe in Jesus.

Barron also recalls that when Christian-Jewish people witness to Jewish people, Christians see in them the "remnant of Israel"[43] and the Jewish people are challenged to consider the compatibility of being a Jew and yet believing in Jesus as Messiah at the same time.[44] I will have opportunity to deal with the theme of the remnant later on. JFJ is especially keen to denounce two concepts as heresies: *universalism* ("Jews are already saved just because they are part of a Covenant with Abraham") and *dual-covenant theory*[45] ("one covenant for Jews and another one for Gentiles").[46] These two concepts, seen rightly as threats by JFJ, are abundantly refuted by many evangelical scholars and do not need to be treated in the present work.[47]

---

42. Barron, *BBJE*, Introduction.

43. For Glaser, this idea of remnant (Rom 9:27; 11:15) is crucial: "That's one of the reasons why it is also so important to maintain our Jewish identity after coming to faith, to keep the testimony visible to both the church, and to our people—to make that statement that the gospel is still for the Jews." Cf. Glaser, *BBJE*, IV.

44. Barron, *BBJE*, III.

45. Or two-covenant theology. See chapter 4 below.

46. Cf. John 3:3; 14:6; Acts 4:12, as well as the promises of the OT toward the Jewish people and the fact that "most of the 'Law of Moses' can no longer be kept because the Temple is not standing." Barron, *BBJE*, I.

47. Cf., for instance, Kjær-Hansen, et al., "The Uniqueness of Christ."

To the Jew First or to the Jew at Last?

THE ABRAHAMIC COVENANT

> 1 Now the Lord said to Abram, "Go from your country and your kindred and your father's house to the land that I will show you. 2 I will make of you a great nation, and I will bless you, and make your name great, so that you will be a blessing. 3 I will bless those who bless you, and the one who curses you I will curse; and in you all the families of the earth shall be blessed." (Gen 12:1–3)

As touched on in the article of David Brickner, the election of Israel and the covenant of God with Abraham are clearly the major framework of the *MP* thesis: "The biblical mandate to prioritize Jewish evangelism rests upon her position as an elect nation," declares Glaser,[48] because the aim of God in choosing Abraham and his descendants was to save the whole world through them:[49] The LORD says, "It is too light a thing that you should be my servant to raise up the tribes of Jacob and to restore the survivors of Israel; I will give you as a light to the nations, that my salvation may reach to the end of the earth."[50]

According to Avi Snyder, European Director of JFJ, as well as according to others I will mention later one,[51] the Jewish people are still called to be a light for the nations:

> The call—the only call that Israel has ever received—remains to this day. It's seen in the evidence of Scripture. It's seen in the methodology of the Apostle Paul. . . . No wonder so many of us throughout history have felt driven to pioneer some new endeavour or to champion some new cause. *We were created to proclaim* . . .[52]

Snyder has obviously Romans 11:28–29 in mind:[53]

48. Glaser, *BBJE*, I.1. Cf. Gen 12:1–3 and Deut 7:6–7.

49. Ibid., I.2.a. and Barron, *BBJE*, II. Cf. also Wright, *New Testament*, 267–68.

50. Isa 49:6. Cf. also 42:6; 51:4; Luke 2:32 and Acts 13:47.

51. Cf. R. M. M'Cheyne, A. Bonar, C. H. Spurgeon, C. Hodge, J. Jocz, J. Murray, R. H. Hicks and W. A. Brindle. Others are going so far in their understanding of an enduring call that their conclusions lead virtually to a Jewish universalism and a call (addressed to the Gentiles) to not evangelize the Jewish people, let alone evangelize them first. Cf. Kinzer, *Postmissionary Messianic Judaism*, 214: here, Kinzer is speaking of "an apparent Jewish no to Yeshua." Cf. also Soulen, *God of Israel*, 173: "Nothing in the Apostolic Witness remotely suggests the validity of a gentile-Christian mission to non-Christian Jews."

52. Snyder, *Created to Proclaim*, 16 in my pagination (in "The irrevocable call" part). Italics mine.

53. Cf. ibid., 15.

> As regards the gospel they are enemies of God for your sake; but as regards election [*tēn eklogēn*] they are beloved, for the sake of their ancestors; for the gifts and the calling of God are irrevocable [*ametamelēta gar ta charismata kai hē klēsis tou theou*].

However, we have to consider what is in question here. In this last passage, the issue is the salvation of the Jewish people after God's intervention and not the proclamation of the gospel to the nations. And indeed, I believe that one day, "for the sake of their ancestors [*dia tous pateras*]"—and because it is God who gives, chooses and calls—God will intervene powerfully among the Jewish people to save them in great numbers (see chapter 4). But, in effect, the call of Genesis 12:3 and the promise of Isaiah 42:6 to be a blessing and a light to the nations were realized in the first century, when the gospel was extended to all the other nations through Jesus and his disciples: "And the scripture, foreseeing that God would justify the Gentiles by faith, declared the gospel beforehand to Abraham, saying, 'All the Gentiles shall be blessed in you.' For this reason, those who believe are blessed with Abraham who believed" (Gal. 3:8–9). Consequently, this call, tied to the covenant of God with Abraham to be a light to the nations, is since then shared by all the Jewish and Gentile Christians who have been chosen, called, gifted, with the responsibility to bring the gospel to all the nations:

> 1 I therefore, the prisoner in the Lord, beg you to lead a life worthy of the calling [*tēs klēseōs*] to which you have been called [*eklēthēte*], ... 4 There is one body and one Spirit, just as you were called to the one hope of your calling [*eklēthēte en mia elpidi tēs klēseōs umōn*], ... 7 But each of us was given grace [*hē charis*] according to the measure of Christ's gift [*tēs dōreas tou Christou*]. 8 Therefore it is said, "When he ascended on high he made captivity itself a captive; he gave gifts to his people[54] [*edōken domata tois anthrōpois*]." ... 11 The gifts he gave [*Kai autos edōken tous men apostolous*] were that some would be apostles, some prophets, some evangelists, some pastors and teachers, 12 to equip the saints for the work of ministry, for building up the body of Christ, 13 until all of us come to the unity of the faith and of the knowledge of the Son of God, to maturity, to the measure of the full stature of Christ.[55]

---

54. The Greek actually reads: "he gave gifts to men." For the discussion on this *crux interpretum*, see O'Brien, *Ephesians*, 286–93.

55. Eph 4:1–13. Cf also 2 Thess 1:11–12; 2 Tim 1:8–9; 2 Pet 1:10 with a "synonymous word-pair," *tēn klēsin kai eklogēn* (Cf. Davids, *2 Peter & Jude*, 187).

To the Jew First or to the Jew at Last?

The fact that the call to be a light to the nations has been shared by Jews and Gentile believers in Jesus, in the Church which is the people God has always planned to have, does not mean that God has forsaken the Jewish people (cf. Rom 11:1): there has been and there still exists a remnant of Jewish people who believe in Jesus. Moreover, God keeps the Jewish people particularly close to his heart because of the first covenant with Abraham and his descendants; it is the reason why he will intervene for them (Rom 11:30–32):

> What, then, is the significance of the Christian axiom of v. 29 that the gifts and calling of God are irrevocable? According to the development of its meaning in vv. 30–32 it contains the consolation which the Church and the Synagogue have in common, but which also they can hear and receive only in common.[56]

Daniel E. Sims, an American pastor currently ministering in Greece, insists on the fact that God, while beginning with Israel in the Old Testament, is far from forgetting the Gentiles: Rahab (Josh 2), the Gentiles who worshipped in Solomon's (1 Kgs 8:41–43) and in Herod's Temple (Gentiles' court), the Assyrian king (2 Kgs 17), the Gentile widow with Elijah (1 Kgs 17), Naaman cleansed by Elishah (2 Kgs 5), Ruth, Jonah and Nineveh, Obadiah, and Nahum are all witnesses of God's grace toward the Gentiles.[57] Regarding Isaiah 49:6, he comments, however, that, although the salvation was supposed to be proclaimed to the Gentiles of the world, the tribes of Jacob are still put first.[58] Glaser, linking Isaiah 49:6 and Exodus 19:6, calls Israel "a nation of 'missionary-priests'" who ultimately has to bring the Messiah.[59] Elias E. Hidalgo, founder and director of Shalom Scripture Studies Inc., is keen to affirm that the Jewish people are not only "chosen," but according to Deuteronomy 7:6, "holy" and "special"; they are the "apple of the eye of God" (Zech 2:12).[60] As for Charles Henry Titterton, president of the Prophecy Investigation Society, he discerns a "fivefold mission":

> i   to witness to the Unity of God (Deut. 6. 4);
>
> ii to witness to the blessedness of serving the true God (Deut. 33. 26–29; 1 Chron 17. 20, 21; Ps. 144. 15);
>
> iii to receive, preserve and transmit the Holy Scriptures (Deut. 4. 5–8; Rom. 3.);

---

56. Barth, *CD II.2*, 303.

57. Cf. Sims, *Jew First*, 23. Jeremias, considering Palestinian exegesis dealing with the Gentiles who came in contact with Israel, seems to follow the same path of interpretation. Cf. Jeremias, *Jesus' Promise*, 13–14.

58. Sims, *Jew First*, 24–30.

59. Glaser, *BBJE*, I.2.a.

60. Hidalgo, "Jew First," no page.

iv to be the earthly progenitors of the Messiah through the line of David (Gen. 3. 15; 12. 3, etc.; 2 Sam. 7. 12–16; Is. 7. 14; 9. 6; Matt. 1. 1; Rom. 1. 3);

v to be witnesses to the Resurrection of Jesus Christ (Acts 1. 22; 2. 32).[61]

Unfortunately, Israel failed in her mission and "did not live or preach the Torah."[62] Glaser quotes Judges 2:1–3 in support of this idea;[63] the episode of the visit of Jerusalem by the queen of Sheba would, in my opinion, have been a better illustration: Solomon, at the height of his glory, was a light to the nation of Sheba; but in the next chapter of his life, he fell into the trap of foreign women (1 Kgs 10–11).

Arthur F. Glasser, Dean Emeritus of the School of Intercultural Studies at Fuller Theological Seminary, in one of the articles of the JFJ *Newsletter*, explains this failure by proposing some mitigating circumstances. For him, if Israel, despite her early welcome of proselytes, did not really engage in missionary activities over the centuries (no mission societies, no translations of the Scriptures for non-Jews, etc.), it should not be forgotten that the Gentile world does know the God of Holy Scripture thanks to Jesus, a Jew, and his "band of Jewish disciples."[64] For Schoeman, "the Jews did in fact succeed in their mission—although one could say 'despite themselves.'"[65] For the missionary and scholar Bill Bjoraker, the presence of the God-fearers in the synagogues is a proof of Israel being light to the Gentiles.[66] Ray Pritz, current lecturer at the Caspari Center for Biblical and Jewish Studies, notes that Matthew 23:15[67] affirms that the scribes and the Pharisees were very active, crossing even the seas, yet were not very successful.[68]

---

61. Titterton, *Jew First*, 6.

62. Glaser, *BBJE*, I.3.a. Very close to Wright, *Jesus*, 604, 608–9.

63. Glaser, *BBJE*, I.3.a.

64. Glaser, "Nothing?," 6. Jeremias recalls that the term *prosēlytos* means "he who comes forward" and characterizes "a tendency to adopt a passive attitude of waiting for the Gentiles to come forward." In Jeremias, *Jesus' Promise*, 16–17.

65. Schoeman, *Salvation*, 28. Schoeman, while using also biblical arguments from the gospels, Acts and Romans, adopts a historical-covenantal interpretation (see 51–53).

66. Bjoraker, "Jew First," 111–12.

67. "Woe to you, scribes and Pharisees, hypocrites! For you cross sea and land to make a single convert, and you make the new convert twice as much a child of hell as yourselves."

68. Pritz, "Jewish Evangelism and the Gentile World. Morning Session: Acts 17:1–34," 209.

To the Jew First or to the Jew at Last?

Thankfully, as Glaser also recalls, "the mission of Israel was continued by the believing remnant"[69] (a remnant which still exists today), and "whereas the mission was undertaken by the 'new' people, the election was not revoked with the 'old.'"[70] This is an important point because, for JFJ, as already said, the Jewish people are still to be a light to the Gentiles; and as we will see, there will come a time—according to a dispensationalist perspective—when the Messianic Jews will specifically be missionaries among the Gentiles.[71] This is part of the defense against a third threat, supersessionism: if, as believed by JFJ, the church has not replaced Israel, then it follows that Israel has still to be a light to the Gentiles. That is why it is of such importance to evangelize them first.

THE MINISTRY OF JESUS

As already quoted, John Stek is of the opinion that

> [n]o one can read the New Testament without discovering among its dominant themes that one which is epitomized by the Pauline phrase, 'to the Jew first.' This theme is pervasive in the Gospels as a fact of history and a constitutive element in the Divine purpose.[72]

The proponents of the MP are obviously well aware, as I am, of that indisputable fact:

> [Jesus] answered, "I was sent only to the lost sheep of the house of Israel." He said to her, "Let the children be fed first [*prōton*], for it is not fair to take the children's food and throw it to the dogs." (Mark 7:27; cf. also Matt 15:24)

> These twelve Jesus sent out with the following instructions: "Go nowhere among the Gentiles, and enter no town of the Samaritans, but go rather to the lost sheep of the house of Israel." (Matt 10:5–6)

Perhaps because of their obvious meaning, JFJ does not make an effort to quote these two verses in the documents I studied. Sims recalls that although Jesus asked his disciples not to go among the Gentiles, he

---

69. Glaser, *BBJE*, I.3.b.
70. Ibid., I.3.c. Cf. Rom 11:28–29 and Jer 31:31–33. Cf. also Bjoraker, "Jew First," 114.
71. Barron, *BBJE*, II. Gen 12:1–3 is still valid today: see Cooper, *Jew Still First*, 35–36. See chapter 4 below.
72. Stek, "Jew First," 15–16.

had already healed the Gentile servant of the Centurion soldier (Matt 8), showing his interest in Gentiles.[73] After the disciples had fulfilled their obligation to reach the Jewish people, Jesus sent them to all the nations (Matt 28:19–20).[74]

Rudy González, Dean of the William R. Marshall Center for Theological Studies and Professor of New Testament at the Southwestern Baptist Theological Seminary, proposed recently an original—but unconvincing— interpretation which considers that "Matthew 10 and 28:18-20 should be seen as a whole and comprehensive commission that sets the pattern the disciples were to follow."[75] For him, it was a mistake not to recognize the order of Jesus not to go to the Gentiles (Matt 10) as part of a global missional pattern and he pleads that, in Matthew 28, *panta ta ethnē* does not include the Jewish people.[76] Mitch Triestman, missionary with the ABMJ and then with Friends of Israel, also understands Matthew 10 this way, though he does consider that "all nations" in Matt 28:19 includes also the Jewish people.[77] Having myself been tempted to consider the proposition that *panta ta ethnē*, does not include the Jewish people, I am now convinced that the formula in Matthew always includes the Jewish people.[78] Regarding the apparent contradiction of a Jesus who expected the salvation of the Gentiles while going first to his people, I have to point out that there are clearly two successive events in *salvation history*: God's good news was first issued to Israel, then also to the Gentiles.[79] Even though Jesus limited his ministry to Israel, the Gentiles were already in his mind, and eventually the time came for them to also be the recipients of this grace. As he was asking his disciples

---

73. However, his quote of Matt 8:11 ("I tell you, many will come from east and west and will eat with Abraham and Isaac and Jacob in the kingdom of heaven") may be more likely related to Jesus' post-ministry.

74. Cf. Sims, *Jew First*, 31–33, here 32. Mosher, *Romans*, 41, links Rom 1:16 and Heb 1:2; 2:3.

75. González, "Jew First I," 52–68.

76. At the same time, according to González, *panta ta ethnē* in 25:32 does include the Jewish people. We think González is inconsistent regarding this point and it shows that he is lead by his desire to make the "Great Commission" fit with his thesis.

77. Cf. Triestman, *Jew First*, 12–13: "In the 'Great Commission,' the disciples are actually being recommissioned."

78. Cf. Matt 24:9, 14; 25:32; 28:19. For the demonstration, see France, *Matthew*, 235–37. Cf. also the statement of the *Norwegian Mission to Israel* which denounces the objection that "*the Great Commission was given to Jesus' Jewish disciples and only concerns ministry to the Gentiles.*" in DNI, "Jew First," 54.

79. So also Jeremias, *Jesus' Promise*, 71; Stek, *Jew First: Exegetical Examination*, 55.

to go to preach to all the nations (Matt 28:19–20), the ministry formerly limited to Israel was expanded to all the other nations.[80]

THE PATTERN IN ACTS[81]

This is certainly the point most argued by the proponents of the *MP* and I need to discuss it in more detail. According to the proponents, each time Paul—or any other disciple—did go to a new place, he went first to the Jewish people. As stated by Glaser, "The Pauline understanding of the use of 'proton' in Romans 1:16 is demonstrated in the Book of Acts."[82]

The word *prōton* appears five times as an adverb in Acts: 3:26; 7:12; 13:46; 15:14; 26:20.[83] Besides quoting some of its use, Sims does a survey of almost all the situations where the idea of Paul going first to the Jewish people before the Gentiles can be observed. As we will see later in this part, the American Lutheran pastor Joseph P. Gudel often goes beyond Sims in his use of Acts.[84] González uses another strategy, quoting all the verses in Acts which reflect the different aspects of Jesus' orders in Matthew 10 (preaching, healing, ruptures, receptive homes, etc.), realized in a Jewish as well as in a Gentile context; but many of his quotations are doubtful and not very helpful to sustain the missional pattern.[85] However, he recognizes rightly that "there are two occasions where the outreach is directly to the Gentile people," namely in Lystra (Acts 14:8–18) and Malta (Acts 28:1–10).[86]

Pentecost

In this study of Acts, it is important not to turn directly to the pattern, but to take some time to integrate Pentecost into this presentation. Indeed, the ministry of Jesus' disciples really began at Pentecost.

---

80. So Goldsmith, *Matthew & Mission*, 201.

81. W. C. Kaiser picked out Mark D. Nanos' expression "two-step missionary pattern." In Kaiser Jr, "Jewish Evangelism," 40. Cf. Nanos, *Romans*, 239–47.

82. Glaser, *BBJE*, II.B.3. For Dauermann, "Jew of Course," 5, this argument is a *cum hoc ergo propter hoc*.

83. We will not consider 7:12 where *prōton* expresses the idea of a "first visit" (because of *en tō deuterō* in the following verse). Cf. Peterson, *Acts*, 252.

84. Cf. Gudel, "Jew First," 36–42.

85. Cf. González, "Jew First II," 20–29, here 21.

86. Ibid., 22, note 5: in theses places, Paul's ministry "shows no apparent outreach to Jews."

Status Quaestionis

But you will receive power when the Holy Spirit has come upon you; and you will be my witnesses in Jerusalem, in all Judea and Samaria, and to the ends of the earth [*esesthe mou martyres en te Ierousalēm kai [en] pasē tē Ioudaia kai Samareia kai eōs eschatou tēs gēs*]. (Acts 1:8)

Despite the importance of the verse, it is only cited briefly in Barron's conclusion, and never in Glaser's. The reason may be that, contrary to how it has been often quoted, there is no mention of being witnesses "beginning with Jerusalem" in this verse.[87] However, Brickner does not hesitate to quote it in his sermon, stating: "Now you are to be my witnesses, *beginning* in Jerusalem, and in Judea, in Samaria and to the uttermost parts of the earth."[88]

In fact, the phrase "beginning with Jerusalem" occurs only in Luke 24:46–48,[89] though in a similar context:

and he [Jesus] said to them, "Thus it is written, that the Messiah is to suffer and to rise from the dead on the third day, and that repentance and forgiveness of sins is to be proclaimed in his name to all nations, beginning from Jerusalem [*arxamenoi apo Ierousalēm*]. You are witnesses of these things."[90]

For Hoffman Cohn, former general secretary of The American Board of Missions to the Jews (ABMJ),[91] Luke 24:47 is of capital importance: it does not mean "begin with your home field" but give the gospel literally "to

---

87. González, ibid., 22, falls into the trap.

88. Brickner, "Chosen for What," italics meaning a change of tone in his voice in order to insist on the word.

89. Not even Rom 15:19 can be evoked (as in the *Weymouth New Testament*) with *apo Ierousalēm*: "But—to speak simply of my own labours—*beginning* in Jerusalem and the outlying districts, I have proclaimed without reserve, even as far as Illyricum, the Good News of the Christ;" (italics mine; cf. Bible Study Tools website. Online: http://www.biblestudytools.com/wnt/romans/15-19.html, accessed April 2012).

90. Cf. Aland et al., *GNT*, reads: "47 . . . εἰς ἄφεσιν ἁμαρτιῶν εἰς πάντα τὰ ἔθνη. ἀρξάμενοι ἀπὸ Ἰερουσαλὴμ 48 ὑμεῖς μάρτυρες τούτων." But there is no major difference in the meaning.

91. From 1919 to 1948, he wrote the January editorials of the magazine *Chosen People*, based on "To the Jew first" and collected them in a book (Hoffman Cohn, *Beginning*), where he himself depicted this mission as "the largest, the most respected, the most beloved, and, yes, the most hated, Jewish mission agency in all the world" (ibid., 233). We take the opportunity to recall that Moishe Rosen was a former missionary with the ABMJ, which was founded in 1894 as The Brownsville Mission to the Jews and became Chosen People Ministries (CPM) in 1984.

To the Jew First or to the Jew at Last?

the Jew first."[92] Gudel quotes these verses to show that Peter "addressed his message specifically to the Jewish people."[93]

What is at stake here is of course Pentecost, the gift of the Spirit and the proclamation to all the nations that were there in Jerusalem, represented primarily by those "devout Jews from every nation under heaven living in Jerusalem" and visitors present for the feast "both Jews and proselytes" (Acts 2:5–22). By reason of circumstances, Pentecost was celebrated in Jerusalem (Judaea), and the Spirit—and with him the power to understand salvation in Christ—began his ministry in Jerusalem among all the people who were in the city at that time, mostly Jewish people. The time also came for the Samaritans (Acts 8) and then for the Gentiles (Acts 10–11) to have their particular Pentecost. This event must then be understood in a historical way: "Acts provides only selected illustrations of the way God's purpose was advanced in the first few decades, and the narrative concludes with the task uncompleted."[94]

Acts 3:26

> You are the descendants of the prophets and of the covenant that God gave to your ancestors, saying to Abraham, "And in your descendants all the families of the earth shall be blessed." When God raised up his servant, he sent him first to you [*hymin prōton anestēsas ho theos ton paida autou apesteilen auton*], to bless you by turning each of you from your wicked ways.[95]

It is interesting to note that this verse is also reluctantly quoted by the proponents of the *MP*.[96] Glaser, referring to it in a later section of the

---

92. Hoffman Cohn, *Beginning*, 12–13. *Contra*, for instance, Paterson, *Great Commission*, 37–38. For a presentation of the biblical movement from the particular to the universal (temporal, spatial & peoples), see Bauckham, *Bible & Mission*, 13–48.

93. Gudel, "Jew First," 40.

94. Peterson, *Acts*, 113.

95. Another translation is preferable: "For you first, God raised up His Servant and sent Him to bless you by turning every one of you from your wicked ways" (NASV, 1995). In the phrase *hymin prōton anestēsas*, *prōton* is to be linked to *hymin* rather than *anastēsas*; see Barrett, *A Critical and Exegetical Commentary on the Acts of the Apostles*, 213. See also 13:26, wich also has an aorist: "My brothers, you descendants of Abraham's family, and others who fear God, to us the message of this salvation has been sent [*hēmin ho logos tēs sōtērias tautēs exapestalē*]."

96. Sims, who refers most to Acts, does not quote it. Gudel, "Jew First," 40, uses it to show that the Apostles were preaching to the Jewish people, as he does with Acts 4:5–22; 5:27—42; 7:1–53.

lecture, concludes that "as the original offer of the Kingdom by the King was made to Israel first during the 'days of his flesh,' so now again, having been raised from the dead, He is offered 'first' to the chosen nation for the purpose of turning them away from their iniquities."[97]

This verse is clearly to be understood in historical terms. The use of the aorist tense can indeed leave no place for an ongoing action. In this discourse to the Jewish people, Peter indicated clearly that God, in sending Jesus to die on the cross and rise again, had primarily the Jewish people in mind. As David G. Peterson formulates it, "The use of the word 'first' (*prōton*) implies the sort of sequence portrayed in Isaiah 49:5–6, where the Servant of the Lord is used to "restore the tribes of Jacob" so that they can be "a light for the Gentiles" and bring God's salvation 'to the ends of the earth.'"[98]

The Call of Paul and His Practice: Acts 9:15–20

Although Paul was a missionary to the Gentiles,[99] Glaser thinks that he established a "pattern" to first go to the Jewish people, a pattern that still needs to be followed today.[100] For Snyder, this habit was more than an act of obedience, "it was the outworking of Paul's continued love and concern for the Jewish people."[101] Within this practice lies, according to Brickner, also the following idea that he expresses in a phrase that he is fond of: "When you preach the gospel loud enough for Jews to hear, a whole lot of other folk listen in."[102] González recognizes, however, that "there is no necessary correlation between Jewish outreach and immediate success among Gentiles" and that the pattern "is adopted for more than pragmatic motives to maximize evangelistic efforts."[103] In Acts 9:15–20, we read:

> 15 But the Lord said to him [Ananias], "Go, for he is an instrument whom I have chosen to bring my name before Gentiles and kings and before the people of Israel [*enōpion ethnōn te kai basileōn huiōn te Israēl*];"[104]

97. Glaser, *BBJE*, III.6. Barron does not quote it.
98. Peterson, *Acts*, 185.
99. Cf. Rom 11:13–14; Gal 2:7–9.
100. Glaser, *BBJE*, II.B.3.
101. Snyder, *Paul Founder*, 5–6. Cf. Rom 10:1.
102. Brickner, "Chosen for What," "the folks" meaning in the time of Paul the "God-fearers." Cf. also Rosen, "Why first?," 2.
103. González, "Jew First II," 23–24.
104. It is interesting to see that Israel is in the third position in this verse, the

> 19 ... and after taking some food, he regained his strength. 20 For several days he was with the disciples in Damascus, and immediately he began to proclaim Jesus in the synagogues [*kai eutheōs en tais sunagōgais ekēryssen ton Iēsoun*], saying, "He is the Son of God."

For Sims, if Acts 9:15 attests that Paul was called into Gentile mission, Acts 9:20 confirms that he nevertheless preached to the Jewish people first.[105] This verse is indeed a typical verse quoted to sustain the *MP* thesis. As soon as Paul recovered his strength, he went *immediately* to preach in the synagogues. However, the reason for this action is not mentioned. Did Luke want to stress that Paul went first to the Jewish people or that, as soon as he was converted and had taken a little time to recover, he went to preach? The latter seems the more likely explanation since it would, indeed, be typical of Paul's very strong character to desire to see his fellow Jews participate in the same salvation.

Other verses are quoted for the same purpose: for instance, Acts 13:5–6; Sims is of the opinion that the disciples found a Jew at Salamis because "they made a special effort to look for him."[106] With regard to Acts 13:13–15 Sims believes—due to the lack of any reference to evangelization in Perga—that Paul missed out "this huge city full of Gentiles!" because he "couldn't go to the Gentiles until he had preached to the Jews there!"[107] Regarding Acts 16:11–13 Arnold Fruchtenbaum, founder and director of Ariel Ministries, believes that this Jewish community, too small to finance a synagogue, was gathered by the river: "Paul, knowing this, waited until the Sabbath before he preached elsewhere because he knew that the gospel must go out to the Jew first."[108] I am obliged to say that these conclusions are *argumentum e silentio*: in fact, we do not know the exact schedule of Paul and his companions during these days for which Acts is understandably silent.[109]

The Gospel Accepted by Many Gentiles: Acts 11:1–3

> Now the apostles and the believers who were in Judea heard that the Gentiles had also accepted the word of God [*ta ethnē*

Gentiles are first.
105. Sims, *Jew First*, 8.
106. Ibid., 10. Idem for Acts 18:2 with the Jew Aquila.
107. Ibid., 11–12.
108. Fruchtenbaum, "Romans 1:16," 9 and Fruchtenbaum, "Jew First," 210.
109. So González, "Jew First II," 22–23.

edexanto ton logon tou theou]. So when Peter went up to Jerusalem, the circumcised believers criticized him, saying, "Why did you go to uncircumcised men and eat with them?"

For Gudel, it is not until Acts 10 that we have any mention of an attempt to bring the gospel to the Gentiles: "In fact, immediately after Peter brought the gospel to Cornelius and his household, he was criticized for sharing the message of salvation with Gentiles."[110] But Gudel misunderstands this passage, which does not imply that the message in itself was only now accessible to the Gentiles—this would contradict all the times Gentiles received salvation prior to Cornelius—but that the Gentiles from now on had access to the Good News through faith without having to fulfill certain requirements, especially circumcision and table fellowship.[111]

Regarding Acts 11:19 it needs to be noted that, contrary to all appearances, it does not refer to our issue: "Now those who were scattered because of the persecution that took place over Stephen traveled as far as Phoenicia, Cyprus, and Antioch, and they spoke the word to no one except Jews." Paterson, who deals at length with this matter in his book, has rightly noticed that Luke reports these words "preach to the Jews only" to express their fear of persecution.[112]

The Gospel Refused by Many Jewish People: Acts 13:46 and 14:1[113]

> 13:46 Then both Paul and Barnabas spoke out boldly, saying, "It was necessary that the word of God should be spoken first [*Hymin ēn anankaion prōton lalēthēnai ton logon tou theou*] to you. Since you reject it and judge yourselves to be unworthy of eternal life, we are now turning to the Gentiles." ... 14:1 The same thing occurred in Iconium, where Paul and Barnabas went into the Jewish synagogue and spoke in such a way that a great number of both Jews and Greeks became believers.

Neither Glaser nor Barron quote the essential verse of Acts 13:46, but instead only Acts 14:1.[114] Acts 14:1 is indeed usually mentioned to counter the accusation that Acts 13:46 attests that the gospel needed to be preached

---

110. Gudel, "Jew First," 40.
111. Cf. Jeremias, *Jesus' Promise*, 25. The proselyte Nicolas was already a member of the Jerusalem community (Acts 6:5).
112. Cf. Paterson, *Great Commission*, 23, 68–72, 81–83.
113. Same arguments apply to Acts 18:6 and 19:6. Cf. Sims, *Jew First*, 15–16.
114. Cf. Barron, *BBJE*, II or Glaser, *BBJE*, B.3.

to the Jewish people first but that this priority is no longer relevant today. The proponents of the *MP* thesis claim that the proof that these Pauline words of Acts 13:46 were not intended to put a brake on Jewish evangelism can be found in the next chapter, where it is explicitly mentioned that Paul went to the synagogue of Iconium[115] and, moreover, "spent considerable time there."[116]

González considers that the shift in Acts 13:46 means three things: a witness against the continued obstinacy of the Jewish people, a reference to their failure not to have been a blessing for the nations and a hope to stir them to jealousy.[117] For Redar Hvalvik, former lecturer in New Testament Theology at the Free Faculty of Theology in Oslo, who wrote in my opinion the most engaging article on the academic question, Acts 13:46 is very important: "This seems to be more than a mere missionary strategy. According to Acts 13:46, Paul says to the Jews that it 'was necessary (*anangkaion*) that the word of God should be spoken first to you.' Unfortunately, we are not told the reason for this necessity."[118]

Indeed, we have in Acts 13:46 the heart of the reason why Paul went first to the Jewish people.[119] If we are not told of this necessity, I agree with Stek that Paul grounded it in the divine will and in the Scriptures, "even though he appeals to no specific passage."[120] Actually, Acts 13:46 supports the notion that the gospel had to be addressed first to the Jewish people but also warns them that due to their rejection of it the gospel will be preached to the Gentiles. This does not mean that Paul never preached to the Jewish people anymore, but it does mean that the extension of the mission to the Gentiles was already there, as Acts 28:25b–28 reports by quoting Isaiah 6:9–10 (see my point on these verses further on).

---

115. Cf. Sims, Jew First, 11–12. Further, Sims uses the same argument with Acts 17:1–2, 10, 16–17; 19:1–8; 28:16–17. See Sims, Jew First, 14–16, 19.

116. Gudel, "Jew First," 40. Cf. also Oduor, *Jew First*, 10. I agree here with Haacker that "often though only the words regarding the orientation towards the Gentiles are taken into account (v. 46) and then unduly radicalised." My translation. See Haacker, "Juden zuerst!," 90: "Weithin werden jedoch hier nur die Worte von des Hinwendung zu den Heiden (V. 46) beachtet und dazu noch unzulässig radikalisiert."

117. González, "Jew First II," 24.

118. Hvalvik, "Jew First," 3.

119. For Haacker, "Verse [13:]46 declares the Jews to be the primary addresses of the gospel; a literal allusion to Rom 1:16; 2:9." My translation. See Haacker, "Juden zuerst!," 90: "V. 46 erklärt die Juden zu den primären Adressaten des Evangeliums; ein wörtlicher Anklang an Röm 1,16; 2,9.)"

120. Stek, *Jew First: Exegetical Examination*, 165.

Acts 15:14

> Simeon has related how God first [*prōton*] looked favorably on the Gentiles, to take from among them a people [*ex ethnōn laon*] for his name.

Hoffman Cohn is the only one—with Cooper[121]—who makes reference to this verse, which deals with the event of Peter and Cornelius (Acts 10): "In Acts 15:14 the noteworthy point is not that the Gentiles were to be made exclusive believers in Christ but that for the first time in history Gentiles *also* were to become partakers with Jews in the gift of the Holy Ghost."[122] In this verse, *prōton* actually refers to "the early days" (*aph' hēmerōn archaiōn*) of Acts 15:7: "in the early days God made a choice among you, that I [Peter] should be the one through whom the Gentiles would hear the message of the good news and become believers."[123]

According to Jeremias, "two prior conditions must be fulfilled before God's call could go out to the Gentiles":[124] (1) "The promise of salvation given to 'the fathers' (Rom 15:8), and to 'the sons of the prophets and of the covenant' (Acts 3:25), must first be fulfilled"[125] and "the dwelling of David, which has fallen" must first be restored (Acts 15:16–18)[126] and (2) "The blood of the true passover Lamb must first be shed for 'many' (Mark 14.24), the ransom must be paid for 'many' (Mark 10.45)."[127]

Both to the Jewish People and to the Gentiles: Acts 20:21; 26:19–20

> 20:21 as I testified to both Jews and Greeks [*diamartupomenos Ioudaios te kai Hellēsin*] about repentance towards God and faith towards our Lord Jesus.[128] ... 26:19 After that, King Agrippa, I was not disobedient to the heavenly vision, 20 but declared first to those in Damascus, then

---

121. Cooper, *Jew Still First*, 2.
122. Hoffman Cohn, *Beginning*, 240.
123. Peterson, *Acts*, 429–30.
124. Jeremias, *Jesus' Promise*, 71.
125. Ibid.
126. Cf. ibid., 72. So also Jervell, *Theology Acts*, 39–40.
127. Cf. Jeremias, *Jesus' Promise*, 72–73, where Jeremias considers *pollōn* as referring to "a great multitude" that includes the ingathered Gentiles.
128. This verse, where *prōton* is not added as in Romans 1:16, shows that the Roman formula was not every time used by Paul. Cf also Acts 14:1, 5; 19:10, 17.

> in Jerusalem and throughout the countryside of Judea, [*tois en Damaskō prōtov te kai Hierosolymois, pasan te tēn chōran tēs Ioudaias*] and also to the Gentiles [*kai tois ethnesin*], that they should repent and turn to God and do deeds consistent with repentance.[129]

In order to support his thesis with Scripture, Sims links Acts 1:8 and 26:20—showing the similarity of construction—to argue that the phrase "and then to the Gentiles" shows that Paul went to the Jewish people first.[130] As a matter of fact, he is right to notice a similarity in the construction; the Greek construction is even almost the same as in Romans 1:16: *Ioudaiō te prōton kai Hellēni*. However, it is interesting to note that Paul specifically did not go first to the *Jews* of Jerusalem, but to the *disciples* in Damascus, although he preached to Jewish people there, as we know from Acts 9:19b–20.[131] Moreover, the formula *prōton te kai* in this verse is highly indicative of how Romans 1:16, at least at first glance, should be understood. If Paul, recounting his own story of the beginning of his Christian life, mentioned that after Arabia he went first to Damascus and then to Jerusalem, this does *not* mean that he needed to go to Damascus each time he wanted to go to Jerusalem.[132] Hvalvik, who notices this point, concludes that "the meaning of *proton* is obviously temporal."[133]

Acts 28:25b–28

> Paul made one further statement: "The Holy Spirit was right in saying to your ancestors through the prophet Isaiah, 'Go to this people and say, You will indeed listen [*Akoē akousete*], but never understand [*mē synēte*], and you will indeed look, but never perceive. . . .' Let it be known to you then that this salvation of God has been sent to the Gentiles; they will listen [*autoi kai akousontai*]."[134]

---

129. On the incomprehensible presence of the accusative (*pasan te tēn chōran tēs Ioudaias*) between two datives, and the fact that Acts does not deal with a mission in Judaea, see the possibilities in Haenchen, *Acts*, 686–87 or Peterson, *Acts*, 670. It could be an accusative of place or extent to describe all the activity of Paul in the region.

130. Cf. Sims, *Jew First*, 18; 34–35.

131. Cf. also Gal 1:16b–17. Regarding the question of where to place Arabia among these events, see Peterson, *Acts*, 312.

132. It neither means an *Arab Missional Priority*.

133. Hvalvik, "Jew First," 3.

134. A minor problem of translation can be raised here. Should we translate *akouō* in verse 28 as "hear" or "listen": "they will also hear" (Stek, *Jew First: Exegetical Examination* 168 & *NASB*) or "and they will listen" (*NIV 1984*)? Paul does not say that they

Regarding this text Sims argues that Paul was not teaching that God had turned from the Jewish people. "He was teaching that in every city God's order is to reach the Jews first, and then to also try to reach the Gentiles."[135] For David, L. Cooper, President of The Biblical Research Society in 1935, Paul, through the citation of Isaiah, "was simply saying to the Jews at Rome that they were of like mind and heart as those to whom the great prophet Isaiah ministered. He did his duty by giving them the truth of the gospel which hardened their hearts for judgment."[136] For him, this "turning from the Jews" was identical to the one reported of Jewish people in Ephesus (Acts 19:8-10). However, Isaiah 6:9-10 seems to announce the divine hardening of Israel. If the prophet was asked to be active in this hardening (imperatives used in the MT),[137] it reminds us of the fact that Jesus deliberately spoke in parables in order that only the ones belonging to him could understand.[138] In Acts 28:26-27, Paul only acknowledges the fact of this divine hardening and "assumes this prophetic task."[139] B. S. Childs, commenting on Isaiah 6, declares that "Israel's *Heilgeschichte* has become Israel's *Unheilgeschichte* [sic]" and he also sees Isaiah's commissioning in this chapter as "a turning point (*Wende*) in God's history with Israel."[140] However, the same Isaiah predicted that there would be a remnant (6:13; 10:20) and "Luke's narrative suggests the same for the Jews in Rome."[141] What is also interesting to note here is the use—as in Acts 13:26—of the formula *ho logos tēs sōtērias*: the message of salvation has been sent (*apostellō* in the two cases) to the descendants of Abraham's family and God-fearers in 13:26 and to the Gentiles in 28:28.[142]

---

will understand, despite the fact that ἀκούω can also have this meaning (cf. Balz and Schneider, *EDNT* 1, definition 5d, 54). However, if we consider the contrast between verse 27 and verse 28 intended by Paul, we can only understand that "Israel collectively will not hear, but Gentiles will hear and understand and be saved. There is more to this contrast than simply 'to the Jew first and then to the Gentiles'" (Peterson, *Acts*, 718 (note 103)).

135. Sims, *Jew First*, 19-20.

136. Cooper, *Jew Still First*, 13.

137. *šimě'û šāmôa'* and *ûrě'û rā'ô*; in the LXX, which is used for the quotations in the NT, verbs are in the indicative: *epachunthē, ēkousan, ekammusan*.

138. Matt 13:10-17 and par.; John 12:37-43.

139. Peterson, *Acts*, 715-16. Cf. Acts 9:15-16: the sufferings of Paul recall those of Isaiah.

140. Childs, *Isaiah*, 57.

141. Peterson, *Acts*, 716.

142. Cf. ibid., 718.

To the Jew First or to the Jew at Last?

Diaspora

Before ending this important part, I need to look at the Diaspora. In his book *Jesus and the Land*, Gary M. Burge, Professor of New Testament at Wheaton College and Graduate School, gathers sources to evaluate the Diaspora at the time of Jesus. Despite the difficulty of the task, his conclusion is decisive: "*more Jews were living outside the Holy Land than were living in it.*"[143] For the proponents of the MP, the pattern "to the Jew first" applies also to the Diaspora.

Lon Solomon, member of the Board of Directors of JFJ as well as the Pastor of McLean Bible Church in Virginia, for instance, writes: "Scripture records the four missionary journeys of the Apostle Paul, and it is striking how, in all four cases, his itinerary fell precisely within the areas where the Jewish Diaspora was concentrated."[144] At the same time, we do not know a lot about the Alexandrian and North African Diaspora. E. P. Sanders suggests:

> It seems to me conceivable, in fact to be the best answer to a question which may have no certain answer, that Paul, Peter, and the others, in their urgent desire to carry out their representative missions, made no special provision for Diaspora Jews. We should note that those who formed what was perhaps the largest single group, the Jews of Alexandria, are not mentioned at all in the New Testament, and certainly not in the division of labor referred to in Gal. 2:9.[145]

Hippolytus of Rome reports that John, called Mark,[146] was the first bishop of Alexandria,[147] and so possibly the one who brought the gospel there. There is no way to evaluate whether or not Mark preached the gospel to Jewish people first there, but it seems likely that he did.

Considering today's Diaspora, some argue that if we try to reach the Jewish people, who are currently scattered throughout the world, we will inevitably reach non-Jews.[148] Dr Robert H. Hicks, minister of Family Life—Church of Savior at Wayne, PA—develops this point in the "practical argu-

---

143. Burge, *Jesus & Land*, 18. Italics his.

144. Solomon, "Paul & BYG," 8.

145. Sanders, *Paul, the law, and the Jewish people*, 189. Cf. also Pearson, "Christians and Jews," 206–13.

146. Cf. Acts 12:12, 25; 15:37–39.

147. Cf. Gates et al., "Mark the Evangelist" (online at http://www.dacb.org/stories/egypt/markthe_evang.html, accessed April 2012).

148. See the third argument of the twenty-fifth sermon of M'Cheyne, preached on the 17th November 1840, entitled "Our Duty to Israel: 'To the Jew first'—Rom. 1:16" in Bonar, *M'Cheyne*, 489–97.

ment" of his *MP* interpretation. According to him, four observations can help to spread the gospel in the whole world if we first go to the Jewish people: due to the Diaspora the Jewish people are everywhere, the Jewish people are concentrated in cities (a decision to reach them will boost church planting in these cities), the Messianic Jews know the price of following Jesus (they are therefore committed to evangelization) and finally the secular Jews—who are the majority—are very open.[149] Triestman, anticipating, however, the possible argument that the Jewish people are not everywhere, states:[150]

> The Lord has done an amazingly good job of scattering the Jewish people. I marvel at where we have been able to locate our people in our travels. I have always found that where there is a burden in a believer's heart to reach the Jews, there are also Jewish people to be reached nearby.[151]

Facing this argument, I must recognize the fact that the Jewish people represent only 0.0022 percent of the world population and that they cannot be everywhere and concentrated in all the cities at the same time. To follow through with this argument, it would be more productive to concentrate our efforts on China, which is currently conquering the whole world.[152]

Conclusion

The proponents of the *MP* are right to point out that Paul used a pattern that is clearly presented by Luke in Acts. The Apostle seemed hence to follow the paths of his master and Messiah Jesus who became "a servant of the circumcised" in order to fulfill the promises given to the patriarchs (Rom 15:8). The gospel had to be preached first to them: "this priority should not be regarded as merely pragmatically strategic, but based on deep theological reflection on the divine promises to Abraham."[153] But if they are the "natural heirs and recipients"[154] of the gospel, Paul is also convinced that "the Gen-

---

149. Cf. Hicks, "Romans 1:16," 12–13.

150. It can be deduced from Hidalgo, "Jew first," in the paragraph entitled "In Romans 1:16," that if there are no Jewish people nearby, prayer and financial support are always a good way to support the *MP*.

151. Triestman, *Jew First*, 30.

152. According to the *Joshua Project*, "Jews are found in 126 countries, Arabs in 130 countries, and Chinese groups in 127 countries." Cf. "People Group Facts," Joshua Project website. Online: http://www.joshuaproject.net/great-commission-statistics.php, accessed April 2012. Cf. also Paterson, *Heartcry*.

153. Barnett, "Paul's Grace," 103.

154. Pakula, *First for Jews*, 8.

tiles have become fellow heirs, members of the same body, and sharers in the promise in Christ Jesus through the gospel" (Eph 3:6).[155] This is why he can tell those who reject his gospel: "It was necessary that the word of God should be spoken first to you. Since you reject it and judge yourselves to be unworthy of eternal life, we are now turning to the Gentiles" (Acts 13:46).

I cannot reject the idea that it may have been a normal habit for Paul to go to the synagogue merely to worship his Lord,[156] or a practical way for him to begin his ministry by the usual Jewish place of worship "since the synagogue provided the most obvious platform for his message—'to the synagogue first and so to the God-fearing Gentile.'"[157] Some suggest that it was a good way for him to develop a kind of "church-planting strategy of preaching in synagogues first, so as to divide the congregation, win some God-fearing Gentiles, and start a Gentile-dominated church with these new believers."[158] A newcomer to a foreign country may also be tempted to join his fellow countrymen. However, any of these reasons, if true, would be stronger than the historico-covenantal one, which meant Paul was forced—by necessity—to go to the Israelites first because of the covenant of God with Abraham. Since he was facing hostility in large measure, he had, however, to accomplish this mission to the Jewish people before expanding it to the Greeks in order that Jewish people and Gentiles could become part of the same body.

THE FORMULA IN ROMANS

The Epistle to the Romans is obviously a core reference in our study. The adverb, *prōton*, is used 5 times in the Letter: 1:8, 16; 2:9, 10; 3:2; 15:24.[159] And indeed, for Sims as well as for many others, if Romans is Paul's "'magna carta' of salvation,"[160] Romans 1:16 is the "apostolic *didache*"[161] of the *MP*.

---

155. Cf. Eph 1:12, "so that we, who were the first to set our hope [*tous proēlpikotas*] on Christ, might live for the praise of his glory," contrary to all appearances, does not concern our issue. For the discussion, see Thielmann, *Ephesians*, 74–76.

156. This was suggested to me by Maurice Rubin, a messianic Jew, PhD colleague, during a conference that I gave in March 2012 at the London School of Theology.

157. Dunn, *Romans 1–8*, 40. Cf. also Schnabel, *Early Christian Mission: Jesus*, 1300–1301.

158. Cf. the consideration of this supposition in Brindle, "Jew First," 222.

159. 1:8 and 15:24 will not be taken into consideration, since they are not directly linked to my study.

160. Brindle, "Jew First," 222.

161. To reuse a phrase of Stek, "Jew First," 17.

Status Quaestionis

The Formula of Romans 1:16

"Nuclear Christianity"

Moishe Rosen promoted an original image not found elsewhere among other proponents of the missional interpretation. Regarding Romans 1:16 and the power of the gospel, Rosen thought of "explosion."[162] The July 2009 JFJ *Newsletter* teaches us that this image first came to him after hearing about the Evangelism Explosion mission.[163] The idea is fairly simple and strong: as a car utilizes the explosion in its internal combustion engine, the mission and the church should utilize the "gunpowder of God"—i.e., "the gospel"— whose "formula is to bring the gospel to the Jew first (Rom. 1:16)."[164] If the church, as well as the Jewish people, is scared of an explosion,[165] then "The power of evangelism is explosive. If it destroys anything, it is our delusions of self-sufficiency."[166] Finally, recognizing that the Jewish people represented the hardest part of the mission task,[167] Rosen thought they should be the priority: "My thesis is that if we plan a strategy to reach Jews, we will have a strategy to reach anyone."[168]

It is true that the JFJ "Behold your God" campaigns[169] attest that, over the years, two to three more non-Jews have been reached than Jewish people.[170] I must recognize that the name Jews for Jesus puzzles the crowds in Western countries, but would this be the case deep in the countryside of India? I recognize also that JFJ has a very innovative and efficient way of evangelizing. But does this mean than any other mission not orientated to-

---

162. Hoffman Cohn thinks about a similar image, namely the image of fire needing first paper, then light pieces of wood, then heavier wood and finally coal: if the order is not respected, there will not be any fire. In Hoffman Cohn, *Beginning*, 145–46.

163. Cf. Rosen, "Nuclear Christianity," 7. Evangelism Explosion (*EE*) is an effective training and discipling ministry that equips people to share the gospel using simple Bible verses and lively illustrations. It was founded by Dr. D. James Kennedy in the sixties and is active in 212 [*sic*] countries. Cf. Evangelism Explosion Canadian website. Online: http://www.eecanada.org/history.html, accessed January 2011.

164. Rosen, "Jewish evangelism," 380. Cf. also Rosen, "Nuclear Christianity," 7. Surprisingly, Rosen does not use the word dynamite, which comes etymologically from the very word *dynamis* used in Romans 1:16.

165. Cf. Rosen, "Jewish evangelism," 380.

166. Rosen, "Nuclear Christianity," 7.

167. Today, JFJ argues that Jewish people are more open than we think.

168. Rosen, "Jewish evangelism," 382.

169. The JFJ operation "Behold your God" produced 55 campaigns in worldwide cities with more than 25,000 Jewish people, except Israel.

170. Brickner, "Jews Proclaim," 2. See also Brickner, "Gospel Shout," 2.

ward Jewish people and with the same dynamism would not touch as many Gentiles—and Jewish people? Similarly, if the mission among the Jewish people is the hardest mission, and if you are trained to reach religious Jews, will you be able to deal with fundamentalist Muslims? Unfortunately I will have to leave these socio-missiological questions to another researcher; they require statistical studies that fall outside of the scope of this present book.

The Three Readings of Prōton

As expected, three readings of *prōton* are generally considered by the proponents of the *MP*, which are very close to those presented in my introduction. For example, Glaser calls them "Historical Priority (in time)," "Covenant Priority (in Historical importance)" and "Present Priority (in a positional sense)." The Greek lexicon of Bauer, Arndt, and Gingrich is often quoted to support the thesis that *prōton* has in Romans 1:16 the meaning of "first, foremost, most important, most prominent" or "in the first place, above all, especially."[171]

HISTORICAL PRIORITY

For Glaser, who quotes Charles Hodge as a characteristic proponent of the *HP*,[172] the "tragic flaw of this argument is that, if stretched to its logical conclusion, it would discourage any form of testimony to the Jewish people today."[173] This inference, which may be legitimate when we consider history,[174] is particularly linked to what JFJ and other missions will regard as a third threat: the *replacement theology*. This theory, also called *supersessionism*, is understood as claiming that "the promises made by God to Israel, are actually fulfilled by the 'Church' (believers) and that Israel no longer holds a special place in God's plan."[175] For Rosen, this omission to reach the Jewish people leads to the first two threats already mentioned: *universalism* and the *two-covenant theology*.[176]

---

171. Bauer, et al., *Greek-English Lexicon*, 732–34. Cf. Hvalvik, "Jew First," 3; Bjoraker, "Jew First," 111.

172. Hodge, *Romans*, 27–29. Barth, *Romans*, is also mentioned.

173. Glaser, *BBJE*, II.A.1.

174. Cf. chapter 1 and Wertheim, *Romans 1:16* 2, who insists especially on this point: "The actual history of modern Jewish evangelism is only about 300 years old."

175. Barron, *BBJE*, II. Cf. chapter 4.

176. Rosen, "Jewish evangelism," 382–83. Wertheim, *Romans 1:16* expresses this idea in an odd way: "Do you believe as Paul did that the gospel needs to go to the Jews first? Or, have you bought the lie that the Jews have their own way to God and don't

I acknowledge that the concept of Israel not having a place anymore in the plan of God will lead logically to a lack of evangelism. Although this concept can encourage *universalism* and the *two-covenant theology*, these theologies did not originate from the idea that Jewish people should not be evangelized. Universalism has its roots at least as far back as Origen and his *apokatastasis*,[177] while the *two-covenant theology* is linked to Franz Rosenzweig at the beginning of the twentieth century, his theory gaining popularity in the aftermath of the Shoah.[178] Hence today, it is more the idea of the *two-covenant theology* and *postmodernist universalism* that discourages the evangelization of the Jewish people after the Shoah than the other way round.

Covenant Priority

To characterize this position, Glaser quotes John Murray,[179] Gifford,[180] Sanday and Headlam,[181] Calvin,[182] Johnson,[183] Barrett,[184] and Käsemann.[185] As we have already seen in the introduction, those go further than Hodge in the way that they affirm that the priority in Romans 1:16 is not merely a question of time but is linked with the status of the Jewish people as chosen people, according to the covenant of God with Abraham. This covenant priority, just like "historical priority," is recognized by all the proponents.[186]

Present Priority[187]

In the *BBJE* document, no scholars are quoted to endorse this view, which is considered to be the most difficult to comprehend and apply: "It proposes

---

need Jesus?"

177. Dodd, "Universalism," 1188.

178. Cf. Rosenzweig, *Star of Redemption*.

179. Murray, *Romans*, 28. However, while recognizing the vagueness of the commentary, Glaser is close to place Murray in his *Present Priority* (MP).

180. Gifford, *Romans*, 61.

181. Sanday and Headlam, *Romans*, 24.

182. Calvin, *Romans & Thessalonians*, 27.

183. Johnson, *Romans*, 30.

184. Barrett, *Romans*, 29.

185. Käsemann, *Romans*, 23.

186. See Wilks Jr, "Jew First," second point, who quotes Romans 11:28–29 in support.

187. Bjoraker uses "Positional Priority" and even "meaningful present priority," because "The Jewish people were called, cultivated and conditioned to be a missionary people" (cf. Bjoraker, "Jew First," 111–12). As already said, we prefer "Missional Priority."

that even today, the gospel must always be brought first to the Jew, before the Greek. The problem is not with the soundness of the view, as with the difficulty of the commission."[188] At the same time, Glaser goes on to consider that requiring a church to witness to Jewish people first in a given community before going to the Gentiles "is only one possible implication."[189] I find the formulation rather ambiguous. If applying the *Present Priority* in evangelism does not require witnessing to Jewish people before witnessing to the Gentiles, I do not really understand what it implies. Moishe Rosen shows the same ambiguity: "I don't mean that no one in a community should hear the gospel until the Jews have all heard it; I mean that Paul set an evangelism pattern for a reason."[190] Martin Goldsmith, JFJ European Board member, observes:

> Having served as a missionary in parts of South East Asia where there were no Jews (except me!), I have come to see that some times [sic] the truth of Rom. 1.16 may not be relevant in every situation. For those I worked with the priority was evangelism among other peoples, among Muslims, Buddhists, etc. In theory they might note the teaching of Rom. 1.16 and therefore have a love in theory for us as Jews, but in practice other biblical truths and demands take precedence.[191]

John Piper, the famous Pastor for Preaching and Vision at Bethlehem Baptist Church in Minneapolis, is one of the few[192] who coherently pushes the conclusion to its end in saying that "Jews have a priority in the order of frontier missions when the gospel comes to a new place."[193]

Glaser considers the *Present Priority* to be the best exegetical analysis of the passage.[194] He recognizes that the adverb *prōton* can have a temporal sense as in Mark 4:28 ("The earth produces of itself, first the stalk, then [*prōton chorton eita*] the head, then [*eita*] the full grain in the head."). But in Romans 1:16,

---

188. Glaser, *BBJE*, II.A.3.

189. Ibid., Cf. also COWE, "Christian Witness," 5.

190. Rosen, "Nuclear Christianity," 7.

191. Goldsmith, "Jew of Course," 1.

192. Cf. also Fruchtenbaum, "Romans 1:16," 6: "What is true of the local church is also true of the missionary in the field. He must first take the gospel to any Jews who may be in the field where he is working."

193. Piper, "Jew First," no page. However, Piper, *Nations be Glad*, besides two mentions of the power of God for salvation in Rom 1:16 (85, 170), does not mention the MP. He is even presenting a clear HCP (27): "A fundamental change happened with the coming of Christ into the world. Until that time, God has focused his redemptive work on Israel with occasional works among the nations.... Now the focus has shifted from Israel to the nations," with a reference to Matt 21:43.

194. Glaser, *BBJE*, II.B.

it has according to him a positional sense—"above all" or "especially"—as in Matthew 6:33 ("But strive first for the kingdom of God and his righteousness [*Zēteite de prōton tēn basileian [tou theou] kai tēn dikaiosynēn autou]*").[195] These last two Bible quotations are worthy of interest regarding the structure in Romans 1:16 (*Ioudaiō te prōton kai Hellēni*): the first one mentions explicitly *eita* and the other indicates by the position of *prōton*—contrary to Romans 1:16—that it is both *tēn basileian* and *tēn dikaiosynēn autou* which are the object of the priority.[196] As for Hvalvik, he chooses 2 Corinthians 8:5 to support this idea: "they gave themselves first to the Lord and, by the will of God, to us [*all' heautous edōkan prōtov tō kyriō kai hēmin*])."[197] However, this last verse is clearly part of a historical situation, while Paul is describing the generosity of the churches in Macedonia (cf. v. 1–4).

Regarding these examples I need to say that the precise phrase *te prōton kai* of Romans 1:16 is absent, contra Acts 1:8 where it can be found with an inversion, as I have already noticed. They demonstrate that *prōton* has a wide range of meaning and that the exact Roman phrase is difficult to find in other parts of the Bible. I will deal with this question in my third chapter.

The Present Tense of the Phrase

Not textually mentioned in the texts of JFJ, although it is in the background of the choice of the expression "present priority" by Glaser and Barron,[198] is the fact that the present tense of the phrase is proof for Sims and others that the gospel *is* (*estin*), for all time, "the power of God for salvation to the Jew first and also to the Greek."[199] As Fruchtenbaum puts it: "To interpret this verse historically . . . is also to say that the gospel was the power of God, but it is no longer that."[200] Potentially, this argument is the weightiest. Indeed, the present tense challenges us to consider if the pattern used by the disciples to go "to the Jew first" stopped sometime in history; and if yes, when? "I have never found one person who gave me a satisfactory answer to this question," claims Hoffman Cohn.[201]

195. See also Arndt and Gingrich, *A Greek-English Lexicon*. Cf. Glaser, *BBJE*, II.B. Luke 12:31, parallel to Matt 6:33, does not mention *prōton*.

196. Certainly a hendiadys; cf. Luke 12:31, which omits *dikaiosynē*. Cf. Hagner, *Matthew I*, 166.

197. Cf. Hvalvik, "Jew First," 3.

198. Cf. Glaser, *BBJE*, II.A.3, Barron, *BBJE*, II.

199. Cf. Sims, *Jew First*, 39–40.

200. Fruchtenbaum, "Romans 1:16," 6 or Fruchtenbaum, "Jew First," 206. See also the introduction by Mitch Glaser in Bock and Glaser, *Jew First*, 16.

201. Hoffman Cohn, *Beginning*, 146–47.

To the Jew First or to the Jew at Last?

I recognize that here is a strong potential argument that I could express this way: if "the gospel has primary relevance to Jews in the first century," to use a phrase by Brindle,[202] which event determined that this relevance had ended? Considering the Jewish people today and their history and roots, are they not still the logical recipients of grace? I need to state in my third chapter in which way *estin* is directly linked to *Ioudaiō te prōton kai Hellēni* and if *euangelion* is the subject of *estin* or not. I also need to understand Romans 9–11 within the history of salvation.

The Translation of Te Prōton Kai

The phrase *te prōton kai* in Romans 1:16 is generally translated by the proponents of the MP as "first and also" rather than "first and then."[203] Sims lays emphasis on the fact that, otherwise, Paul would have used other words, such as "then," "afterwards," or "subsequently."[204] Hvalvik also thinks that the construction is worth considering. If a simple connection *kai* had pointed to the difference between "Jews" and "Greeks" (as in 1 Cor 10:32: "Give no offense to Jews or to Greeks or to the church of God [*aproskopoi kai Ioudaiois ginesthe kai Hellēsin kai tē ekklēsia tou theou*]," the *te kai* implies that "the distinction is set aside."[205] The addition of *prōton*, therefore, indicates "that Jews seem to have some sort of priority."[206]

The Formula in Romans 2:9–10

> There will be anguish and distress for everyone who does evil, the Jew first and also the Greek [*Ioudaiou te prōton kai Hellēnos*], but glory and honor and peace for everyone who does good, the Jew first and also the Greek [*Ioudaiō te prōton kai Hellēni*]. For God shows no partiality.

Romans 2:9–10, where the same expression as in 1:16 appears, is of course mentioned by Sims and others.[207] They argue that, as *prōton* is not

---

202. Brindle, "Jew First," 225. Cf. also Murray, *Romans*, 28. Brindle talks about a "theological priority" (ibid., 226). To avoid an unclear terminology, we prefer not to use this adjective, which can cover infinite senses.

203. Moo, surprisingly, chose to keep "first and then." Cf. Moo, *Romans*, 68.

204. Sims, *Jew First*, 40.

205. Hvalvik, "Jew First," 2, Hvalvik is quoting Blass and Debrunner, *Grammar*, 444.

206. Hvalvik, "Jew First," 2. See my discussion in chapter 3.

207. Again, the texts of JFJ that we studied do not make that point, but I know from

used in these two verses for a historical purpose, the same should logically apply to Romans 1:16. Sims even declares—certainly too hastily—having "never read a single commentary that said the word 'first' in this verse [Rom 2:9] indicates a chronological appearance that has been done away with."[208] Actually, Hvalvik rightly notices that some texts do talk about a chronological judgment, i.e., in priority on Jerusalem (Jer 25:29), the Temple (Ezek 9:6-7, cf. also 1 Pet 4:17) or Israel (*Testament of the Twelve Patriarchs* 10:8-9: "for the Lord first judges Israel for the wrong she has committed and then He shall do the same for all the nations").[209] However, he concludes that it is "improbable that in Romans 2:9-10, Paul has in mind a kind of temporal priority, the context indicating otherwise."[210] Considering verse 12, he states that there is a difference between Jewish people and Gentiles according to the law: "the Jews have the law (cf. 2:14. 17f), so they will be judged by law."[211] For Hoffman Cohn, this time of judgment corresponds to the great tribulation whose tortures will be experienced first by the Jewish people, and he concludes: therefore, "let us have the kindness of heart and the decency of fair play to give now in the present age of grace, the Gospel 'to the Jew first.'"[212]

My exegetical chapter will deal with this important issue of the judgment of Israel and the nations and attempt to answer whether it concerns a historical judgment, for instance in AD 70, or a "Final Judgment" at the end of time or a kind of qualitative judgment.

The Advantage of the Jew (Rom 3:1-2)

"Then what advantage has the Jew? Or what is the value of circumcision? Much, in every way. For in the first place the Jews were entrusted with the oracles of God [*prōton men* [gar] *hoti episteuthēsan ta logia tou theou*]" (Rom 3:1-2).

Sims quotes this passage to assert rather inconclusively that "[h]ere the connection is seen between something being first in order and first in importance. The chief, or first, advantage of being a Jew is possession of the

---

a conversation with Stephen Pacht, current JFJ missionary in Switzerland, that it is one of their arguments.

208. Sims, *Jew First*, 77.

209. Cf. Hvalvik, "Jew First," 4. Test. Ben. 10:8-9 quoted by Hvalvik. Brindle, "Jew First," 228, adds Amos 3:2.

210. Hvalvik, "Jew First," 4.

211. Ibid., Cf. also Brindle, "Jew First," 228: "Spiritual privilege brings spiritual responsability."

212. Hoffman Cohn, *Beginning*, 56.

Holy Writings and their enlightenment."²¹³ At the same time, it is interesting to see how *prōton* is clearly used here in a historical manner: the Jewish people *had* been entrusted (again aorist) with the oracles of God. I understand why this argument is rarely evoked among the proponents of the MP.

ESCHATOLOGICAL PERSPECTIVES ACCORDING TO ROMANS 9–11

As we will have already seen in the first chapter, Romans 1:16 has been linked throughout history with the chapters 9–11 of the same Epistle. Obviously, the proponents of the *MP* do not make an exception.

Israel's Need

Sims argues that, according to Romans 9–11, the Jewish people have greater need for the gospel. This is therefore a very good reason to continue bringing the gospel to the Jewish people first today: "being so deeply fallen, and having sinned against such glorious privileges; they are much more accountable than the Gentiles."²¹⁴ This theme, developed especially by Robert Murray M'Cheyne, is taken up by others such as Hoffman Cohn or Fruchtenbaum.²¹⁵ For M'Cheyne, the gospel should be preached first to the Jewish people,

1. *Because judgement will begin with them. . . . In an [sic] hospital, the kind physician runs first to that bed where the sick man lies who is nearest to die. (. . .)*
2. *It is like God to care first for the Jews. . . . We should be like [God] in understanding, in will, in holiness, and also in His peculiar affections.*²¹⁶

Regarding Romans 2:9-10, we need to know which judgment is at stake (see chapter 3). At the same time, we have previously seen how God has extended his affection to the whole world, to all the other nations, without forgetting Israel. Based on the same logic, it might be fair to conclude that those who do not have the Scriptures in their own language even today are in greatest need.²¹⁷

---

213. Sims, *Jew First*, 42–43.
214. Ibid., 77–78. Cf. Luke 12:48.
215. Hoffman Cohn, *Beginning*, 37–41; Fruchtenbaum, "Eschatology," 252–53.
216. Bonar, *M'Cheyne*, 489–97. A clear allusion to Rom 2:9-10.
217. See, for instance, the heartbreaking speech in defence of evangelizing the lost Asian Gentiles in Yohannan, *Revolution*. I will come back to this point in my final conclusion.

Israel's Restoration

For Hvalvik, Romans 9–11 is important, because it indicates that Paul does not think the salvation of the Jewish people is a temporal priority; indeed, it is not the Jewish people who will be saved first, but "the 'full number of the Gentiles' will be saved prior to the salvation of the great majority of the Jewish people."[218] This last interpretation, however, meets an obstacle: historically, it is a fact that the first to be saved were the Jewish people, as witnessed in the Gospels and in Acts.

Hicks develops a "theological argument" for the *MP* regarding Romans 9–11 using three points: provoke the Jewish people to jealousy (Rom 11:11, 14), call the remnant of Israel to faith in her Messiah (Rom 10:9–21) and bring about the national restoration of Israel (Rom 11:25–27).[219] But if the Jewish people become jealous because Paul preaches the gospel to the Gentiles who accept it, why insist on preaching the gospel to the Jewish people? If it is true that one can only hear the gospel if we preach it, does Romans 10:18 not also say that the Jewish people have already "heard? Indeed they have." Finally, the restoration of Israel according to Romans 11:25 is conditional upon the "full number of the Gentiles." Will this fullness arrive if we do not go to the Gentiles? These questions will be studied in the fourth chapter.

To illustrate that this restoration is already here, some, such as Geoffrey Cohen, Associate Pastor in Jewish Ministries at Gateway Church, argue that there have never been as many Messianic Jews at any point in history compared with today.[220] However, if I consider the current conservative number of Messianic Jews today, 150,000,[221] I discover that this number is not greater than the one estimated for the time prior to the Shoah, at least up to 250,000.[222]

---

218. Hvalvik, "Jew First," 6.

219. Hicks, "Romans 1:16," 11–12.

220. Cohen, "Jew First II," no page. He believes that there have been more Jewish people saved in these last twenty years than in all the preceding centuries!

221. Cf. Harvey, *Mapping Messianic*, 2. 350,000 in Schoeman, *Salvation*, 351.

222. This is one estimation of the number of Messianic Jews killed in the Shoah. Cf. Blocher, "Post-Holocaust/Shoah Theology," 7. According to Hoffman Cohn in 1934, after Hitler ordered a census among the 560,000 German Jews, "over 200,000 members of Christian Churches in Germany were of Jewish extraction! Of these, more than 60,000 were full blooded Jews, converts of the present generation!" In Hoffman Cohn, *Beginning*, 91–92. Hoffmann Cohn uses these numbers to prove that when a country follows the order to preach the gospel to the Jewish people first, God blesses it. Schonfield, *History*, 174, is close to these numbers: "The [First World] war was thus regarded as an instrument for the carrying out of the divine plan, another instance of God making the wrath of man to praise Him. . . . When it became possible to gather reliable statistics, it was found that 97,000 Jews had joined the church in Hungary, 17,000 in

To the Jew First or to the Jew at Last?

If the "hardening" of the Jewish people will last "until the full number of the Gentiles has come in" (Rom 11:25), how can we imagine a Jewish revival before this "full number"? Moreover, how can we imagine, after this "full number" is obtained, a Jewish people being particularly mission-oriented toward Gentiles whose "full number" is attained? This question needs to be clarified and put in its eschatological context (see chapter 4 below).

The Salvation of Israel and the Second Coming of Christ

This argument is linked with Romans 9–11 but adds other texts to support the idea of a national repentance of the Jewish people determining the return of Jesus. The aim is to encourage the mission among the Jewish people to activate the return of Jesus: a "national repentance" should precede the return of Jesus; but none of the texts quoted by Glaser support this idea.[223] Indeed, Deuteronomy 4:30–31, part of the covenant of God with his people, refers first of all to a restoration after the exile. This is parallel to Deuteronomy 30:1–10, where the return to the land is promised with the circumcision of the heart—circumcision which will only occur through the work of Christ.[224] Regarding the prophecy of Zechariah 12:10[225] ("when they look on the one whom they have pierced [LXX: *anth' ōn katōrchēsanto*], they shall mourn for him"), it was fulfilled in the first century as the executioners were dealing with the dead body of Christ (*opsontai eis hon exekentēsan*; John 19:37). It is used again in Revelation 1:7 ("He is coming with the clouds; every eye will see him, even those who pierced him [*kai hoitines auton exekentēsan*]."), but it remains difficult to understand if this reference concerns the Fall

---

Austria, 35,000 in Poland, 60,000 in Russia, over 20,000 in America, and smaller numbers in other countries." According to Glaser, the number of Jewish people who became believers in Jesus during the first third of the twentieth century is upward of 230,000. See Glaser, "Lessons," 229–31. As already seen, according to De le Roi, there was a "quarter of a million Jews . . . won for Christ during this [nineteenth] century" (Schonfield, *History*, 154). Hoffman Cohn notes that the church historian Neander "estimates that there were fully a million Jews who accepted the Lord Jesus Christ as Saviour, in the first century of the Christian era." In Hoffman Cohn, *Beginning*, 32. Finally, Dr Dalman of Leipsic claimed that "if all the Jews who have embraced Christianity had remained a distinct people, instead of being absorbed by the nations among whom they dwelt, their descendants would be counted in millions." Stock, *A Short Handbook of Missions*, 155, quoted in Robinson, *History of Christian Missions*, 473–74.

223. Glaser, *BBJE*, III.

224. Cf. Wright, *New Testament*, 261.

225. See also Hoffman Cohn, *Beginning*, 163. Cooper, *Jew Still First*, 18, links Zech 12:10 with Hos 5:15 where "the prophet was speaking of Israel's confession at the close of the Great Tribulation."

Status Quaestionis

of Jerusalem in AD 70 or the second coming of Christ at the end of time. "Whether repentance will follow, John does not say; only that sorrow will be one outcome of the divine judgement which is arriving."[226] Finally, since Matthew 3:2 and 4:17, on the nearness of the kingdom of God, refer to the fact that the kingdom came with Jesus—and it is in this way that it is near, and even in the midst of the disciples in Luke 17:21—these verses cannot thus be used to refer to the second coming.[227]

However, two other texts seem to anticipate a time when the spiritual Jewish leaders—and the Jewish people following them—will repent and welcome Jesus, announcing that the kingdom taken from the spiritual leaders will be giving back.[228]

Firstly, in Matthew 23:37–39, Jesus says to the scribes and Pharisees: "See, your house is left to you, desolate. For I tell you, you will not see me again until you say, 'Blessed is the one who comes in the name of the Lord.'"[229] I will need to understand in my following chapters to which event Psalm 118:26 is referring.[230]

Secondly, commenting on Acts 3:17-26 ("Repent therefore, . . . that he may send the Messiah appointed for you, that is, Jesus, who must remain in heaven until the time of universal restoration [*achri chronōn apokatastaseōs pantōn*]"), Glaser links the word "restitution" with the related Greek verb used by the disciples in Acts 1:6 ("Lord, is this the time when you will restore the kingdom to Israel? [*ei en tō chronō toutō apokathistaneis tēn basileian tō Israēl*;]" Here again, there is still the question whether the kingdom had already been established, for instance in AD 70, or if it shall be established during for a future event, such as the return in power of the Jewish people in Jerusalem in 1967, a possible realization of the prophesy of Jesus in Luke 21:24.[231]

As Fruchtenbaum argues, eschatology was a catalyst for Jewish evangelism. Traditionally in the USA, the "primary motivating factor" has been premillennial dispensationalism, whereas on the British scene it has been postmillennial theology, expecting the "future and national regeneration of Israel"; as for amillennialists, "they are not motivated by their eschatology, but are motivated from the general pattern of the need to evangelize

---

226. Smalley, *Revelation*, 38.
227. See Wright, *Jesus*, 198–474.
228. Cf. Matt 21:33–46; Mark 12:1–12; Luke 20:9–19.
229. Cf. Hoffman Cohn, *Beginning*, 19–20, 68–69.
230. Cf. Wright, *New Testament*, 570–72.
231. Cf. Brickner, "Chosen for What," as well as Brickner, *Future Hope*, 7.

and Jews should not be excluded as objects of evangelism."[232] Yet again, will we see a massive conversion of Jewish people after "the full number of the Gentiles has come in" (Rom 11:25)? And if so, should evangelistic priority be given to the Gentiles, a kind of *reverse missional priority*? We will see in chapter 4 and conclusion that this is not exactly the case.

The Evangelization of the World by the Jewish People

My concern to deal with the idea that priority should be given to the preaching of the gospel to the Jewish people forces me to come to an important argument regarding the thesis, viz. that the gospel has to be preached first to the Jewish people because it is the mission of the Jewish people to become the greatest evangelists ever seen, according to a certain interpretation of Romans and Revelation. It will be a restoration to Israel's divine mission and role in the evangelization of the world: "Paul is saying that Israel's disobedience cannot ultimately thwart the plan of God. He also seems to be implying, and many today believe, that the salvation of the world still 'hinges' in some sense upon the salvation of the Jewish nation."[233] Sims thinks that "[we] are to be ever-conscious of the priority of Jewish evangelism because the salvation of the Jewish people will bring great blessing to the world."[234] Hoffman Cohn thinks that God will use the messianic Jews—like him—to prepare the 144,000 Jewish evangelists: "And may it not be that He will use us if we are yielded to His will for Israel, to prepare those 144,000 Jews for the tribulation days so that through their testimony many thousands of your Gentile relatives may be saved . . . ?"[235] González, who is not a dispensationalist, argues that "Romans 11:12 fleshes out the missional strategy stated first in 1:14–16. . . . When Jews reject the gospel, Gentile conversions, nevertheless, follow and when Israel finally acknowledges Jesus as Messiah, Gentile conversion will happen like never before."[236] It will be the "life from the dead" of Rom 11:15.[237]

---

232. See Fruchtenbaum, "Eschatology," 251.
233. Glaser, *BBJE*, I.4.
234. Sims, "Jew First Online," end of the chapter "Paul and the Jew First Principle."
235. Hoffman Cohn, *Beginning*, 92; cf. also 227 and Ariel, *Evangelizing*, 18.
236. González, "Jew First II," 26.
237. Cf. M'Cheyne's fourth argument (with reference to Zech 8:23) in Bonar, *M'Cheyne*, 489–97 and Rev. Patterson's twelfth argument, written before 1948, linked with Isa 66:8 ("a nation born in a day") in Patterson, *Jew First*, 4. Cf. also Hoffman Cohn, *Beginning*, 197–98.

When will this event take place? For Brickner, the revival will be at the end of the Tribulation and therefore after the rapture of all the faithful Christians on earth at this time:[238]

> But the time is coming when Israel will not only embrace Y'shua, they will become the greatest evangelists for their Messiah the world has ever seen. Think about it. God used a minority of Jews who believed in Jesus to turn the first-century world upside down with an amazing message of hope and life. Is it possible that in the last days, God will again empower Jewish people with that message of hope and life in Jesus? I believe so.[239]

This world-wide task of evangelization will indeed be accomplished following the testimony of "the two witnesses" of Revelation 11:3–13 and by "the 144,000" of Revelation 7:4–8.[240] One question arises: if the Jewish revival will occur at the end of the Tribulation and hence after the rapture, why encourage the mission to the Jewish people on the basis of this event *before* the Tribulation? Lindsay points to this issue when he says:

> It is logical to ask at this point, how is he [the Antichrist] going to make war with the saints when they are gone from the earth? "The saints" are the people who are going to believe in Christ during this great period of conflict. After the Christians are gone God is going to reveal Himself in a special way to 144,000 physical, literal Jews who are going to believe with a vengeance that Jesus is the Messiah. They are going to be 144,000 Jewish Billy Grahams turned loose on this earth—the earth will never know a period of evangelism like this period. These Jewish people are going to make up for lost time. They are going to have the greatest number of converts in all history. Revelation 7:9–14 says they bring so many to Christ that they can't be numbered.[241]

Moreover, the passages in question are, as many believe, very difficult to interpret.[242] It appears dangerous to assert a thesis on their basis. On Revelation 11:1–14, Tom Wright remarks in a humorous way:

---

238. Brickner, *Future Hope*, 35: "Zechariah predicts a staggering level of fatalities in this final conflict. But in the end, those who survive will return to God. When that happens, there will be a spiritual renewal of the people of Israel, the likes of which the world has never seen."
239. Ibid., 36. See also Lindsay and Carlson, *Late Planet*, 142–43.
240. See Brickner, *Future Hope*, 36–39; 49–51
241. Lindsay and Carlson, *Late Planet*, 111.
242. See Aune, *Revelation 6–16*, for an overview of the contemporary debate.

> People find many books puzzling, but the Bible is often the most puzzling of all. People find many parts of the Bible puzzling, but Revelation is often seen as the most puzzling book of all. And people find Revelation puzzling, but the first half of chapter 11 . . . is, for many, the most puzzling part of all.[243]

As for Revelation, 7:4–8, Ryrie himself declares: "Some groups do deem it best for their ministry to have a pretribulation Rapture clause in their doctrinal statements, but I have never seen a creedal statement that considered it necessary to include the identification of the 144,000."[244] Indeed, there is no clear mention in these verses that these 144,000 will be evangelists.

According to his eschatological scheme, Brickner surprisingly refutes the idea that the Jewish people need to believe in Jesus—I imagine that he is talking about "revival" and not "individual conversions"—before the second coming of Christ: "It was never part of the Christian belief that Jesus would return in the year 2000, nor is it now part of the Christian belief that Jewish people must believe in him before he can return."[245] Doing so, he may certainly refer to the "first second coming" of Jesus at the rapture, rather than the "second second coming" after the seven weeks of Daniel 9. In fact, the director of JFJ rightly wants to underline the sovereignty of God (as in the passage of Lindsay quoted above), but in my view draws the wrong conclusion:

> If there are Christians who believe that people can hasten the return of Messiah by their actions or beliefs, they are a decided minority and sorely misinformed. Those who believe the Bible know that on such matters God is sovereign. In other words, he is calling the shots and we are not in any position to either move him along any faster or delay his hand concerning the Messiah's return. To think otherwise is to make the same mistake that our matriarch, Sarah made. . . . God doesn't need our help to accomplish his plans. His timing is perfect and it rarely coincides with our wishes. Most Christians who urgently share their faith with Jews or Gentiles, do so out of a strong conviction that God wants them to. They are also compelled by care and concern because they truly believe that following Jesus is the path to joy, peace and forgiveness—and that a choice for him is the greatest choice that any human being could make.[246]

---

243. Wright, *Revelation for Everyone*, 97.
244. Ryrie, *Dispensationalism*, 18.
245. Brickner, *Future Hope*, 143.
246. Ibid., 143–44.

While largely agreeing with this last statement, I argue, instead, that the second coming of Jesus is delayed because of the incompleteness of the mission: "And the good news must first be proclaimed to all nations [*eis panta ta ethnē prōton*]" (Mark 13:10 and par.).[247] I will have the opportunity to come back to this point in chapter 4 ("Eschatological perspectives") as it is part of a more global eschatological development.

THE DEBT OF CHRISTIANS TO THE JEWISH PEOPLE

As a son is thankful to his mother who gave him life and took care of her in her last days, Christians should be thankful to the Jewish people and bring them the gospel first. In his hundred year old little leaflet of four pages, Rev. Alexander Patterson lists twelve arguments for the *MP* and after considering the pattern of Paul, the ministry of Jesus and the place of the Jewish people in the Bible, he approaches the 4th argument with Romans 9:4–5 in mind: "They gave us our Scriptures, having preserved them most carefully and with infinite pains kept them from error. . . . Above all it was the Jewish Nation that gave us our Christ and His apostles, and all that Christianity means to us."[248]

For the same reason, Bjoraker encourages donations to the missions among the Jewish people and cites Romans 15:27 as support for his request: "for if the Gentiles have come to share in their spiritual blessings, they ought also to be of service to them in material things."[249] The non-Jew Stephen Madden, who wrote a little leaflet for The British Society for the Propagation of the Gospel among the Jews,[250] is grateful to the Jewish people for the Sabbath and recalls that somebody said: "Had Judaism given nothing more to mankind than the establishment of a weekly day of rest we should still be forced to proclaim her one of the greatest benefactors of humanity."[251]

This point is more complicated than it at first appears. I acknowledge that the oracles of God have been entrusted to the Jewish people, and I am thankful for those, both Jewish and Christian, who preserved the Scriptures until today (the Masoretes in particular). I acknowledge also that the Gentiles have been grafted onto the "cultivated olive tree" (Rom 11:24), namely believing Israel, to participate in its spiritual blessings. However, we have

---

247. Cf. also 2 Pet 3:9.
248. Patterson, *Jew First*, 2.
249. Bjoraker, "Jew First," 112–13.
250. Cf. Madden, *Jew First*.
251. Ibid., 4. Madden declares wishing to be Jew: "Sir, I am half-English, half-Irish—there is no Scotch in me; but I would to God I had some Jewish blood in me then I could be proud" (ibid., 6).

to question whether the historical circumstances of Romans 15:27 are the same today. Moo writes:

> Gentiles' status as members of the people of God is inextricably tied to a salvation history that has an indelible OT/Jewish cast. Gentile Christians, many with no previous ties to Judaism and living far from Jerusalem, need to understand this also; and their giving of money to the "saints in Jerusalem" will go a long way toward solidifying this sense of "indebtedness."[252]

We have to be careful not to mix different ideas that do not belong to the same period. Historically, the Gentiles were able to benefit from the message of God thanks to the Israelites who kept the Scriptures and thanks to the first Messianic Jews who preached the gospel to them. Paul used this argument to encourage the Gentiles to give to the church in Jerusalem. However, we cannot transpose this argument to today's mission to the Jewish people. Yes, I am deeply thankful for my salvation through Jesus the Jew. But if we have to be thankful for the preservation of Scriptures by the Jewish people, we have also to be thankful for the preservation of Scriptures by the monks throughout history. Moreover, I have never met any Gentile Christian converted to Christianity by unbelieving Jews. Finally, I cannot say that the gospel, received first by the Jewish people at the beginning of the church, is still entrusted to them today. The gospel is now entrusted to the church, composed of all the Jewish people and Gentiles who put their trust in Jesus.

We also need to be careful not to use a positive argument—the Patterson's Jewish motherhood—in the same way a negative one as been used for centuries—the accusation of deicide. No scholar today will claim with 1 Thessalonians 2:14–15, for instance, that today's Jews (or "Judeans") are responsible for the death of Jesus. Yet saying that we are indebted to today's Jews for the gift of the gospel to the Gentiles in the first century is equally untrue. Unfortunately, as we have already seen with Rabbi Poupko, the Jewish people today (believers and unbelievers)—and Gentile Christians—are often brandishing the Christian persecutions of the past as Christians have brandished the charge of deicide in the past.

THE CHRISTIAN PERSECUTIONS OF THE JEWISH PEOPLE THROUGHOUT HISTORY

This argument considers the acts of violence perpetrated towards the Jewish people in the name of Christianity to encourage the proclamation of the

---

252. Moo, *Romans*, 905.

gospel to the Jewish people as a kind of reparation. For Patterson, we should have "the most sympathetic feelings" for the Jewish people considering the past persecutions of the Jewish people (Patterson is writing before the Shoah).[253] This argument is not often used by the contemporary proponents of the *MP*, but I suspect it may have been uppermost in their minds. The past persecutions (and especially the Shoah) have led Christians to act in an empathetic way towards the Jewish people: either to affirm that those who perpetrated the Shoah were not *real* Christians[254] or to show them love and kindness, both politically and financially, in all circumstances.[255] Hoffman Cohn is bold enough to say in 1943, that "Satan himself really believes in the doctrine of 'To the Jew first.' Yes, the devil believes this, and together with Hitler, practices it! Only they do this *in reverse!* For has not the Jew been always first in every explosion of world hate?"[256]

Current missions to the Jewish people find themselves in an embarrassing and difficult position, where evangelization of the Jewish people is seen by the Jewish people themselves as an anti-Semitic act. To face this situation and as Richard Mouw, president of the *Fuller Theological Seminary*, expresses it, "[w]e cannot simply quote Paul—who wrote when the church was a minority religion struggling to clarify both continuities and differences with a Jewish majority—without recognizing that we do so from the side of Auschwitz."[257] However, we as Christians need to especially try and understand the Jewish people in order to restore dialogue and receive forgiveness:

> If we want to tell of the power of the gospel "to the Jew first" (Rom. 1:16) in our context, we may need to draw near to our Jewish friends, first of all, in order to learn from them and work with them on matters of profound significance in our contemporary world.[258]

In point of fact, as I have touched on in my first chapter, arguments like Mouw's encouraged many not to evangelize the Jewish people.

---

253. Patterson, *Jew First*, 2. Cf. also Hoffman Cohn, *Beginning*, 17–19 and LCWE, "Jewish Evangelism," 1–2.

254. Patterson, *Jew First*, 2–3.

255. See, for instance, *The International Christian Embassy Jerusalem* "founded in 1980 as an evangelical Christian response to the need to comfort Zion according to the command of Scripture found in Isaiah 40:1–2: 'Comfort, comfort my people, says your God. Speak tenderly to Jerusalem.'" Cf. International Christian Ambassy website. Online: www.icej.org, accessed April 2011. Cf. also Oduor, *Jew First*, 143–49.

256. Hoffman Cohn, *Beginning*, 175.

257. Mouw, "Jew First," 13. Cf. also Leventhal, "Holocaust," 122–54.

258. Mouw, "Jew First," 13.

To the Jew First or to the Jew at Last?

THE BLESSINGS WITHIN THE MISSIONAL PRIORITY

"God deals favorably with those who are good to the Jews":[259] this is a widely developed notion stemming from Genesis 12:1–3. Sims' argument blurs the distinction between evangelism and philo-Semitism, when he refers to the fact that Egypt was blessed when Pharaoh blessed Joseph. He argues that the pyramids were built during Joseph's life, but when the Jewish people were made slaves, "the curse of Genesis 12:3 went into effect," resulting in the plagues.[260] He continues to apply his idea to Babylon, Persia, Greece, Rome, Germany, and the British Empire, all countries that have been blessed when they were blessing Israel and then cursed when they denigrated her.[261] He even adds: "Is it a coincidence that America, the Jews' second homeland, is the only remaining superpower today?"[262] These national blessings prove, according to Sims, that the same would happen to the church which evangelizes the Jew first: "If a church would trust God and bless Israel, God would be faithful and bless that church."[263]

Hoffman Cohn considers the "marvellous growth of the great Free Church of Scotland" and recalls how Horatius Bonar, during the first great convention that established the *Free Church of Scotland* in 1843, "made an impassioned plea that God could not bless the new united Free Churches of Scotland unless they then and there established as a part of their doctrinal program the divine order in Missions as being 'To the Jew First.'"[264] He also recalls the blessings harvested by the *London Jewish Missionary Society* as this mission led, for instance, Samuel Isaac Joseph Schereschewsky to Christ: "How many millions of dollars will you put as the value of Bishop Schereschewsky's translation of the English Bible into the Mandarin tongue, a translation which enabled the Christian Church to reach in one sweep a

---

259. Sims, *Jew First*, 45. See also Gen 21:12; 28:14–15. Cf. also argument 11 in Patterson, *Jew First*, 4 and last argument of M'Cheyne in Bonar, *M'Cheyne*, 489–97.

260. Sims, *Jew First*, 48.

261. Ibid., 48–54.

262. Ibid., 54. With identical arguments, see Oduor, *Jew First*, 116–22. Today, however, although America is still the major supporter of Israel, the nation is fading.

263. Sims, *Jew First*, 54. The same idea is expressed by Fruchtenbaum, "Romans 1:16," 10.

264. Hoffman Cohn, *Beginning*, 26–27. See also Robertson, *Jew First*. David W. Torrance, retired Church of Scotland pastor, affirms that "[t]oday, the Church of Scotland along with most other mainstream churches has lost the vision of taking the Gospel 'to the Jew first.'" In Torrance and Taylor, *Israel*, 7–8. "George Taylor" is a pseudonym.

population of Chinese numbering 250,000,000?"²⁶⁵ This last point is sometimes associated with the idea of the superiority of Jewish intelligence.²⁶⁶

The first way of support that is generally accepted is prayer. As Reginald Oduor, lecturer of philosophy at Kikuyu Campus of the University of Nairobi and the national chairman of Prayer for Israel Kenya, expresses it on behalf of many: "God has a very clear order in world evangelism—'To the Jew **first**, and also to the Greek' (Rom. 1.16c). . . . We must therefore give first priority to praying for evangelism among the Jewish people, . . ."²⁶⁷ And he adds: "One of the best ways in which to bless Israel and thus be blessed in turn is to uphold her before the Lord through intercessory prayer."²⁶⁸ But blessing also involves money. Hoffman Cohn, quoting from 1Kings 17:13, appeals to the "Divine arithmetic": "God had put His plus sign over against the poor widow's minus barrel, and lo and behold! the addition became multiplication, and multiplication reached infinity!"²⁶⁹ Yet, in 1930, The Barbican Mission to the Jews, founded in 1871 and which became after merging with The International Society for Evangelisation of the Jews the mission Christian Witness to Israel, published the little tract "To the Jew First" in order to raise money for the mission.²⁷⁰ The January 2011 JFJ *Newsletter* that I considered at the beginning of this chapter is not a call for money and I have to admit that the slogan "To the Jew First" is used rarely by JFJ to encourage people to prioritize giving to the mission among the Jewish people. However, here is an example:

> Every January Jews for Jesus hears from at least a few friends who say they want to start the new year with a gift to bring the message of the Messiah to Jewish people. . . . I suspect that our Jews for Jesus friends who follow this example of giving "to the Jew first" probably receive even more blessing from giving those gifts than we do from receiving them. Aside from the gifts themselves, the accompanying letters always make me happy. I rejoice in them because I like to see Christians acting upon what they regard as biblical principles.²⁷¹

Other missions, such as Chosen People Ministries, often used and still use the slogan for fundraising and testify that people who gave first to

265. Hoffman Cohn, *Beginning*, 27–29, where he quotes many more Messianic Jews.
266. Cf. Cooper, *Jew Still First*, 21, 28.
267. Oduor, *Jew First*, 127.
268. Ibid., 129.
269. Hoffman Cohn, *Beginning*, 45.
270. Anonymous, *Jew First*, 4.
271. Rosen, "Why first?" 1. Cf. also Brickner, "Expect?," 1 and Brickner, "Russia," 2

the Jewish people have received blessing and joy.[272] In the September 2011 UK edition of *The Chosen People*, Newsletter of CPM, one can find a little colorful square on its back cover, at the bottom right, encouraging: "Please remember Chosen People Ministries in your will. 'I will bless those who bless you' (Genesis 12:3)."[273] For Hoffman Cohn, money is better invested in Jewish missions than Gentile missions: "The astonishing truth is that where Jewish mission work is efficiently and ably carried on, the actual conversions are some 3½ to 1 as compared to Gentile results—money, population and effort being equal!"[274] Despite the difficulty of checking the effective validity of this proposition—especially this last calculation—I can understand the important financial implication of the *MP* thesis, which does not seem to be far from the "Prosperity Gospel."[275] However, as already seen, I believe that Genesis 12:3 has been realized in the first century when the gospel has been extended to all the other nations (Cf. Gal 3:8-9). As for the other blessings in the Old Testament, we have to be reminded that they were "conditional on diligent keeping of the Law and commandments."[276]

FIGURES OF HISTORY

The proponents of the *MP* interpretation are keen to learn from missionary figures in history to sustain their thesis, the most well-known being Hudson Taylor and his habit of sending on the first day of every year a check to the president of the Mildmay Mission, John Wilkinson, with the comment: "to the Jew first." Wilkinson also had the habit of immediately sending a check to the China Inland Mission with the comment: "and also to the Gentile."[277] Besides Robert Murray M'Cheyne, mentioned above, also Andrew Bonar, Charles Haddon Spurgeon, Charles Hodge, and John Murray are all seen as

---

272. Cf. Hoffman Cohn, *Beginning*, 13 or Glaser, "His Power Changed My Life," 1–4. Hoffman Cohn declares in page 24: "While all around us they are crying 'deficits,' 'retrenchment,' 'bankruptcy,' the Lord has given this Mission the largest income of its history."

273. Nessim, "Director's Letter," 4. Daniel Nessim is the UK director of CPM.

274. Hoffman Cohn, *Beginning*, 231–32.

275. Cf., for a good example of the Prosperity Gospel, the following best-seller book which encourages to pronounce daily Jabez prayer (1 Chr 4.10) to be blessed: Wilkinson and Kopp, *Prayer of Jabez*.

276. Martin, *Jew First*, 6. Cf. Deut 11:26–28, for instance.

277. Glaser, *BBJE*, II.B.5. Cf. also Mitch Glaser in Bock and Glaser, *Jew First*, 17 or Hoffman Cohn, *Beginning*, 73 and Rosen, "Why first?" 1. It is not said if the amount of the checks were similar!

advocates of the priority of evangelism among the Jewish people.[278] Hoffman Cohn adds Horatius Bonar, Andrew Murray (pastor and founder of mission societies), Jonathan Goforth (missionary to China), and James M. Gray (Moody Bible Institute) to the list.[279] As for Arthur Glasser, Jakób Jocz, missionary in Poland, embodies the "principle."[280]

It is interesting to observe that the missionary revival of the nineteenth century—which touched also the mission among the Jewish people[281]—leads Patterson to claim the support of the church as an argument for the *MP*: "There are 200 societies with 750 workers now at work. In the United States there are 48 with 147 workers. All this shows that the churches have placed the mark of their approval upon this work."[282] Today, despite American support, the missions among the Jewish people are often struggling to convince the church to engage with the Jewish people first.[283] Anyway, the concept of appealing to figures of history to sustain a thesis is, to say the least, fragile. Many other "figures" have not gone in this direction, as we have seen in my first chapter.

THE WAY NOT TO FORGET THE JEWISH PEOPLE IN OUR EVANGELISM

This widely held concern states that, generally, when someone remarks that he does not want to prioritize evangelism of the Jewish people over that of the Gentiles, it means that he does evangelize everybody but the Jewish people.[284] Cohen compares it with marketing: "if you don't market a particular product towards a particular people group, you're not going to reach them."[285]

---

278. Cf. Sims, *Jew First*, 55–62. It is possible that Sims confuses Andrew Bonar with Horatius Bonar.

279. Hoffman Cohn, *Beginning*, 26–27; 124–25; 127–28.

280. Glasser, "Jocz," 523–31. See also his statement promoting the present priority of Rom 1:16 in Glasser, *Fuller Theological Seminary News Release, 12th May 1976*, no page.

281. Cf. Thompson, *Century of Jewish Missions* and chapter 1.

282. Patterson, *Jew First*, 3.

283. Cf. Cohen, "Jew First II," where Cohen mixes optimism and pessimism.

284. See, for instance, Hoffman Cohn, *Beginning*, 224. And at the opposite end, the proponents like to say, as Kjær-Hansen did: "*If the gospel is not, or no longer is, for Jews, then it is also not, or no longer is, good news for Gentiles.*" In Kjær-Hansen, "One Way," 293. See also Anderson, "Jew First," 310.

285. Cohen, "Jew First II," against Mouw, "Jew First," 12: "I oppose treating Jews as if they were only 'targets' for evangelism."

To the Jew First or to the Jew at Last?

This argument is reinforced if one considers that the Jewish people usually think that the gospel is only for the Gentiles.[286]

However, this argument is quite simply wrong. Otherwise, the same would be true for any other targeted population. The fact that an individual or a church does not attest that it is a priority to preach the gospel to a particular group is not identical to the claim that he does not want to target this group. I believe that any church should welcome anyone in building and try to reach everybody while evangelizing on the street.

Having said that, I do agree that a ministry has the legitimacy to target a population group (the students by the Christian Union, the children by the Child Evangelism Fellowship, the Arabs by the Arab World Ministries, etc.), as does JFJ. I recognize also that a ministry that focuses its attention on a particular group may indeed overlook the others; this is the case for JFJ too, and it is an understandable fact. In this way, I would agree with the argument: if Arab World Ministries is targeting the Arabs, it is not giving priority to the Jewish people. But this ministry is not claiming that the Arabs should be evangelized prior to any other people, as the *MP* would claim.

THE IMPARTIALITY OF GOD

This point is not an argument of the proponents of the *MP* itself, but more an observation while evaluating their defense.[287] Challenged with the biblical declaration of the impartiality of God,[288] the proponents often need to justify themselves, as Rosen felt he had to:

> I believe our Heavenly Father takes no more joy in a Jew coming to Christ than He does in a Hindu or a Buddhist or a pagan. Every soul is equally precious in His sight. Nevertheless, Jewish evangelism is crucial—perhaps it is the most significant issue on which the church will prove its character, conviction and commitment to evangelism.[289]

Fruchtenbaum expresses it like this: "In relation to missions, the gospel must be to the Jew first. This is not a matter of preference, but a matter of procedure."[290] Sims feels the need to say "that every verse stating that there

---

286. Cf. Cohen, "Jew First II," and his testimony.
287. However, Sims writes a chapter on it: "Is God a Respecter of Persons?" Cf. Sims, *Jew First*, 71–78.
288. Cf. Rom 2:11; Gal 3:28; Acts 10:34.
289. Rosen, "You Asked," 6.
290. Fruchtenbaum, "Romans 1:16," 10.

is no difference between the Jew and the Greek is ALWAYS in the context of salvation and never in the context of evangelism."²⁹¹ It would be like thinking of a wreck where the first people to be asked to leave and be saved would be the women and the children—because of their greatest need—but not forgetting that there are enough dinghies for the men too. But what about the time needed for the rescue? Is prioritizing the women and children not showing partiality? At the same time, Sims recognizes that "the Jews do not have priority in righteousness or merit" or "in how they are saved" but that they "are still a special people."²⁹²

Patterson states that, because of the persecution by his own people and their treachery, "[t]he Jew is worth saving. While all men are also worth saving, the Jew has special value as a witness for Christ. The cross that the converted Jew carries is a heavier one than that carried by any other."²⁹³ I do not know if a Muslim convert in an Arab country would agree with that statement.

These comments show the natural uneasiness felt by the proponents of the MP when they want to associate their thesis with the fact that "God shows no partiality" (Rom 2:11). It seems, rather, that if God has shown and will show partiality regarding salvation of the Jewish people and Gentiles, it is only according to his sovereign order of salvation in the history (see chapter 4).

OTHER PERIPHERAL ARGUMENTS

The Gospel of John

The Gospel of John offers a well-known and often quoted verse, 4:22: "You worship what you do not know; we worship what we know, for salvation is from the Jews." However, this verse is used more as a slogan than an argument for the *MP*.²⁹⁴ David Zadok, Director of *HaGefen Publishing*,

---

291. Sims, *Jew First*, 71. See also Wallace, "Jew First," no page, who leaning on Stern, *Jewish New Testament Commentary*, 329, quote Rom 2:7–12; 3:9–31; 4:9–12; 5:12, 17–19; 9:24; 10:12–13; 11:30–32 to say that "[a]s far as salvation is concerned, they are equal before God."

292. Sims, *Jew First*, 73–75. See Piper, "Jew First," who is the only one who, while promoting the *MP*, also chooses to consider the following in his section "In What Ways Do the Jews Not Have Priority?": "Paul wants to humble both Jew and Greek and make them deeply aware that they depend entirely on mercy, not on themselves or their tradition or ethnic connections."

293. Patterson, *Jew First*, 2.

294. See, however, Hoffman Cohn, *Beginning*, 121–30.

proposes—hopefully with caution—an original but hardly convincing idea that John, in his gospel, expresses a priority for Jewish evangelism. For him, the fact that the famous verse of John 3:16 is placed "right in between the conversations with a Jew first [Nicodemus] and then a Samaritan" could show that "perhaps Romans 1:16 and Acts 1:8 are not the only places in the New Testament that emphasize the priority of the mission to the Jews."[295] However, as in the case of Genesis 12:3/Galatians 3:8–9, I argue that this verse in John refers to the fact that Jewish people understand the object of worship, "for they were elected as the people from whom the salvation of the world would come, i.e., through the Messiah."[296]

The Land of Israel

Eighty years before the creation of the State of Israel, Helen MacLachlan had already called her book, which deals with the future land, *Notes on the Unfulfilled Prophecies of Isaiah. Addressed to "the Jew First, and Also to the Gentile."*[297] In 1996, Oduor devotes large sections in his book to the topic of the land of Israel,[298] although without making a link between the formula "To the Jew first" and the land itself. But it is Torrance and Taylor who develop a theology of the land within the formula.[299] Considering that Israel is the focus of world attention and that she still has to be the light of the world, the only way for a revival in the Middle East—and finally an end of this conflict—would be the conversion of the Jewish people:

> As the late Dr Zwemer,[300] perhaps the greatest authority on the ministry of the gospel to the Islamic world, said, "the converted Jews make the best missionary to the Arab. Their conversion to Christ should be the abiding passion and concern of the church." . . . The very presence of the State of Israel, and all that has happened in recent years, has shaken the Islamic world. God

---

295. Zadok, "Mission Priority from the Gospel of John," 3.

296. Beasley-Murray, *John*, 62.

297. MacLachlan, *Unfulfilled Prophecies: to the Jew First*, cover.

298. Oduor, *Jew First*, the land Israel is mentioned from the first words of the introduction and almost throughout the whole book, but esp. 81–91.

299. Torrance and Taylor, *Israel*, 158–60, in their chapter 12 "To the Jew First" (157–64), but also 62–63. See also Nadge, *Juden zuerst!*, 42–62.

300. Dr Samuel M. Zwemer (1867–1952) was lecturer at Princeton Theological Seminary from 1929 to 1952

is challenging Islam through Israel, and confronting the Islamic peoples with himself.[301]

For Brickner, "the modern day state of Israel is a miracle of God and a fulfillment of Bible prophecy."[302] JFJ has concentrated its efforts on Israel in these last years, and, at the time of writing, a new building is being established in the land called the *Moishe Rosen Center*:[303]

> Jesus clearly said that "Jerusalem would be trodden down by the Gentiles until the time of the nations is fulfilled" (Luke 21:24). It has been 50 years since the founding of that state, but only 30 years since Jerusalem came under the control of Jews for the first time since Jesus made that prediction. Could it be that "this generation shall not pass until all these things are fulfilled?"[304]

I believe that God has sovereignly allowed the Jewish people to come back to the land of their ancestors, although not to fulfill Old Testament prophecies I regard to have already been fulfilled. But considering geopolitical issues to support an exegesis is dangerous,[305] and the past is full of misleading interpretations based on political events.[306] Should we likewise concentrate our mission among the Arabs in order to resolve the conflict? Rather, as will become clear in chapter 4, the "great reversal keenly felt throughout Jesus' ministry—the last will be first!—has now been applied to the land, this land of inheritance, the land of Judah, no doubt the most precious commodity fought for in Jesus' day."[307]

---

301. Torrance and Taylor, *Israel*, 160

302. Brickner, "About modern Israel," quoted in Burge, *Jesus & Land*, 112.

303. Cf. Brickner, "Under Construction," no page. Since the worldwide BYG campaign finished in the summer of 2006, Israel has been and is still the target of biannual campaigns. (See http://jewsforjesus.org/programs/byg, accessed January 2001).

304. Burge, *Jesus & Land*, 112.

305. Like Nadge who declares: "If it is our commission to bring the Gospel to the Gentiles how much more to the Jews considering the political situation." My translation. See Nadge, *Juden zuerst!*, 60: "Darum: Wenn es schon der Auftrag ist, Heiden das Evangelium zu bringen, um wieviel mehr den Juden unter der heutigen politischen Situation?"

306. See, for instance, the eschatological understanding of the *European Common Market* as the "beginning of ten nation confederacy predicted by Daniel and the Book of Revelation" in Lindsay and Carlson, *Late Planet*, 94.

307. Burge, *Jesus & Land*, 35.

To the Jew First or to the Jew at Last?

The First Fruits of the Harvest

We owe the original interpretation of "The first fruits of the harvest" to Ari Sorko-Ram, founder of *Maoz Israel Ministries*, as outlined in his little booklet *To the Jew First*.[308] Basing his argument on Exodus 4:22b ("Israel is my son, my firstborn")[309] and on Romans 11:12, he finds a parallel with the *Counting of the Omer*: "It is important for the Body of Messiah today to recognize Israel's position in the body as the first fruits. Remember, what we do with the first fruit determines what God will do with the harvest."[310] To support this idea, he recalls a conversation he had with the famous German evangelist Reinhard Bonnke (called to Africa many years ago) whom God once asked to pray for Israel:

> And I said, "But Lord, I am not going to Israel . . ." and I got really quiet for a moment and heard the Lord again saying, "Reinhard, pray for Israel." Again I said, "Lord, if I am not going to Israel, why pray for Israel?" Finally the Lord responded saying, "Reinhard, if you pray for Israel, I will give you Africa!"[311]

As this point is related to Romans 9–11, I will deal with it in chapter 4.

CONCLUSION

Considering this survey of the arguments from JFJ and other proponents for the *MP*, I outline a few conclusions, which will form the framework of my two following chapters. I do agree that the Jewish people need to be saved today and therefore evangelized, that Jesus went first to his fellow Jews, that the aim of God was to bring the gospel first to them and that the disciples of Jesus went also first to the Jewish people. However, the verses usually quoted to express the *Jewish missional priority* in Acts are not conclusive and could equally be interpreted in a historical way, i.e., the Jewish people receive first the gospel in history, as Acts reveal to us. For that matter, Fruchtenbaum is cautious regarding the use of the second book of Luke:

> Since Romans 1:16 is prescriptive, we should make Jewish evangelism our priority today. However, since Paul's practice in the Book of Acts is descriptive, it may or may not be essential

---

308. Sorko-Ram, *Jew First*, 44.
309. *NASB* 1995.
310. Sorko-Ram, *Jew First*, 17–20.
311. Ibid., 29; italics and bold in the original.

to make Jewish evangelism the first thing one should do when entering a new city or area.[312]

In fact, this priority in Jewish evangelism is often ambiguous and the proponents usually state that the practice is more difficult than the theory. The proponents are as uncomfortable in applying the priority too literally as are the ones they accuse of not quoting the "nine words" of Romans. In fact, I wonder if the *MP* was not born from an attempt to get things back into balance, expressed, however, with some ambiguity, in the *Lausanne Occasional Paper 7*:

> We do not suggest that there should be a radical application of "to the Jew first" in calling on all the evangelists, missionaries, and Christians to seek out the Jews within their sphere of witness before speaking to non-Jews! Yet we do call the church to restore ministry among this covenanted people of God to its biblical place in its strategy of world evangelization.[313]

At the same time, the New Testament clearly expresses that, because of the unbelief of a number of Jewish people, the gospel went to the Gentiles, as can be seen in Acts 13:46 and Romans 11:25–31. I need to undertake an exegetical study to determine the full sense of Romans 1:16 and explore if this adverb calls for the priority of Jewish evangelism over non-Jewish evangelism. Behind the entire issue lie eschatology and a particular understanding of the role of the mission to the Jew in the salvation of the world. How should Romans 9–11 be understood? Major systematic work needs to be done to define the real relationship between Israel and the church, as well as the general plan of God in the story of salvation.

Other, more popular arguments have also shown their weaknesses. They rather appear to have been added because of the thesis than as support of the thesis itself. Through the work I will now undertake exegetically, I hope to shed some more light on this issue from another perspective.

---

312. Fruchtenbaum, "Romans 1:16," 10.

313. COWE, "Christian Witness," 5. The committee recognizes earlier (4) that "[i]t might be difficult to be precise about what Paul understood by the phrase, 'to the Jew first.'"

III

Propositio
Exegesis of Romans 1:16–17

I AM CURRENTLY LIVING in the London Borough of Hillingdon, County of Middlesex, England. This borough is ruled by the Conservative Party whose aim, among others, is "Putting Residents First."[1] In order to apply this principle they have issued all responsible adults resident in the borough a "*HillingdonFirst* card." This card offers many "discounts or rewards on goods and services" to the Hillingdon residents.[2] For example, parking is much cheaper if you own the card. If you want to use a domestic rubbish tip in Hillingdon without producing the card, you would have to pay £10 before depositing any rubbish, etc. The *HillingdonFirst* principle is fairly simple to understand: the Conservative Party chose to favor those residents living in the borough. Incidentally, it can help for the future election. If a resident of another borough comes into Hillingdon to make the most of various Hillingdon facilities, he will be accepted but unfavored, because the residents are given priority over non-residents.

What about "The Jew first Principle"?[3] The proponents of the *missional priority* (*MP*) claim that Jewish people and Gentiles have the same rights with regard to salvation. However, they also believe that Jewish people should be the ones to be informed first of this good news, before

---

1. Puddifoot, "Hillingdon Leads the Way," 1.
2. Cf. LBH, *Hillingdon First Directory*.
3. This phrase is particularly dear to Daniel E. Sims (cf. chapter 2).

Propositio

the non-Jews. Could it be seen as if the gospel was going more freely, more appropriately to Jewish people, and that non-Jews would have to overcome the hurdle of their non-Jewishness before they are allowed to benefit from the gospel? "The Jew first principle" is, according to its advocates, expressed particularly in Romans 1:16 (see chapter 2). If it is fairly clear that the Jewish people were the ones to receive the gospel first in history, my concern is to evaluate how Christian theology should respond to those who argue that the uncontested *historical priority* (*HP*) enjoyed by Israel in the earliest years of the church should translate into a continuing *missional* priority today with Romans 1:16 as the biblical endorsement of their view. It is my aim now to enter into exegesis of this verse.

My exegetical study will take Romans 1:16–17 as a starting point and then be extended to the whole letter, the New Testament, and the rest of the Scriptures. As an explorer whose desire is to drink the water from the source, I will attempt to discover the essence of the "theme of the letter"[4] or the "*propositio*."[5] At this point, I am going to define the role played by Romans 1:16–17 in the whole Epistle and according to the aim of Paul. Actually, it appears that the expression "to the Jew first and also to the Greek" (*Ioudaiō te prōton kai Hellēni*) needs to be understood more in connection with Romans 2:9–10 and 3:1–31 than with chapters 9–11. These last chapters, which deal with salvation history, will however be considered in due time in chapter 4 below.

THE PURPOSE OF ROMANS

As N. T. Wright once wrote, "anyone who claimed to have read all the commentaries (let alone all the secondary literature) on Romans would be lying."[6] Indeed, despite the fact that the question regarding the author of Romans has—for once—not been much challenged,[7] the sole question of the purpose of Romans has been the object of many studies and theories, as the book edited by Karl P. Donfried, *The Romans Debate*, attests.[8] And yet,

---

4. As many used this term: Dodd, *Romans*, 9; Nygren, *Romans*, 72; Kuss, *Römerbrief*, 27; Murray, *Romans*, 28; Cranfield, *Romans I*, 90, Moo, *Romans*, 68 or Hultgren, *Romans*, 70.

5. See Jewett, *Romans*, 135.

6. Wright, *Romans*, 395.

7. Cf. Moo, *Romans*, 1–3. Cf., however, J. C. O'Neill: "I believe, with one or two isolated men like Weisse and Loisy, . . . that the words of the epistle handed down to us were not written by one man, were not written at one time, were not written to one audience." O'Neill, *Romans*, ii.

8. Cf. Donfried, *Romans Debate*.

we need to have at least a general understanding as to Paul's intentions when he wrote this Epistle to be better able to understand Romans 1:16 in its context. Since Donfried's book—which, despite being far from new (1977), was revised and expanded in 1991 and has been reprinted as recently as 2009, a proof of its value—others have still tried to resolve the problem of the aim and the destination of the letter.[9] To begin with, I do not claim to have solved the problem! However, some agreement or consensus—presented in the following pages in *"italics"*[10]—can be expressed between the major specialists, agreement upon which I can build my study, leaving other details that are irrelevant for the case to the side.

A Letter Addressed to a Christian Community in Rome

Between the writings of Melanchthon in 1521 and Anders Nygren in 1944,[11] Romans has usually been understood as "a compendium of Christian doctrine."[12] More recently, *"[w]ithout question a consensus has been reached that Romans is addressed to the Christian community in Rome which finds itself in a particular historical situation."*[13]

This point is important because it is part of the argument of the proponents of the *MP* to consider that Romans 1:16 expresses a conviction of Paul with systematic features: it adds some weight to the affirmation that the gospel is (forever) for the Jew first.[14] And indeed, Paul would more likely have written this letter during a stay in Corinth (Rom 16:1–2; 23) *circa* AD 57,[15] after many controversies among the churches of Corinth, and in Galatia and Macedonia.[16] This may explain the *manifesto* feature of the letter: while addressed to the Romans, it contains a systematic development of his ideas that could fit other communities[17] and that could be considered as a "historical testament of the Apostle."[18]

---

9. See, for instance, A. Andrew Das and his presumptuously entitled *Solving the Romans Debate*, xii, 324.

10. For this consensus, see Donfried, *Romans Debate*, xix–lxx.

11. Wedderburn recalls that F. C. Baur has already challenged this view in 1836; see Wedderburn, *Reasons*, 4.

12. Pauck, *Melanchthon and Bucer*, 22.

13. Donfried, *Romans Debate*, lxix, italics mine.

14. See chapter 2, "The formula in Romans" ("Present Priority").

15. Cf. Moo, *Romans*, 3.

16. Cf. Manson, "St. Paul's Letter," 14.

17. Cf. ibid., 15.

18. Bornkamm, "Last Will," 27.

Propositio

However, the historical context of Romans should not be dismissed so easily. The context is more understandable if one considers the promulgation of the edict of the Emperor Claudius in AD 49 by which the Jewish people—Jewish Christians included[19]—were expelled from Rome, since they "constantly made disturbances at the instigation of Chrestus."[20] If, at the death of the Emperor in AD 54 and the rescinding of the decree by Nero, they were allowed to return, we can understand that this gap of five years may have changed the relationship between Gentiles and Jewish Christians in the church. The belief that God excluded the Jewish people and transferred the promises and privileges from the Jewish people to the Gentiles could easily have been developed,[21] based possibly on the teaching of Jesus, most especially the Parable of the Wicked Tenants.[22] Among other issues regarding the law, Paul needed to shed light on this.

A Multiple Purpose

Romans is thus not only a systematic development of Paul's ideas that could have been addressed to any first-century church of the Roman Empire, but a letter for a community that appears to have been organized in house-churches (16:5). *"There also appears to be a developing agreement that it is unwise to speak of a single purpose in Paul's writing to Rome."*[23] First, as Paul plans to visit Rome, as well as Jerusalem and Spain, he seeks the support of the Romans. He asks for prayer because he seems afraid of the Judeans regarding the collection he wants to bring to Jerusalem (15:30–31); since it is a collection of Gentile provenance to a Jewish destination, the unity of Jewish people and Gentiles in the church is at stake;[24] he wants the support

---

19. As Priscilla and Aquila (Acts 18:2). Cf. Donfried, "Short Note," 46–47.

20. Suetonius, "The Deified Claudius," Book V, XXV:4, 53. According to Dio Cassius, Claudius already had problems with the Jewish people whom he banned in AD 41 from meeting because he could not expel them given their great number: "As for the Jews, who had again increased so greatly that by reason of their multitude it would have been hard without raising a tumult to bar them from the city, he did not drive them out, but ordered them, while continuing their traditional mode of life, not to hold meetings." Cf. Dio, *Roman History*, Book 60, 6:6, 383. For Das, who assumes a Jewish population of between 20,000 and 50,000, the two events are not necessarily contradictory; cf. Das, *Solving*, 149–202; esp. 163 and 167.

21. See Wright, *Fresh*, 127. An attitude which, according to him, "really would deserve the name 'supersessionism.'"

22. See chapter 4, "The Witness of the Gospels," for this discussion.

23. Donfried, *Romans Debate*, lxx, italics mine.

24. See Bornkamm, "Last Will," 17–18.

of the "West."[25] Secondly, he needs the Christians of Rome to be on his side as he plans to enlarge his ministry toward Spain. The capital city was an ideal operational base, if only to learn to speak the language required for an effective work in the Iberian Peninsula: Latin.[26] As Rome is not one of *his* churches, he has to gain its confidence.

Since Paul Minear's monograph, *The Obedience of Faith*,[27] distinguished between five communities among the Roman addresses—"the weak" (Jewish Christians), "the strong" (Gentile Christians), "the doubters," "the weak in faith who did not condemn the strong" and "the strong in faith who did not despise the weak"—scholars today are less keen to compartmentalize the Roman house-church and tend to consider only two kinds of Christians in Rome. It seems more likely that those among them, who understood that the practice of the works of the law[28] was no longer compulsory, are in that respect called by Paul the "strong" and seem to be more generally of Gentile provenance (I imagine that some of Jewish provenance, like Priscilla and Aquila, were also part of this group). The others, probably Jewish Christians—but also probably former God-fearers and proselytes—who were having difficulties facing the novelty of the gospel brought by Paul, were reluctant to leave the works of the law and seem to have been called the "weak" by Paul. At the same time, both the Gentile and Jewish members of the community have to learn not to boast—the Gentiles, whom grace has been given following the blindness and the persecution affecting the Jewish people, and the Jewish people and proselytes who still tend to boast in their Jewishness acquired by birth, circumcision and practice of the works of the law—and to welcome one another.[29]

An important question for our issue is whether Paul wants to come to Rome to evangelize, despite the fact that he does not want to "build on someone else's foundation" (15:20).[30] Verses 1:13–15 seem indeed to declare

25. See Jervell, "Letter to Jerusalem," 48.

26. Cf. Bruce, "Continued," 187. Jewett, "Argument," 266–67.

27. Cf. Minear, *Obedience*.

28. Especially circumcision, Sabbath, and kosher laws (distinctive badges of membership; cf. 3:20–30). Without entering into the whole debate new/old perspective, we follow here the understanding of "works of the Law" developed, for instance, by Wright, *New Testament*, 237, while being open to an enlargement of their definition. These works of the law are different in status from the "Law" understood as the right practice of the commandments (cf. the Decalogue in Rom 2:17–24 reread through the teaching of Jesus in the "Sermon of the Mount," Matthew 5–7).

29. Cf. Rom 14. See Donfried, *Romans Debate*, for all the sample groups of interpretation.

30. If indeed we know that it was not Paul who founded the church in Rome, we can only, with Stuhlmacher, "surmise that the gospel was brought to Rome from Antioch

that Paul wants to "reap some harvest" among them as he has among the rest of the Nations, being "a debtor both to Greeks and to barbarians, both to the wise and to the foolish," hence also a debtor to the Romans. Wright does not see a contradiction here, for Paul "has been eager to come for a long time" and "his sense of obligation includes that city also," two very personal reasons.[31] As for Stuhlmacher, verse 15 "in no way indicates that Paul is still intending to come as a missionary to preach his gospel in Rome"—he wants to come to "share some spiritual gift" and "be mutually encouraged" (12–13)—but expresses rather what he *would have done* if no church had existed in the area: hence, the verse could be translated "Therefore for my part I was prepared to preach the gospel to you in Rome as well."[32] What can be said is that evangelization in Rome may not be the main purpose of Paul's coming to Rome. As already said, he has Jerusalem and Spain in mind, as well as the edification of the church in dealing with the internal problems.

An Integral Letter (including Chapter 16)

Since the letter presents few textual criticism problems, especially concerning its last chapter, *"Romans 16 . . . is now viewed by the majority as being an integral part of Paul's original letter."*[33] This is an important detail if one considers all those who are mentioned in this chapter of greetings, both Jewish people and Gentiles, names that shed some light on the house-churches. While Francis Watson thinks that "Paul is writing chiefly to persuade the Jewish group to recognize the legitimacy of the Gentile group"[34] and Das suggests an exclusive Gentile audience for Romans[35]—both on the basis of Romans 1:5–6—I would propose, considering the admonition of Paul to both the "strong" and the "weak" in chapter 14 and because of a broad consensus among scholars, that the letter was addressed to a mixed community with a Gentile majority, if I take into account the historical context of the church.[36]

---

or Jerusalem by anonymous missionaries, merchants, or artisans, and took root there among the large Jewish population and the so-called God-fearers." Cf. Stuhlmacher, "Purpose," 235.

31. Wright, *Romans*, 422–23.
32. Stuhlmacher, "Purpose," 237. Stuhlmacher is indebted to Käsemann and Zeller.
33. Donfried, *Romans Debate*, lxx, italics mine.
34 Watson, "Congregations," 212.
35. Cf. Das, *Solving*, 6. See also Stowers, *Rereading*, 21–22, 30–33.
36. See for example Bruce, "Continued," 180.

A Series of Rhetorical Devices Rather Than a "Diatribe" in Itself

Although many of the parts of Romans have been, since Rudolph Bultmann's 1910 doctoral dissertation,[37] identified as part of a first-century Greek diatribe, it is usually believed today that Paul is not imprisoned by any literary scheme but rather uses many rhetorical devices for his purpose.[38] "The so-called diatribe is not a literary genre but rather a series of rhetorical devices."[39] However, the brief outline of the letter I will employ for this study is by and large taken from rhetorical features as presented, for instance, by Robert Jewett:[40]

- 1:1–7: *exordium* or introduction;[41]
- 1:8–15: brief *narratio* or narration of the background of Paul's intended visit to Rome;[42]
- 1:16–17: *propositio* or brief statement of the thesis or enumeration of the issues;
- 1:18—15:13: *probatio* or proof of the case being argued:
- 1:18—4:25: *confirmatio* of the thesis: "Paul confirms the basic thesis of 1:16–17 by showing that the impartial righteousness of God provides righteousness for Jews and Gentiles alike, by faith";[43]
- 5:1—8:39: *exornatio* where "Paul deals with a series of implications and objections to the doctrine of the righteousness of God conveyed by Christ";[44]
- 9:1—11:36: *comparatio* where "Paul takes up the case of unbelieving Israel to demonstrate that the righteousness of God will still be triumphant, that the gospel in the end will not fail";[45]

---

37. Bultmann, "Der Stil," but see Stowers, *Rereading*, for a contemporary example.

38. See Donfried, "False Presuppositions," 112–24; Donfried views *Romans* to be a "letter-essay."

39. Donfried, *Romans Debate*, lxx, italics mine.

40. See Jewett, "Argument," 267–76, based on J. P. Louw and to a lesser extent Wuellner, "Paul's Rhetoric," 128–46.

41. Jewett, "Argument," 267, considers instead the introduction continuing until verse 15.

42. Jewett (ibid.) reduces the narration to verses 13–15.

43. Ibid., 273.

44. Ibid., 273.

45. Ibid., 273–74.

- 12:1—15:13: *exhortatio* where "Paul lays out ethical guidelines for living in righteousness, thus developing the final proof of the thesis in 1:17 that the righteousness shall *live* by faith";[46]
- *refutatio* or rebuttal of opposing views; because Romans is not "a forensic letter requiring a rebuttal of charges" this section is replaced by "diatribal components within several proofs";[47]
- 15:14—16:24: *peroratio* or conclusion that provides the practical appeal for the cooperation of the Roman house-churches in missionary activities in Jerusalem, Rome, and Spain.

Other structural and literary features could certainly be mentioned, such as the observation of Johannes N. Vorster, who sees 1:16–17 "simply as *transitus*, while acknowledging propositional elements";[48] for my purpose it may suffice to say that Paul seems to have used rhetorical schemes rather freely in order to build a very strong defense, and that verses 1:16–17 are considered as particularly important in his development.[49]

Romans 9–11 As an Integral Part of the Letter

"With regard to Romans 9–11 there is today a wide-ranging agreement that these chapters form an integral part of the main argument and that they are not simply a Pauline afterthought."[50] It is a major concern for Paul to define in Romans (and particularly in chapters 9–11) the relationship between Jew and Gentile in God's plan for salvation. This agreement will be particularly important as I will study the relationship between 1:16 and this part of the letter in chapter 4 below.

---

46. Ibid., 274.

47. Ibid., 267–68. See for example Rom 3:1, 3, 5, 9, 27; 4:1; 6:1, 15, 21; 7:7; 8:31; 9:14, 20, etc.

48. Vorster, "Strategies," 155.

49. Étienne Trocmé has these beautiful words: "In this epistle, much more than in any other, Paul composes; instead of being led by emotion of eloquence . . . he borrows his plan to God." My translation. See Trocmé, "Méthode Missionnaire," 148 (note 3): "Dans cette épître, beaucoup plus que dans les autres, Paul compose; au lieu de se laisser entraîner par l'émotion ou l'éloquence, il y . . . emprunte son plan à Dieu."

50. Donfried, *Romans Debate*, lxx, italics mine.

To the Jew First or to the Jew at Last?

Conclusion

Considering this debate, I conclude that Romans is a letter from Paul, addressed entirely to the Roman community in a specific historical situation. If it contains some systematic features, it should not be forgotten that its purposes are to look for Western support before going to Jerusalem, expand the work toward Spain, as well as to reprimand Christians of Gentile and Jewish origins[51] who have difficulties in living together because of their conception of the law. Except for the impression that they were already meeting in different home-churches,[52] we do not know whether or not this was as a result of their difficulties.[53] Nevertheless, I assume that Paul wants to address both. For these aims, Paul uses all the possible rhetorical features he can. As for the different subjects broached by Paul, I will deal with them in the course of the discussion. I especially have to define if one of Paul's purposes in Romans is to encourage evangelization, and if he gives priority to evangelization among the Jewish people. And if it is found to be so, I need to examine how Paul goes about it.

ELEMENTS OF STRUCTURE IN ROMANS

Having set the scene, we need to determine if Romans 1:16 is part of the historical context of the letter—dealing more with the first-century Roman situation—or part of its more systematic features, which would have systematic implications for any church, anywhere and possibly for anytime. On the one hand, with Watson, I will state that 1:16, like 1:8–15, "is still referring to the Roman situation":[54] "'For the Jew first' expresses Paul's acknowledgment of the priority and the pre-eminence of the Roman Jewish Christian congregation, whereas 'and also for the Greek' asserts the legitimacy of the group of Pauline Gentile Christians in Rome."[55]

---

51. Stuhlmacher, "Theme," 334 characterized this community as of a "'lower middle class' and (at the most) 'middle class.'"

52. Wright thinks that the Roman community might have been composed of an average of a hundred people: "If we were to guess at a maximum of twenty for each group of Christians, that would still only give us a hundred, plus a few stray names whose allegiance we do not know. It may well have been fewer." In Wright, *Romans for Everyone 2*, 133. See also Wright, *Romans*, 422 where he agrees to go up to two hundred.

53. See Das, *Solving*, 1–8, who suggests that Paul is addressing the "Gentile" community.

54. Watson, "Congregations," 214.

55. Ibid.

Propositio

On the other hand, because of the importance and the place of these verses as *propositio* in this masterpiece of Paul and the repetition of the expression "to the Jew first, as well as to the Greek," in 2:9–10, I suspect that they have a more universal purpose. Romans 1:16–17 is really part of the introduction, concluding the section where Paul expresses his desire to come to Rome, as well as a good résumé of what he is going to develop in the letter. I suggest that these two verses are like a gateway that allows us to enter into Romans.[56] It functions as a sign posted on a door.[57]

Structurally, I record that 1:8–17 displays a chiastic movement underlining the importance of faith present at the beginning, the middle, and the end of the passage:[58]

8 your faith — *Faith*
　9 announcing the gospel of his Son — *Gospel*
　　10 I may somehow at last succeed in coming to you — *Trip*
　　　11 *so that I may share with you some spiritual gift* — *Gift*
12 (be mutually encouraged by each other's faith, both yours and mine) — *Faith*
　　　13 I have often intended to come to you — *Trip*
　　14–16 proclaim the gospel . . . For I am not ashamed of the gospel — *Gospel*
　17 through faith for faith; . . . "The one who is righteous will live by faith." — *Faith*

Andrew Perriman, in his latest book, disapproves of the "tendency amongst commentators to regard only 1:16–17 as the *propositio*, reflecting a general inclination to marginalize the theme of wrath."[59] For him, Habakkuk's quotation "presupposes judgment, first on Israel, then on the Chaldeans, which makes it appropriate to include the statement about the revelation of the wrath of God in the *propositio*."[60] This argument is reinforced by the use of *gar* ("For") and *apokaluptetai* ("revealed") in Romans

---

56. See Wilckens, *Römer*, 77, and Nygren, *Romans*, 65, who consider the two verses as a fluid and good transition. Hultgren, *Romans*, 71, uses the expression "bridge passage."

57. Vorster's *transitus* also recognizes this "transitional character of 1.16–17." Cf. Vorster, "Strategies," 156.

58. I owe this chiasm to my supervisor, Steve Motyer. I am not aware of a commentator who mentions it.

59. Perriman, *Future People*, 29 (note 1).

60. Ibid.

1:18.[61] Perriman also selects this judicious remark by Fitzmyer who draws out the parallel between the *ap' ouranou* ("from heaven") of Romans 1:18 and the *en autō* ("in it") of 1:17.[62] I perceive in these three verses the entire sovereign power of God acting through his word in history. Regarding the link between 1:16–17 and the first three chapters of Romans, we discover a fair amount of similarities, as the little structural sketch on the next page shows, while 2:9–10 is acting like a "chorus."[63]

Commentators have noticed that 1:16–17 is mainly developed in the first part of Romans as Jewett points out:

> One might visualize the structure of the argument as a thesis in 1:16–17 followed by an initial circle of proof in 1:18—4:25 that confirms the thesis. The next three proofs in Romans provide extensive developments of this thesis, answering relevant and ethical objections while amplifying important themes and implications.[64]

---

61. Cf. Snodgrass, "Gospel in Romans," 301–2.

62. Fitzmyer, *Romans*, 277. Cf. Perriman, *Future People*, 31 (note 4).

63. The term "chorus" is mine. It is rather surprising that none of the commentators have used it before, though the concept has certainly been thought of before.

64. Jewett, "Argument," 271. Nygren, *Romans*, 86, even suggests that the theme of Romans, i.e., *ho dikaios ek pisteōs zēsetai*, is developed first in chapters 1–4 (*dikaios ek pisteōs*) and secondly in chapters 5–8 (*zēsetai*).

Propositio

Salutation and God's Gospel

1:1 Παῦλος δοῦλος Χριστοῦ Ἰησοῦ,
κλητὸς ἀπόστολος ἀφωρισμένος εἰς **εὐαγγέλιον** θεοῦ, ² ὃ προεπηγγείλατο διὰ τῶν προφητῶν αὐτοῦ ἐν γραφαῖς ἁγίαις ³ περὶ τοῦ υἱοῦ αὐτοῦ τοῦ γενομένου ἐκ σπέρματος Δαυὶδ κατὰ σάρκα, ⁴ τοῦ ὁρισθέντος υἱοῦ θεοῦ ἐν **δυνάμει** κατὰ πνεῦμα ἁγιωσύνης ἐξ ἀναστάσεως νεκρῶν, Ἰησοῦ Χριστοῦ τοῦ κυρίου ἡμῶν, ⁵ δι' οὗ ἐλάβομεν χάριν καὶ ἀποστολὴν εἰς ὑπακοὴν **πίστεως** ἐν πᾶσιν τοῖς ἔθνεσιν ὑπὲρ τοῦ ὀνόματος αὐτοῦ, ⁶ ἐν οἷς ἐστε καὶ ὑμεῖς κλητοὶ Ἰησοῦ Χριστοῦ,
⁷ πᾶσιν τοῖς οὖσιν ἐν Ῥώμῃ
ἀγαπητοῖς θεοῦ, κλητοῖς ἁγίοις, χάρις ὑμῖν καὶ εἰρήνη ἀπὸ θεοῦ πατρὸς ἡμῶν καὶ κυρίου Ἰησοῦ Χριστοῦ.

The desire of Paul to come to Rome

⁸ Πρῶτον μὲν εὐχαριστῶ τῷ θεῷ μου διὰ Ἰησοῦ Χριστοῦ περὶ πάντων ὑμῶν ὅτι ἡ **πίστις** ὑμῶν καταγγέλλεται ἐν ὅλῳ τῷ κόσμῳ. ⁹ μάρτυς γάρ μού ἐστιν ὁ θεός, ᾧ λατρεύω ἐν τῷ πνεύματί μου ἐν τῷ **εὐαγγελίῳ** τοῦ υἱοῦ αὐτοῦ, ὡς ἀδιαλείπτως μνείαν ὑμῶν ποιοῦμαι ¹⁰ πάντοτε ἐπὶ τῶν προσευχῶν μου δεόμενος εἴ πως ἤδη ποτὲ εὐοδωθήσομαι ἐν τῷ θελήματι τοῦ θεοῦ ἐλθεῖν πρὸς ὑμᾶς. ¹¹ ἐπιποθῶ γὰρ ἰδεῖν ὑμᾶς, ἵνα τι μεταδῶ χάρισμα ὑμῖν πνευματικὸν εἰς τὸ στηριχθῆναι ὑμᾶς, ¹² τοῦτο δέ ἐστιν συμπαρακληθῆναι ἐν ὑμῖν διὰ τῆς ἐν ἀλλήλοις **πίστεως** ὑμῶν τε καὶ ἐμοῦ. ¹³ οὐ θέλω δὲ ὑμᾶς ἀγνοεῖν, ἀδελφοί, ὅτι πολλάκις προεθέμην ἐλθεῖν πρὸς ὑμᾶς, καὶ ἐκωλύθην ἄχρι τοῦ δεῦρο, ἵνα τινὰ καρπὸν σχῶ καὶ ἐν ὑμῖν καθὼς καὶ ἐν τοῖς λοιποῖς ἔθνεσιν. ¹⁴ Ἕλλησίν τε καὶ βαρβάροις, σοφοῖς τε καὶ ἀνοήτοις ὀφειλέτης εἰμί, ¹⁵ οὕτως τὸ κατ' ἐμὲ πρόθυμον καὶ ὑμῖν τοῖς ἐν Ῥώμῃ **εὐαγγελίσασθαι**.

Statement

¹⁶ Οὐ γὰρ ἐπαισχύνομαι τὸ **εὐαγγέλιον**,
δύναμις γὰρ θεοῦ ἐστιν εἰς σωτηρίαν παντὶ τῷ πιστεύοντι,
Ἰουδαίῳ τε **πρῶτον** καὶ **Ἕλληνι**.
¹⁷ **δικαιοσύνη** γὰρ θεοῦ ἐν αὐτῷ **ἀποκαλύπτεται ἐκ πίστεως εἰς πίστιν**,
καθὼς γέγραπται, Ὁ δὲ **δίκαιος ἐκ πίστεως** ζήσεται.

Development

¹⁸ **Ἀποκαλύπτεται** γὰρ ὀργὴ θεοῦ ἀπ' οὐρανοῦ ἐπὶ πᾶσαν ἀσέβειαν

2:⁹ θλῖψις καὶ στενοχωρία ἐπὶ πᾶσαν ψυχὴν ἀνθρώπου τοῦ κατεργαζομένου τὸ κακόν,
Ἰουδαίου τε **πρῶτον** καὶ **Ἕλληνος**·
¹⁰ δόξα δὲ καὶ τιμὴ καὶ εἰρήνη παντὶ τῷ ἐργαζομένῳ τὸ ἀγαθόν,
Ἰουδαίῳ τε **πρῶτον** καὶ **Ἕλληνι**·

3:¹ Τί οὖν τὸ περισσὸν τοῦ Ἰουδαίου ἢ τίς ἡ ὠφέλεια τῆς **περιτομῆς**; ² πολὺ κατὰ πάντα τρόπον. **πρῶτον** μὲν [γὰρ] ὅτι ἐπιστεύθησαν τὰ λόγια τοῦ θεοῦ. ³ τί γάρ, εἰ ἠπίστησάν τινες, μὴ ἡ ἀπιστία αὐτῶν τὴν πίστιν τοῦ θεοῦ καταργήσει;...
²¹ Νυνὶ δὲ χωρὶς νόμου **δικαιοσύνη** θεοῦ **πεφανέρωται** μαρτυρουμένη ὑπὸ τοῦ νόμου καὶ τῶν προφητῶν, ²² **δικαιοσύνη** δὲ θεοῦ διὰ **πίστεως** Ἰησοῦ Χριστοῦ εἰς **πάντας τοὺς πιστεύοντας**. οὐ γάρ ἐστιν διαστολή, ²³ πάντες γὰρ ἥμαρτον καὶ ὑστεροῦνται τῆς δόξης τοῦ θεοῦ ²⁴ **δικαιούμενοι** δωρεὰν τῇ αὐτοῦ χάριτι διὰ τῆς ἀπολυτρώσεως τῆς ἐν Χριστῷ Ἰησοῦ· ²⁵ ὃν προέθετο ὁ θεὸς ἱλαστήριον διὰ [τῆς] **πίστεως** ἐν τῷ αὐτοῦ αἵματι εἰς ἔνδειξιν τῆς **δικαιοσύνης** αὐτοῦ διὰ τὴν πάρεσιν τῶν προγεγονότων ἁμαρτημάτων ²⁶ ἐν τῇ ἀνοχῇ τοῦ θεοῦ, πρὸς τὴν ἔνδειξιν τῆς **δικαιοσύνης** αὐτοῦ ἐν τῷ νῦν καιρῷ, εἰς τὸ εἶναι αὐτὸν **δίκαιον** καὶ **δικαιοῦντα** τὸν **ἐκ πίστεως** Ἰησοῦ. ²⁷ Ποῦ οὖν ἡ καύχησις; ἐξεκλείσθη. διὰ ποίου νόμου; τῶν ἔργων; οὐχί, ἀλλὰ διὰ νόμου **πίστεως**. ²⁸ λογιζόμεθα γὰρ **δικαιοῦσθαι πίστει** ἄνθρωπον χωρὶς ἔργων νόμου. ²⁹ ἢ Ἰουδαίων ὁ θεὸς μόνον; οὐχὶ καὶ ἐθνῶν; ναὶ καὶ ἐθνῶν, ³⁰ εἴπερ εἷς ὁ θεὸς ὃς **δικαιώσει** περιτομὴν ἐκ πίστεως καὶ ἀκροβυστίαν διὰ τῆς πίστεως. ³¹ νόμον οὖν καταργοῦμεν διὰ τῆς πίστεως; μὴ γένοιτο· ἀλλὰ νόμον ἱστάνομεν.

109

To the Jew First or to the Jew at Last?

These elements of structure suggest again that Romans 1:16–17 is acting as the gateway to Romans. These two verses are containing all the themes introduced by the precedent verses and developed in the following chapters of the Epistle: the gospel, salvation, faith/faithfulness, righteousness, and the wrath of God. These observations are important considering the fact that "Rom. 1.16–17 can be seen as a nucleus in which many of the letter's problems and arguments are condensed and anticipated":[65] understanding the first part of Romans will help us to apprehend "our" adverb *prōton*, "first."

ROMANS 1:16–17 AND 2:9–10

After a few considerations regarding textual criticism—we obviously need to know if *prōton* is to be kept in Romans 1:16—I will consider verses 16–17 in more detail in an attempt to comprehend the whole sense of the *propositio* of Romans.

Textual Criticism

Since the important adverb *prōton* is omitted in the Vaticanus and the Dresden Manuscripts, in the Old Latin version (called "Italag") as well as in the Sahidic version and by Marcion (according to Tertullian[66] and Ephraem[67]), it is necessary to settle this issue first.[68]

Concerning Marcion, we should not be surprised by this omission: for him, "the privilege of the Jews was unacceptable."[69] In his thorough study on Marcion, Harnack writes:

> In 1:16 Marcion did not have the "first" after "to the Jew" in his text. Since this is obviously a tendentious excision, and yet the word is missing also in G g and in fact even in B, therefore an influence of the Marcionite text upon the catholic text here is to

---

65. Vorster, "Strategies," 153.

66. "Non enim me pudet evangelii, virtus enim dei est in salutem omni credenti, Iudaeo et Graeco" (*primum* is missing). Tertullian, *Adversus Marcionem*, 590. NB: Vulgate has "non enim erubesco evangelium virtus enim Dei est in salutem omni credenti Iudaeo primum et Graeco." Cf. Weber and Gryson, *Biblia Sacra*, 1750.

67. We have, however, not found any allusion to Rom 1:16 in Mitchell et al., *S. Ephraim's Refutations of Mani, Marcion, and Bardaisan*, xxiii–lxv.

68. Cf. Nestle, et al., *NA27*, 410. For the reference to Ephraem, see Anonymous, *He Kaine Diatheke*, 468.

69. Metzger, *A Textual Commentary*, 447.

Propositio

be assumed.... [He also eliminated] the entire section 9:1–33, because of its friendliness toward the Jews and its Old Testament references, and finally also the long section 10:5—11:32, which must have appeared to him as intolerable for the good God.[70]

In order to win the church to his ideas, Marcion literally bought it with 200,000 sesterces![71] His rival church enjoyed a lot of success for centuries. Considering that it was the work of Marcion to remove the word "first" in order to make The Epistle to the Romans fit with his theological pattern, all the modern commentators I have consulted agree in saying that *prōton* is in the original text. In the fourth revised version of *The Greek New Testament*,[72] the issue is not even raised. Here is the text kept: *Ou gar epaischynomai to euangelion, dynamis gar theou estin eis sōtērian panti tō pisteuonti, Ioudaiō te prōton kai Hellēni*.

Regarding the other versions omitting the word, as F. Godet says, "[i]ts rejection in the two MSS. B and G is more difficult to explain."[73] Is it then a corruption coming from Marcion, a copyist error or an interpolation from 2:9–10?[74] Consulting Swanson's *Variant Readings Arranged in Horizontal Lines against Codex Vaticanus*,[75] I can observe that, although Codex Vaticanus is considered to be the best manuscript, all the other manuscripts (except, as already mentioned, *Dresden*) have the word *prōton*, some write it even with a spelling mistake.[76] The ninth century Dresden manuscript (G) has also got two great mistakes in the first part of verse 16 and, in the second part, the expression *eis sōtērian* is also missing: "Οὐ γὰρ ἐπαισχύνομαι ἐπί εὐαγγέλιον, δύναμεις γὰρ θεοῦ ἐστιν εἰς παντὶ τῷ πιστεύοντι, Ἰουδαίῳ τε καὶ Ἕλληνι."[77] This late manuscript regarding this verse is obviously difficult to trust. The minuscule 1611 (twelfth century) is interesting regarding the second part of verse 16: it omits the end of *pisteuonti* as well as the two

---

70. Harnack, *Marcion*, 33–34. Harnack dates his corrected text between 139 and 144.

71. Cf. ibid., 15–20. One of the theses of Harnack is that Marcion, even known as a son of a bishop, seems to come out of Judaism: "his entire attitude toward the Old Testament and Judaism can best be understood as one of resentment" (ibid., 15).

72. Cf. Aland et al., *GNT*, 520.

73. Godet, *Romans I*, 153.

74. See Johannes Weiss quoted in Käsemann, *Romans*, 23 who makes the following mistake: "2:1-2" instead of "2:9-10" (same mistake in the original German).

75. Swanson, *NT Greek Manuscripts*, 8–9.

76. That is to say, seventy manuscripts (the reason Swanson mentions only sixty-eight manuscripts is that he does not consider the church fathers, except Clement of Alexandria who does not quote verse 16). Minuscule 1319 has the spelling mistake *te prōtō*, minuscules 1646 and 2464 have the spelling mistake *te proton*.

77. Swanson, *Greek Manuscripts: Romans*, 8–9.

words *Ioudaiō te*, but keeps at the same time *prōton*. Although the Greek is nonsense here, it still keeps the word: "σωτηρίαν παντὶ τῷ πιστεύον πρῶτον καὶ Ἕλληνι."[78]

Thus, the idea that it is a Marcionite corruption should not be dismissed. Regarding the theory that "first" is an interpolation from 2:9–10, which depends on the fact that the word *prōton* presents no textual difficulty in these two verses, it seems too speculative in light of the many manuscripts in favor of the presence of the word in Romans 1:16 and is no longer proposed. As Cranfield expresses it, the "presence of πρῶτον in 2.9 and 10 is itself a very strong reason for thinking it likely that Paul would also have inserted it here [in 1:16], and the probability is confirmed by much else in the epistle."[79] If it can be concluded that the word *prōton* was very likely present in the original, this textual problem shows that it was able to aggravate some of the first readers of The Letter of St. Paul to the Romans.

Structure of Romans 1:16–17

As already seen, because of the stream of words in Paul's thought, we do not know if 16a is strictly connected to the end of verse 15 or needs to be kept with 16b. This point is particularly important for the issue: indeed, we have to understand the links between the different elements of verse 16 and especially the one between *euangelion* ("gospel") and *dynamis theou* ("power of God"). As a matter of fact, we have to decide if there should be a "full stop" after *euangelisasthai* (end v. 15) or after *euangelion* (end v. 16a), and if *dynamis theou* is to be considered as predicate of *euangelion*.[80]

A Full Stop After Euangelisasthai

The majority of the translations of Romans chose this option.[81] It allows verses 16 and 17 to be particularly highlighted and acknowledged as sig-

---

78. Ibid., 9.

79. Cranfield, *Romans I*, 91.

80. We are well aware that the original manuscripts had no punctuation. Contrary to Sims, *Jew First*, 37–39, who uses the semicolon present in Romans 1:16 in the King James Bible to support his argument.

81. According to Aland et al., *GNT*, 520, four editions and/or translations relate 16a to 15 by omitting the full stop after *euangelisasthai*: the *Textus Receptus* (Oxford 1889), *The New Testament in the Original Greek* by Wescott and Hort (1881), the *Apostoliki Diakonia* (1988) and the Revised English Bible (1989). It is also the choice of the 1898 *Young's Literal Translation* by Robert Young. Cf. also Cranfield, *Romans I*, 87.

nificant in the Epistle. However, it does not seem to be the best option if I consider the chiasm already shown in verses 8–17. Indeed, the translation without interruption makes sense: "hence my eagerness to proclaim the gospel to you also who are in Rome, for I am not ashamed of the gospel . . ." This is the position of N. T. Wright: "[1:8–15] actually runs on without a break into the next one [v. 16]."[82]

A Full Stop After Euangelion

This option takes into account my previous observation but also considers the great emphasis expressed by *dynamis gar theou* ("for the power of God") in 16b and *dikaiosynē gar theou* ("for the righteousness of God") in 17a, as correctly observed by Michel.[83] We could then translate:

. . . for I am not ashamed of the gospel.

1. For the power of God is for the salvation of everyone who has faith, to the Jew first and also to the Greek.

2. For the righteousness of God is revealed in it (in him?) through faith for faith, as it is written, "The one who is righteous will live by faith."

Hence the importance of establishing which word is the subject of *estin* ("is"): *euangelion* or *dynamis theou*? We need to clarify if *dynamis theou* is indeed the predicate of *euangelion* as it is usually translated. If not, it means that the last translation weakens the link between *euangelion* and *dynamis theou* and puts a brake on our discussion. The central focus of my research issue is to determine, in essence, if the gospel is for the Jew first. If it appears that it is rather the power of salvation which is for the Jew first, it may lead me to a slightly different path, i.e., the one which would insist more on the sovereignty of God's salvation than on the human part of evangelization. If I believe that God is sovereign and with sovereign power chose those who will be saved, I also believe that he requests his people to preach the gospel. Even though, at the end of the day, this might not fundamentally change the result, putting the focus on God instead of the gospel would, however, change the debate.

---

82. Wright, *Romans*, 421. Wright however chose to keep the full stop in his own translation in Wright, *Romans for Everyone* 1, 9.

83. Michel, *Römer*, 51.

To the Jew First or to the Jew at Last?

Dynamis Theou as Predicate

As a matter of fact, no translation throughout history seems to have translated Romans 1:16–17 with *dynamis theou* as the subject of *estin*. According to Daniel B. Wallace, who briefly touches upon our issue,[84] *dynamis theou* in Romans 1:16 fits in the category of the "definitive anarthrous pre-verbal predicate nominatives," which "usually fall within the qualitative-definite range."[85] One example that resembles Romans 1:16 is 1 Corinthians 1:18:

> *Ho logos gar ho tou staurou tois men apollymenois mōria estin,*
> (For the message about the cross is foolishness to those who are perishing,)
> *tois de sōzomenois hēmin dynamis theou estin.*
> (but to us who are being saved it is the power of God)

As Wallace expresses it, "'The word of the cross is foolishness' . . . does not mean 'foolishness is the word of the cross,' for there are other kinds of foolishness."[86] I could probably say the same of the second part of the verse: "the power of God" is not "the word of the cross." To come back to Romans 1:16, it seems hence more likely to translate: "the gospel is a/the power of God."[87] Moreover, the fact that verse 17 includes also *en autō* and seems to relate it to *euangelion* leads me to link both 16b and 17 to this word. Otherwise, I would need to understand something else or someone else behind *en autō*, such as, for instance, Jesus.

As a matter of fact, verses 1:16–17 seem to be rigorously structured by three *gar* (for) which allow me to discern four clauses:[88]

A. *Ou gar epaischynomai to euangelion,* (16a)

B. *dynamis gar theou estin eis sōtērian panti tō pisteuonti,* (16b)
 Ioudaiō te prōton kai Hellēni. (16c)

C. *dikaiosynē gar theou en autō apokalyptetai ek pisteōs eis pistin,* (17a)

D. *kathōs gegraptai, Ho dikaios ek pisteōs zēsetai* (17b)

Wright concludes, "A is so because B; B is so because C; C is so because D; and D is thus the foundation of the whole sequence. This is undoubtedly

---

84. Wallace, "Jew First," but his article is more on anti-Semitism than *MP*.
85. Wallace, *Grammar*, 263–64.
86. Ibid., 41.
87. "A" or "the" power? Both translations are legitimate according to the Greek. However, it seems that the "qualitative" translation should be preferred to the "indefinite" one. See Colwell's rule in ibid., 257.
88. Cf. Michel, *Römer*, 51.

Propositio

the pattern here."[89] While drawing this sequence, we can see that our expression is right in the middle. However, since we do not face a chiasm, I cannot jump to a premature conclusion. The structure of 1:16–17 is taking up, again, "the concept of faith, which concept is to occupy so decisive a place in what follows."[90] In fact, the whole demonstration of the structure of Romans 1:1–17 expresses, highlights, emphasizes the theme of faith, concluding the quotation of Habakkuk. We have to be careful in our consideration of these verses and take them as they are, i.e., as explanation of an important statement about faith; in this development, *Ioudaiō te prōton kai Hellēni* occupies a secondary place.

I Am Not Ashamed of the Gospel

The word *euangelion* or "gospel"/"good news" has today lost some of its original significance, when limited for instance to the words: "salvation in Jesus Christ." The preachers are usually keen to recall that it means "good news," announcing that, despite our state as sinners, we can have life in Jesus Christ. Yet, as Wright reminds us, if in early Christianity *euangelion* had this meaning of "the proclamation about Jesus,"[91] it meant at the same time "the announcement of the accession or the birthday of a ruler or emperor."[92] Paul was "at the interface of his two worlds,"[93] and it is important to have in mind both of these senses, two senses which can be summarized in this way: "'the gospel' itself, strictly speaking, is the narrative proclamation of King Jesus."[94]

---

89. Wright, *Romans*, 423. Vorster, "Strategies,"162, sees in the relationship between 1:16b–c and 1:17a a *dissociation*: "It can be visually expressed as a pair consisting of term I [1:16b–c] and term II [1:17a], the latter being the criterion for the former. Term I is usually that which is to be disputed and is depicted as the illusionary, the immediate, while term II is depicted as authentic truth."

90. Nygren, *Romans*, 67.

91. Wright, *Romans*, 415. Cf. Isa 40:9 (*ho euangelizomenos Siōn, ho euangelizomenos Ierousalēm*); 52:7 quoted in Rom 10:15 (*hōs hōra epi tōn opeōn hōs podes euangelizomenou akoēn eirēnēs hōs euangelizomenos agatha hoti akoustēn poiēsō tēn sōtērian sou legōn Sion basileusei sou ho theos*), "where the messenger was to bring to Jerusalem the good news of Babylon's defeat, the end of Israel's exile, and the personal return of yhwh to Zion." Ibid., 415.

92. Ibid., 415.

93. Ibid.

94. Wright, *What St Paul*, 45.

To the Jew First or to the Jew at Last?

A question arises whether the "gospel" that Paul is talking about here is "the narrative proclamation of King Jesus"[95] or the "gospel of Paul,"[96] the gospel for which he has to fight as revealed to him on the road of Damascus.[97] So Stuhlmacher:

> In this letter he [Paul] attempts to convince the Roman Christians of the substance of his controverted gospel. The letter is an exposition and clarification of that gospel vis-à-vis the criticism Paul knows to be rampant in Rome. . . . That is why he engages in chapters 1–16 in a detailed discussion of problems and questions which the Christians at Rome are asking about the Pauline gospel—as Paul himself knows from the reports of his friends.[98]

For Stuhlmacher, Paul does not intend to do missionary work in Rome but wants to clarify *his* gospel in order to have the support of Rome for his missionary expansion towards Spain. Hence, "[w]hen the Apostle emphasizes in 1:16 that he is not ashamed of the gospel, he is signalling to friend and foe alike among his recipients that he intends to stick to his embattled cause in Rome as elsewhere."[99]

The definition of the gospel in 1:1–6 seems to allow us to go in both directions ("general gospel" and "*Pauline gospel*"):

> . . . the gospel of God, which he promised beforehand through his prophets in the holy scriptures, the gospel concerning his Son, who was descended from David according to the flesh and was declared to be Son of God with power according to the spirit of holiness by resurrection from the dead, Jesus Christ our Lord, *through whom we have received grace and apostleship to bring about the obedience of faith among all the Gentiles for the*

---

95. As in 1 Cor 15:1–9 or Col 1:21–23, for instance.

96. Cf. 2:16; 16:25: *to euangelion mou*, certainly in echo of the cutting remarks of the Romans (and certainly other Christians from other churches): "For when one says, 'I belong to Paul,' and another, 'I belong to Apollos,' are you not merely human?" (1 Cor 3:4).

97. Cf. Stuhlmacher, "Theme," 334–45. See Kim, *Origin*, for a thorough study on the issue, as he suggests that this vocation to go to the Gentiles was given to Paul on the "Road of Damascus." Regarding the conversion of Paul, Cooper, *Jew Still First*, 16, has a strange understanding of the words of Paul in 1 Tim 1:15, saying that he is the "chief" (*prōtos*) of sinners: for Cooper, this does not mean that Paul is the lowest but that, "in speaking of himself as the first of the sinners of Israel, he was thinking of the conversion of the nation in terms of his own. From this angle we can see that Paul's accepting the Lord as Saviour and Messiah was typical of that of the Hebrew race when it turns to the Lord."

98. Stuhlmacher, "Purpose," 236. Before him, see Michel, *Römer*, 51.

99. Stuhlmacher, "Purpose," 239.

sake of his name, including yourselves who are called to belong to Jesus Christ . . ."[100]

Paul, as well as telling "the narrative proclamation of King Jesus," has been called to the Gentiles, and in this way it is *his* gospel. As Simon Gathercole shows, the "gospel of Paul" is not very different from the one presented in the *Gospels* in accordance with three key themes: "(1) the identity of Jesus as the Messiah, (2) his work of atoning sacrifice and justification, and (3) his inauguration of a new dominion. These lie at the heart of the apostolic gospel."[101] A third important understanding of the gospel sits alongside both these definitions: *euangelion*, in its state of "verbal noun,"[102] can connote an *activity* as well as a *content*: Paul is not ashamed of the *preaching* of the gospel, for it is in the *preaching* of the gospel that the power of God is manifested to the Jew first and also to the Greek. As Stuhlmacher expresses it from the above quotation, it is Paul's "cause."[103] I will come back to this point when I consider the effect of the adverb *prōton* on the whole sentence.

A word must be said about the litotes "I am not ashamed."[104] Paul could have said "I am proud,"[105] a theme which would have corresponded well with other passages in Romans.[106] If he chose this formulation, it is certainly not to cloud the issue. For Cranfield, this litotes should not be compared with the litotes used in Acts,[107] but may be compared with the terrifying warning of Mark 8:38 (or Luke 9:26, in connection with 2 Timothy 1:8): "Those who are ashamed of me and of my words in this adulterous and sinful generation, of them the Son of Man will also be ashamed when he comes in the glory of his Father with the holy angels." *Ou epaischynomai* may act as an introductory formula to a first century confession, comparable to the phrase "I acknowledge," a formulation which may have been used as a dominical

---

100. Italics mine.

101. Gathercole, "Gospel of Paul," 154. However, Gathercole does not deal with the fact that the extension of the gospel to the Gentiles leads to important modifications in the way the law has to be handled by both "Jews" and "Greeks."

102. Cf. Blass and Debrunner, *Grammar*, § 119 (1), 64.

103. Cf. Rom 1:15; Phil 4:5 (*en archē tou euangeliou*), where "in the early days of the gospel" must mean "when I was first preaching the Gospel" or "when you first heard the Gospel preached by me."

104. Not many commentaries deal with this detail. See the short notice in Moo, *Romans*, 65.

105. See Vorster, "Strategies,"158: 'I am boasting about the good news . . ."

106. Cf. 2:17, 23; 3:27; 4:2; 5:2–11; 15:17.

107. In Cranfield, *Romans I*, 86. Cf. Acts 12:18; 14:28; 17:4, 12; 19:11, 23–24; 20:12; 21:39; 27:20 and 28:2 as examples.

saying in the church of the first century.[108] Paul acknowledges his "double" gospel—which obviously is one—he believes in it, he is not ashamed of it, he has no fear to proclaim it, not even to proclaim it to the Romans.

The Power of God

Dynamis theou has quite a wide range of meaning in the Scriptures: "power," "might," "strength," "force," "capability," "ability," "deed of power," "miracle," "wonder," "resource," "power as a personal transcendent spirit or heavenly agent/angel," and even "meaning" (1 Cor 14:11).[109] While links between *dynamis* and *doxa* ("glory"), *aphtharsia* ("incorruptibility"), *pneuma* ("spirit"), *sophia* ("wisdom"), *logos* ("word"), *charis* ("grace"), *archē* ("origin"), *exousia* ("authority"), *kyriotēs* ("lordship"), and *angelos* ("messenger") can be found,[110] two of the main links—worth emphasizing regarding the issue—are with *sōtēria* ("salvation"; cf. LXX Pss 20:2; 139:8, 1 Pet 1:5, 1 Cor 1:18)[111] and *anastasis* ("resurrection"): "The essential demonstration of God's power was in the resurrection of Jesus (2 Cor 13:4) and of the Christians (1 Cor 6:14)."[112]

Concerning the use of *dynamis* (*theou*) in Romans 1:16, Luther thinks it "is to be understood as 'potency' or 'power,' or as 'Muglickeit [Möglichkeit],' which means 'possibility,'"[113] or as "the strength, *of God*."[114] For Barth, "[b]eing completely different, it is the krisis of all power."[115] Michel sees it as "the sign of God, his appearance and his mighty deeds; through his *dunamis*, God wins through against all opposition and against all failures of the people and all powers."[116] As for Leenhardt, he links it with the exodus.[117] Most of the recent commentators simply qualify this power "of salvation,"

---

108. It was Michel, *Römer*, 51, leaning also on Matt 8:38 and 2 Tim 1:8, who noticed it.

109. Cf. Bauer, et al., *BDAG*, 262–63, which classes Rom 1:16 surprisingly in the category of "capability."

110. Cf. Balz and Schneider, *EDNT 1*, 355–58.

111. See J. Weiß and his *Heilskraft*, "healing power/power of salvation" in Michel, *Römer*, 51–52, note 5.

112. Balz and Schneider, *EDNT 1*, 356. Cf. Rom 1:4; Mark 12:23–24, Matt 22:29. See also Wright, *Resurrection*, 232–35, 309.

113. Luther, *Lectures on Romans*, 15–16.

114. Ibid., 8.

115. Barth, *Romans*, 36.

116. My translation. See Michel, *Römer*, 51: "das Zeichen Gottes, seiner Erscheinung und seiner Machttaten; durch seine δύναμις setzt sich Gott gegen allen Widerstand und gegen alles Unvermögen der Menschen und Mächte durch."

117. Cf. Leenhardt, *Romans*, 48–49.

but I need to insist that it is more than that. It is the magnificent and cosmic strength of God through his mighty Spirit, which is already seen operating in creation and which will be seen again in the recreation/resurrection.[118] It expresses God's divinity and his capability to perform the immeasurable wonder of a mighty exodus. This exodus, characterized by the liberation of the slavery of sin, is exemplified in the life, death, and resurrection of King Jesus. It is the promise of salvation and the resurrection of everyone who believes in him as mighty savior, as well as the resurrection of the whole universe. The *dynamis theou* of Romans 1:16 is the final victory over human and spiritual powers through Jesus on the cross, accomplishing the most powerful and grace-filled act that had ever existed for our salvation and his glory! And for this reason, I plead that if *to euangelion*, the "narrative proclamation of King Jesus," can be associated with the power of God; it does not mean that it is—strictly speaking—the power of God in itself. As Wright expresses it, "1.16–17 is a claim about the *effect* of the gospel: when it is preached, God's power goes to work and people are saved."[119] K. H. Schelkle, in defining *sōtēria*, proposes: "Just as the word mediates the truth it teaches, so the gospel not only proclaims salvation but also effects it."[120]

Salvation of Everyone

Eis Sōtērian

Sōtēria expresses the ideas of deliverance (Acts 7:25) and preservation (2 Macc 3:32)[121] and can refer to "welfare, well-being" in extra biblical secular Greek.[122] Klaus Haacker recalls the connection between salvation and faith; the miracles of healing are an experience of faith in the ministry of Jesus: "Daughter, your faith has made you well / has saved you."[123] Even if the healings of Jesus were real physical healings, we know that they were a sign for spiritual healing,[124] giving a foretaste of the *sōtēria* that Paul is talking

---

118. Cf. Wright, *Resurrection*, 421.
119. Wright, *Justification*, 156–57.
120. Balz and Schneider, *EDNT* 3, 328.
121. Cf. Ibid., 327–29.
122. Bauer et al., *BDAG*, 985–86. *Sōzō* itself has the double meaning of saving and healing (Balz and Schneider, *EDNT* 3, 319–20).
123. Mark 5:34. Cf. Haacker, *Römer*, 38. See also par. Matt 9:22, but also Luke 8:48, Mark 10:52 (and par. Luke 18:42), Luke 7:50; 17:19.
124. Cf. the use of *sēmeion* by John (e.g., John 4:54).

about here: the deliverance from sin for a new life of well-being leading to resurrection and eternal life on the new earth.[125]

Panti

The singular form of this adjective (indefinite dative masculine singular *panti*, in *panti tō pisteuonti*, "everyone who has faith")[126] expresses a gospel for individuals in a welcoming and inclusive way[127] as well as the universality of the gospel.[128] For Beker, its "basic climax is reached prior to the paraenesis of Romans 12–15 in 11:32: 'For God has consigned all people to disobedience, that he may have mercy upon all.'"[129] It is the "*pas argument*,"[130] and indeed, one of the major foci of the letter is to affirm that all, Jewish people and Gentiles, are sinners, but also that all, Jewish people and Gentiles, can be saved. The idea is that, if for a long time salvation has been more or less restricted to the people of Israel,[131] Paul is proclaiming an enlargement of the hope of salvation to everybody, including the Gentiles. As Vorster noted, "[t]he inclusion of the Jew is presupposed, the inclusion of the Greek is new information."[132]

Tō Pisteuonti

Pisteuō is "to consider something to be true and therefore worthy of one's trust" (believe) and, consequently, "to entrust oneself to an entity in complete confidence" (put your faith in).[133] *Pistis* and *pisteuō* are "*the* central theological terms for the appropriate relationship to God and for the Christian religion itself."[134] In *tō pisteuonti*, the two main senses of *pisteuō* are related: human beings are called to believe that the gospel is true, i.e., that

---

125. A great deal could be said on this subject, but I do not have the space to expand on it. Cf. Wright, *Surprised by Hope*, 206–13.

126. See also Rom 10:4.

127. Cf. Schreiner, *Romans*, 62.

128. Cf. Beker, "Faithfulness of God," 329.

129. Ibid., 329.

130. 25 uses of *pas* and cognates throughout the epistle.

131. If some like Rahab or Ruth—to quote the most famous—and other God-fearers or proselytes were saved before the ministry of Christ, we can say that this was rather the exception than the rule, even if it was quite a frequent exception.

132. Vorster, "Strategies," 160.

133. Bauer, et al., *BDAG*, 816–17.

134. Balz and Schneider, *EDNT* 3, 92.

Propositio

Jesus is the proclaimed King, who died and rose again for the forgiveness of sins, and thus put their trust in Jesus for their salvation.

To the Jew First, But Also to the Gentile

The reality of this power of God for salvation for everyone who has faith is *Ioudaiō te prōton kai Hellēni*. Here at last I arrive at the center of my study; I needed to follow the right progression in my journey in order to understand the context and not be misguided.

Ioudaios & Hellēn

As result of the Paul's use of *Hellēn* two verses before, in which he compares the Greeks with the barbarians (*barbaroi*), many discussions have been raised to understand what *Hellēn* means in our verse: does it have the same sense as in verse 14, i.e., "the wise" or "the educated"? Some consented to this, for instance, H. W. Schmidt. For him, Paul is attempting to express the following: "Particularly those who claim a special advantage (a religious one like the Jews or a cultural one like the Greeks) need the saving power of God the most."[135] It is true that "[s]ince *ca.* 700 b.c., the designation 'Hellene' united the Greek tribes and city-states through language, culture, and religion" and that it was common to also call non-Greeks who have language and education "Hellenes," as opposed to the "barbarians," who according to the Greeks included the Jewish people.[136]

However, it would be misleading not to consider that Paul, between the two verses, uses a different comparison: in the first instance, he obviously compares two categories of people separated by language and culture;[137] in the second, he refers to the well-known Jewish limitation made between Jewish people and Greeks/non-Jews/Gentiles, as in the courts of the Temple. As Stowers summarizes it: "The gentile is the ethnic-religious other of Jews just as the barbarian is the ethnic-religious other of Greeks."[138]

---

135. My translation. See Schmidt, *Römer*, 27: "Gerade diejenigen, welche einen besonderen Vorzug anmelden (einen religiösen wie die Juden oder einen kulturellen wie die Hellenen), bedürfen der rettenden Gotteskraft am meisten."

136. Cf. Balz and Schneider, *EDNT* 1, 435.

137. When using the word "foolish" (*anoētois*), Paul does not make a judgment: the barbarians, because of their language, which was not understood by the Greeks, and because of the fact they were not speaking Greek, were like "foolish people." Even the brightest man would be like a fool in a country where he does not speak the language!

138. Stowers, *Rereading*, 34. He depends here on Hall, *Inventing the Barbarian*.

To the Jew First or to the Jew at Last?

The fact that Paul characterizes the first people group as having some kind of priority is obviously important: as we will see, it would have been nonsense for him to say "to the Greek first and also to the barbarian" despite the fact that it was certainly his habit to first address people who speak Greek, before people who were barbarians for him.

The two terms "Jew and Greek" form a regular combination in Paul.[139] But why did Paul not use the combination "Jews and Nations"? The issue, as expressed by H. Schlier, seems more that "Paul does not know the singular of *ta ethnē*."[140] Despite the fact he could have used *ethnikos*,[141] above all, he does not want to use *ethnos*, which would have been completely misleading, the proof of this being that the people of Israel can themselves be considered a nation.[142] Also, *ethnikos* may have been understood as our current word "pagan" as in 3 John 7. It seems that Paul really wants to differentiate these two groups in a formal, religious, cultural, and ethnic way.[143]

Te Kai

The two particles *te* and *kai* linked in this verse seem to guard the word *prōton* and are there to express equality between "Jews" and "Greeks":[144] *te* suggests the fundamental equality between Jew and Gentiles before the gospel.[145] Indeed, the coordinating conjunction *te*, an enclitic always used in postpositive position, functions here in combination with another coordinating conjunction, *kai*; these "signal a closer connection between two sentence parts than either particle can alone, for which English has no simple equivalent."[146] Louw and Nida suggest "both . . . and."[147] I prefer the English

---

139. Cf. 1 Cor 1:22-24; 10:32; 12:13; Gal 2:14-15; 3:28; Col 3:11; see also Rom 3:1-4 and 11:18, 28-29. Cf. Dunn, *Romans 1-8*, 40, and Zeller, *Juden*, 13-18.

140. My translation. See Schlier, *Römerbrief*, 43-44: "Paulus kennt keinen Singular von τὰ ἔθνη." Before him, Kuss, *Römerbrief*, 21-22.

141. Matt 5:47; 6:7; 18:17.

142. Cf. John 11:48, for instance.

143. *Ioudaios* is mentioned in Romans in 2:17, 28, 29; 3:1, esp. in relation to circumcision.

144. Cf. Wilckens, *Römer*, 85-86.

145. Cf. Cranfield, *Romans I*, 91.

146. Balz and Schneider, *EDNT* 3, 339.

147. Louw, et al., *GELNTBSD*, entry 89.102. Cf., for instance, 1 Cor 1:24: *Ioudaios te kai Hellēsin*: "both Jews and Greeks."

Propositio

equivalent "and also" or "as well as"[148] instead of the commonly used but wrong "and then," which Moo surprisingly keeps.[149]

Prōton

The *prōton* used in Romans 1:16 is an adverbial neuter and not an adjective ordinal masculine accusative singular or nominative/accusative neuter singular. Otherwise, it would have taken the dative case of *Ioudaios* or *Hellēn* and would also likely have been accompanied by an article in the dative singular case.[150]

In fact, the expression *te prōton kai* is unique to Romans, nowhere else found in the Greek New Testament and the LXX, even if, as I have already noted, there is *almost* the same phrase in Acts 26:20.[151] Looking for it in other first century writings, I have only found it once in Philo—*prōton* being, however, used as adjective with article—where the philosopher deals with flights: ". . . and the others he has appointed for the curses, namely, *the first and last sons* of Leah (*ton te prōton kai ton hystaton tōn Leias*), Reuben, and Zabulon, and the four bastard sons by the handmaidens . . ."[152] Unless the expression *te prōton kai* was used in the time of Paul as a short formula for *ton te prōton kai ton hystaton*, which does not seem to be the case, this extract of Philo unfortunately does not help me in my inquiry.

Despite the original interpretation of R. C. H. Lenski, who does not believe that *prōton* applies only to the "Jew" but also to the "Greek" ("The Gospel is the power of God for salvation 'in the first place for both Jew and Greek'"),[153] commentators usually correctly assume that it exclusively concerns the Jew. In fact, for Schlier, even if *prōton* was to be deleted, "the

---

148. As Godet, *Romans I*, 153.

149. Moo, *Romans*, 68. S. Lewis Johnson, Jr. uses as an argument the absence of the idea of "then" to choose the HCP: "The other view [MP] would seem also to require an expressed *then* with the phrase 'to the Greek.'" Cf. Johnson Jr., "Gospel Paul Preached," 332.

150. Despite the fact that the "article is still sometimes omitted with ordinals (mostly in designations of time) following an earlier usage" as in Acts 20:18, *apo prōtēs hēmeras*] ("from the first day"). See Blass and Debrunner, *Grammar*, 134.

151. Cf. Zeller, *Juden*, 143, note 10. Many quote also 2 Cor 8:5 (*alla heautous edōkan prōton tō kyriō kai hēmin dia thelēmatos theou*). See, for instance, Lietzmann, *Römer*, 30, note on verse 16.

152. *De Fuga et inventione* 1:73 in Philo, *Works of Philo Judaeus*, based on Borgen, et al., *Philo Concordance*, in *BibleWorks 8* software. Italics mine.

153. Lenski, *Romans*, 76.

same priority of history of salvation would be shown through the placing of Ioudaios at the beginning."[154]

As an adverb, *prōton* can have different meanings. The BDAG suggests:

1. "pert. to being first in a sequence, inclusive of time, set (number), or space"; this first meaning is twice as commonly found as the second meaning. As an adverb, the lexicon is precise in that it means first in time, i.e. "first, in the first place, before, earlier, to begin with"; in this category, we can find Mark 7:27 ("Let the children be fed first");

2. "pert. to prominence, first, foremost, most important, most prominent"; as an adverb, there is an indication of degree, i.e. "in the first place, above all, especially"; Romans 1:16 is placed in this category, but also surprisingly Acts 3:26 ("When God raised up his servant, he sent him first to you").[155]

As H. Langkammer states in the EDNT:

> Πρῶτον appears in the sense of temporal priority in Rom 1:16. The addressees of the gospel were *first* Jews. But Greeks (Gentiles) are placed on an equal salvation-historical level with παντὶ τῷ πιστεύοντι. ... Πρῶτον demonstrates here a "nuance of rank" (Zeller 142) and should therefore not be translated "and then to the Greeks" but "also to the Greeks." Temporal priority is, however maintained (cf. Acts 3:26; 13:46). In Rom 2:1–11 Paul emphasizes this priority, both in the prediction of tribulation (v. 9) and in the blessing (v. 10).[156]

It is quite striking to consider the following two lexicons and realize that they are more or less opposite in their consideration of the *prōton* of Romans 1:16. The Friberg Lexicon classifies it under the category of time "*at first, to begin with, (for) the first time*"[157] and the Thayer's Greek-English Lexicon of the New Testament files it under "*first, at the first*; a. in order of time," more precisely, "first and also (or afterward), i.e. as well as."[158] The other lexicons I referred to earlier do not deal with our verse.[159] Actually,

---

154. My translation. See Schlier, *Römerbrief*, 43–44: "würde derselbe heilsgeschichtliche Vorrang durch die Voranstellung des Ἰουδαίοις [sic] zum Ausdruck gebracht." Compare, for instance, the order "Barnabas and Paul" that sometimes changes to "Paul and Barnabas" if, in Acts, Luke wants to place more importance on one and then on the other.

155. Bauer et al., *BDAG*, 892–94.

156. Balz and Schneider, *EDNT* 3, 188.

157. Friberg et al., *ALNT*, entry 23711.

158. Grimm and Wilke, *Greek-English Lexicon*, entry 4566.

159. Cf. Louw et al., *GELNTBSD*, entry 60.46 and Abbott-Smith, *ASL*, 389–90.

Propositio

despite its recognized authority, the BDAG appears isolated in this case. On balance the interpretations in dictionaries seem to favor the *HP*, but I must recall that dictionaries, just like commentaries, decide on the meaning according to their own exegesis.

To come to the contemporary commentaries on Romans and their interpretation of *prōton*, I can divide them into three categories for my purpose:[160]

1. *Historico-covenantal priority* interpretation (HCP);[161]
2. *Missional priority* interpretation (MP, with sometimes an element of ambiguity);[162]
3. Silence on the issue.[163]

Historico-covenantal Interpretation

The *HCP* proponents usually consider that the adverb *prōton* describes the privilege that the Jewish people had in the *Heilsgeschichte* (because of their election). The supporters of this thesis add that the gospel is for the Jew

---

Moulton and Milligan, *VGT*, 557. Liddell et al., *LSL*, 1535.

160. We are talking expressly of commentaries written by scholars before 2012. There are of course articles on the subject, which have been considered in the chapter 2 above.

161. In our contemporary academic world, no-one states that *prōton* expresses purely a historical priority. Also, a lot of commentaries are dealing with the situation of Paul in the first century and do not deal with this modern issue.

162. For instance, Martin Pakula thinks that Moo and Cranfield are proponents of the *MP*. Steve Motyer, however, is of the opinion that they are in favor of the *HCP*. I wrote to Moo to have the final answer but, after another attempt, I am still waiting for it! There is therefore a degree of subjectivity in my judgement when considering the two main interpretations. Cf. Pakula, *First for Jews*, 3: "Two excellent modern commentaries on Romans are the ones by C. E. B. Cranfield and Douglas Moo. In their comments on the meaning of the phrase: "first for the Jew", they assert that this phrase cannot be merely an historical assertion: that the gospel went first to the Jew (which is true enough), but that the gospel is first for the Jew in a sense that must still be relevant today." Also, we need to remember that the proponents of the *MP* are including the *HCP* in their understanding, which is not the case the other way round. In the same way, cf. Hultgren, *Romans*, 74, note 133: "In various ways this viewpoint [*MP*] is found in the works of C. K. Barrett, *Romans*, 29; E. Käsemann, *Romans*, 23; C. Cranfield, *Romans*, 91; J. Fitzmyer, *Romans*, 257; and P. Stuhlmacher, *Romans*, 28; D. Moo, Romans, 68–69."

163. Among them: Robinson, *Romans*, 15–16; Pilch, *Galatians and Romans*, 31; Briscoe, *Romans*, 34–37; Heil, *Romans*, 13–16; Morgan, *Romans*, 18–22; Shulam and Le Cornu, *Romans*, 41–42. Bruce, *Romans*, 78–79, despite the fact that he expresses his position in another writing (see below).

To the Jew First or to the Jew at Last?

as well as the Gentile (universality of the gospel). André Feuillet expertly sums it up:

> To explain this phrase: "to the Jew first, then to the Greek," it is certainly suitable to put forward this undisputable historical fact: before the Gentiles the Jews first received the Good News of the Gospel, as testified by the evangelic tradition and the Acts of the Apostles of a common accord ... Regarding the doctrine of salvation, the text of Rom 1:16 rather confronts us with this surprising paradox: on one side the most absolute universalism because the salvation brought by Christ is offered free to each human being who believes; on the other side however, thanks to the little word "first," the Apostle fully keeps the special role played by Israel in the History of salvation.[164]

Other proponents of the *HCP* are: E. Käsemann,[165] M. Black,[166] R. Bowen,[167] A. Viard,[168] H. Schlier,[169] U. Wilckens,[170] W. Hendriksen,[171] F. F. Bruce,[172] D. M. Lloyd-Jones,[173] D. Zeller,[174] L. Morris,[175] J. Ziesler,[176] J. R.

---

164. My translation. Cf. Feuillet, "Situation privilégiée," 40: "Pour rendre compte de ce langage : 'd'abord le Juif, puis le Grec,' il convient certes d'invoquer ce fait historique incontestable : antérieurement aux Gentils les Juifs les premiers ont reçu la Bonne Nouvelle de l'Evangile, ainsi que l'attestent d'un commun accord la tradition évangélique et les Actes des Apôtres ... En ce qui concerne la doctrine du salut, le texte de *Rm* 1,16 nous met bien plutôt en présence de cet étonnant paradoxe : d'un côté l'universalisme le plus absolu, puisque le salut apporté par le Christ est offert gratuitement à tout homme qui croit; par ailleurs, néanmoins, grâce au petit mot 'd'abord,' l'Apôtre maintient intégralement le rôle privilégié joué par Israël dans l'Histoire du salut."

165. Käsemann, *Romans*, 23.

166. Black, *Romans*, 44.

167. Bowen, *Romans*, 18.

168. Viard, *Romains*, 46–47.

169. Schlier, *Römerbrief*, 43–44.

170. Wilckens, *Römer*, 85–86.

171. Hendriksen, *Romans*, 61.

172. Bruce, "Continued," 184.

173. Llyod-Jones, *Romans*, 292–93.

174. Zeller, *Römer*, 43.

175. Morris, *Romans*, 68.

176. Ziesler, *Romans*, 70.

Propositio

Edwards,[177] J. A. Fitzmyer,[178] J. Cottrell,[179] K. Grayston,[180] C. R. Hume,[181] K. Haacker,[182] N. T. Wright,[183] W. MacDonald,[184] D. Coffey,[185] E. Lohse,[186] L. E. Keck,[187] B. Dickson,[188] R. Jewett,[189] C. S. Keener,[190] F. J. Matera,[191] among others. Because of the polemic raised with the *MP*, some prefer to be extremely clear:

> This does not mean that every Jew must be evangelized before the gospel can be presented to Gentiles. But it does mean that God, after having dealt in a special way with the Jew in OT days and having followed this by sending his Son to the lost sheep of the house of Israel, could not pass by this people.[192]

> There is no distinction between them in respect of salvation. The priority of the Jews ("first for the Jew") is both theological, because God chose them and made his covenant with them, and therefore historical ("We had to speak the word of God to you first" [Acts 13:46]).[193]

Steve Mosher has an original interpretation; for him, the phrase concerns Jesus: "Jesus was the first Jew to have faith in God's new saving power. Out of Jesus' faith, others also came to faith."[194] Dunn, in a unique way, feels that the phrase "to the Jew first" was not even a strategic formula for the beginning of Paul's ministry but that everything needs to be put back in its context:

---

177. Edwards, *Romans*, 41–42.
178. Fitzmyer, *Romans*, 256–57.
179. Cottrell, *Romans*, 106–7.
180. Grayston, *Romans*, 4–5, but he touches lightly the issue.
181. Hume, *Romans*, 23–24.
182. Haacker, *Römer*, 38.
183. Wright, *Romans*, 424.
184. MacDonald, *Believer's Bible Commentary*, 1677.
185. Coffey, *Romans*, 38.
186. Lohse, *Römer*, 77–78.
187. Keck, *Romans*, 51, 89–94.
188. Dickson, *Romains*, 44.
189. Jewett, *Romans*, 139–40.
190. Keener, *Romans*, 26.
191. Matera, *Romans*, 35.
192. Harrison, *Romans*, 19.
193. Stott, *Romans*, 60–61.
194. Mosher, *Romans*, 40.

To the Jew First or to the Jew at Last?

> The sequence "Jew first but also Gentile" should not be taken as directly indicative of Paul's missionary strategy, since he saw himself as first and foremost "apostle to the Gentiles" (11:13; 15:16); but since his natural constituency was the body of Gentiles who had already been attracted to or influenced by Judaism (proselytes and "God-worshipers"—see *Introduction* §2.2.2), it has some bearing on his evangelistic practice since the synagogue provided the most obvious platform for his message—"to the synagogue first and so to the God-fearing Gentile."[195]

MISSIONAL INTERPRETATION

The supporters of the *MP* agree with the *HCP* in thinking that the gospel is for Jewish people and Gentiles alike, but state that the Jewish people still have the right to hear the gospel before the Gentiles. In this context, A. J. Hultgren, the writer of the most recent commentary on Romans that I have consulted for this study, is worth quoting: "It is to them [the Jewish people] that the gospel was 'promised beforehand through [God's] prophets in the holy scriptures' (Rom 1:2). Now that the promise has been fulfilled, they are the ones to whom the gospel should be proclaimed first."[196] I also file under this interpretation P. Stuhlmacher,[197] G. N. Davies,[198] S. Mosher,[199] and M. D. Nanos.[200] But other commentators are not so straightforward: it seems that they regard *prōton* as indicating the necessity for the gospel to be preached to the Jewish people first, then and now. However, the way they express the idea may show that this was the case only in the first century. Among them:

---

195. Dunn, *Romans 1–8*, 40.

196. Hultgren, *Romans*, 74.

197. Stuhlmacher, *Romans*, "Moreover, the precedence of Israel over the Gentiles in terms of salvation history, established by God through election (cf. Rom. 3:2; 9:4f.), is not annulled by the gospel, but confirmed."

198. Davies, *Faith & Obedience*, 36: "For it is unlikely that Paul is thinking of a temporal priority here, but rather, a priority concerning God's promises to save Israel."

199. Mosher, *Romans*, 42: "There is still a place for world mission to continue the pattern of Jesus and Paul of going to the Jew first. Like Paul, who continually tried to 'win Jews' (1 Cor. 9:20) as part of his God-given mission, many now can also make known God's special call to Jewish people."

200. Nanos, *Romans*, 21: "For Paul, the pattern of salvation history has been and always will be, even in the midst of confronting misguided exclusivity on the part of some of the children of Jacob, 'to the Jew *first* and *also* to the Greek.'"

Propositio

C. E. B. Cranfield,[201] D. Moo,[202] S. Bénétreau,[203] T. R. Schreiner,[204] G. R. Osborne,[205] and R. Mohrlang.[206]

The main issue here concerns obviously the role one should give to *prōton* as adverb. If we know that it is an adverb in Romans 1:16, the way it is used is obviously more complex. Unfortunately, "[t]he adverb has been treated by the grammars as a sort of printer's devil in the sentence. It has

201. Cranfield, *Romans I*, 90–91: "the word πρῶτον indicates that within the framework of this basic equality there is a certain undeniable priority of the Jew. In view of chapters nine to eleven it is hardly admissible to explain this πρῶτον as referring merely to the historical fact that the gospel was preached to the Jews before it was preached to the Gentiles, or, while allowing a reference to the special position of the Jews in the Heilsgeschichte, to cite Gal 3.28 and Eph 2.14f as proof that this πρῶτον is, in Paul's view, something now abolished, as Nygren does. Rather must we see it in the light of Paul's confident statement in 11.29 that ἀμεταμέλητα . . . τὰ χαρίσματα καὶ ἡ κλῆσις τοῦ θεοῦ." Nygren, *Romans*, 72–74 has indeed an original but not so fanciful comment regarding the fact that the Jewish people believed they were saved only by being a Jew: "But the explanation of his eagerness ['to the Jew first'] is his purpose to make clear that salvation is the same for them too." See also Schmidt, *Römer*, 27, referring to E. Klostermann, T. Zahn, E. Kühl, "not to describe them as particularly privileged, but as particularly needy ([cf. Rom] 3.9)."

202. Moo, *Romans*, 68–69: "However much the church may seem to be dominated by Gentiles, Paul insists that promises of God realized in the gospel are 'first of all' for the Jew. To Israel the promises were first given, and to the Jews they still particularly apply."

203. "The practice, clearly underlined in the Acts of the Apostles, that Paul was first preaching the gospel in the synagogue when arriving in a town, was not only a matter of appropriateness and commodity, but meant a legitimate order, a priority to observe." My translation. See Bénétreau, *Romains 1*, 55–56: "La pratique, clairement soulignée dans le livre des Actes, selon laquelle Paul commençait l'annonce de l'Evangile dans une ville par une prédication dans la synagogue, relevait non seulement de considérations d'opportunité et de commodité, mais du sens d'un ordre légitime, d'une priorité à respecter." Ambiguity removed since a correspondance with him the 20th July 2010: Bénétreau is an *HCP* proponent, even if he thinks that "The Jewish believers need to be inspired by Paul's example. For them, the duty not to neglect their Jewish brothers and to favor prayer and witness toward them appears to me established." My translation ("Les croyants juifs doivent s'inspirer de l'exemple de Paul. Pour eux le devoir de ne pas négliger leurs frères juifs et de privilégier la prière et le témoignage auprès d'eux m'apparaît établi.")

204. Schreiner, *Romans*, 62: "The priority of the Jews was not merely a historical reality that had now lapsed for Paul."

205. Osborne, *Romans*, 41: "It is debated how extensively this priority of Jewish evangelism is binding on the church today. But the reasoning behind Paul's statement here still applies in our day, so the priority should still stand. It does not mean, however, that every Christian is to go to the synagogue first. Rather, Jewish mission must have visibility and emphasis in the mission of the church worldwide, in terms both of prayer and of action."

206. Mohrlang, *Romans*, 40: "As his chosen people, Jews have a prior claim to the Good News."

been given the bone that was left for the dog, if it was left"[207] and this still seems to be the case: Wallace's grammar book, for instance, has no section on adverbs in his 1996 edition.[208] If I follow Robertson's grammar book, I can consider for our case three uses of *prōton*:[209] with a verb, a substantive, or an adjective. "The context must often decide the exact idea of an adverb"[210] and we have to be careful not to insert an idea in the *prōton* of Romans 1:16.

Prōton as an Adverb Modulating a Verb

Etymologically, the usual function of an adverb is to modulate a verb. This is how it is used in Matthew 6:33: "But strive first for the kingdom [*zēteite de prōton tēn basileian*] of God and his righteousness, and all these things will be given to you as well." In this example, the adverb clearly qualifies the verb *zēteō* and hence the way we have to seek the kingdom. In Romans 1:16, we have two verbs: *eimi*, "to be" (indicative present active 3rd person singular) and *pisteuō*, "to have faith" (participle present dative masculine singular). Since *tō pisteuonti* is used as a noun to designate "the believer" in the sentence, I will deal with it in the next section. The modification of *estin* by the adverb *prōton* is doubtless the strongest argument in favor of the MP. In this case, Paul would be emphasizing in a very declarative and systematic way that *the gospel is first for the Jew*. The implied action expressed in the verbal noun *euangelion* ("preach the gospel") would consolidate the idea that the preaching of the gospel is directed (and should be directed) first to the Jewish people.

One could also argue that *prōton* modifies the implied action expressed in "power unto salvation," i.e., that God's power is active to save first the Jewish people. In that case it would express the idea that the Jewish people who followed Jesus in the first century understood much of the fulfillment of the prophecies, and that it would have certainly helped them to grasp the gospel, despite the rejection of many religious leaders. However, considering the battle of Paul to convince his countrymen of the salvation only by faith, this seems unlikely.

---

207. Robertson, *Grammar*, 545.

208. Wallace, *Grammar*, mentions adverbs here and there, a dozen of times, but does not write a section on them.

209. See Robertson, *Grammar*, 544–52.

210. Ibid., 549.

Propositio

PRŌTON AS AN ADVERB MODIFYING A SUBSTANTIVE AND AN ADJECTIVE

As already noticed by many commentators, *Ioudaiō te prōton kai Hellēni* is explaining *panti tō pisteuonti*.[211] The modification of *tō pisteuonti* (used as a noun) by the adverb *prōton* leads more towards an *HCP*. Who is this "everyone who has faith"? It is the Jew first and also the Greek. In that case, *prōton*, as adverb modifying the noun "believer" and giving an indication of priority to the noun "Jew," would characterize the people saved first through the power of God: the Jewish people. *Prōton* would then be simply used as a temporal adverb, adding temporal information to a fact. It would then not be a question of evangelization, but a question of history, as in Acts 3:26: "When God raised up his servant, he sent him first to you [*hymin prōton anastēsas*], to bless you by turning each of you from your wicked ways."[212] In a more informative and factual way, Paul would signify that even though the Jewish people were the first to believe, they were not the only ones to do so, since the gospel is for everyone, including the Greeks.

THE *PRŌTON* OF ROMANS 3:2

Having expounded these two possible modifications of *prōton* in Romans 1:16, my contention is that the answer to the problem is to be found two chapters further on. This is doubtless the strongest argument in favor of an *HCP* interpretation. Even though commentators make an obvious link between 1:16 and 3:1-2 or 9:4-5,[213] the use of *prōton* in 3:2 has not been emphasized as it should regarding the understanding of *prōton* in 1:16.[214] For example, if I consider one of the last commentaries published on Romans by Hultgren, a proponent of the *MP* interpretation, it seems that he is ignoring the repetition of *prōton* in 3:2:

---

211. Cf. Lenski, *Romans*, 76; Cranfield, *Romans I*, 91; Dunn, *Romans 1-8*, 40; Schreiner, *Romans*, 62; Haacker, *Römer*, 38; *contra* Schmidt, *Römer*, 27.

212. Robertson, *Grammar*, 549, is using Acts 3:26 and Rom 2:9 to distinguish the adverb *prōton* from the adjective *prōtos*.

213. See, for instance, Sanday and Headlam, *Romans*, 24, Barth, *Romans*, 40; Wilckens, *Römer*, 85-86; Viard, *Romains*, 46-47; Schlier, *Römerbrief*, 43-44; Feuillet, "Situation privilégiée," 40; Zeller, *Römer*, 43; Ziesler, *Romans*, 70; Lohse, "Juden zuerst," 203; Moo, *Romans*, 68-69; Haacker, *Römer*, 38. Douglas A. Campbell is certainly the one who links the most the two *prōton*. Cf. Campbell, "Determining," 315-36, esp. 334.

214. See, however, Lietzmann, *Römer*, 30, note on v. 16; Zeller, *Römer*, 43; Stuhlmacher, *Romans*, 28; Cottrell, *Romans*, 106-7.

To the Jew First or to the Jew at Last?

The phrase "to begin with" is a translation of πρῶτον μὲν, which could be translated as "first." But as at 1:8 (and 1 Cor 11:18), there are no succeeding points (second, third, etc.). The term can have the meaning "to begin with," "above all," or "first of all" to mark a transition to what follows.[215]

As I have already mentioned, Romans 1:8—4:25 (and especially 3:1–31) is a development of the rather condensed verses 1:16–17. And indeed, if we look at a comparison of 1:16–17 and chapter 3, the similarities are striking:

1:16–17	3:1–2, 21–29
16 it is the power of God for salvation to everyone who has faith (*dynamis gar theou estin eis sōtērian panti tō pisteuonti*)	22 the righteousness of God through faith in Jesus Christ for all who believe. (*dikaiosynē de theou dia pisteōs Iēsou Christou eis pantas tous pisteuontas*)
to the Jew first and also to the Greek. (*Ioudaiō te prōton kai Hellēni*)	1 Then what advantage has the Jew? Or what is the value of circumcision? (*Ti oun to perisson tou Ioudaiou*) 2 Much, in every way. For in the first place the Jews were entrusted with the oracles of God. (*Prōton men [gar] hoti episteuthēsan ta logia tou theou.*)
17 For in it the righteousness of God is revealed (*dikaiosynē gar theou en autō apokalyptetai*)	21 the righteousness of God has been disclosed, (*dikaiosynē theou pephanerōtai*)
through faith for faith; as it is written, "The one who is righteous will live by faith." (*ek pisteōs eis pistin, kathōs gegraptai: ho de dikaios ek pisteōs zēsetai.*)	30 he [God] will justify the circumcised on the ground of faith and the uncircumcised through that same faith. (*ho theos hos dikaiōsei peritomēn ek pisteōs kai akrobustian dia tēs pisteōs*) 26 he justifies the one who has faith in Jesus. (*dikaiounta ton ek pisteōs Iēsou*)
3:29 Or is God the God of Jews only? Is he not the God of Gentiles also? Yes, of Gentiles also (*ē Ioudaiōn ho theos monon; ouchi kai ethnōn; nai kai ethnōn*)	

Romans 3 is very valuable in aiding the understanding of 1:16–17. It confirms that "power of God" (*dynamis theou*) and "righteousness of God" (*dikaiosynē theou*) are linked for a similar divine deed. The covenantal and just faithfulness of God is expressed through the power of a cosmic resurrection and victory over evil. Most importantly for our issue, *prōton* in 1:16 can be read in the light of *prōton* in 3:2: the privilege of the Jewish people lies in the fact that they have been entrusted with the oracles of God: the idea of a

---

215. Hultgren, *Romans*, 133.

Propositio

priority regarding evangelism is not the point of 1:16. Also, the righteousness of God is revealed through faith, for the circumcised (embodied by Abraham, as chapter 4 recalls) as well as the uncircumcised (the Greek; cf. 3:30); as we will see, it helps us to understand the real significance of "through faith for faith" (*ek pisteōs eis pistin*) dealing with the faith of individuals, "Jews" as well as "Greeks." Finally, it concludes with a "translation" of the formula that we have been studying: "Or is God the God of Jews only? Is he not the God of Gentiles also? Yes, of Gentiles also."[216] This time round, the question was not to understand if the gospel was for the Jew (it was obviously),[217] but if it was rather also for the Greek. Actually, we could translate the formula as follows: "To the Jew, of course, but also to the Greek."[218]

As a matter of fact, the entire thrust of Romans is Paul's argument that the gospel is *also* for the Gentiles, as 15:8-9 reminds us:[219] "For I tell you that Christ has become a servant of the circumcised on behalf of the truth of God in order that he might confirm the promises given to the patriarchs, and in order that the Gentiles might glorify God for his mercy." Following the *propositio* of 1:16-17, Paul is advocating at length that sin possesses all men and that judgment is for both Jewish people and Gentiles (with, however, a bright interval in 2:10). Considering this universality, which seems to deny the specialness of the Jewish people, Paul needs to explain what he meant by the *prōton* of 1:16.[220] If both Jewish people and Gentiles are equal, Jewish people are excelling—expressed with the word *perissos* in 3:1. They have an advantage that Paul wants to explain in a rhetorical way:[221] "Then

216. Cf. also 9:24: *ex Ioudaiōn alla kai ex ethnōn*.

217. For Goldsmith, if the phrase "to the Jew first" was present simply to state that the gospel went first to the Jewish people, it would add "nothing to what the Roman Christians already believed. It is much more likely that the phrase 'first for the Jew' has a sense of priority." Cf. Goldsmith, *Good News*, 121.

218. Gaston, *Paul and the Torah*, 118: "It is then possible to take full account of the *te* and *prōton* and translate, somewhat provocatively, 'for the Jews of course, but also for the Greek.' This can be supported by the 'not only . . . but also' pattern, later in the epistle. God is God not only of Jews but also of Gentiles (3:29)." See also Bauer et al., *BDAG*, 993 who suggests the same meaning as τέ—τέ.

219. Cf. Stuhlmacher, *Romans*, 28.

220. In his lecture given on *Romans* on the 7th December 2011 at the London School of Theology, Robert Willoughby suggested that Paul looked to "win" the Jewish people by writing 1:3-4 and "to the Jew first." It would back up the rhetorical question of Paul.

221. Cf. Stowers, *Rereading*, 16-17; 159-67, and his development of the "Speech-in-Character." For him, 3:1 is a question expressed by a Jewish Teacher. Even though I have learned a great deal from his study of the diatribe, I will not follow him on all points, the main criticism being that it sounds strange to use a Jewish objection when Paul is addressing mainly Gentiles.

what advantage has the Jew? Or what is the value of circumcision? Much in every way! [Or *Why did I say 'to the Jew first'? I have a very good reason!*] First [to the Jew], because the Jews were entrusted with the oracles of God." As remarks Campbell, "[t]hese questions are pointed rephrasings of the statement in 1.16b."[222]

One might reply that *prōton* in 3:2 has a different meaning than in 1:16, introducing a list of advantages. But if Paul seems to introduce a list, he does not continue it as we have already seen with Hultgren, except maybe in 9:4–5, which might be another development of this "entrusted with the oracles of God."[223] The formula *prōton men [gar] hoti* in 3:2 is again unique in the whole Bible and presents some text-critical problems regarding each of these words.

According to Swanson,[224] *prōton* as adverb is original. Only minuscule 1646 has a spelling mistake, *proton*, certainly due to the proximity of *tropon*; more of interest is that minuscules 6 and 1739 and the Sahidic version have *prōtoi*, a reading adopted by Eusebius of Caesarea and Origen:[225] even though it is obviously not the reading to follow,[226] it shows the idea of "they [the Jewish people] are first" was in the mind of the scribe, maybe linked with the parables of "the first will be the last and the last will be the first," which I will consider in my fourth chapter.[227] Moreover, *men* is absent from a few minuscules (6, 1739, 424c and 1881); however, it is not really relevant for the understanding of the phrase, often left untranslated. The absence of *gar* in some good manuscripts (B, D*, G, 9 minuscules, as well as a few Latin and Bohairic manuscripts and the Peshitta) is more problematic and debatable; but as the same manuscripts all keep *hoti*, the idea of causality remains, even if weakened. As for *hoti*, it is missing from the manuscripts that have *prōtoi*, certainly to make the sentence more fluid, and from one isolated minuscule (424c), which also omits *men*.

Hence, textual criticism reveals that the adverb is to be kept but also that the turn of phrase used by Paul brings some difficulties: the readers, facing this unusual use of *prōton*, seem to have been upset. Indeed, more surprising is the fact that Paul, beginning with this expression, should have

---

222. Campbell, "Determining," 334. For Campbell, "the slogan 'Jew first and then Greek' is not Paul's invention," but "have originated within the Judaizers' coherent convictions." Cf. Campbell, "Determining," 335. I think he goes too far.

223. See Williams, "Righteousness," 269, and the parallelisms presented between Romans 3 and 9.

224. Swanson, *NT Greek Manuscripts*, 34.

225. Cf. Nestle, et al., *NA27*, 413 and Anonymous, *He Kaine Diatheke*, 473.

226. Blass and Debrunner, *Grammar*, 232, however think it is the best reading.

227. Cf. Matt 19:30; 20:10; 20:16, Mark 10:31, Luke 13:30; the only places where *prōtoi* is used without a genitive complement in the New Testament.

Propositio

continued a list. According to my software *BibleWorks 8*,[228] Philo, who often uses the formula *prōton men hoti* and never *prōton men gar hoti*—which may confirm that the *gar* should not be kept—is interesting for our study. Out of the seventeen times he uses *prōton men hoti*, fourteen times, it is very clear that it is a list, following on with "secondly" (*deuteron*; four times)[229] and sometimes "thirdly" (*triton*; six times),[230] or "then" (*epeita*; three times),[231] or "after these things" (*meta de tauta*; once);[232] three times, it is less clear, even if the following logical structure makes possible the idea of a list: using the cunjunctive particles *de* (twice)[233] and *kai* (once).[234]

I will not consider, as Hultgren does, that the *prōton* of 1:8 has no subsequent second point as seems to be the case in 3:2. Actually, 1:13, "I want you to know, brothers and sisters" (*ou thelō de hymas agnoein, adelphoi*) could very naturally be considered as a second point. For Calvin, *prōton* does not show an order[235] "but simply means *chiefly* or *especially*, and is to be taken in this sense: 'The fact of their being entrusted with the oracles of God alone ought to be sufficient to secure their dignity.'"[236] Because of the lack of other advantages listed for six chapters (Rom 3–8), I tend to follow Calvin in his proposition; it leads me to another possible translation of *Ioudaiō te prōton kai Hellēni*: "to the Jew especially, but also to the Greek."[237] Hence, the

228. Philo, *Works of Philo Judaeus*, based on Borgen et al., *Philo Concordance*, in *BibleWorks 8*.

229. Philo, *De opificio mundi*, 1:170–71; *De somniis*, 2:69; *De specialibus legibus*, 2:168–69; 4:53.

230. Philo, *De Josepho*, 1:216; *De specialibus legibus* 1:74; 1:126–28; 2:140–41; 4:5; Q & A on Genesis—Paramelle 1:5.

231. Philo, *De specialibus legibus*, 2:166; *Quod omnis probus liber sit* 1:63; *De aeternitate mundi* 1:94.

232. Philo, *De vita Mosis*, 1:110.

233. Philo, *Quis rerum divinarum heres sit*, 1:267–72 (in 267, Philo, is quoting a verse after his *prōton men hoti*, and in 271–72 he is saying "but [*de*] . . . for we read in the next verse"); cf. *Quaestiones in Genesim* (fragment. 2:12), where *de* is translated "also." We may put *Prōton men* of Romans 1:8 in this category—even if *hoti* is missing—where Paul is dealing with his dialogue with God concerning the Romans, before introducing the idea of a visit to them, which takes him to the second point: *ou thelō de hymas agnoein* of 1:13, again with *de* (even if the delimitation of the different points of the list is more difficult to determine).

234. Philo, *De decalogo* 1:2–5, where *kai* is translated "also."

235. As, for instance, in 1 Cor 12:28.

236. Calvin, *Romans & Thessalonians*, 58. Calvin is followed by Godet, *Romans I*, 221–22 and Haldane, *Romans*, 107. The KJV also chooses this option: "chiefly."

237. Zeller, *Juden*, 144, suggests also the philological possibility to translate *prōton* as "'particularly,' 'especially,' 'primarily.'" ("'besonders,' 'gerade,' in erster Linie." My translation).

advantage that the Jewish people have, expressing the reason why Paul uses "first" in the formula "to the Jew first," lies mainly in the fact that they were entrusted with the oracles of God.[238] This link between 1:16 and 3:2 shows also the link between "the gospel" (*to euangelion*) and "the oracles of God" (*ta logia tou theou*):[239] it is the gospel that the whole of Scripture points to, which existed in embryonic form in the Old Testament.[240] It seems that we have here the most convincing explanation of Romans 1:16. The good news was announced firstly and directly to the people of Israel through the covenant of God with Abraham and through the prophets. Moreover, this good news was completed and also announced firstly to the Jewish people in the period of the New Testament: God spoke through Jesus, who came firstly for his people, but also for all the nations. And indeed, Abraham had his faith considered as righteousness (Rom 4:3) and foresaw the day of Jesus, hence the salvation in him.[241] This is also the case for all the Israelites who have believed since the coming of Jesus, who are part of the remnant described by Paul in Romans 11:5, and is still the case today (as it is also today for the Gentiles).[242] In this way, Blocher even wonders:

> The complications of the human heart, however, and those further complications which a painful story has produced through bloody centuries, make it permissible to conjecture a situation in which a Jew would be gripped in his/her heart by the gospel as already revealed in the Tanakh and be led to trust, "through the fog," in the God of grace, the God of Jesus Christ. Normally, such a person would overcome this ignorance when presented with the clear and explicit truth of Jesus Christ.[243]

---

238. Cf. Deut 4:7–8 ("For what other great nation has a god so near to it as the LORD our God is whenever we call to him? And what other great nation has statutes and ordinances as just as this entire law that I am setting before you today?"); Ps 147:19–20 ("He declares his word to Jacob, his statutes and ordinances to Israel. He has not dealt thus with any other nation; they do not know his ordinances. Praise the LORD!"); Rom 9:4.

239. Zeller, *Juden*, 144–45 does this link.

240. Cf. 10:4–13, where Paul says that "the word of faith that we preach" is precisely what Moses was writing about in Deut 30; Heb 4:1–7, 1 Pet 4:6, Gal 3:8; 2 Tim 3:14–15. For the understanding of *ta logia tou theou* as the Law and the Prophets, see Bell, *No One Seeks*, 203.

241. Cf. John 8:56.

242. *Contra* Stowers, *Rereading*, 296–97.

243. Blocher, "Two Covenant Theology," 206.

Propositio

Hence, considering the parallel between 1:16 and 3:2, I conclude that *prōton* should be read in an *HCP* way, since it modifies *Ioudaiō* to specify *tō pisteuonti*.

Romans 1:17

Much more has been said on Romans 1:17 than on 1:16 and it is not my aim to study it in detail here. Delving into these huge areas of "righteousness of God" (*dikaiosynē theou*) and "faith/faithfulness" (*pistis*), let alone discussing their respective objective or subjective senses, will bring me too far from the cause.[244] To allow me to go on in our exploration without too much interruption, I need to give some principal directions.

As already said, the emphasis of 1:16–17 is on *pistis*, the salvation of everybody through this *pistis* and the revelation of the *dikaiosynē theou*. Whether *pistis* refers to "faith" or "faithfulness," of Christ, God or the believer, or whether the righteousness is God's, from God or given by God are not questions I need to tackle for the issue. My concern is to understand how the gospel is the power of God for salvation to everyone who has faith—to the Jew first and also to the Greek—and how this is linked with the fact that the *dikaiosynē theou* is revealed through faith for faith; as it is written, "The one who is righteous will live by faith."

Dikaiosynē theou is a key phrase, with "a consistent apocalyptic meaning," as J. C. Beker, leaning on Käsemann, explains:

> As God's eschatological salvation power, it [*dikaiosynē theou*] claims the creation for God's lordship and sovereignty which the Christ-event has proleptically manifested. It denotes the victory of God and his cosmic act of redemption. . . . The term gathers up in itself the rich connotations of Israel's covenant terminology: *hesed* (steadfast love), *emet* (truth), and *zedakah* (righteousness), especially in its eschatological dimensions as documented, for instance, in 2 Isaiah and the Psalms. . . . In this function the *dikaiosynē theou* must be understood both as God's faithfulness to himself and as his redemptive activity in accordance with his faithfulness.[245]

It recalls the link already shown between "power of God" (*dynamis theou*) and "righteousness of God" (*dikaiosynē theou*): the parallel between these two expressions in Romans 1:16–17 is very obvious. N. T. Wright and

---

244. See, for instance, Heliso, *Pistis*.
245. Beker, "Faithfulness of God," 331.

To the Jew First or to the Jew at Last?

John Piper, in their recent open dispute, while considering their opposing views are both insisting on faithfulness. For Wright, *dikaiosynē theou* is "God's covenant faithfulness"[246] or "God's faithful covenant justice,"[247] and, for Piper, it is "God's inviolable faithfulness to uphold the value of his glory."[248] And indeed, what was at stake since the fall in the mind of God was to find a solution to make the world and humankind recover their original state. If Israel was chosen, it was to be a light to the Gentiles. As Israel has failed, God had to send his own son, "King of the Jews" (Matt 2:2), as representative of Israel, to fulfill the covenant promise to Abraham in a cosmic act of power through his death and resurrection. Through the work of Jesus, the love, truth, faithfulness, justice and glory of God are revealed for the salvation of everyone who believes, the Jew first and also the Greek.

Considering this fact, it was quite natural that this salvation promise to Israel was for centuries firstly addressed to her. Good news is always revealed in a certain historical and spatial context. As a matter of fact, Israel, who was for centuries expecting the coming of the Messiah, had already heard of this salvation before, even if the coming of the Messiah was only completely revealed in the first century of our era. This news had been received—or should have been received—with gladness, as one hears of the birth of the son of the King![249] It is why Paul can say that the *dikaiosynē theou* has been revealed in this good news, exposing the reality of the power of the resurrection, for a new exodus, for sin having being defeated through the punishment of Jesus, for the satisfaction of the justice of God and the appeasement of his wrath.

The point at stake is the fact that everybody can be saved through this *pistis*, both Jewish people and Gentiles, even if the Jewish people had the *first* opportunity to experience it. As a matter of fact, God has not changed, neither has his way of salvation: from Abraham and Genesis 15:6 (see also Deut 30:11–14) to Paul and Romans 4:3 (see also 10:5–10), salvation comes from trust in God and confession of the tongue! In this matter, I suggest that the likelier understanding of 1:17 could be: "For in it the righteousness of God is revealed through faith (of the Israelite in the OT) for faith (of the Jew and the Greek in the new covenant); as it is written, 'The one who is righteous will live by faith.'" The translators of the NIV, by reading "by faith,

---

246. Wright, *Justification*, 49.
247. Wright, *Fresh*, 25.
248. Piper, *Future of Justification*, 69.
249. See the enthusiasm of the crowd (Matt 13:2 or 14:14, for instance) *contra* the scepticism of the religious leaders.

Propositio

from first to last," also envisage a parallel between 16c and 17a and seem to have also understood the expression "through faith for faith" in this way.

The quotation of Habakkuk 2:4, despite its difficulties, seems to consolidate my point of view. The historical context of this prophecy is more likely to be the blossoming of the Chaldean Empire, which covets the territory of Judah, whose king at that time is Jehoiakim (Hab 1:5–11).[250] After the fall of the Assyrians, Habakkuk is certainly hoping that better days were ahead, and behold, now the Babylonians! Facing this crisis, the prophet has good reason to question the covenant between God and his people: "Habakkuk witnesses of the call into question of the covenant between YHWH and Israel; maybe he has the feeling of the closeness of the breach, by Israel, of the Sinai covenant, [as well as the closeness of] the Babylonian exile."[251] Habakkuk is wrestling with the fact that the priority of Israel seems to have been called into question: her status of being the loved nation in the heart of God is challenged in a world where YHWH seemed to have abolished the preference, treating Israel as cannon-fodder for the Babylonians, just like any other nations in their path. It is during these difficulties that Habakkuk encourages the people of Israel by saying that the righteous will live *ek pisteōs* [*mou*][252] and has the vision that God will indeed come "to save his people, to save his anointed" (3:13: eis sōtērian *laou sou tou sōsai tous christous sou*; in non-italics, same formula as in Romans 1:16).

To sum up, Habakkuk asserts that God will come to deliver the righteous from the wicked,[253] hence answering his question formulated at the beginning of his prophecy (1:2). The one who will put his trust in YHWH and continue to obey his law faithfully will live, even if the salvation seems delayed.[254] As a matter of fact, the context of Habakkuk is not related to any kind of "evangelism," if I may use this anachronistic term for seventh century BC. The question is not whether or not to be "a light among the Gentiles," but to preach salvation in the midst of the difficulties of this Gentile

---

250. See Tidiman, *Nahoum, Habaquq, Sophonie*, 135–37.

251. My translation. See Tidiman, *Nahoum, Habaquq, Sophonie*, 144: "Habaquq assiste à la remise en question de l'alliance entre Yahvé et Israël; sans doute pressent-il la proximité de la rupture, par Israël, de l'alliance du Sinaï et l'exile babylonien."

252. I am well aware of all the debate concerning this verse but will not engage with it here because it is not directly relevant for our topic.

253. I will define the "righteous" in the OT as the one who is recognized by God as "in the right," saved by faith through the covenant and keeping the Law to honor his God. Cf. Gal 3 (the formula is in verse 11) and Wright, *Justification*, 59–87. The "wicked" is more likely to qualify the Israelite who does scorn the Law than the Chaldean; see Hab 1:4. See Hiebert, *Habakkuk*, 625–26.

254. See the use of the formula in Heb 10:37–38.

invasion and to lean on God who will save his people, namely his anointed.[255] An interesting point regarding the issue is the fact that Habakkuk 1:5 is quoted by Paul in Acts 13:41,[256] before the controversial verse 46.[257] I suggest the following parallel: just as, during the time of Habakkuk announcing the destruction of Judah, Israel was called to look at the nations from where the judgment will come—during which the arrogant would perish and the righteous would live by faith (cf. 2:4)—so Paul, announcing the destruction of the Holy City by the Nations, also calls the arrogant Israelites to look at the nations who will now be saved. In any case, *ek pisteōs eis pistin*, the righteous shall live by faith! Facing the judgment which is to come, physically preceded by the destruction of Jerusalem, everyone who will put his faith in Jesus, Jew as well as Gentile will be faithful and will be saved.[258]

The Formula of Romans 2:9–10

The two verses of Romans 2:9–10 are obviously important in our study, recalling the chorus, which is the main object of our study.

Structure

Similar features of parallelism, lead me to link verses 9–10 with verses 6–8 (chiasm):[259]

---

255. *Contra* the modern commentaries that we consulted, I believe that due to the apparent parallelism "Messiah" refers to the people themselves (cf. Ps 28:8)—the chosen people—rather than an individual, a king or the Messiah Jesus.

256. According to the MT Habakkuk declares: "Look at the nations (*rĕ'û baggôyim*), and see! Be astonished! Be astounded! For a work is being done in your days that you would not believe if you were told." But according to the LXX, he is saying: "Look, you scoffers and see, be really amazed and perish, for in your days I am doing a work, a work that you will never believe, even if someone tells you" (*idete oi kataphronētai kai epiblepsate kai thaumasate thaumasia kai aphanisthēte*). The translators of the LXX seem to have confused the word *baggôyim* with *bōgĕdîm*; cf. Elliger et al., *BHS*, 1049.

257. Controversial in our present study. See chapter 2, "The pattern in Acts" ("The gospel refused by many Jewish people").

258. Cf. Matt 24:13: "But the one who endures to the end will be saved." These events are being understood as either realized in the Destruction of Jerusalem or the end of the world. See Wright, *Jesus*, 339–68.

259. Cf. Moo, *Romans*, 135 or Matera, *Romans*, 63.

Propositio

A   6 For he will repay according to each one's deeds:
- B   7 to those who by patiently doing good [*ergou agathou*] seek for glory and honor and immortality he will give eternal life;
  - C   8 while for those who are self-seeking and who obey not the truth but wickedness [*adikia*], there will be wrath and fury.
  - C'   9 There will be anguish and distress for everyone who does evil [*kakon*], the Jew first and also the Greek.
- B'   10 but glory and honor and peace for everyone who does good [*to agathon*], the Jew first and also the Greek.

A'   11 For God shows no partiality.

This structure also allows me to link more clearly the anguish and distress promised to those who seek injustice with wrath and fury, and the glory and honor promised to those who seek glory, honor, and immortality with eternal life.

Anguish and Distress

As Paul is pointing out to his contemporaries that "God's wrath has overtaken them [the Jewish people] at last" (1 Thess 2:16),[260] it seems that spiritual judgment has already fallen on the people of Israel.[261] Romans 11:7–11 talks of what was sought by Israel and that only the elect (from Israel) obtain it while the rest are hardened.[262] At the same time, it seems that we have here two other times of tribulations which jumble together: the judgment of the destruction of Jerusalem in AD 70 and the final judgment, the first foreshadowing the second. Indeed, the judgment of the son of man (Matt 16:27) fell "physically" on the whole structure of Judaism with the destruction of the Temple in the first century[263] while Paul is also referring to a future day of judgment (2:5, 16). The situation of the Jewish people regarding the Greco-Roman Empire in the first century AD is parallel to the situation of the Judeans regarding the Chaldean Empire in the sixth or seventh century

---

260. Cf. Moo, *Romans*, 141: "the revelation of God's wrath of which Paul is speaking is addressed clearly to Jews and Greeks in Paul's own day." Cf. also 2 Thess 1:6.

261. Part of that judgment is demonstrated by Jesus in the use of the parables and the realization of the prophecy expressed in Isa 6:9–10 (Mark 4:12; Matt 13:13–15; Luke 8:10). Cf. Wright, *Jesus*, 236–39.

262. Cf. also John 12:40; 2 Cor 3:15.

263. Cf. Amos 3:2 mentioned by e.g. Haacker, *Römer*, 38; Hendriksen, *Romans*, 61. Brindle, "Jew First," 228, quotes Jer 25:29, which "declares that when God begins to bring a sword against all those who inhabit the earth, He will begin at the 'city which is called by my name.'" See also Luke 11:47–51, 1 Pet 4:17.

To the Jew First or to the Jew at Last?

BC: there will be a judgment first on the people of God, then on the nation that was used by God to punish his people.[264] God judged the people of Israel in AD 70 and he will judge the nations throughout history[265] and every human being at the end.[266]

N. T. Wright clearly demonstrates how several acts and words of Jesus were predicting this judgment on the Temple and the coming of Jesus as king:[267] "when Jesus came to Jerusalem, he symbolically and prophetically enacted judgment upon it—a judgment which, both before and after, he announced verbally as well as in action."[268] And it is certainly the Parable of the wicked tenants (Matt 21:33–46 and parallels) that give me the best insight into the events:

> the day of the spiritual leadership of the 'chief priests, scribes, and elders' was brought to an end. They would be destroyed and the care of the vineyard would be entrusted to others. (. . .), the twelve are seen to be *Christ's new shepherds for Israel*.[269]

Having a priority in the last judgment would indeed mean nothing (God does not have a waiting room in his law court):

> not only that the Jew also stands under God's judgment, but that he stands in the first rank of those who are to be judged. Jewish priority (in the history of salvation) is also a priority of judgment—first to receive God's wrath as well as first to receive his blessing.[270]

---

264. See the very interesting narrative explained by Perriman, *Future People*, 44–60.

265. The nations which were used in the past to punish Israel have always been punished in return: Assyria, Babylon, Medo-Persia, and Rome. Regarding this last one, should we consider the fall of AD 476? Perriman, which proposes no date for this judgment in his book, writes in a response to our e-mail: "in order to understand Romans we do not have to know exactly how things worked out."

266. Cf. Rom 14:12; Jer 17:10; Ps 62:12–13 (LXX 61:13); 2 Cor 11:15; 2 Tim 4:14; Rev 2:23. And this despite the fact that Paul uses *zōen aiōnion* in Rom 2:7. "Eternal life" begins on the earth; see John 3:36, for instance.

267. See Wright, *Jesus*, 405–28, 489–528, 612–53. See "The Cleansing of the Temple" (Matt 21:12–17), "The Fig-Tree cursed and the (Temple)-Mount thrown in the sea" (Matt 21:18–19 and parallels); "The Prophecy of the destruction of the Temple" (Matt 24:1–44 and parallels); Story of the talents (Matt 25:14–30 and parallels). However, if Wright convinced me that the coming of the son of man is foretold in this last passage, I think that it is as a foreshadowing of the second coming of Jesus. The judgment of Jerusalem is a foretaste of the last judgment. The parables of "the first and the last" will be considered in chapter 4 below.

268. Ibid., 417.

269. Stek, *Jew First: Exegetical Examination*, 80.

270. Dunn, *Romans 1–8*, 93.

Propositio

If the wrath of God went first to the Jewish people at the time of Paul, I can legitimately consider that the *prōton* of Romans 1:16—as it parallels 2:9—refers to the opportunity the Jewish people had to receive the gospel first in the time of Paul too.

But the idea of priority is not only historical regarding this understanding. The Jew of the first century is judged first and condemned according to his works because the law is for him the measure of judgment: condemned "first" is synonymous with "will be judged by the law [*dia nomou krithēnai*]."[271] "The responsibility, which they have due to the knowledge of the divine commandments, puts the Jews in first place when they have to come to court."[272] I catch in the words of Paul a glimpse of the Sermon of the Mount where Jesus is giving the law its real significance (Matt 5:21–48):[273] the Jew described in Romans 2:17–24 is still living under the old legalistic understanding of the law, which has not been transcended yet. He boasts because of the Law, he is therefore judged by it, because before the holy God, his transgressions are clearly visible. This is why the *prōton* of 2:9–10 also signifies that, due to their knowledge of the law,[274] the judgment is particularly addressed to the Jewish people.[275] As for the Gentiles, who have the law written in their heart (2:14–15) but who were not entrusted with it as the Jewish people were—they are in this way disadvantaged compared to the Jewish people—they will also have their works judged accordingly. However, in both cases only the one, who put his faith in Jesus, first the Jew, but also the Greek, will be saved.

Glory and Honor

In the same way, honor and eternal life are first for the heirs who do good, as Ephesians 1:11–12, noticed by Hume,[276] expresses it:

---

271. Cf. Zeller: "To be condemned as 'first' is here synonymous with διὰ νόμου κριθῆναι." My translation. See Zeller, *Juden*, 151: "Als 'erster' verurteilt werden ist da gleichbedeutend mit διὰ νόμου κριθῆναι."

272. My translation. See Lohse, "Juden zuerst," 205: "Die Verantwortung, die ihnen aus der Kenntnis der göttlichen Gebote zukommt, rückt die Juden an die erste Stelle, an die sie im Gericht zu treten haben."

273. Cf. Cranfield, *Romans I*, 169.

274. This is not so much the case today since secularization has spread to the Jewish community. If the law was defining the Jew at the time of Paul, we cannot affirm the same for today.

275. See Moo, *Romans*, 139: "As the word of the promise has gone 'first' to the Jew, so does punishment for failure to respond to that word go 'first' to the Jew."

276. Hume, *Romans*, 23–24. Hume quotes also Rom 15:8–9.

11 In Christ we have also obtained an inheritance, having been destined according to the purpose of him who accomplishes all things according to his counsel and will, 12 so that we, who were the first to set our hope on Christ [*tous proēlpikotas en tō Christō*], might live for the praise of his glory.[277]

Since the gospel was preached first to the Jewish people, it was natural that they were the first to be able to respond to it. The first disciples (and all the believers before them, who, as Abraham, saw the day of Jesus)[278] were the witnesses of this life changed through the gospel. It is a new life demonstrating good works, not done in order to be saved but because of the reality of salvation. The fact that these works are or will be judged does not mean that the salvation of humanity is based on works but that "a person in Christ does meet these conditions as the fruit of faith comes to expression in his life."[279] As for the Gentile, if he can practice good works because of the law written in his heart, he has to understand that his good works do not save him (they are spoilt by sin)[280] and that only faith in Jesus will give him eternal life. Having put his faith in Jesus, he will do good, and his good works will also be judged one day.[281]

CONCLUSION

Hence these two verses of Romans 1:16–17, the *propositio* of the Epistle, are a résumé of the powerful action of God who, to fulfill his promises and his covenant with Abraham and to show his faithfulness, has deployed his strength through the cosmic acts of the death and the resurrection of the King Jesus. Jesus is the Lord—more powerful than Caesar—and he allows everybody who has faith in him to be saved from the wrath of God. This good news of the rising of the Lord Jesus has been first addressed to the people of Israel who were aware of the prophecies announced by the prophets

---

277. Eph 2:11 states that Paul is using "you" to talk to the Gentiles ("So then, remember that at one time you Gentiles by birth . . .") and I can conclude that in Eph 1:11–12 Paul is speaking of the Jewish people of whom he is a representative. Cf. O'Brien, *Ephesians*, 116. For the larger debate and an understanding of the "we" as being "Paul and those with him" and the "you" as the "Ephesians believers," see Hoehner, *Ephesians*, 231–34.

278. Cf. Luke 16:31.

279. Moo, *Romans*, 142.

280. See Isa 64:6: "We have all become like one who is unclean, and all our righteous deeds are like a filthy cloth." or Eccl 10:1: "Dead flies make the perfumer's ointment give off a foul odor."

281. Cf. 1 Cor 4:5; 2 Cor 5:10; Eph 6:8; 1 Tim 5:24–25; 2 Tim 4:8

Propositio

centuries before, predicting the coming of a Messiah to save his people from their sins (Matt 1:21) and "that repentance and forgiveness of sins is to be proclaimed in his name to all nations, beginning from Jerusalem."[282]

To try to figure how to grasp this whole issue, I attempt an allegory, which as all allegories has its limits: In 19th century France, the people were suffering from rabies and hundreds were dying each year of this virus. But the French people, brought up with the divine promise that through them the victory will come, were putting their trust in their scientists who were working on this disease: it was said that one of them would find the remedy. In particular, God had made a promise to a poor tanner in Arbois (Eastern France) assuring him that through one of his descendants the evil would be defeated. All the French population was hoping for this salvation which was sure to come, but when? In 1885, finally, Louis Pasteur found the cure. The good news spread like wildfire all over the country and everybody rejoiced! Of course, the discovery soon became a benefit for all Europe, good news for other nations too. But today, if in Africa and Asia there are still between 40,000 to 70,000 people dying of rabies per year, there is no need to have on the headlines of French newspapers "Rabies defeated!" even if each Frenchman still needs to be aware of the risk of rabies and be vaccinated. If a Frenchman is beaten in the country side by a rabid dog, and is unaware of the vaccine, the word of his doctor telling him about the remedy will certainly be good news for him!

For the people of the Roman Empire in the first century, the good news of the risen Lord needed to be proclaimed to the Jewish people first but also to the Gentiles, and for a very good reason. The Jewish people had an advantage: for centuries, their prophets had predicted the coming of the Messiah for their salvation but more—and contrary to the case of rabies!—they had the opportunity to be saved by him in advance, even before his coming. They knew the story of salvation and were obliged to spread it so as to be a light for the Gentiles. For the Gentiles of the first century, it was obviously also good news that someone had come to save them from their sins as announced by the prophets in the Scriptures; but they were unaware of all the preceding narrative of salvation through Israel. In the same way, there still might be today French people affected by rabies, but they should know that there is a cure.

As Paul was preaching in the first century, the main focus was the good news of a salvation without the practice of works of the law, but by faith alone; this was opening a way for the Gentiles too. Faith had always

---

282. Luke 24:46–47. See also Ps 98 (1–3, 8–9), which is regarded by Leenhard as to have been the inspiration of Rom 1:16. See Leenhardt, *Romans*, 46.

been part of the salvation plan for Israel since Abraham; however, the Jewish people needed to be reminded of that, tempted as they were to put their trust in their ancestry and religious practice. It would be the same for the French people who, because they are French, would think that they will never be touched by rabies because Louis Pasteur was French! They would be wrong, the French people still need to be vaccinated (and in this way, they need to have faith in Pasteur and his work done through the rabies vaccine) in order not to be affected by this evil. And indeed, if someone should really know about rabies, it should be French people! Today, the Jewish people still need to be reminded of the good news of their Messiah, but the "priority" or advantage expressed by Romans 1:16 is not to be found in the context of evangelization of the Jewish people, but to be understood in the first century context. As a matter of fact, Paul does not habitually appeal in his letters to the churches to evangelize, and *The Epistle to the Romans* is not an exception.[283] If the intention of Paul was to appeal to his readers to evangelize the Jewish people first, he would have made it clear and would have dealt with it;[284] but his intention was rather to assert this extraordinary new truth: the gospel was indeed the power of God for the Jewish people (because with them were entrusted his oracles), but not only for them, for the Gentiles too, as the works of the law, which had been separating Jewish people and Gentiles, were no more relevant.

To complete my study, I need now to turn to Romans 9–11 and evaluate the Jewish missional priority through the salvation history presented in these chapters.

---

283. For a very good résumé of the whole debate on this issue, see Keown, *Congregational Evangelism*, 1–36. Keown himself suggests a "corporate general proclamatory evangelism" in Philippians (Ibid., 1). Alan Kreider observed that the same was true for the early Christian writings: "In my reading of early Christian materials with missionary eyes, I have been amazed at the absence of pastoral admonitions to evangelise." Kreider, "Worship & Evangelism," 8. See also O'Brien, *Gospel & Mission*. O'Brien while acknowledging this fact, pleads that Paul encourages to mission, for instance in his letter to the Corinthians: "The apostle may not have expected his converts at Corinth to be engaged in missionary initiatives of the kind he was furthering; but each *in his or her own way and according to their personal gifts* was to have the same goal and ambitions as Paul himself, that is, that of seeking by all possible means to save many" (Ibid., 106). As for Goldsmith, "[a]s followers of Christ, all of us are sent out in mission" (Goldsmith, *Grip on Mission*, 15).

284. The proponents of the *MP* often consider Romans 9–11 to be such an appeal. We will study this issue soon.

IV

Heilsgeschichte
Evaluation of the Jewish Missional Priority through the Salvation History Presented in Romans 9–11

From September 2001 until August 2002, I ministered at a little Baptist church in a small city of the French Bourgogne: Le Creusot (23,000 inhabitants today). The history of this city is closely linked with the Schneider family, which allowed this place to flourish between 1836 to 1960, based upon a very good quality steel business forging locomotives, rails, cannons, and armor plating. The Schneider dynasty developed a paternalism that ruled the daily life of the inhabitants, since at least one member of each family was employed by the company (at its zenith some 20,000 people—schools and hospital employees included). It goes without saying how profoundly the inhabitants loved this rich family that generously provided everything they needed. One of the Schneider's privileges was to transform a royal glassworks built in 1786, *La Cristallerie de la Reine*, into their residence, a castle then named *Le Château de la Verrerie*. Nobody in the city was allowed to enter the park adjoined to the castle, let alone to enter the castle—except members of the family and, I assume, some friends—until the 9th September 1972. Following the death of the last son, Charles, in 1960, the city council acquired *Le Parc de la Verrerie* in 1969 and declared it open to the general public three years later. For many months following the announcement of this news, many inhabitants dared not walk upon the grass of the estate: it was quasi-holy. When in 2001 I was going for a walk in this park, I had no idea how important this place was for many of the inhabitants, now unemployed or retired. We were simply enjoying the beautiful green area full of many different trees and animals and overshadowed by an amazing castle transformed into a museum.

The history of *Le Creusot* makes me think of the salvation history. The Lord of the universe, who in his common grace is making his sun rise and is sending rain on the righteous and on the unrighteous (Matt 5:45), has chosen one people to operate his cosmic mission: Israel.[1] His one privileged people he blessed with many riches others could not even dream of sharing, except a few God-fearers and proselytes:

> the adoption, the glory, the covenants, the giving of the law, the worship, and the promises; to them belong the patriarchs, and from them, according to the flesh, comes the Messiah, who is over all, God blessed forever.[2]

But the aim of the Lord from the beginning was to bless "all the families of the earth" (Gen 12:3), and one day, through the death of his only begotten son, salvation was open to everybody.[3] If, since the coming of Jesus, the Jewish people have in great number refused this salvation, this is not the end of the story of "Paul's kindred according to the flesh."[4] This chapter will deal with the next steps of my research and especially the study of Romans 1:16 in connection with chapters 9–11.

If I have called this chapter "*Heilsgeschichte*," it is to acknowledge that German theology in the past has made an impressive contribution to this field, as the important work of Dieter Zeller, *Juden and Heiden in der Mission des Paulus*, demonstrates.[5] In his work, Zeller provides a synthesis of the thought of Oscar Cullmann, Johannes Munck, Rudolph Bultmann, Gunther Klein, Charles Müller, Ernst Käsemann, Peter Stuhlmacher, Ulrich Luz, and Christian Dietzfelbinger. It is not my purpose to repeat what has already been put forward; however, the understanding of Cullmann as summarized by Zeller is worth quoting, since it offers a definition:

> Salvation History is for him [Cullmann] selection and sequence of events in history that are determined and connected by a

---

1. Cf. Wright, *Mission of God*, 57–65.
2. Rom 9:4–5. Interestingly, the land is not part of this list. It seems to have been a habit of Paul not to refer to the land in his writings. See Davies, *Gospel & Land*, 167.
3. Cf. John 3:16.
4. Cf. Rom 9:3.
5. Zeller, *Juden*, 18–33.

Heilsgeschichte

divine plan. Through revelation, these are being unveiled to humankind so that in faith man can "become part" of them. Despite the constancy of the divine plan, the Salvation History reveals a progressive movement because new events of salvation put the earlier revelations in a new light and because the resistance of man causes new turns in the salvation plan. The act of the new interpretation belongs also to the Salvation History.[6]

This definition reminds us also that it is God who is in charge when we deal with mission. In his sovereignty, he leads it: it is *his* mission, despite the fact that he allows us to share in it:

> Certainly, the mission of God is the prior reality out of which flows any mission that we get involved in. Or, as has been nicely put, it is not so much the case that God has a mission for his church in the world but that God has a church for his mission in the world. Mission was not made for the church; the church was made for mission—God's mission.[7]

If the German theologians to whom Zeller refers to differ here and there in their understanding of salvation history, particularly how Israel according to the flesh fits into it, they all think that this Israel has a role to play as Cullmann expresses it clearly: "The Israel *kata sarka* remains the point of departure and the way for the history of salvation, but it also remains from Christ on—in the focus as the elected nation—where it expanded to the nation of believers."[8]

It will also be my task to deal with this role, looking at it, however, from the angle of the Jewish people and the matters of order and priority. My aim is not to enter into all the issues covered by these three important

---

6. My translation. See ibid., 18–20: "Heilsgeschichte ist ihm [Cullmann] eine Auswahl und Abfolge von Ereignissen in der Geschichte, die durch einen göttlichen Plan bestimmt sind und zusammenhängen. Durch Offenbarung werden sie dem Menschen erschlossen, damit er sich im Glauben in sie 'einreihe.' Trotz der Konstante des göttlichen Plans weist die Heilsgeschichte eine fortschreitende Bewegung auf, weil neue Heilsereignisse die früheren Offenbarungen in ein neues Licht rücken und der Widerstand des Menschen neue Wendungen im Heilsplan bedingt. Der Akt der Neuinterpretation gehört mit zur Heilsgeschichte."

7. Wright, *Mission of God*, 62. Cf. also Gaventa, "Mission of God," 65–66: "I argue that in Romans God not only sends Paul and his co-workers on a mission, but God has God's own mission of rescuing the world from the powers of Sin and Death so that a newly created humanity—Jew and Gentile—is released for the praise of God in community."

8. My translation. See Cullmann, *Heil*, 241: "Das Israel κατὰ σάρκα bleibt der Ausgangspunkt und der Weg der Heilsgeschichte; es bleibt aber auch von Christus an, wo es sich zum Volk der Gläubigen ausweitet, im Blickfeld als das Erwählungsvolk."

chapters, since I have no room for that and besides, others already have admirably dealt with them.[9] As a matter of fact, I claim that Romans 9–11 confirms that the *prōton* of Romans 1:16 is to be understood as a priority in the order of the salvation history, and not as a priority of evangelism today. Other texts, such as the parables of Jesus regarding "The first will be the last and the last will be the first,"[10] will also be examined as evidence in the debate; as we will see, if some have made a connection between these texts, I will highlight them in an unprecedented way regarding our issue.

As we have seen in my second chapter, one of the arguments of the proponents of the *missional priority* interpretation (*MP*) is to argue that the priority of Jewish evangelization is supported by Romans 9–11 through the themes of Israel's need, Israel's restoration, and the evangelization of the world by the Jewish people.[11] I have already critically exposed these themes and I need now to look at the text itself. Which scheme of salvation history can be deduced from it? Is there a missional *modus operandi* which needs to be followed for the evangelization of the world? The aim of this chapter is to shed light on these issues.

EVANGELISM IN ROMANS 9–11

Evangelism is not the main theme of Romans 9–11; it is "the faithfulness of God to his covenant word"[12] despite "the Jews' failure to believe the gospel."[13] There is no direct order to evangelize whoever, whenever and wherever; we have already seen that this absence of exhortation to evangelize is a usual habit of Paul.[14] However, there are a few passages that need to be considered regarding evangelism. As Zeller expresses it, "because even the salvation of Israel according to 1.16 depends on the gospel, the sentence contains factually the explanation of chapters 9–11 in itself, showing how the special vocation of the Jews with regard to the gospel and through the gospel can still come true eschatologically."[15]

---

9. See, for instance, Motyer, *Israel*. For a more detailed study in connection with our issue, see the thorough work of Bell, *Provoked*. Cf. also Ellison, *Mystery of Israel*.

10. Matt 19:16–30 (Mark 10:17–31; Luke 18:18–30); Matt 20:1–16; Luke 13:22–30. Then called "The first/last sayings."

11. See chapter 2, "Eschatological perspectives according to Romans 9–11."

12. Abasciano, *Paul's Use*, 107.

13. Wright, *Climax of Covenant*, 235.

14. See again Keown, *Congregational Evangelism*, 1–36. The case of Romans 10:14 will be considered in due course.

15. My translation. See Zeller, *Juden*, 145: "weil auch das Heil Israels nach 1,16 am Ev hängt, birgt der Satz sachlich die Ausführungen von Kap. 9–11 in sich, die zeigen,

Heilsgeschichte

God Has Not Forgotten His People: Romans 11:1

My first point is obviously important, and Paul is hopefully very clear concerning this issue: "I ask, then, has God rejected [*mē apōsato*] his people? By no means! I myself am an Israelite, a descendant of Abraham, a member of the tribe of Benjamin" (Rom 11:1). The proof that God has not rejected the Jewish people is that Jewish people like Paul can be part of the New Covenant. This was the case for Paul and also for the 150,000 Messianic Jews living today.[16] This verse alone is sufficient evidence to state that Jewish people can be the object of God's grace revealed in Jesus Christ and hence to encourage mission among the Jewish people today.

The Jewish People and the Gentiles Heard the Gospel: Romans 10:5–21

This first important passage concerns the way the gospel was heard by Jewish people and Gentiles.

Romans 10:5–13

As already seen in my previous chapter, Romans 10:5–13 reminds us that salvation is by faith, first to last, either for the Jew or the Greek, because God does not change:[17] "12 For there is no distinction between Jew and Greek; the same Lord is Lord of all and is generous to all who call on him. 13 For, 'Everyone who calls on the name of the Lord shall be saved.'"

Indeed, the important message of Moses in Deuteronomy 30 was that "this commandment that I am commanding you today is not too hard for you, nor is it too far away" (Deut 30:11), because it does not require any effort to save oneself anymore through following the commandments but rather a faithful desire of the heart to receive salvation by grace alone. Avoiding the huge debate related to these texts and reading them missiologically—as I will read Romans 9–11 missiologically—I can say that the emphasis lies on the fact that salvation can be applied to both Jewish people and Greeks because of the theological principle which states that God has no favorites, even if a positive discrimination was first applied to Israelites and the Jewish people. The word of faith that Paul is proclaiming is the same

---

wie die besondere Berufung der Juden dem Ev gegenüber und durch das Ev doch noch eschatologisch wahr werden können [*sic*]."

16. Still according to Harvey, *Mapping Messianic*, 2.
17. See chapter 3, "Romans 1:16–17 and 2:9–10" ("Romans 1:17").

as the one Moses was proclaiming, however, without any distinction between Jew and Greek.

Romans 10:14–21

Following his point regarding the salvation by faith for all, what does Paul say?

> 14 And how are they to believe in one of whom they have never heard? . . . 18 But I ask, have they not heard? Indeed they have; for "Their voice has gone out to all the earth, and their words to the ends of the world." 19 Again I ask, did Israel not understand? First Moses says, "I will make you jealous of those who are not a nation; with a foolish nation I will make you angry."

One question arises: Of whom is Paul speaking in this passage? Having considered for a long while that "they" was referring to "the Jews,"[18] I have to admit that Bell has convinced me on this point: the "they" concerns "Gentiles as well as Jews."[19] And this point is very important in our issue because it states that there is no question about the facts that, at the time Paul is speaking, both Jewish people and Gentiles had the good news: "When Paul wrote Romans, he clearly saw his mission as a universal one. He had fully preached the gospel from Jerusalem to Illyricum, and there was no more room in the east. He therefore hoped to preach the gospel in Spain after his visit to Jerusalem."[20] However, if these verses apply to both Jewish people and Greeks, they apply first—or particularly—to the Jewish people.[21] How has the gospel been heard by Jewish people and Gentiles? The message of salvation had been preached either through the prophets of Israel who proclaimed the good news of the kingship of their God and of peace (Isa 52:7; Nah 2:1), or through creation (Ps 19:4).[22] But who believed when Jesus rose like a young plant (Isa 53:1–2)?[23] Some have, but many have not. God has revealed himself to those who were not seeking him (Isa 65:1) and Israel should have understood this fundamental point, because Moses himself prophesied that they would be made jealous by another nation (Deut

---

18. As Hultgren, *Romans*, 389, does, for instance.
19. Cf. Bell, *Provoked*, 83–87. Cf. also Motyer, *Israel*, 119: vv. 18 and 20 addressed to the Gentiles; vv. 19 and 21 addressed to the Jewish people.
20. Bell, *Provoked*, 336–37.
21. Cf. Moo, *Romans*, 662.
22. Cf. Rom 1:18–32.
23. Cf. John 12:38–43 which refers here directly to the Jewish people.

Heilsgeschichte

32:21). Constantly God held out his hand to his disobedient people (Isa 65:2) and he still does it today.

The aim of Paul in this passage is not primarily to encourage the mission to the Jewish people but to make the Jewish people aware of two important facts. Firstly, that salvation was already present in creation and the Scriptures and that Israelites and Jewish people had the opportunity to respond to it by faith (and a few Gentiles too). Secondly, that salvation, fulfilled in Jesus, has also been revealed to the Jewish people and has been announced to the Gentiles also. It was prophesied a long time ago that those who are not a nation will respond to it. The Jewish people should not be surprised by this new reality.

If verses 14–15 clearly concern mission, I suggest that the aim of Paul here is more to defend himself against the objections of his opponents than to encourage his listeners/readers to evangelize. He wants indeed to defend his mission to the Gentiles. The Jewish people needed to recognize that, in order for the Gentiles to believe, these Gentiles needed someone to tell them the good news in a special way so they could hear it.[24] As the Jewish people had the opportunity to call on the name of the Lord in the past—and this opportunity is still available (Rom 11:1)—Gentiles need also to have this opportunity to access this salvation, a salvation by faith without the works of the law. Hence, Jewish people and Gentiles would have had the chance to hear the good news. Therefore, as Bell proposes,

> the best way to understand 10.19 is that having described the universal scope of the Christian mission, Paul now asks "Did Israel not know or understand that the gospel was for Gentiles as well as Jews, that God's purposes for salvation were universal?"[25]

The Jewish People Provoked to Jealousy for Their Salvation: Romans 11:11–15

This second important passage, which continues to discuss jealousy, deals at the same time with the salvation of the Jewish people today and at the end of time:

> 11 So I ask, have they stumbled [*eptaisan*] so as to fall [*pesōsin*]? By no means! . . . 12 Now if their stumbling [*to paraptōma*

---

24. The general revelation happened through creation. Cf. Demarest, "General Revelation," 944–45; Henry, "Special Revelation," 945–48.

25. Bell, *Provoked*, 86; cf. Motyer, *Israel*, 124. Among all the different interpretations, this is the simplest.

autōn] means riches for the world, and if their defeat [*to hēttēma autōn*] means riches for Gentiles, how much more will their full inclusion mean [*to plērōma autōn*]!

We are first reminded here that God has not forgotten or rejected his people, their stumbling is not a fall: "The one who falls down in a race loses. The one who merely stumbles may be able to continue."[26] I will talk about the metaphor of race, as well as the *plērōma* and the *proslēmpsis* of Israel, in the next section.

Bell demonstrates basically that the jealousy in question in Romans has Deuteronomy 32 as its "primary source."[27] Just before his death, Moses is told that the people will be unfaithful and will break the covenant (Deut 31:16): "They made me jealous with what is no god, provoked me with their idols. So I will make them jealous with what is no people, provoke them with a foolish nation" (Deut 32:21). Similarly, Paul refers to the consequences of this jealousy both for his present evangelization and the future restoration of Israel. In both cases, it is not a matter of evangelizing the Jewish people, let alone of a mission to the Jewish people first, but on the contrary to the Gentiles! Paul is stirring up Jewish jealousy by his ministry to the Gentiles: "Paul incites [Israel] by reversing his own order 'to the Jew first and then to the Greek,' and now apportions salvation first to the Gentile, in order to make Israel 'jealous.'"[28]

If the theoretical reasons for jealousy are easy to understand, i.e., that the Jewish people, seeing that their God has turned to the Gentiles are wanting to win him back again,[29] it is quite difficult to apply these reasons for Jewish evangelism today. Bell discerns two kinds of jealousy: "For Paul, Israel's jealousy in Rom. 10.19 is something that produces '*Leiden*' (pain): Israel is provoked to jealous anger. However, in Rom. 11.11, 14, the meaning changes to 'provoke to jealousy,' but jealousy in the good sense of the word, emulation."[30] In JFJ's brochure *Pointers on Witnessing to Jews*, David Brickner gives seven "Practical Tips" for witness to Jewish people, the fourth being:

> Give a personal testimony. The reality of God in your life is a powerful witness. Many Jewish people think that you were born a Christian, in the same way that they were born Jewish.

---

26. Stowers, *Rereading*, 313.
27. Bell, *Provoked*, 285–86.
28. Bornkamm, *Paul*, 151.
29. Cf. Bell, *Provoked*, 7.
30. Ibid., 43. An emulation which needs to be distinguished from the jealous anger of the Jewish people following the success of the apostles in their preaching: cf. Acts 5:17; 9:23–30; 13:45; 14:1–7; 14:19; 17:5; 17:13–14; 18:6, 12–17; 19:9. See Bell, *Provoked*, 315.

> Hearing how you became a follower of Jesus, how God answers your prayers, can provoke your Jewish friend to jealousy. (Rom. 11:11)[31]

Ruth Rosen goes deeper and fights against the idea that Romans 11:11 discourages us from talking clearly about Jesus to our Jewish friends. If many Jewish believers recognize as an important step in their journey to faith the obvious joy and peace of their witnessing friends (before knowing they were Christian), "this does not mean that the Jewish friend has been provoked to jealousy as described in the verse."[32] But for the daughter of the founder of JFJ, "[i]f Christian friends truly desire to live out this verse, they will be clear about what they have and how they got it: a relationship with God through the Jewish Messiah, Jesus. This is indeed provocative to a Jewish person."[33] However, we have to admit that this notion of jealousy is a hard concept to handle in the modern era, considering all the Christian anti-Semitism in history.

ORDER OF SALVATION IN ROMANS 9–11

As a matter of fact, dealing with evangelism, Paul seems to expound an order of salvation of this type: the Jewish people saved first, then the Gentiles and the Jewish people again. This *Heilsgeschichte* is totally governed by the sovereignty of God, acting according to his grace and mastering present and future:

> 14 What then are we to say? Is there injustice on God's part? By no means! 15 For he says to Moses, "I will have mercy on whom I have mercy, and I will have compassion on whom I have compassion." 16 So it depends not on human will or exertion, but on God who shows mercy. (9:14–16)

If this is the case, it will support the idea that the priority expressed in Romans 1:16 is more likely to be an *HCP*.

A Race between Jewish People and Gentiles

Commenting on Romans 11:11–15, Stanley Kent Stowers develops a very fascinating comparison between this passage and a race to illustrate the way

---

31. Brickner, *Pointers*, 3.
32. Rosen, "Provoking to Jealousy," 7.
33. Ibid.

the Jewish people may receive a prize despite their stumble: "Philo, another Jew, describes how athletes that he himself has seen have transcended bodily weakness and trauma by means of the mind's zeal for victory and fear of defeat (*hētta*)."[34] In *Quod omnis probus liber sit* 1:111, Philo indeed declares:

> Then, if those who exercise their bodily vigour have surmounted the fear of death whether in the hope of victory or to avoid seeing themselves defeated [*tēn idian hēttan*], can we suppose that those who drill the invisible mind within them, the veritable man, housed within the form which the senses perceive,—those who train it with words of philosophy and deeds of virtue will not be willing to die for their freedom and so complete their appointed pilgrimage with a spirit that defies enslavement![35]

Despite the fact that the word used by Paul (*hēttēma*) is not the same as used by Philo (*hētta*)—*hēttēma* does not seem to exist in classical Greek[36]—the comparison can be striking, all the more when Stowers continues with identifying Israel's *plērōma* with her completion of the race. He links this also to Homer's race in the book XXIII of *The Iliade*:

> The race in the funeral games has three contestants—Antilochus, Ajax, and Odysseus—instead of two. In Homer's race too, a god trips a runner. As the runners reach the homestretch, Ajax is in the lead with Odysseus on his heels. Approaching the finish line, Odysseus prays to Athena for greater speed. The goddess answers not only by giving the second place runner additional speed but also causing Ajax to slip and fall into the disgusting filth left from a cattle sacrifice made by Achilles. Although Odysseus passes Ajax and takes first prize, Ajax manages to get up and finish ahead of Antilochus. The god trips the runner who is on the verge of winning; the second place runner unexpectedly comes in first, but the runner who was tripped manages to finish the race and share the prize.[37]

The relevance of this analogy between Homer and Paul is very interesting and the impact of the Greek poet on Paul should not be dismissed.[38]

---

34. Stowers, *Rereading*, 313–14.
35. Philo, *Quod Omnis*, 1.111, 72–75.
36. Berry, *Classic Greek Dictionary*, 310.
37. Stowers, *Rereading*, 314.
38. Cf. Winter, *Philo & Paul*, 77: "Indeed, the influence of Homer on Jewish literature may reach well beyond Philo if F. E. Halleway is correct that aggadic works 'resemble Greek and Hellenistic commentaries to the poems of Homer.'" See also Wright, *Resurrection*, 32: "In so far as the ancient non-Jewish world had a Bible, its Old

Heilsgeschichte

Were the Israelites (here Ajax) not the first in the course, as Romans 9:4–5 reminds us, and seem to have been overtaken by the Gentiles (Odysseus)? Have the Israelites who rejected Jesus not slipped in the filthy sacrifice of the ox—i.e., the former sacrificial system—but managed to finish the race through the remnant (cf. Rom 11:5) and/or the Israelites grafted back into the olive tree (cf. Rom 11:24)? But who is Antilochus representing? There are many differences between Paul and Homer's text, as the following quote by Homer shows:

> But when they were now about to dart forth to win the prize, then Aias [Ajax] slipped as he ran—for Athene hampered [*blapsen*] him—where was strewn the filth from slaying of the loud-bellowing bulls.... So then much enduring, goodly Odysseus took up the bowl, seeing he came in the first [*phthamenos*], and glorious Aias took the ox.... Then Antilochus bare away the last prize [*loistheion*] ... and gave glory to the son of Peleus [Achilles], swift of foot. And Achilles made answer, and spake to him, saying: "Antilochus, not in vain shall thy word of praise be spoken; nay, I will add to thy prize a half-talent of gold."[39]

First, Homer does not talk about jealousy, despite the fact Odysseus might have felt it being in second place for the major part of the course. Secondly, Paul's letter attributes the fall to the Israelites and not to a god—or God—worshipped by the Gentiles, even if one can argue about the divine origin of the hardening of Romans 11:25. Thirdly, the vocabulary used by Homer is stranger than Paul's: *blaptō* is not used in Romans neither is there a reference to "first" or "last,"[40] let alone the words *phthanō* or *loistheios*.[41] Finally, the Jewish people did not slip in a filthy sacrifice but stumbled on a stone (*lithon proskommatos kai petran scandalous*; Rom. 9:33), i.e., Jesus.

Even though this analogy appears to be debatable, it gives us an insight into the kind of narrative that existed in Paul's time, a narrative that might have had an influence on the understanding of our issue. It would not be the first time that God would have used images and concepts known by the people living at the time his Scriptures were written.[42]

Testament was Homer."

39. Homer, *The Iliad*, Book XXIII, 552–53.

40. The case of the *aparchē* ("first fruits") in Rom 11:16 is, however, to mention; see next point.

41. If *blaptō* and *phthavō* are present in the LXX, they are not used in the NT; as for *loistheios*, it is not used in the whole Bible. The case of *hysteron* in Romans 11:31 will be examined in the next section.

42. See the elements regarding the snake in Genesis, for instance, in Blocher, *Beginning*, 142–46, or the covenants between Lord and suzerains in Deuteronomy in Vogt,

The Jewish People Are the "first Fruits": Romans 11:16

Romans 11:16 is germane to our issue: "If the part of the dough offered as first fruits is holy [*hē aparchē agia*], then the whole batch is holy; and if the root is holy, then the branches also are holy." We have already alluded to the use of this theme by Ari Sorko-Ram to encourage the mission to the Jewish people in priority.[43] However, *aparchē* in this verse is really to be taken in the context of the olive tree whose roots—i.e., Abraham and the patriarchs who first had the grace to believe and are, in this way, bearing the branches of the remnant or the believing Gentiles—are holy (cf. Num 15:17–21). In a way, two metaphors are mixed here—the reason for difficulties regarding the interpretation—but there is a clear parallel: the first fruits, like the roots, can be assimilated with the patriarchs.[44] Hence, the first fruits, being already part of the olive tree, are representing believing Jewish people who do not need to be evangelized. As a matter of fact, this points in favor of an *HCP* interpretation of Romans 1:16.

It should be noted that Paul is saying of the Thessalonians that they are his "first fruits" in 2 Thessalonians 2:13:

> But we must always give thanks to God for you, brothers and sisters beloved by the Lord, because God chose you as the first fruits for salvation [*aparchēn eis sōtērian*] through sanctification by the Spirit and through belief in the truth.

It shows at least some flexibility in the use of the word *aparchē*, since it sometimes characterizes Gentiles too.[45]

The Salvation of Israel: Romans 11:23–32

This is certainly the most debated passage regarding the final destiny of Israel according to the flesh. The exegesis of this passage is worthy of a monograph in itself, and the work has already been done.[46] I have had the opportunity myself to study this passage previously in the context of the time-schedule of the salvation of Israel,[47] and we need to keep here our focus on the issue

---

Deuteronomic Theology, 15–28.

43. Cf. chapter 2, "Other peripheral arguments" ("The first fruits of the harvest").
44. Cf. Moo, *Romans*, 698–701 for the debate and this conclusion.
45. Cf. also Rom 16:5; 1 Cor 16:15; Jas 1:18; Rev 14:4.
46. See, for instance, the thorough study of Refoulé, *Tout Israël*, 292.
47. See Fritz, "Le poids d'un mot," 42–58.

Heilsgeschichte

we raised all along: Does Romans 11:23-32 indicate the priority of Jewish evangelism today?

The mystery developed in Romans 11:25-32 follows a very studied structure:[48]

25 Οὐ γὰρ θέλω ὑμᾶς ἀγνοεῖν, ἀδελφοί, τὸ μυστήριον τοῦτο, ἵνα μὴ ἦτε [παρ'] ἑαυτοῖς φρόνιμοι,
So that you may not claim to be wiser than you are, brothers and sisters, I want you to understand this mystery:

ὅτι πώρωσις ἀπὸ μέρους τῷ Ἰσραὴλ γέγονεν **Salvation for Gentiles while Jewish hardening**
a hardening has come upon part of Israel,
ἄχρις οὗ τὸ πλήρωμα τῶν ἐθνῶν εἰσέλθῃ, **Salvation for Israel when end of Gentile salvation**
until the full number of the Gentiles has come in.
26 καὶ οὕτως **πᾶς Ἰσραὴλ** σωθήσεται· **Result: Salvation for All—Jewish people and Gentiles**
And so all Israel will be saved;

καθὼς γέγραπται, Ἥξει ἐκ Σιὼν ὁ ῥυόμενος, ἀποστρέψει ἀσεβείας ἀπὸ Ἰακώβ·
27 καὶ αὕτη αὐτοῖς ἡ παρ' ἐμοῦ διαθήκη, ὅταν ἀφέλωμαι τὰς ἁμαρτίας αὐτῶν.
as it is written, 'Out of Zion will come the Deliverer; he will banish ungodliness from Jacob.' And this is my covenant with them, when I take away their sins.'

28 κατὰ μὲν τὸ εὐαγγέλιον ἐχθροὶ δι' ὑμᾶς,
As regards the gospel they are enemies of God for your sake;
κατὰ δὲ τὴν ἐκλογὴν ἀγαπητοὶ διὰ τοὺς πατέρας·
but as regards election they are beloved, for the sake of their ancestors;

29 ἀμεταμέλητα γὰρ τὰ χαρίσματα καὶ ἡ κλῆσις τοῦ θεοῦ.
for the gifts and the calling of God are irrevocable.

30 ὥσπερ γὰρ ὑμεῖς ποτε ἠπειθήσατε τῷ θεῷ, νῦν δὲ ἠλεήθητε τῇ τούτων ἀπειθείᾳ,
Just as you were once disobedient to God but [you] have now received mercy because of their disobedience
Disobedience of the Gentiles | **Salvation of the Gentiles**
31 οὕτως καὶ οὗτοι νῦν ἠπείθησαν τῷ ὑμετέρῳ ἐλέει, ἵνα καὶ αὐτοὶ [νῦν] ἐλεηθῶσιν·
so they have now been disobedient by the mercy shown to you, so that they too may (now)* receive mercy.
Disobedience of Israel | **Salvation of Israel**
32 συνέκλεισεν γὰρ ὁ θεὸς τοὺς πάντας εἰς ἀπείθειαν, ἵνα τοὺς πάντας [...]** ἐλεήσῃ
For God has imprisoned all in disobedience so that he may be merciful to all.
Disobedience of all | **Salvation for All**

* The *NRSV*, which I have slightly changed in this verse, has decided to keep the word "now", wrongly in my judgement.
** These three dots are there to express the lack of parallelism had the second *nyn* (νῦν, "now") of Rom 11:31 be there.

It is my contention that this structure reveals a parallelism between verses 25b-26a and 30-32 and that these two passages both express three important ideas, which allow verses 25v-16a to be understood in the light of verses 30-32:

1. "a hardening has come upon part of Israel [*hoti pōrōsis apo merous tō Israēl gegonen*],"[49] which allowed the salvation of the Gentiles. This is parallel to verse 30 where it is said that the Gentiles, once disobedient, have now received mercy because of the disobedience of the Jewish

---

48. Ibid., 47.

49. Cf. Acts 7:51-53; 28:25-28; 2 Cor 3:14-15. During this period, a remnant is still saved.

people. This parallelism already recalls that the gospel went first to the Jewish people, and now to the Gentiles;

2. "until the full number of the Gentiles has come in [*achris hou to plērōma tōn ethnōn eiselthē*]": the hardening will stop, which suggests that once again large proportions of the Jewish population will be saved (not just a remnant) when the number of Gentiles that should be saved will be reached.[50] Verse 31 suggests that if they are now disobedient, it is in order that they one day receive mercy.[51] During this time of Jewish revival, the Gentiles will be seduced by Satan;[52]

3. "And so all Israel will be saved [*kai outōs pas Israēl sōthēsetai*]": if the full number (*plērōma* of 11:25) of the Gentiles has come in and if the full number (*plērōma* of 11:12) of the Jewish people has come in following this great Jewish revival, all Israel chosen by God will thus be saved, composed of all the believers from Israel and from the other nations, i.e., the spiritual descendants of Abraham, "the Israel of God" (Gal 6:16):

> *And so all Israel shall be saved.* Many understand this of the Jewish people, as if Paul were saying that religion was to be restored to them again as before. But I extend the word *Israel* to include all the people of God, in this sense, "When the Gentiles have come in, the Jews will at the same time return from their defection to the obedience of faith. The salvation of the whole Israel of God, which must be drawn from both, will thus be completed, and yet in such a way that the Jews, as the first born in the family of God, may obtain the first place.[53]

This statement is also parallel to verse 32, where Paul states that Gentiles and Jewish people have been disobedient in order to receive all—Jewish people and Gentiles—mercy.

These events will coincide with the return of Jesus Christ and with the completion of the promises given to the chosen people in history (11:29). I propose that this Deliverer coming from Zion is Jesus ("salvation is from the Jews;" John 4:22), whose death enabled the salvation of everyone who

---

50. Regarding this notion of numbers to be reached, see Rev 6:11; 7:4; Heb 11:40.

51. In my Master's dissertation, I have shown that the second *nyn* of Romans 11:31 is not the reading that should be upheld. The absence of *nyn* is attested by some old and good manuscripts and could also be considered as a *lectio difficilior* (its presence is generally considered as the *lectio difficilior*). The structure I have emphasized indicates that this *nyn* does not fit with the three intersecting parallelisms in verses 30–32.

52. See further on my eschatological considerations.

53. Calvin, *Romans & Thessalonians*, 255.

has faith in him throughout history. For the Jewish people, this salvation will be particularly powerful at the end of time, when the hardening will cease, when the full number of Gentiles will have come in, when Jesus will come back.

Having said that, I do understand that in such a debated passage some have other views, but, on the whole, I think that a balanced conclusion will at least be the one expressed by Moo: "His [Paul's] point seems to be that the present situation in salvation history, in which so few Jews are being saved, cannot finally do full justice to the scriptural expectations about Israel's future."[54] Again, Romans 11:25–32 does not seem to deal with evangelism but rather with salvation history. These verses are expressing a sovereign plan of salvation, freely decided by God himself.

These conclusions do not mean that some Jewish people will not be saved, as part of the remnant, before this massive conversion of Jewish people takes place—some will.[55] However, they lead me to discern a paradigm in salvation history: if the Jewish people were the first to be saved, they will also be the last. I do understand that this sovereign plan of salvation in its deterministic aspects and Jewish enmity regarding the gospel (11:28)[56] has led some to conclude that no evangelization of the Jewish people is necessary.[57] As for me, if the enmity toward God concerns a big part of the Jewish people, and in particular their leaders, I believe that there is still a remnant that may respond positively to the mercy of God. Moreover, because of their election, the Jewish people will know this mercy on a great scale. Hence, I understand that the Epistle to the Romans, while developing the salvation history, aims neither to discourage evangelization of the Jewish people nor to encourage evangelization of them first.

The Witness of the Gospels

In his commentary, C. E. B. Cranfield states that Romans 9–11 obliges us to consider the *prōton* of 1:16 as referring to something other than the historical predominance of the Jewish people in the *Heilsgeschichte* (especially in

---

54. Moo, *Romans*, 724.

55. In this way, the return of Israel to their land can be the preparation of this Jewish and geographical revival. Cf. Blocher, *Espérance chrétienne*, 53. Cf. also Schonfield, *History*, 174: "Before the great culmination it was necessary for the Jews to be gathered back to their own land, where finally they would repentantly accept Jesus as their true Messiah and become a missionary nation to the whole world."

56. As a verbal noun, *euangelion* may imply "the preaching of the gospel."

57. Two-covenant theology, for instance.

regards to verse 11:29).⁵⁸ At the same time, he remarks: "The paradoxical insistence both on the fact that there is no διαστολή ["distinction"] (3.22; 10.12) and also at the same time on the continuing validity of the Ἰουδαίῳ ... πρῶτον (*in spite of the actual order of salvation disclosed in 11.25f*) belongs to the substance of the epistle."⁵⁹ This well-respected scholar, considered by the missiologist Martin Pakula as a proponent of the *MP*,⁶⁰ recognizes that Romans 11 depicts a particular order of salvation: if the Jew has to be the first at the end, the salvation of the Gentiles will precede the final salvation of the Jewish people.

Furthermore, if there is one thing clearly developed in Romans 9–11 it is this: if the Jewish people were saved before the Gentiles—i.e., if they were saved first—it is also in God's plan to save them in the end, in memory of the covenant made firstly with them, *via* Abraham: "The first shall be last and the last first."⁶¹ However, I have **not** found any of the proponents of the *MP* interpretation referring, even in a footnote, to the first/last sayings.⁶² I believe the reason is that if they recognize this, they might be **forced to agree with the proponents of the *HCP* and hence understand** *prōton* in Romans 1:16 only in historical terms. I recognize that the issue raised by the first/last sayings is not an easy one exegetically. But it needs, however, to be studied in the context of this study. It is true also that Paul does not use the word "last" in Romans. Romans 11:31 would have indeed been a good place to find *hysteron* ("later")—as is the case in 11 minuscules, some Slavonic, Coptic (Sahidic and Fayyumic) manuscripts and the Ambrosiaster⁶³—instead of the disputed second *nyn* ("now"); but I have to admit that the *hysteron* reading should not be upheld (because of textual criticism and structure).⁶⁴ I think for the same reasons that the second *nyn* should not be upheld. However, even if I have to keep the second *nyn*, I believe the idea of Israel being saved later is definitely there, had this *nyn* be considered as "eschatological":⁶⁵

58. Cranfield, *Romans I*, 91.

59. Ibid., Italics mine.

60. Cf. Pakula, *First for Jews*, 3.

61. Matt 19:27-30, 20:1-16; Mark 10:28-31; cf. also Luke 13.28-30.

62. Stek, *Jew First: Exegetical Examination*, 118-30 (NB: page 123 does not exist), has rightly judged that they should be studied regarding our issue.

63. The minuscules are 33, 256, 263, 365, 1319, 1573, 1852, 1912, 1962, 2127, according to Aland et al., *GNT*, 551. Swanson, *Greek manuscripts: Romans*, 185, surprisingly, counts only five minuscules, of whom two are different (88, 1735) and, for him, the minuscule 1573 has *hymin heteron* instead of *hysteron*.

64. Cf. Fritz, "Le poids d'un mot," 25-29; 45-48.

65. Cf. Cranfield, *Romans I*, 586.

Heilsgeschichte

it seems best to treat Paul's "now" as an expression of imminence, expressing his conviction that this final manifestation of God's mercy to Israel could take place "now, at any time." ... The salvation experienced by the Gentiles means that Israel is "now" in the position to experience again God's mercy.[66]

Finally, as noticed by Bell, if "[t]he jealousy motif is unique to Romans,"[67] three strands are related to this theme in the Synoptic Gospels and hence to our issue:

4. "the rejection of Israel and the acceptance of the Gentiles,"[68] reflected in the parables of the wedding/great banquet[69] and the wicked tenants;[70]

5. "Jesus praising the faith of the Gentiles and Samaritans in the context of the unbelief of the Jews";[71]

6. "the calling of the Gentiles followed by that of the Jews, a pattern we have seen in Rom. 11.11–14 and 11.25–32, which is reflected in the synoptic saying 'The first shall be the last and the last first.'"[72]

As a matter of fact, it is my contention that these first/last sayings and earlier parables, along with the Parable of the Two Sons[73] and the episode of "The fig tree cursed,"[74] are now important to consider in our study. These passages of the Gospels deal at the same time with the covenant made between God and Israel and the shift operated since the coming of Jesus and the disobedience of many in Israel, especially the religious leaders. These texts speak of the priority of the Jewish people in salvation history as well as, for some of them, a Jewish revival at the end of time.

---

66. Moo, *Romans*, 735, who interprets the second *nyn* as "eschatological," though not using the epithet.
67. Bell, *Provoked*, 166.
68. Ibid.
69. Cf. Matt 22:1–14; Luke 14:16–24.
70. Cf. Matt 21:33–44; Mark 12:1–11; Luke 20:9–18.
71. Bell, *Provoked*, 166. Cf. Matt 8:10–12, 15:28; Luke 10:33–37, 17:16.
72. Ibid.
73. Cf. Matt 21:28–32 (cf. also Luke 15:11–32). Snodgrass notices also the connection between the Parable of the Wicked Tenants and the parables of the two sons and the wedding feast, which bracket it. Cf. Snodgrass, *Wicked Tenants*, 73.
74. Cf. Matt 21:18–22; Mark 11:12–14, 20–25. Cf. also Luke 13:6–9.

To the Jew First or to the Jew at Last?

The First/last Sayings

As already seen, I am not the first to propose a connection between Romans 9–11 and the first/last sayings. Karl Barth, in his *Church Dogmatics*, remarked the following:[75]

> But the fulness of the Gentiles—and this is the mystery of the divine decree—is to be the first to enter. That which, according to Rom. 116, naturally belongs "to the Jew first and also to the Greeks [sic]" will and must actually accrue (apart from the remnant of Israel) to the Greek first and only then to the Jew. The first are to be the last and the last first (Mk. 1031). The children of the household are to be thrust out and to be made to wait whilst strangers gathered from the four corners of the earth already sit down in the kingdom of God with Abraham, Isaac and Jacob (Lk. 1328f.). And it corresponds to this on the political level that "Jerusalem shall be trodden down of the Gentiles, until the times of the Gentiles be fulfilled" (Lk. 2124).[76]

For Barth, "the restraining and the delaying of the first of His elect to be called, and therefore the mysterious closing of their eyes, ears and hearts, is proper and necessary" because it attests and establishes "the genuineness of the election of the people of Israel as such by the restoration of the natural order."[77] For him—as for me—"All Israel" in Romans 11:26 is therefore this elected community, composed of both Jewish people and Gentiles. All Israel will be saved in the way the first will be the last in order to characterize the divine mercy, which exalts the lowly and brings low the exalted. In fact, "[t]he Jews would not be the last unless they were really the first."[78]

Similarly, Käsemann, dealing with Paul's mission, continues the same theme:

> The mission of the apostle is a colossal detour to the salvation of Israel, whereby the first become last. Still, world history cannot end until those first called have also found their way home as the last. On this tour and detour, however, Paul himself is nothing other than John the Baptist claimed to be, namely the forerunner of the end of the world.[79]

---

75. We have to admit at the same time that the thought of Barth regarding Israel can appear relatively complex to handle. Cf. the reflexion of the Jewish philosopher Michael Wyschogrod on Barth's doctrine of Israel in Wyschogrod, "Barth," 219–24.

76. Barth, *CD II.2*, 300.

77. Ibid.

78. Ibid., 301.

79. Käsemann and Bunge, "Paul and Early Catholicism," 241.

Heilsgeschichte

The formula of the first/last sayings is presented differently in the following verses:

- Luke 13:30: "Indeed, some are last who will be first, and some are first who will be last [*kai idou eisin eschatoi hoi esontai prōtoi kai eisin prōtoi hoi esontai eschatoi*]."
- Matthew 19:30: "But many who are first will be last, and the last will be first [*Polloi de esontai prōtoi eschatoi kai eschatoi prōtoi*]."
- Matthew 20:16: "So the last will be first, and the first will be last [*Houtōs esontai oi eschatoi prōtoi kai hoi prōtoi eschatoi*]."
- Mark 10:31: "But many who are first will be last, and the last will be first [*Polloi de esontai prōtoi eschatoi kai hoi eschatoi prōtoi*]."

This formula can also be found in the *Epistle of Barnabas* 6:13, though regarding things instead of persons: "And the Lord says, 'See! I am making the final things like the first [*Idou poiō ta eschata ōs ta prōta*].'"[80] Finally, in 4 Ezra 5:42, during the time of exile, Ezra asks the Lord (who appears as an angel) about the coming judgment on Jacob, and the Lord answers: "just as for those who are last there is no slowness, so for those who are first there is no haste [*sicut non novissimorum tarditas, sic nec priorum velocitas*]."[81] This last formula is quite different though—when comparing the Latin with each text—from Luke 13:30: "et ecce sunt novissimi qui erunt primi et sunt primi qui erunt novissimi," for instance.[82]

I think that the first/last sayings should neither be linked to the characterization of Jesus or the Lord as "first and last" in Isaiah (41:4-6; 48:12) and Revelation (1:17; 2:8; 22:13)—"implying that, since he is both extremes, he encompasses the continuum defined by the antithetical terms"[83]—nor to the comparison of the "first" and the "last" Adam in 1 Corinthians 15:15. It is, however, true that in some sense Jesus was first in his glory and decided to become last to serve us and die on the cross for us. Philippians 2:1–11 presents well this journey of humility.[84] We can deduce that when he rose again, he became first again in his glory. Jesus, who through his incarnation became the servant Israel of Isaiah,[85] first, then last, then first, may also parallel the fate of Israel according to the flesh, who was first, then last, and who is called to be first again.

80. Ehrman, *Apostolic Fathers*, 35.
81. Weber and Gryson, *Biblia Sacra*, 1940.
82. Ibid., 1636.
83. Aune, *Revelation 17–22*, 1219.
84. See also Isa 52:13—53:12.
85. Cf. Blocher, *Songs of Servant*.

To the Jew First or to the Jew at Last?

Luke 13:22–30

The teaching of Jesus relating to the "narrow door" (cf. also Matt 7:13–14) is announcing this shift that will occur in the first century as many among Israel will be rejected from the kingdom of God, despite their status of "sons of the kingdom" (*hoi huioi tēs basileias* in Matt 8:11–12), while the Gentiles will eat with Abraham, Isaac and Jacob: "Then people will come from east and west, from north and south, and will eat in the kingdom of God" (Luke 13:29). The identity of those coming from everywhere to eat with Abraham is quite clear.[86] Only those having accepted the grace of God without depending on their merits will be saved. This teaching is not without reference to the Parable of the Ten Virgins (Matt 25:1–13). The conclusion of Jesus is presented in this way: "Indeed, some who are last will be first, and some who are first will be last."

It is important to note that there can indeed be two ideas present in the first/last sayings: the idea of an order of time sequence as well as that of an order of rank. As a matter of fact, the last in time regarding salvation, i.e., the Gentiles, appear at the same time to be last in the sense of humility, the sinners who recognize that they do not deserve any salvation, since they are not part of Israel.[87] In contrast, those to whom the grace of God appears to have been offered first have the tendency to reject it, leaning on their works instead of counting on faith alone: they are first in the sense of their rank in the lineage of Abraham. It does not mean that all Jewish people in the first century were unfaithful, neither does it mean that all Gentiles believed, but it shows a tendency for it to be the case. This trend is reaffirmed in other passages containing the first/last sayings, although with some differences.

Hence, Luke 13:30 is at the same time expressing two ideas:

1. *Salvation History*: "Jesus closes with a saying that marks the eschatological reversal he has just described."[88] The Jewish people were the first to be saved and the saying might suggest that they will be the last, at the end of time (*reverse eschatological priority*).

2. A humbling experience as in Mark 9:35 ("Whoever wants to be first [*prōtos*] must be last [*eschatos*] of all and servant [*diakonos*] of all")[89] or in Luke 14:7–11:

---

86. Cf. Bock, *Luke II*, 1239.
87. See the Canaanite woman's faith in Matt 15:21–28.
88. Bock, *Luke II*, 1239.
89. Cf. also Mark 10:44; Matt 20: 27 ("and whoever wishes to be first [*prōtos*] among you must be your slave [*doulos*]"); 23:11–12; Luke 14:11.

Heilsgeschichte

> 7 When he noticed how the guests chose the places of honor [*tas prōtoklisias*], he told them a parable. . . . 10 "But when you are invited, go and sit down at the lowest place [*eschaton topon*], so that when your host comes, he may say to you, "Friend, move up higher"; . . . 11 For all who exalt themselves will be humbled, and those who humble themselves will be exalted."

Many among the Jewish people, who were the first according to their rank, will due to their pride be last, i.e., humbled, and the kingdom will be offered to those who consider themselves as last and who are humble.

Matthew 19:27—20:16[90]

These first/last sayings are not easy to interpret.[91] They need to be placed in the wider context of Jesus' teaching on the kingdom, a kingdom which needs to be received as a child—and not as the rich man or the two sons of Zebedee.[92] They also need to be studied in line with the Parable of The Laborers in the Vineyard" (Matt 20:1–16). In contrast to the heart of a child, the heart of the rich young man, held back by his wealth, is not fully consecrated to God: he is worshipping Mammon.[93] As for Peter, James and John, they have to learn to serve as Jesus showed them, by being the last or the servant (Mark 6:35).

Thankfully, despite their brief episode of pride and contrary to this rich young man, it is clear that the first disciples of Jesus left all to follow Jesus. If the rich young man represents the Jewish people who did not follow Jesus, the disciples represent those who followed him. Referring now to "The laborers in the vineyard," Peter, the Jew, and the other disciples, were one of the first to be hired to work in the vineyard, with the other disciples (Judas omitted).[94] According to this parable, all who are hired are saved and receive their wage. The main point is that they are hired at different times. The last hired represent those who are not worthy of being hired; they are analogous to the tax collectors and harlots invited to the kingdom of God in the Parable of The Two Sons (Matt 21:31; see further on).[95] By extension, the Gentile believers are also among them: they too will receive the same

---

90. Cf. also par. to Matt 19:27–30: Mark 10:28–31; Luke 18:28–30.
91. See Snodgrass, *Stories*, 370–81, for the different interpretations.
92. These episodes bracket our text. Cf. Matt 19:13–26 (Mark 10:13–27; Luke 18:15–27) and Matt 20:20–28 (Mark 10:35–45; Luke 22:24–27).
93. Cf. Matt 6:24; Luke 16:13.
94. So Hagner, *Matthew II*, 572 and Hultgren, *Parables*, 41.
95. Cf. Hagner, *Matthew II*, 571.

salvation as the first,[96] and it is for this very reason that those who work all day complain because they think they were not being treated fairly. It is the very grace of God that has not always been understood by the disciples.[97]

Peter, by asking Jesus what will be his recompense, claiming to be the first, arouses the lesson of "The laborers in the vineyard." Peter needed to be reminded that he was saved by grace and not because of his merits.[98] His attitude stands for those who think they are saved because of their own righteousness. By inference, Peter symbolizes all the Jewish people who thought that the "sinners" and the Gentiles would not be part of the kingdom of God. Jesus teaches him that these last are in fact first, getting ahead of them in the Kingdom. The issue is not about the order of payment ("beginning with the last and then going to the first." Matt 20:8), which is not contested, but more the idea to let the first witness the payment of the last,[99] and therefore the grace of God and their humiliation. The disciples of Jesus, who were the first to be hired and saved, will have their recompense: "you who have followed me will also sit on twelve thrones, judging the twelve tribes of Israel" (Matt 19:28).[100] But at the same time Peter needed to be reprimanded.

These sayings remind us that the offer of salvation was given first to the Jewish people and that some believed and were not led astray by the religious leaders. The good news, in my opinion, is that, since they are the first ones in terms of salvation history, they will also be the last to enter into the kingdom. I propose that Paul might have read these sayings feeling more hopeful, refusing to see them as indicating the end of the covenant with Israel. Indeed, this is what he is expressing in Romans 11:11: "So I ask, have they stumbled so as to fall? By no means! But through their stumbling salvation has come to the Gentiles, so as to make Israel jealous." They have stumbled, they will be jealous (as those who will see the Gentiles at the table with Abraham in Luke 13) but I cannot say that they have stumbled *so as to fall* finally. Paul, in Romans 11:17–24, would hence also oppose the reading of these first/last sayings by Gentile Christians who might have thought that

---

96. What they received was the equivalent of a day's wages, the amount of money necessary to live. Cf. Jeremias, *Parables*, 37.

97. Even until the end the disciples did not understand God's grace. Cf. Luke 24:25.

98. The use of *hetairos* ("friend") is not especially friendly. See its use in 22:12 (wedding banquet parable) or 26:50 (Judas' betrayal).

99. Cf. Jeremias, *Parables*, 35.

100. For Snodgrass, *Stories*, 368, it means being "told of their participation with the exalted Son of Man in leading a reconstituted Israel." See Jervell, *Theology Acts*, 75–76 and 79–80 (note 144) regarding the meaning of *krinontes* in the parallel text (Luke 22:24–30): "judging" or "ruling"?

Heilsgeschichte

they were this new nation, the nation to whom the kingdom has been given because Israel failed to produce the fruit, the last who have been made first.

I can then imagine that it is in God's plan that, at the end of time, a large proportion of Jewish people living then will recognize their need of salvation, repenting and leaning on the grace of God and their faith alone, as these first disciples of Jesus did. These sayings would then support more an *HCP* interpretation of Romans 1:16. However, Paul seems to express in Romans 11 a reverse historical order accordingly. The revival will be taking place when the "fullness" (*plērōma*) of the Gentiles has come in. The sovereignty of God remains fully present in this plan of salvation. It is God who saves and will decide this revival. We therefore need to concentrate on all the nations who have not yet heard of the gospel (as we will see, 154 Jewish peoples are considered as "unreached" today): this should take priority. The missions among the Jewish people are therefore not meaningless: we need to preach the gospel to the Jewish people today because of the remnant, and we need to be prepared for this Jewish revival, a revival which will involve the whole church but with the precious support of the missions among the Jewish people.

We are currently in the period described by Jesus in Matthew 23:37–39, as he is addressing the scribes and Pharisees: "See, your house is left to you, desolate. For I tell you, you will not see me again until you say, 'Blessed is the one who comes in the name of the Lord.'" Jerusalem "was bent upon refusing, but the offer remained open. Ironically, of course, the crowds in Jerusalem welcomed him (as one might have expected) with Psalm 118:26; but by then it was apparently too late."[101] As for me, I believe that one day, the Jewish people will be able to welcome their savior with this phrase and in this attitude:

> Repent therefore, and turn to God so that your sins may be wiped out, so that times of refreshing may come from the presence of the Lord, and that he may send the Messiah appointed for you, that is, Jesus, who must remain in heaven until the time of universal restoration that God announced long ago through his holy prophets. (Acts 3:19–21)

---

101. Wright, *Jesus*, 572.

To the Jew First or to the Jew at Last?

The Parables of the Two/Lost Sons

The parables of The Prodigal Son (Luke 15:11–32) and The Two Sons (Matt 21:28–32) are not identical, but very similar.[102] Similar to the first sayings, they use a kind of "first/last" vocabulary. For N. T. Wright, they echo in their entirety the right way to address God as "father":

> Jesus, in inviting his hearers to think of their god explicitly this way, was emphasizing a strand in Jewish tradition which implicitly carried forward his claim: those who possessed this "faith" in yhwh as "father" [faith characterized for Wright as "the appropriate stance of the covenant people before the rightful god . . . the thing which marks out the true people of Israel at a time of crisis and judgment" and which "will characterize the people who are restored after the exile"] were defining themselves as the eschatological Israel."[103]

The Parable of the Two Sons possesses major textual problems expertly highlighted by Hultgren.[104] Ancient manuscripts tend to support the reading that identifies the "first" son as the one who refuses to go at first. However, it is easy to understand the correction of some scribes who had rightly understood the identification of the chief priests (and the elders) with the son who said "yes" but did not go to the vineyard. I would propose that the "first" (*ho prōtos*) of the two sons (*tekna duo*) is in fact to be compared to the "younger" (*ho neōteros*) of the two sons (*duo huioi*) in the Parable of the Prodigal Son. In both cases the younger represents the one who did not seem to obey the father but finally did, by repenting and recognizing the sufficient grace of the father. Conversely, in the Parable of the Two Sons, the "second" (*ho heteros*) of them is in fact to be compared to the "elder" (*ho presbuteros*) in the Parable of the Prodigal Son.

These two parables express two kinds of independence the younger son desires, either by not obeying when asked to go to the vineyard, or by asking for his share of the property. If in the Parable of The Two Sons the younger is first asked to go to the vineyard, it does not mean that he is the first, i.e., the elder, but that it was customary to ask the younger first to do a task. It was certainly the usual habit in Eastern countries, as it is still the case today, depending, however, on the task asked: if it is a small task, the father will go to the younger one; if it is a task which requires responsibility

---

102. Cf. Blomberg, *Interpreting*, 186; Snodgrass, *Stories*, 268.

103. Wright, *Jesus*, 263 [261].

104. Hultgren, *Parables*, 218–19. For more details, see Swanson, *Greek manuscripts: Matthew*, 207–9.

Heilsgeschichte

(because the father is the owner of the vineyard and has slaves to take care of), he will go to the elder. In our case, it is difficult to know if "working" (*ergazomai*) in the vineyard refers to a task that requires responsibility. I would be tempted to think that, because Jesus refers to the religious leaders, the elder is concerned, and it therefore was a minor task.[105] Hence, in both of these parables, the elder is the one who is really first in the sense of rank among the children.

Hence the elder son, representing the religious chiefs as well as those who hypocritically follow the law, is the one who says he will obey but does not, or the one who appears to be faithful to the father but is not, because, "surely, to obey is better than sacrifice" (1 Sam 15:22). The younger is the one who disobeys but "later" (*hysteron*) repents and is accepted. In the Parable of the Prodigal Son he receives the first robe (*stolēn tēn prōtēn*) and enters before (*proagō*: "go first") the elder into the kingdom of God. Here, a hope of the elder going "after" the younger into the kingdom can be imagined, a hope which can be interpreted as a final revival among the Jewish leaders who, for once, will lead many to faith in Jesus.

If in these parables it is more a question of the outcasts of Jewish society (prostitutes, tax-collectors) recognizing their sin and need of salvation—represented by the lost son in the second parable—*versus* the religious leaders who consider themselves as righteous—represented by the elder son—I propose that the lesson can be extended to the Gentiles[106] who were considered worse than the worse among the Jewish people. Jewish and Gentile believers are forming, I believe, the "true people of Israel."

The Parables of the Wedding/Great Banquet[107]

In the first century, pondering the teaching of John the Baptist or Jesus, two kinds of responses were possible, dividing people into two groups: those who rejected the teaching and those who accepted it and participated in the feast.[108] If the "banquet is the symbol for salvation,"[109] the wedding banquet for the son recalls the end-time marriage of the church with the lamb.[110] In

---

105. Snodgrass, *Stories*, 270, who usually presents the "cultural information" regarding each parable, is surprisingly silent on the issue.
106. Cf. Wright, *Jesus*, 127–28.
107. Matt 22:1–14; Luke 14:16–24.
108. Cf. Hultgren, *Parables*, 220–23.
109. Bailey, "Peasant Eyes," 89.
110. Rev. 21:9. Cf. also Blomberg, *Interpreting*, 233.

each of these parables, the family and the key figures are invited,[111] but refuse the invitation, which encourages the king or the father to invite those who were not supposed to come, strangers, "both good and bad," "the poor, the crippled, the blind, and the lame"—in other words, all those who were considered by the religious leaders to be sinners and the scum of Jewish society. This is exactly what occurs as the prostitutes and the tax collectors accept the message of John (Matt 21:31-32) while the "chief priests, the scribes, and the leaders of the people" want to kill Jesus (Luke 19:47). But beyond this differentiation between these two typological groups, there is the announcement of the salvation of Gentiles, as Isaiah 25:6-9 foretells: "On this mountain the Lord of hosts will make for all peoples [lĕkol-hā'ammîm] a feast of rich food, a feast of well-aged wines, of rich food filled with marrow, of well-aged wines strained clear." For who was at this time the sinner among the sinners if not the Gentile (Gal 2:15)? Stek goes even further:

> In this it is assumed that since all Israel had been made the object of God's redemptive works and revelations in the past, the original invitees must refer to Israel as a people. If this is so, then the later wedding guests gleaned from the highways and crossroads of the realm cannot refer to "the publicans and the harlots" since these would have been included in the earlier invitation. Consequently, the gleanings from the highways and crossroads must refer to the Gentiles, and the original invitees who are rejected are Israel as a people.[112]

As a matter of fact, the banquet parables are easier to understand than Romans 11. It is easier to understand that, because the first guests refused the invitation, *therefore* there was room for the others. We have all experienced this in the organization of our own wedding or in the last minute invitation we received to another's wedding. The image of the olive tree is in this way similar: "These to-ings and fro-ings of the [divine] mercy [Rom 11:30-31] have been enlightened previously, in particular with the Olive's illustration."[113] You need to make room on the tree (pruning) in order to be able to graft other branches in (Rom 11:23). But I have to be careful not to press the meaning of the parable. It was in the plan of God from the begin-

---

111. Cf. 1QSa 2: 11-22, where it is a question of a messianic banquet: "men of renown": "priests," "chiefs of the [clans of Israel]," "heads of [family of the congreg]ation," "wise men of [the holy congregation]." Cf. Vermes, *Dead Sea Scrolls*, 159.

112. Stek, *Jew First: Exegetical Examination*, 127.

113. My translation. See Bénétreau, *Romains 2*, 122: "Ce chassé-croisé de la miséricorde a déjà été mis en lumière précédemment, en particulier dans l'illustration de l'olivier."

Heilsgeschichte

ning to save Jewish people and Gentiles; to reduce the issue to a question of room on the tree misses the point, the proof being that God is able to graft the Jewish people in again! Even if the gospel needed to be preached first to the Jewish people, the fact that the gospel Paul was preaching was rejected by the Jewish people pushed him to go to the Gentiles (Acts 13:46). Also, Moses had prophesied that God would make Israel jealous of another nation. This is where the salvation of the Gentiles enters into the plan.

At the same time, the sacrifice of Christ is linked to the rejection of the Jewish people in a very mysterious way:[114] "And now, friends, I know that you acted in ignorance, as did also your rulers. In this way God fulfilled what he had foretold through all the prophets, that his Messiah would suffer" (Acts 3:17–18). For Christ's death to be effective as a sacrifice, Christ needed not only to die, nailed to a Roman cross, but that the religious leaders, especially in the person of the priest, would present him as the innocent victim for the sin of all the people.[115] It is this death, putting an end to the sacrificial system and to the identity markers of the works of the law, which brings salvation to the Jewish people first, but also to the Gentiles. This is the new covenant. As Judah—a name highly symbolic—was delivering his master, the people as a whole finally followed their leaders and a whole generation became the accomplices of a crime which at the same time was for the salvation of all (Matt 27:25). As Israel failed to be the light of the Gentiles, Jesus took his place in this cosmic demonstration of the grace of God through his death as the faithful servant of Isaiah 53:

> Within this, the allusions to Isaiah 53 should not be regarded as the *basis* of a theory about Jesus' self-understanding in relation to his death; they may be, rather, the tell-tale signs of a vocation which he could hardly put into words, the vocation to be the "herald" of Isaiah 40.9 and 52.7, and thence to be, himself, the servant, representing the Israel that was called to be the light of the world but had so signally failed to live up to her calling.[116]

---

114. Here, we stumble over what Blocher calls the "'opaque' enigma of evil." Blocher, *Evil & Cross*, 102.

115. Cf. Matt 1:21; John 11:50; Heb 9:15–17.

116. Wright, *Jesus*, 604.

To the Jew First or to the Jew at Last?

The Parable of the Wicked Tenants[117]

The Parable of the Wicked Tenants shares in a way the same ideas but is more difficult to understand. The identification of the *ethnos* in Matt 21:43 has been especially the object of many debates.[118] In this parable the leaders—referred to at times as *hoi prōtoi* in the New Testament[119]—are targeted, who can be identified as the "first" in rank among their peers, bearing responsibility toward the common worshipping people led astray by them: they did not properly take care of the vineyard Israel,[120] and, as their ancestors had killed the prophets, they killed the prophet Jesus. If there is, in the gospels, an overall rejection of the gospel by the ones who are first/the elders and an acceptance of it by the common people at the beginning of Jesus' ministry,[121] in the end the crowds are led by the same religious leaders to despise Jesus, even to the point of death (Matt 27:22-23 and par.), while in the end the Gentiles are the object of God's mercy. The rejection of the gospel by a substantial part of Israel is therefore to the advantage of a sizeable part of the Gentiles, as taught in Romans 11. Through this, the aim of God to save all is achieved: first the majority of Jewish people, then the majority of Gentiles, and then the Jewish people again.

The leaders of the parable will be rejected—the first will be last—and the kingdom will be given to a nation "that produces the fruits of the kingdom [*ethnei poiounti tous karpous autēs*]." According to Snodgrass, this nation cannot be the Gentiles—the "you" of Matthew 21:43 cannot refer to the Jewish people—because otherwise *ethnē* would certainly have been used.[122] For him, *ethnos* cannot refer to the entire church either:[123]

> In this passage ἔθνος can only have a religious sense which is independent of a reference to a nation as a whole and should be understood as indicating the true people of God (as in I Peter 2,9). . . . Matthew and his readers may well have understood that the "new people" made up the Church, but nothing in the

---

117. Cf. Matt 21:33-44; Mark 12:1-11; Luke 20:9-18.

118. See Snodgrass, *Wicked Tenants*, 72-112.

119. Cf. Mark 6:21; Luke 19:47; Acts 13:50; 17:4; 25:2; 28:7; 28:17.

120. For Israel as a vineyard, see Isa 3:14; 5:1-7; 27:2-3; Jer 2:21; 5:10; 6:9; 8:13; 12:10; Ezek 15:1-8; 17:6-10; 19:10-14; Hos 9:10; 10:1; Ps 80:9-17.

121. This acceptance can be seen in Matt 13:2 and it lasts until the triumphant entry in Jerusalem in Matt 21:1-9.

122. Cf. Snodgrass, *Wicked Tenants*, 92.

123. Cf. ibid., 93.

Heilsgeschichte

text makes this explicit; the identification of this new group is left imprecise.[124]

I would suggest that this nation is then likely to be the people composed of all those who have put their trust in Jesus—Jewish or non-Jewish—led by the new shepherds of Israel who are embodied by the twelve disciples.[125] This nation is composed mainly of those who were the outcasts of the Jewish people, the tax collectors, the prostitutes, the humble, the sinners, the Samaritans, the Gentiles, etc., in a word: the last.

The Cursed Fig Tree[126]

The episode of the cursed fig tree should also be considered regarding our issue, not only because it belongs in the movement developed in Matthew 19:13—22:14 or Mark 10:13—12:12, but also because it presents a detail which might suggest a revival among Israel. The image of the fig tree is indeed used, less frequently than the vineyard though, to represent Israel, especially regarding the fruit produced by her.[127] In Jeremiah 24:1-10, the exiles are regarded as the "good figs" (v. 5) and "King Zedekiah of Judah, his officials, the remnant of Jerusalem who remain in this land, and those who live in the land of Egypt" (v. 8), i.e., the chiefs and those from the people who disobeyed God, are regarded as the "bad figs."

The surprising characteristic of "The cursed fig tree" event is that Jesus goes to a fig tree to eat figs out of season (Mark 11:13).[128] The main point that Jesus is trying to make is that the fig tree is cursed because it is fruitless but maybe also to stress that a day will come when it will be in fruit again.

---

124. Ibid., 93–94.

125. Cf. chapter 3, "Romans 1:16–17 and 2:9–10" ("Prōton as an adverb modulating a substantive and an adjective)" and Hagner, *Matthew II*, 623. Or as Turner, "Matthew 21:43 and the Future of Israel," 61, expresses it in the following way: "Matthew 21:33–46 should be interpreted as referring to a transfer of leadership in the kingdom from the fruitless Jerusalem religious establishment to the fruitful Matthean Christian Jewish community, led by Jesus' apostles."

126. Matt 21:18–22; Mark 11:12–14, 20–25. Cf. also Luke 13:6–9.

127. Cf. Jer 8:13, 24:1–10; Hos 9:10; Mic 7:1; Hab 3:17. There is a very close connection between the passage of the fig tree and the one of the vineyard regarding Israel and her fruits.

128. I think that solving the issue as James R. Edwards attempts with his botanical explanation is misleading (cf. Edwards, *Mark*, 339–40, where he differentiates the "early or unripe figs" (*paggim*) from the "mature figs" (*te'enim*)). *Contra* Lagrange: "We have to conclude . . . that Jesus was accomplishing a symbolic act." My translation. See Lagrange, *Marc*, 293–94: "Il faut conclure . . . que Jésus faisait une action symbolique."

To the Jew First or to the Jew at Last?

Because the event is bracketing the cleansing of the Temple,[129] I suggest its aim is to illustrate Jesus' judgment on the Jewish leaders and the unbelieving Israel, embodied particularly in the destruction of Jerusalem in AD 70. At the same time, it seems to indicate a time when Israel, at last, will respond positively to the message of Jesus, an event corresponding to the revival mentioned in Romans 11, as Richard H. Hiers points out:[130] "The term 'ever' ('may no one ever eat fruit from you' [Mark 11:14; or 'may no fruit ever come from you again!' in Matt 21:19]) translates the Greek idiom, εἰς τὸν αἰῶνα which, in turn, may render the Hebraic לְעֹלָם or עַד־עוֹלְמֵי עַד [Isa 45:17]: 'to' or 'until' the 'age (to come)' or the 'eternal age.'"[131] I will not follow Hiers in all his conclusions, but his remark may encourage the idea that the day will come when Israel will produce fruit.

The Barren Fig Tree (Luke 13:6–9)

The Parable of the Cursing of the Fig Tree calls to my mind the one of the barren fig tree, which is still more difficult to understand. "The barren fig tree" should not be linked to "The lesson of the fig tree" in Matthew 24:32–33.[132] I admit that to interpret the words "as soon as its branch becomes tender and puts forth its leaves, you know that summer is near" as referring to the revival of Israel is tempting:

> Fulfilled prophecy comes down to the destruction of Jerusalem and the dispersion of the Jews. Then there is a long interval till the budding of the fig tree will be fulfilled in the partial restoration of the Jews in unbelief to their own land. When that event takes place, all unfulfilled prophecies will be rapidly accomplished in a very brief period of time. In Isaiah, there is no chronological arrangement of visions; but there is no difficulty in pointing out those which are still future.[133]

---

129. Mark 13 and Matt 24—with the (foretelling of the) destruction of the Temple—are not very far off too. For Wright, *Jesus*, 422, the mountain of Mark 22–23, "spoken in Jerusalem, would naturally refer to the Temple mount."

130. However, this parable should not be confused with the "parable" of the olive tree of Romans 11, even if we are dealing with similar issues.

131. Hiers, "Not the Season for Figs," 397.

132. Cf. Kendall, *The Parables of Jesus*, 200. Cf. also Mark 13:28–31; Luke 21:29–33, and despite ApPet 2.

133. MacLachlan, *Unfulfilled Prophecies: to the Jew First*, iv.

Heilsgeschichte

However, as noted rightly by Snodgrass, "there is little connection between the two accounts other than the mention of the fig tree."[134] This last lesson uses the Parable of the Fig Tree without actually dealing with the fig tree, i.e., "Israel": "With this parable [of the barren fig tree] Israel is depicted as in a perilously similar position to the fruitless vineyard. Israel should have been like a fruitful fig tree, the very symbol of divine prosperity; instead she was fruitless and faced judgement."[135]

The question of the addressees of "The barren fig tree" parable is debated: should we distinguish between the vineyard as representing the people of Israel and the fig tree—which is barren—as representing the leaders, as Kenneth E. Bailey suggests?[136] This position may be strengthened by the parallel Parable of The Wicked Tenants, where the tenants also represent the leaders while the vineyard represents the people of Israel led by these leaders. However, if the religious leaders are particularly targeted, the parable aims at an enlargement: "the fig tree would naturally symbolize the religious leaders of Israel, though the principle of judgment on those who do not repent obviously applies universally."[137] Those who are following the leaders are targeted too, as the warning reported by Luke 13:1–5 just before our passage attests: "unless you repent, you will all perish just as they did." The parable shows the patience of the wine grower regarding the fruitlessness of the fig tree and it mentions the announcement that the tree might be cut soon. Snodgrass, however, due to the story of the healing of the crippled woman (Luke 13:10–17) following this text, wonders: "Jesus' ministry of restoration is effective for her, but others resist. She is healed; will Israel be restored?"[138]

Hence I can conclude that the Gospels witness to the idea of the priority of the Jewish people regarding the order of salvation, the judgment pronounced on the Temple and Jerusalem, and the leading astray of the crowds by their leaders. Some of the texts considered might also be announcing a future revival among Israel according to the flesh, as I believe it is developed by Paul in Romans 9 to 11.

ESCHATOLOGICAL PERSPECTIVES

The Jewish revival I have just explored leads me to consider eschatology. As already seen in my first historical chapter, the issue of the priority of Jewish

---

134. Snodgrass, *Stories*, 261.
135. Ibid., 264.
136. Bailey, "Peasant Eyes," 81–82.
137. Blomberg, *Interpreting*, 269.
138. Snodgrass, *Stories*, 258.

evangelization is very strongly linked to the eschatological perspective of the proponents of the *MP*: "I came to the realization that the biblical, premillennialist messianic image of the Jews and the zeal to convert that people were strongly connected—one motivating the other," confesses Yaakov Ariel in his thorough study on Jewish evangelism in America.[139] Since the motto "To the Jew first" of the London Society for Promoting Christianity Amongst the Jews has grown in parallel with the system developed by John Nelson Darby, i.e., dispensationalism, these two developments have tended to be promoted by the same teaching. And indeed, many of the proponents of the *MP* I have considered are in some way connected to dispensationalism: "The Protestant missionary efforts, motivated by the dispensationalist messianic understanding of that nation and its role in history, have continued uninterrupted throughout the twentieth century."[140]

Dispensationalism has a great variety of strands: classic dispensationalism, progressive dispensationalism, ultradispensationalism, etc.[141] Jews for Jesus cannot be categorized in that way and this subject is debated among its members. However, the influence of classic dispensationalism (or progressive premillennialism) can definitely be found, with debate between classic/historical premillennialism to dispensational premillennialism to progressive dispensationalism.[142] "Messianic Jews are deeply concerned for the future of Israel and thus eschatology is a topic of much speculation."[143] In the introduction of David Brickner's book *Future Hope*, the editor is careful to put in a disclaimer:

> Most views expressed in this book enjoy wide acceptance by followers of Jesus throughout the world. However, some of the subject matter enters areas where honest differences of opinion

---

139. Ariel, *Evangelizing*, 1.

140. Ibid., 3.

141. See Ryrie, *Dispensationalism*, for one overview of the subject. Dispensationalism is characterized by three important points: (1) a distinction between Israel and the church, (2) a literal reading of the Bible and especially of the prophecies and (3) an emphasis put on the glory of God as his ultimate purpose in the world. (Cf. 46–48)

142. We asked David Brickner the following question by e-mail (14 January 2012): "Having reread your book *Future Hope* and to avoid any confusion, can you tell me if you are classical, revised or progressive dispensationalist (I guess revised but I am not sure)? Or anything else?" Brickner answered straight away (14 January 2012): "I don't know what revised is but I would tend to identify with progressive. I like the concept of the inaugurated kingdom." Some of the differences between these strands relate for instance to the way Israel is to be differentiated from the church, the level of literality one reads the Bible, or the moment when the church will be raptured. For the various views on eschatology among the Messianic Jews, see Harvey, *Mapping Messianic*, 223–61.

143. Ibid., 223.

exist even among believers in Jesus. As to those details, this book expresses the views of the author and not necessarily those of the Jews for Jesus organization.[144]

Despite the above disclaimer, this book published by the publishing house of JFJ and edited by the daughter of Moishe Rosen (Ruth Rosen) is very instructive regarding our subject and is at least representative of the thought of the Executive Director who has a great influence on the mission.[145] This is why, while considering other works, this will be the main substance of our study. I recall that Brickner studied at Moody Bible Institute, a bastion of dispensationalism, where Charles C. Ryrie defended it well in his book *Dispensationalism [Today]*, which became a bestseller (more than 150,000 copies sold) and was reedited three times.[146] Brickner was also influenced by Hal Lindey's book, *The Late Great Planet Earth*,[147] which he says was the "most influential book in bringing Jews for Christ into the Jesus Revolution."[148] Moishe Rosen, despite believing that "Jews weren't interested in end-times prophecy,"[149] also wrote a book on eschatology, which was also steeped in dispensationalism.[150]

In this part, I need to explore how Brickner would apply his eschatological model regarding the salvation and the evangelization of the Jewish people and how his understanding of the end of time directly influences his and JFJ's practice.[151] I will then be able to bring some conclusions on the way JFJ understand the *MP*, in connection with its eschatological perspectives and suggest my proposal based largely on Romans 11 and Revelation 20.[152]

144. Brickner, *Future Hope*, ii.

145. For a presentation of "Dispensational Premillennialism," see Herman A. Hoyt in Clouse et al., *Meaning of Millennium*, 63–92.

146. Ryrie, *Dispensationalism*. Today, the stronghold of dispensationalism among theological schools would probably be Dallas Theological Seminary. It, however, supports a progressive dispensationalism incarnated by its Research Professor of New Testament Studies, Darell L. Bock (see Blaising and Bock, *Progressive Dispensationalism*, 336).

147. Lindsay and Carlson, *Late Planet*. Over 15 million copies sold.

148. Brickner, "Jesus' Return," 265.

149. Ibid., 266.

150. Rosen and Massie, *Armageddon*. Three questions are shown on the cover: "Is Israel in jeopardy? Will a Saddam Hussein rise again? What is the role of the West in the 'New World Order'?" The content of the book only reflects in part these very specific questions.

151. I speak of "End of time" instead of "Last days," an expression preferred by Brickner (see Brickner, *Future Hope*, 3) because I think that the last days began with the first coming of Jesus (Acts 2:17).

152. I had the opportunity to express this in my master's dissertation. Cf. Fritz, "Le poids d'un mot," 56–57.

To the Jew First or to the Jew at Last?

The Background

For Brickner, we are in the "last days" as depicted in Matthew 24:4–8; the actual status of the State of Israel shows that the "Time of the Gentiles" has come to an end (Luke 21:24) and the large number of Jewish people who have become believers indicates the imminent return of Christ (Matt 23:39),[153] prefiguring the prophecy of Zechariah 12:10, which will be fulfilled at the second coming of Jesus:

> The nation of Israel has turned away from Y'shua for 2000 years. But when he comes back, there will be no more turning away. The whole world will acknowledge him as the King of Israel and the Savior of the world. He will bring together Jews and Gentiles into his kingdom on the earth.[154]

Many prophecies concerning Israel according to the flesh have not yet been fulfilled, waiting for the end of the church dispensation—a parenthesis in the plan of God—and the establishment of the millennium (Rev 20):[155]

> The Millennium contains some special provisions for Israel. You see, God made some promises to the Jewish people that have not yet be [sic] fulfilled, and part of his purpose in this reign will be to keep those promises. For example:
>
> On the same day the Lord made a covenant with Abram, saying, "To your descendants I have given this land, from the river of Egypt to the great river, the river Euphrates" (Genesis 15:18).[156]

At the end of the church's parenthesis, i.e., at the beginning of the last week of Daniel 9:27, a "ruler" will make a covenant with many Jewish people. None of the believers will hopefully have to live through this awful week, but instead be taken away directly to heaven.[157] According to Brickner, in the middle of this week, the same ruler will put an end to the practice of sacrifice (which supposes a previously built third Temple) and inaugurate the Tribulation,[158] characterized by the Battle of Gog and Magog, as understood in Ezekiel 38:1–2, 8, and 9:

---

153. Cf. Brickner, *Future Hope*, 3.
154. Ibid., 86–87.
155. Cf. ibid., 18.
156. Ibid., 90.
157. Hence "The pretribulation Rapture" in Ryrie, *Dispensationalism*, 18.
158. Cf. Brickner, *Future Hope*, 18.

Heilsgeschichte

Magog, Meshech and Tubal were tribes of the ancient world between the Black and Caspian Seas, which today is southern Russia. The tribes of Meshech and Tubal have given their names to cities of today, Moscow and Tobolsk. Rosh is believed by some to be where the name "Russia" came from. When you consider that Moscow is almost a straight line due north from Jerusalem, it could very well be that a confederation of nations led by Russia are behind this first Tribulation battle. Ezekiel tells us that three other countries join with them: Persia, Ethiopia and Put. We know that Persia is Iran. The others appear to be African nations, perhaps including Libya. Together these nations attack the Land of Israel in the mountains of Israel. Their armies are placed from the northern end of the valley of Jezreel down into the areas of the south, Beer Sheva and the Negev. Jerusalem is in the middle of these mountains, and this is where the armies converge in a massive invasion.[159]

At the end of the Tribulation,[160] after the final battle of Armageddon,[161] as Jesus Christ is coming back, "Israel, so long in unbelief, now recognizes her Messiah."[162] It will be the beginning of the seventh dispensation, "The millennium," during which the Fourth Temple might be built, according to Ezekiel 40:1—43:27:[163] "In the Kingdom of God, the blessings of Israel will become a shared blessing with all of the nations of the world. God will actually restore the fortunes, not only of Jacob, but of the *goyim*, the nations."[164] Finally, at the end of the millennium, the Great Judgment occurs, inaugurating eternity, the new earth, and the new heavens of Revelation 21.

---

159. Ibid., 71. This last quotation illustrates the degree of literality the director of JFJ wants to keep to understand the end time events in perfect harmony with those biblical texts that are not yet believed to have been fulfilled. It does not mean that Brickner is rejecting symbolism in some of them, but that he does it rather rarely (Cf. 36, 117).

160. This tribulation has the aim to refine Israel. Cf. ibid., 19. For similar interpretation, see Lindsay and Carlson, *Late Planet*, 59–97.

161. Cf. Brickner, *Future Hope*, 72–75.

162. Ibid., 86.

163. Cf. ibid., 94 and *Appendix 5*, 136–37. Brickner is prudent regarding the understanding of this Fourth Temple (see the question mark in the appendix) and does not talk about the sacrifices starting again.

164. Ibid., 97.

To the Jew First or to the Jew at Last?

The Salvation of the Jewish People

Regarding the salvation of the Jewish people throughout history, Brickner notices different periods:

> From the fourth century until the 19th century, while there was certainly a small remnant of Jewish believers in Jesus they were not noticed or notable. In the 19th century, just as the Zionist movement was on the rise and present day children of Israel began returning to the Land, once again, Jewish people began coming to faith in Jesus. Since the 1900s, that pace has increased as never before since the first century, particularly in the last three decades. Now, as we enter a new century, more Jews than ever believe in Jesus.[165]

Behind this theme of a great number of Jewish people becoming Christians lies the idea that the Jewish revival is already here. It is for this reason that we should go to the Jew first: when this revival takes place, revival among the Gentiles will follow, and Jesus will be able to come back.[166] I have already dealt with the idea that there have never been as many Messianic Jews as there are today: it is difficult to have reliable data on this issue, but what seems certain is that before the Second World War, there seem to have been more Jewish believers than today.[167] Regarding the concept of the remnant, if I believe what Paul says in Romans, the remnant began to be formed at least in the first and not in the fourth century.

It is also very difficult to apprehend the idea that the church is *only* a parenthesis in the plan of God: I argue that it was in his mind from the beginning; to deny that is to deny his sovereignty. It was his aim to save Jewish people and Gentiles through Jesus: "It is precisely through the ingathering of the nations that God is keeping his promise to Israel."[168] This idea of parenthesis stems from a wrong interpretation of Daniel 9:24–27:

> The past 2000 years have been a parenthesis in Daniel's prophecy and we await that final seven . . . Someone is going to make a covenant or treaty with "the many" for one seven, i.e. seven years. It is important to know the identities of those who are party to this treaty. The context and subject matter of this

---

165. Ibid., 9.

166. Cohen, "Jew First II," as already said in chapter 2, believes that there have been more Jewish people saved in these last twenty years than in all the preceding centuries.

167. See chapter 2, "Eschatological perspectives according to Romans 9–11" (Israel's restoration").

168. Wright, *Mission of God*, 528.

Heilsgeschichte

prophecy clearly indicate that "the many" are the people of Israel. The one who makes the treaty with Israel is "the ruler," the very one whose people destroyed the city and sanctuary. Titus and the Romans were responsible for the first destruction; they were mortal enemies of the Jewish people. So will it be with this future ruler. His "treaty" will be one of treachery.[169]

I admit that the passage is not easy to interpret, but to add a period of at least 2,000 years in the middle of the week mentioned in Daniel 9:27 is to offend the text. This week would more naturally correspond to the time of Christ's ministry on earth completed at his death, with Titus physically destroying the Temple in AD 70.[170] I have no space—and it is not my purpose—to enter into more details. Suffice it to say that this dispensationalist reading of Daniel 9:27 is rather questionable.

My Proposition

Regarding all these eschatological debates, I am surprised by the simplicity of the argument adopted by the amillennialist position, which considers that, literally, there is no "millennium" in the plan of God or that, symbolically, this millennium lasts for 2,000 years and will last until the second coming of Jesus. All Christians who have already died are currently reigning with Christ in heaven.[171] What will happen when the fullness of the Gentiles enters the kingdom of God, when the number of saved Gentiles set by God is reached?[172] For me, the key to understanding this is the destiny of Satan, bound, then unbound, in Revelation 20:1–10:

> God gets the satanic activity to be bound (i.e. limited) during the "thousand years" of the time of the nations; instead of being able to seduce them as he wanted before the coming of Christ (Acts 14:16; cf. 17:30), the Serpent will not be able to prevent the evangelization of the world; toward the term however, the

---

169. Brickner, *Future Hope*, 18. Rosen and Massie, *Armageddon*, do not envisage the millennium nor the rapture.

170. Cf. Blocher, *Les Prophètes: 7e siècles, exil, restauration*, 65–75. I am myself tempted to consider this last symbolic week as seventy years, more detailed than the previous ones: at the beginning of the week takes place the birth of Jesus, at the middle of this week takes place his death on the cross and at the end of the week takes place the destruction of Jerusalem. In a way, the whole life of Jesus as a human being is a covenant with many, Jewish people and Gentiles alike.

171. For a sober presentation, see the little but powerful book of Grier, *Momentus Event*. Also, in the fashion of the "Today books": Cox, *Amillennialism Today*.

172. Cf. Rev 6:11.

paroxysm of his malice will explode (Rev 20:3b, 7–9). The time of the nations means, regarding God's plan, the fulfilment of the salvation of "all" who are expected to be saved among the nations, followed by the coming back of Israel to her God by the faith in the Lord Jesus (Rom 11:25–32). Then the end would be able to arrive.[173]

This interpretation is strengthened by 2 Thessalonians 2:3–11: "What retains the enemy is God's decree which gives to the world a delay in order the evangelization to spread out; the one who retains [the enemy], it is the Missionary."[174] The good news needs to be preached so that evil is restrained: "And this good news of the kingdom will be proclaimed throughout the world, as a testimony to all the nations; and then the end will come" (Matt 24:14). We still live in the "time of the Gentiles" where the Jewish people, apart from a remnant, remain unbelieving. There will come a time when the devil will be unbound, and fuming about the Gentiles, who will be deceived again. This will be the time of the Jewish revival, of an "eschatological revolution,"[175] preceding the second coming of Christ.

This option can be illustrated in the following way. In this salvation history, there is the following sequence:

1. In the old covenant, salvation is granted to Israel according to the flesh, while the Gentiles, seduced by Satan, are given up to their impurity. A few Gentiles, however, were allowed to have access to this salvation.

2. At the first coming of Jesus, Satan has been bound at the cross, no longer able to seduce the nations. However, Israel according to the flesh is blinded and trips on the stumbling block that is Jesus.

3. The grace given to the Gentiles ends when fullness is attained: Satan is unbound and apostasy occurs. At the same time, Israel according to the flesh experiences an end to the blindness, allowing her to

---

173. My translation. See Blocher, "Hâter," 211: "Dieu fait 'lier,' c'est-à-dire limiter, l'activité satanique pendant les 'mille ans,' du temps des nations ; au lieu de les séduire à sa guise, comme avant la venue de Christ (Ac 14.16 ; cf. 17.30), le Serpent ne pourra pas empêcher l'évangélisation du monde ; au terme, cependant, se déchaînera le paroxysme de la malignité (Ap 20.3b, 7ss). Le temps des nations a pour sens, au plan de Dieu, de réaliser l'entrée (dans le salut) de la 'totalité' prévu d'entre les nations, suivie du retour d'Israël à son Dieu par la foi en Jésus le Seigneur (Rm 11.25ss). Alors pourra venir la fin."

174. My translation. See ibid., 210–11: "Ce qui retient l'adversaire, c'est le décret de Dieu qui donne un sursis au monde pour que son évangélisation s'y déploie ; celui qui le retient, c'est le Missionnaire." The enemy is retained through the angel of Revelation 20:1 and his chain.

175. Fritz, "Le poids d'un mot," 57.

Heilsgeschichte

experience a short period of mercy ending with the second coming of Jesus Christ. It is an eschatological and symmetrical[176] revolution.

4. At the second coming of Jesus Christ, Satan is definitively thrown into a lake of fire. All of the dead rise while the last judgment takes place and the new earth and heavens are established.

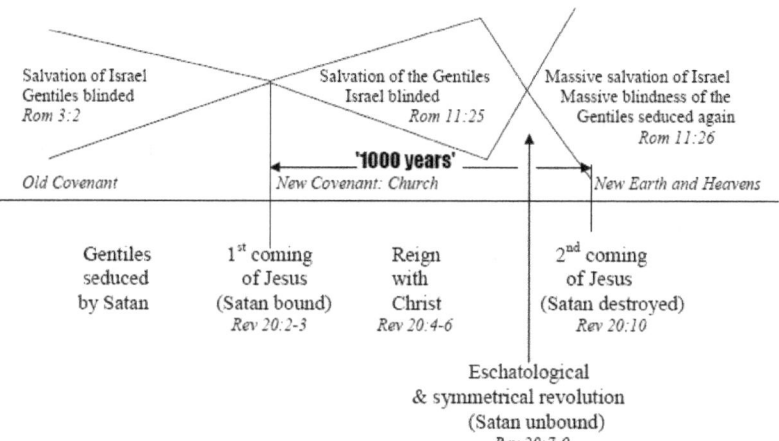

CONCLUSION

Hence, this study of Romans 9–11, whose aim was to illuminate the *MP*, has allowed me to confirm that the *prōton* of Romans 1:16 is more likely to be understood in historical terms or as expressing an advantage. These chapters—which do not have evangelism as their prime focus—do not confirm that we have to preach the gospel to the Jew first, but unveil a mystery of salvation history: if the Jewish people seem at the time of Paul—but also nowadays—hardened, enemies of the gospel, if the Jewish people have lost their primary position, Gentiles should not be too proud,

---

176. Blocher proposes: "The logic of Paul in Romans 11, with his suggestions of symmetry and chronological succession (v. 25: partial and temporary hardening until the fullness of the Gentiles has entered, in all likelihood during the 'time of the nations,' Luke 21:24), as well as other indications, allow in my point of view this thrilling expectation [that a 'great number among the Jewish people will turn towards Christ by the sovereign grace of God']." My translation. See Blocher, "Willowbank et pertinence," 9: "La logique de Paul en Romains 11, avec ses suggestions de symétrie et de succession chronologique (v. 25 : endurcissement partiel et temporaire jusqu'à ce que la plénitude des Gentils soit entrée, vraisemblablement pendant le 'temps des nations,' Lc 21.24), et quelques indices ailleurs, autorisent à mon avis cette prévision exaltante [qu'un 'grand nombre de juifs se tourneront vers le Christ par la grâce souveraine de Dieu']."

because there will come a time when God will intervene in favor of the people with whom his covenant was first made. In the same way, the passages of the gospel I have considered seem also to talk about this reversal of position, either of rank or of time, in the different first/last sayings, parables, and acts of Jesus regarding the Jewish people, especially regarding her leaders who lead many astray.

When the time of the Gentiles is fulfilled, when the full number of the nations is saved, then there will come a time of an unprecedented revival among the Jewish people, an event which will indicate the imminent return of Christ. It would be as if, to retake the Schneider's image, *Le Parc de la Verrerie* becomes the place of a big party organized for all the descendants of Eugene and Adolphe Schneider, the two brothers who started the modern industrialization of Le Creusot. Sure that nobody in the city would dare to prevent the success of the feast!

Conclusion
Study Summary—Self Critique—Further Research

STUDY SUMMARY

THE PLAN IN THIS work was to answer the following question: Must the church today prioritize evangelizing Jews over Gentiles as Jews for Jesus (JFJ) advocates on the basis of Romans 1:16? After extensive research, I must answer in the negative. The *Jewish missional priority* (*MP*), as I chose to name it, which cannot be sustained referring to Romans 1:16, appeared in the history of Christian mission to encourage *at last* the forgotten mission to the Jewish people. It does not mean that the Jewish people should not be evangelized, indeed they should, but it means that the church should consider its mission strategies independently of the *MP* interpretation through a careful consideration of both Jewish people and Gentiles in our world.

This question has been addressed in four chapters, each with different goals: one on *Wirkungsgeschichte* to understand how Romans 1:16 was understood and applied throughout history, one on *Status Quaestionis* to gather and critique all the claims of the proponents of the *MP*, one on *Propositio* to expound the exegesis of Romans 1:16–17 and one on *Heilsgeschichte* to consider salvation history from the angle of the main argument in this study.

Wirkungsgeschichte

The first historical chapter, which dealt with the different contexts the expression had been understood by our predecessors, has shown that until the beginning of the nineteenth century no theologian believed it was a duty for the church to preach the gospel to the Jew first. After many centuries in which the Jewish people had been unfortunately and shamefully put to the side by many, a new love for the chosen people began to emerge with Martin Luther, despite his change of opinion later in life. Pietism made great efforts to reconsider the Jewish people and the mission to the Jewish people, efforts validated by the rediscovery of the fact that Jesus went first to the lost sheep of Israel and that Paul usually went first to the synagogues. Romans 1:16 suddenly became the obvious motto of all these developments and a new systematic argument to sustain a new strategy to reach the Jewish people, as seen in the creation of The London Jews Society in 1809.

Despite a German impulse, the *MP* appears hence to have been largely an Anglo-Saxon movement, emerging in the UK but coming to bloom in the USA and then, evidently through North American influence, to many other nations. To my knowledge, this historical study on Romans 1:16 has never been undertaken so extensively.

Status Quaestionis

The second literary chapter, whose aim was to gather the different arguments of the proponents of the *MP*—beginning with JFJ's—through the study of two centuries of tracts, booklets, articles and books, is also original; this survey has also never been undertaken and no specific work on the subject has been published evaluating, critiquing, and countering the *MP*. This survey allowed me to discern twelve major arguments:

1. The Jewish need of the gospel
2. The Abrahamic covenant
3. The ministry of Jesus
4. The pattern in Acts
5. Romans (1:16; 2:9–10; 9:1–11:36)
6. The debt of Christians to Jewish people
7. The Christian persecutions of Jewish people in history
8. The blessings within the *MP*
9. Figures of history
10. The way not to forget the Jewish people in our evangelism
11. The impartiality of God
12. Other peripheral arguments

Conclusion

Each of these arguments has been evaluated while being detailed. Those connected to Romans appeared to be the strongest arguments to support the *MP*; this is why I chose to study this Pauline Epistle more thoroughly in chapters 3 and 4.

In this second chapter, I discovered how the *MP* had been a very ingenious way to encourage at last the forgotten mission to the Jewish people, using however wrong arguments. The desire was good, but the means were questionable. Moreover, it appears that the proponents of the *MP* are not rigorously putting into practice their thesis.

Propositio

The third chapter was devoted to studying Romans 1:16 exegetically. In Romans, Paul had the heavy assignment of explaining to his fellow countrymen that salvation was by faith alone, without the practice of the works of the law, a teaching that opened the gospel to the Gentiles in a new way. The issue in the first century was not whether the gospel was for the Jewish people—this was obvious—it was whether it was also for the Gentiles without the practice of the works of the law: "For I tell you that Christ has become a servant of the circumcised on behalf of the truth of God in order that he might confirm the promises given to the patriarchs, and in order that the Gentiles might glorify God for his mercy" (Rom 15:8–9). These verses, written by Paul to encourage the Roman Christians to respect one another in their differences, especially ethnic ones, recall that Jesus' mission statement was to come first to the lost sheep of Israel, but also to inaugurate the salvation of the nations, the fulfillment of two aspects of the covenant of God with Abraham in Genesis 12:1–3. By offering his body as a sacrifice for the forgiveness of sins for both Jewish people and Gentiles, Jesus offered a universal salvation that was achieved in effect by the suppression of the works of the law, boundary markers that differentiated Jewish people and Gentiles; since God does not show partiality (Rom 2:11). This is why Paul continued to reinforce his teaching, four times quoting Scriptures that announce this salvation for Gentiles (Rom 15:9–12). If Israel according to the flesh has a priority, it is the obvious and historical priority of being entrusted with the oracles of God as Romans 3:2 explains, oracles which allowed them to be saved first in the old covenant as well as in the new covenant. The originality of this study lies in the discovery of the fact that the *prōton* of Romans 3:2 was directly recalling the one used in Romans 1:16, thereby explaining it.

For Paul, it was necessary that the Jewish people were first made aware of the gospel that Christ had brought in the first century AD (Acts 13:46) in view of the promises given to the patriarchs, which needed to be fulfilled. It was a *historico-covenantal priority* set aside for a particular time; for the judgment on the house of Israel was at hand; as the Jewish people of the first century were the first to benefit from the gospel, they were to be the first to be judged in AD 70 (cf. the use of the *prōton* in Romans 2:9–10). If the Jewish people have been entrusted with the oracles of God first, if they have received the knowledge of God's desire through the Torah, they have also been judged first, as they were held more accountable because they had knowledge of the Torah.

Regarding the missionary practice of the church today, this does not mean that Jewish people should not to be reminded of the good news of their Messiah—they should—but that the "priority" or advantage expressed by Romans 1:16 is not to be seen in the context of a priority regarding the evangelization of the Jewish people today, but to be understood in its first century context.

Heilsgeschichte

The fourth systematic chapter was dedicated to *Salvation History*, with special reference to Romans 9–11. These chapters deal with the favor given to the people of Israel. The Jewish people were the first in time but also in rank. From the first rank they moved to the last one. God covered their eyes with a veil in order that they would not see. But a day will come when they will believe *en masse*, a day when the last will be the first, when the "full number of the Gentiles" (*plērōma tōn ethnōn*) will have come in (Rom 11:25). If chapters 9–11 affirm that the Jewish people need to be evangelized—because of the remnant (Rom 11:5)—they do not mention any priority; they depict the way God chose to deal with the salvation of all, first of the Jewish people, then of the Gentiles, and then again of the Jewish people. If the Jewish people are described by Paul as enemies of the gospel, if the Jewish people have lost their *first* rank, Gentiles should not be too proud, because a time will come when God, *at last*, will intervene favorably towards the people with whom his covenant was first made. The phrase "the first will be the last and the last will be the first," as well as the parables and acts of Jesus regarding the Jewish people that I have considered, seem also to deal with this reversal of position, either of rank or of time, and may have also been understood by Paul in this way (*reverse eschatological priority*). Finally, the eschatological schemes of Jews for Jesus, based on a premillennial dispensationalism, appear to be at least very debatable and not necessarily sustaining the *MP* interpretation, contrary to what the members of the mission might believe.

Conclusion

SELF-CRITIQUE

The interdisciplinary study I have undertaken covers many different subjects, which—for practical reasons only—have not received the attention they might have deserved. I am aware that I have focused throughout on the issues that arise from my particular dialogue with JFJ. I have largely remained within the bounds of the New Testament and have only touched upon features relating to the wider field of theology that are relevant to the discussion with JFJ.

Wirkungsgeschichte

My first chapter, which was a huge historical enterprise, is obviously not exhaustive. I do not claim to have considered all the commentaries written on Romans 1:16 throughout history. I also do not claim to have considered all the aspects of the relationship between Jewish people and Gentiles or the mission to the Jewish people throughout history. However, I think that I have presented in a fair manner the historical tendencies from the commentaries of the theologians and the works of the historians I have consulted. Also, considering the obvious Protestant-evangelical origin of this thesis, I favored this trend over the catholic or orthodox ones for the period following the Reformation.

Status Quaestionis

In my second chapter my aim was to be detailed and exhaustive, though I am aware that I might not have achieved this. I have certainly missed some writings, which, because of their titles, because of their location, had not come to be in my possession. However, I do believe that I gave a very representative idea of what has been written to promote the *MP* and this was done—to my own knowledge—for the first time in biblical studies.

Propositio

As already said in my introduction, I wrote this book more like a missiologist than a New Testament specialist. Some points could have been developed more rigorously according to the latest discoveries within the research of first century languages. Engaging with the new perspective on Paul debate would have certainly illuminated the issue. However, I consider my study of

Romans 1:16 in its context—and its use by JFJ—to be fairly thorough, using evangelical tools that were also employed by the proponents of the *MP*. In this way, I have covered the same ground as they have while going much further than they. Here again, there is such a vast amount of secondary literature that I do not claim to have read everything on the subject.

Heilsgeschichte

My last chapter aimed to link salvation history and thoughts regarding the first/last sayings of Jesus, as well as his parables and some of his public acts. Even though some theologians have made this connection before, I think it was worth developing these themes regarding the *MP*. It shows a divine design to save all via the Jewish people—and their representative Jesus—in order to show no partiality, while saving again the Jewish people *en masse* at the end, in memory of his covenant with Israel. I see here God's sovereignty and the proof that mission belongs to him. The *reverse eschatological priority* remains, however, a suggestion which can obviously be debated.

I was not able to engage with systematic themes such as "election" or "predestination," huge issues that have been the object of numerous books and monographs. Similarly, themes such as dispensational and other eschatological schemes, the impact of the Holocaust or the debate about the *two-covenant theology* would certainly have also deserved to be deepened. However, this would have led us too far astray from our main topic.

FURTHER RESEARCH

Since my work concludes that the mission to the Jewish people is not the priority in mission today, a very important question arises for the church: what is *the* priority in mission today?

Ross Paterson, director of Chinese Church Support Ministries, states it boldly: "I know many dear brothers and sisters who enjoy a bright and fruitful relationship with God, yet somehow miss His number one priority—reaching the unreached."[1] And indeed, what should be our first priority if not to wish everybody on this planet to have a chance to hear the gospel and make a decision according to their conscience? As the 2011 *Cape Town Commitment* expresses it:

> The heart of God longs that *all* people should have access to the knowledge of God's love and of his saving work through Jesus

---

1. Paterson, *Great Commission*, 11.

Christ. We recognize with grief and shame that there are thousands of people groups around the world for whom such access has not yet been made available through Christian witness. These are peoples who are *unreached*, in the sense that there are no known believers and no churches among them. Many of these peoples are also *unengaged*, in the sense that we currently know of no churches or agencies that are even trying to share the gospel with them.[2]

According to The Joshua Project, here are the "ten priority unreached peoples":[3]

People	Country	Population	% Evangel	% Adherent ▲	Primary Religion
Zaza-Dimli	Turkey	1,125,000	0.00 %		Islam
Tihami Arab	Yemen	4,413,000	0.00 %	0.00 %	Islam
Aimaq, Taimani	Afghanistan	563,000	0.00 %	0.00 %	Islam
Garre	Somalia	165,000	0.00 %	0.00 %	Islam
Turkomani	Afghanistan	677,000	0.00 %	0.00 %	Islam
Najdi Bedouin	Iraq	1,437,000		< 5.00 %	Islam
Yemeni, Northern	Yemen	11,380,000	0.01 %	< 5.00 %	Islam
Azeri Turk	Iran	14,657,000	0.00 %	< 5.00 %	Islam
Mazanderani	Iran	4,048,000	0.00 %	< 5.00 %	Islam
Mimi, Amdang	Sudan	111,000	0.00 %	< 5.00 %	Islam
Totals: 10 Peoples-by-Country		38,576,000			

Having noted that, this does not mean that the Jewish people—or should I say the Jewish peoples—do not figure among the "unreached peoples." Actually, among the 6,938 unreached peoples referenced by the quoted project, 154 are Jewish. The Jewish people, having been scattered for centuries among 126 countries,[4] have indeed a good chance to be represent-

2. TLM, *Cape Town*, 52.

3. Cf. "Unreached Listings," Joshua Project website. Online: http://www.joshuaproject.net/unreached.php, accessed April 2012. Some of the columns of this chart have been omitted for reason of clarity.

4. Cf. Joshua Project website. Online: http://www.joshuaproject.net/great-commission-statistics.php, accessed April 2012.

ed in many parts of the world, even if only with a few hundred individuals in some countries: "The traditional way missiologists identify people groups is by counting each group once per country of residence."[5] These Jewish peoples have less than 2 percent of evangelicals or less than 5 percent of Christian adherents—by this fulfilling the criteria of being an unreached people.[6] However, if we consider the size of their population, their possession of the Bible in their respective languages or their access to the "JESUS" film, they are not classified among the top unreached peoples.

This statement leads me to reflect on three practical questions that emerge when applying this priority to the unreached:

1. How should this priority guide us when approaching the evangelization of the Jewish people?

2. How should we handle the tension which could arise in the mind of a missionary facing the priorities in mission today and the call he might have received to evangelize a particular people, the Jewish people for instance?

3. How should we consecrate our time, money, and prayer to satisfy the priorities in mission today?

Reaching the Unreached Jewish People

Having considered that mission to the Jewish people should not have priority, but instead, mission to the unreached peoples, it remains that Jewish people should nevertheless be evangelized, among others, because they are an unreached people in many parts of the world. If the Jewish people are considered today by the majority of the theologians as included in the "nations" of Matthew 28:19,[7] how should we approach their evangelization today? Considering (1) the very good integration of the Jewish people in many parts of the world (which makes for instance a Jew in France a Frenchman),

---

5. Cf. "Peoples," Joshua Project website. Online: http://www.joshuaproject.net/great-commission-statistics.php, accessed April 2012.

6. Cf. "Progress scale," Joshua Project website. Online: http://www.joshuaproject.net/unengaged.php, accessed April 2012.

7. With some exceptions. See R. D. González in chapter 2 above, *ta ethnē* being translated here by "Gentiles." Perriman is bold enough to suggest that in *Romans*, "They [the Jewish people] are bracketed with 'the rest of the nations' in 1:13 (my translation), and Paul provides as the reason for wanting to 'preach the gospel to you also who are in Rome' the fact that he is under obligation both to Greeks and to barbarians, both to the wise and to the foolish, with no mention of the Jews (1:13–14)." See Perriman, *Future People*, 18–19.

(2) their metanarrative rooted in their Hebrew Bible and at the same time (3) their growing secularization, (4) the impact of the Shoah understood as a Christian operation and (5) the important symbolic presence of Christianity in Israel, how should the church consider the "unreachedness" of the Jewish people? This would be the first suggested area of research.

Call

When we think "mission," we think about "calling." How should we consider the calling of the missionary in the context of giving priority to the mission of the unreached? Can this priority, and should this priority, dictate the calling?

During my study of this topic, many told me—for example Ross Paterson—that, however, it is God who calls his missionaries:[8] "I was called sovereignly and unexpectedly to serve the church in China as a student in Cambridge in 1964, and since that time I have been blessed to witness the truly awesome ways the Lord is working in that great nation . . ."[9] The subject of "calling" is difficult to define:[10]

> There are hundreds of strange and radical things God is calling his people to do in the cause of world missions. Not everyone will hear the same call. Yours will be unique. It may be something you never dreamed of doing. It may be something you have only dreamed of doing. But I urge you to listen to the leading of the Spirit . . .[11]

The ways God uses to call someone to mission are varied—some people are even reluctant to admit this.[12] However, in my opinion, stating a preference for one mission over another could influence someone's choice of mission organization, especially if this priority is expressed during a church service or a gathering at a mission conference. The way the church should deal with this tension could be another area of research.

---

8. I had the chance to have a conversation with Ross Paterson on these issues as he visited London School of Theology on the 17th May 2011.

9. Paterson, *Great Commission*, 11.

10. Cf., for instance, Shenk, *God's Call to Mission*, 229.

11. Piper, *Nations be Glad*, 105.

12. See, for instance, Herbert Kane in Moreau et al., *Introducing World Mission*, 159.

To the Jew First or to the Jew at Last?

Time, Money and Prayer

The way we use our time, money, and prayer is an important issue in mission today. Priority is also relevant in these areas. According to their core values Christian missions want to be both efficient and excellent.[13]

At a time when the cost of a newly baptized person is evaluated at $330,000,[14] the issue is all the more important. Missions need to deal with these matters in the wisest possible way. K. P. Yohanan hence pleads for mission in Asia: "Thus, for the Western church today, priority number one must no longer be *going* but rather must be *sending* [meaning "sending money"]. Priority number two, then, should be *going as servants* to train and assist our brothers and sisters in finishing this final task."[15] Other debates regard the way money is to be used. Should we bring material aid to the Jewish people (even the unbelievers)—as does Chosen People Ministries—or only in certain cases to believing Jews—as does JFJ?[16] How should staff salaries be managed? What ministries should be favored?

Money is a delicate but important issue regarding our subject. For if the proponents of the *MP* do not usually put their thesis into practice in a radical way, two points are always strongly encouraged: prayer and money. The proponents of the *MP* will usually encourage people to pray first for and give first to the mission to the Jewish people, and especially to fight against the way churches have forgotten the mission to the Jewish people. A PhD colleague, minister in Hong Kong, was telling me how he is facing the *MP* in his own Christian ministry: some of the Christians want to orientate the church toward an *MP* in the prayer meetings and in the church budget, whereas other Christians would prefer to use the money to reach other peoples in the area. What is usually motivating the former ones is the idea that they will be blessed in return. The *MP* may hence have a powerful influence on the way we use money for mission. As for prayer, in the same way churches may have a tendency to forget the Jewish people when they are praying for mission, *MP* churches are tempted to concentrate their prayer focus on the Jewish people, forgetting the other nations. I think that we need to be balanced regarding this point. Working on this subject of time-money-prayer and priority is a third suggested area of research.

13. For JFJ core values, see JFJ website. Online: http://www.jewsforjesus.org/about/who-we-are/corevalues, accessed May 2012.

14. Cf. Barret and Johnson, *World Christian Trends*, 662. If we consider the money used in mission ($15.2 trillion a year) and the number of baptized people (45 million a year) we arrive at this number.

15. Yohannan, *Reach the World*, 53.

16. Cf. also, for instance, Health missional strategies with Fielding, *Preach & Heal*.

Conclusion

Consequences of the Results of the Study

I am conscious that my conclusions may appear to be dampening the evangelization of the Jewish people today. Obviously, this is not my aim and I would be sad if this were the consequence. I repeat myself, I am *for* the evangelization of the Jewish people today; however, regarding the question of priority, Jewish evangelism should be considered within the context of evangelism of all the nations in the world and according to missiological criteria oriented towards the characteristics of the Jewish people, just as with any other people. I admit that the *MP* has encouraged mission to the Jewish people, but my aim was to evaluate this position. I did not find support for it in the Scriptures, and, because of that, it is doing a disservice to the theological integrity of JFJ.

Will my conclusions encourage anti-Semitism? Here again, if this were the case, it would obviously not be my aim. However, it would not be professional of me to promote an unfounded thesis in order to fight anti-Semitism. Anti-Semitism needs to be fought on its own, without false theologies. Actually, the *MP* may encourage it. While studying this issue, I have heard that some people were surprised, even outraged when they encountered the *MP*. If this thesis were true, it may encourage jealousy from other peoples, jealousy, which might encourage anti-Semitism.

I would finally like to end this conclusion with an excellent statement by Piper that reminds us that the ultimate goal of mission is to worship God. Our whole life should be consecrated to this aim, for the glory of our God:

> Mission is not the ultimate goal of the church. Worship is. Missions exists because worship doesn't. Worship is ultimate, not missions, because God is ultimate, not man. When this age is over, and the countless millions of the redeemed fall on their faces before the throne of God, missions will be no more. It is a temporary necessity. But worship abides forever.[17]

If *MP* was invented to reconsider the evangelization of the Jewish people who had been forgotten, I hope my work will help missions to recover a balance, an equilibrium, regarding evangelization, for the evangelization of all the nations—Jewish people included—and for the glory of our God, for the reconciliation between the particularity of Israel and the universality of God's purpose in Christ.

Five years ago, I asked Jacques Guggenheim, a retired Jewish missionary who had worked among the Jewish people for thirty-six years,[18] if he

---

17. Piper, *Nations be Glad*, 15, 35.
18. Jacques Guggenheim is the former director of the mission *Le Berger d'Israël*

To the Jew First or to the Jew at Last?

believed that the Jewish people should be evangelized first. His short answer sums up my whole book: "Hum, we should not forget them!"[19]

(mission founded in 1936 by the *Fédération des Églises Évangélique Baptistes de France* in collaboration with the American Board of Missions to the Jews, now part of CPM). Cf. Christian Jew Foundation Ministries website. Online: http://www.cjfm.org/about-us/intl-representatives/jacques-guggenheim.html, accessed April 2012 and Le Berger d'Israel website. Online: http://www.lebergerdisrael.org/index.php?page=pages/leberger.php, accessed April 2012.

19. My translation of "Hum, il ne faudrait pas les oublier!" Almost the same conclusion is found in Schaeffer, *Finished*, 24.

Bibliography

Abasciano, B. J. *Paul's Use of the Old Testament in Romans 9:1-9: An Intertextual and Theological Exegesis.* London: T. & T. Clark, 2005.

Abbott-Smith, G. *A Manual Greek Lexicon of the New Testament.* 3rd ed. 1921. Reprint. Edinburgh: T. & T. Clark, 1964.

Abelard, P. *Commentary on the Epistle to the Romans.* Translated by S. R. Cartwright. Mediaeval Continuation, vol. 12. Washington, DC: Catholic University of America, 2011.

Aland, B., et al. *The Greek New Testament.* Reprint. 4th rev. ed. 1966. Stuttgart: Deutsche Bibelgesellschaft-United Bible Societies, 1994.

Althaus, P. *Der Brief an die Römer übersetzt und erklärt.* 1932. Reprint. Göttingen: Vandenhoeck & Ruprecht, 1970.

Anderson, G. H. "To the Jew First." *LCJE Seventh International Conference booklet* (Aug-2003) 304-11.

Anonymous. *He Kaine Diatheke.* 2nd ed. 1904. Reprint. London: British and Foreign Bible Society, 1970.

———. "Jew." In *The Oxford Dictionary of the Jewish Religion*, edited by R. J. Z. Werblowsky and G. Wigoder, 368-69. Oxford: Oxford University Press, 1997.

———. "Proselyte." In *The Oxford Dictionary of the Jewish Religion*, edited by R. J. Z. Werblowsky and G. Wigoder, 550-51. Oxford: Oxford University Press, 1997.

———. *To the Jew First.* London: The Barbican Mission to the Jews, 1930.

Aquinas, T. *Lectures on the Letter to the Romans.* Translated by F. Larcher and edited by J. Holmes. Edited with the support of the Aquinas Center for Theological Renewal. Online: http://nvjournal.net/files/Aquinas_on_Romans.pdf (accessed May 2012).

Ariel, Y. *Evangelizing the Chosen People: Missions to the Jews in America, 1880-2000.* Chapel Hill, NC: University of North Carolina, 2000.

Arndt, W. F., and F. W. Gingrich. *A Greek-English Lexicon of the New Testament.* Chicago: University of Chicago Press, 1952.

Augustine. *Augustine on Romans: Propositions from the Epistle to the Romans.* Translated by P. F. Landes. Chico, CA: Scholars, 1982.

Augustine. *Exposition on the Book of Psalms.* Translated by A. C. Coxe and edited by P. Schaff. A Select Library of the Nicene and the Post-Nicene Fathers of the Christian Church, vol. 8, 2nd repr. 1888. Reprint. Grand Rapids: Eerdmans, 1995.

Augustini, S. A. *Enerrationes In Psalmos.* Patrologia Latina, vol. 36. Edited by J. P. Migne. Paris: Migne Patrologia Latina, 1815-75.

Aune, D. E. *Revelation 6-16.* WBC, vol. 52B. Nashville: Thomas Nelson, 1998.

Bibliography

———. *Revelation 17–22*. WBC, vol. 52C. Nashville: Thomas Nelson, 1998.

Austin, J. L. *How to Do Things with Words: The William James Lectures delivered at Harvard University in 1955*. 1962. Reprint. Oxford: Clarendon, 1965.

Bailey, K. E. "Through Peasant Eyes." In *Poet & Peasant and Through Peasant Eyes: A Literary-Cultural Approach to the Parables in Luke*, 1–187. Grand Rapids: Eerdmans, 1983.

Balz, H., and G. E. Schneider. *Exegetical Dictionary of the New Testament*, vol. 1. 1990. Reprint. Grand Rapids: Eerdmans, 1994.

———. *Exegetical Dictionary of the New Testament*, vol. 3. 1990. Reprint. Grand Rapids: Eerdmans, 1994.

Barclay, W. *The Daily Study Bible: The Letter to the Romans*. 1955. Reprint. Edinburgh: St. Andrew, 1975.

Barnett, P. W. "Was Paul's Grace-Based Gospel True to Jesus?" In *Paul as Missionary: Identity, Activity, Theology, and Practice*, edited by T. J. Burke and B. S. Rosner, 99–111. London: T. & T. Clark, 2011.

Barrett, C. K. *A Commentary on The Epistle to the Romans*. BNTC. London: A. & C. Black, 1957.

———. *A Critical and Exegetical Commentary on the Acts of the Apostles*, vol. 1 on Acts I–XIV. Edinburgh: T. & T. Clark, 1994.

Barrett, D. B. and T. M. Johnson, *World Christian Trends AD 30–AD 2200: Interpreting the Annual Christian Megacensus*. Pasadena, CA: William Carey Library, 2001.

Barron, A. *Biblical Basis for Jewish Evangelism*. Unpublished Jews for Jesus Training Lesson, 1990.

Barth, K. *Church Dogmatics II.2: The Doctrine of God*. Translated by G. W. Bromiley, J. C. Campbell, et al. Edited by G. W. Bromiley and T. F. Torrance. Edinburgh: T. & T. Clark, 1957.

———. *The Epistle to the Romans*. Translated by E. C. Hoskyns. 1933. Reprint. Oxford: Oxford University Press, 1968.

Bauckham, R. *Bible and Mission: Christian Witness in a Postmodern World. Easneye & Frumentius Lectures*. Carlisle, UK: Paternoster, 2003.

Bauer, W., et al. *A Greek-English Lexicon of the New Testament and Other Early Christian Literature*. 3rd ed. 1957. Reprint. Chicago: University of Chicago Press, 2000.

———. *A Greek-English Lexicon of the New Testament and Other Early Christian Literature*. 4th ed. Chicago: University of Chicago Press, 1952.

Baum, G. *The Jews and the Gospel: A Re-examination of The New Testament*. London: Bloomsbury, 1961.

Beasley-Murray, G. R. *John*. WBC, vol. 36. Waco, TX: Word, 1987.

Beker, J. C. "The Faithfulness of God and the Priority of Israel in Paul's Letter to the Romans." In *The Romans Debate*, rev. ed., edited by K. P. Donfried, 327–32. Peabody, MA: Hendrickson, 2009.

Bell, R. H. *No One Seeks for God: An Exegetical and Theological Study of Romans 1.18—3.20*. Tübingen: Mohr, 1998.

———. *Provoked to Jealousy: The Origin and Purpose of the Jealousy Motif in Romans 9–11*. WUNT 2. Reihe 63. Tübingen: Mohr, 1994.

Bénétreau, S. *L'Épître de Paul aux Romains*, vol. 1. CEB. Vaux-sur-Seine: Édifac, 1996.

———. *L'Épître de Paul aux Romains*, vol. 2. CEB. Vaux-sur-Seine: Édifac, 1997.

Berry, G. R. *The Classic Greek Dictionary*. Classic Series, 10th repr. Chicago: Follett, 1948.

Bibliography

Bietz, K. H. *To the Jew First: Romans 1:16*. Eureka, CA: Hebrew Christian, 1973.
Bjoraker, B. "'To the Jew First . . .': The Meaning of Jewish Priority in World Evangelism." *IJFM* 21.3 (2004) 110–16.
Black, M. *Romans*. NCB. London: Oliphants, 1973.
Blaising, C. A. and D. L. Bock. *Progressive Dispensationalism*. 1993. Reprint. Grand Rapids: BridgePoint, 2000.
Blass, F., and A. Debrunner. *A Greek Grammar of the New Testament and Other Early Christian Literature*. Translated by R. W. Funk. Chicago: University of Chicago Press, 1961.
Blocher, H. *Evil and the Cross: Christian Thought and the Problem of Evil*. Translated by D. G. Preston. 1990. Reprint. Leicester, UK: Apollos, 1994.
———. "Hâter la parousie du Christ!" In *La Bible au microscope: Exégèse de théologie biblique du Nouveau Testament*, vol. 2, 209–11. 1997. Reprint. Vaux-sur-Seine: Edifac, 2010.
———. *In the Beginning: The Opening Chapters of Genesis*. Translated by D. G. Preston. 1979. Reprint. Leicester, UK: InterVarsity, 1984.
———. *L'Espérance chrétienne*. Eclairages, Charols-Vaux-sur-Seine: Excelsis-Edifac, 2012.
———. "La déclaration de Willowbank et sa pertinence aujourd'hui." *Théologie Évangélique* 2.1 (2003) 3–20.
———. *Les Prophètes: 7e siècles, exil, restauration*. 3e partie, Vaux-sur-Seine: Cours non plublié (notes de Laurent Clémenceau), 1993.
———. "Post-Holocaust/Shoah Theology." *Mishkan* 65 (2010) 5–19.
———. *Songs of the Servant*. London: InterVarsity, 1975.
———. "Two Covenant Theology and Its Implications for Jewish Missions." In *Jesus, Salvation and the Jewish People: The Uniqueness of Jesus and Jewish Evangelism*, edited by D. Parker, 184–208. Milton Keynes, UK: Paternoster, 2011.
Blomberg, C. L. *Interpreting the Parables*. Downers Grove, IL: InterVarsity, 1990.
Bock, D. L. *Luke, vol. 2: 9:51—24:53*. Grand Rapids: Baker, 1996.
Bock, D. L., and M. Glaser, editors. *To the Jew First: The Case for Jewish Evangelism in Scripture and History*. Grand Rapids: Kregel, 2008.
Bohak, G. "God Fearers." In *The Oxford Dictionary of the Jewish Religion*, edited by R. J. Z. Werblowsky and G. Wigoder, 279. Oxford: Oxford University Press, 1997.
Bonar, A. A. *Memoir and Remains of Robert Murray M'Cheyne*. 1844. Reprint. London: Oliphant, 1892.
Borgen, P., et al. *The Philo Concordance Database, in Greek, with Lemmatization and Morphological Tagging*. Bodø, Norway: Bodø University College, 2005.
Bornkamm, G. "The Letter to the Romans as Paul's Last Will and Testament." 1963. In *The Romans Debate*, rev. ed., edited by K. P. Donfried, 16–28. Peabody, MA: Hendrickson, 2009.
———. *Paul*. Translated by D. M. G. Stalker. London: Hodder and Stoughton, 1969.
Boston, T. *The Whole Works of the Late Reverend Thomas Boston of Ettrick. c. 1710–30*, vol. 3. Edited by S. M'Millan. Reprint. Aberdeen: King, 1848.
Bowen, R. *A Guide to Romans*. TEF Study Guide 11, London: SPCK, 1975.
Bray, G., editor. *Ancient Christian Commentary on Scripture: New Testament, vol. VI: Romans*. Downers Grove, IL: InterVarsity, 1998.
Brickner, D. "Chosen for What." In *Southeast Christian Church*. No pages. Louisville, KY: Sermon audio, n.d.

Bibliography

———. "First and Also." *JFJNL* 5.5771 (2011) 1–2.
———. "First Things." *JFJNL* 5.5765 (2005) 1–2.
———. *Future Hope: A Jewish Christian Look at the End of the World.* 2nd ed. 1999. Reprint. San Francisco: Purple Pomegranate, 2002.
———. "Give a Gospel Shout." *JFJNL* 9.5758 (1998) 1–2.
———. "Jesus' Return, Our Blessed Hope." In *Jews and the Gospel at the End of History: A Tribute to Moishe Rosen*, edited by J. Congdon, 261–71. Grand Rapids: Kregel, 2009.
———. "Jews Proclaim Gospel throughout New York Area!" *JFJNL* 1.5767 (2006) 12.
———. "Moishe Rosen's Yahrzeit." 5th July 2011 *Realtime*. No pages. Online: http://jewsforjesus.org/publications/realtime/95/01 (accessed March 2012).
———. "One Day in Wasilla." Jews for Jesus blog, 9th September 2008. No pages. Online: http://jewsforjesus.org/blog/20080909 (accessed February 2011).
———. *Pointers on Winessing to Jews.* San Francisco: JFJ, 2000.
———. "Reflections on Jews in Russia." *JFJNL* 11.5761 (2011) 1–2.
———. "Still Under Construction." 16th March 2011 *Realtime*. No pages. Online: http://www.jewsforjesus.org/publications/realtime/93/01?rt93 (accessed March 2011).
———. "The What and the Why." *JFJNL* 3.5764 (2003) 1–2.
———. "What Can We Expect?" *JFJNL* 8.5762 (2002) 1–2.
———. "What Do We Think about Modern Israel?" April 1998 *Jews for Jesus Prayer Letter*. No pages. Online: http://www.new-life.net/israel.htm (No longer accessible).
———. "Where Is the Power?" *JFJNL* 11.5767 (2007) 1–2.
Brickner, D. N. "Jewish Resistance to the Gospel." In *Evangelical Missiological Society Conference*, I.A–III. Santa Clara, November 1997.
Brindle, W. A. "'To the Jew First: Rhetoric, Strategy, History, or Theology?'" *BiblSac* 159.634 (2002) 221–33.
Briscoe, D. S. *Romans.* TCC, 6. 1982. Reprint. Waco, TX: Word, 1986.
Broadie, A. *The Mission of Israel.* SI 7. Edinburgh: Handsel, 1989.
Bruce, F. F. *The Epistle of Paul to the Romans: An Introduction and Commentary.* TNTC. London: Tyndale, 1963.
———. *The Hard Sayings of Jesus.* Downers Grove, IL: InterVarsity, 1983.
———. "Interpretation of the Bible." In *EDT*, edited by W. A. Elwell, 565–68. Grand Rapids: Baker, 1995.
———. "The Romans Debate-Continued." 1981–82. In *The Romans Debate*, rev. ed., edited by K. P. Donfried, 175–94. Peabody, MA: Hendrickson, 2009.
Brunner, E. *The Letter to the Romans: A Commentary.* German ed. 1938. Translated by H. A. Kennedy. 1959. Reprint. Philadelphia: Westminster, 1961.
Bultmann, R. C. "Der Stil der paulinischen Predigt und die kynisch-stoische Diatribe." PhD thesis, Göttingen, 1910.
Burchartz, A. "The Heart of Our Mission among the Jews. LCJE European Conference, Bernhäuser Forst, Stuttgart, 30 October 1996." *LCJE Bulletin* 47 (February 1997) 15–18.
Burge, G. M. *Jesus and the Land: The New Testament Challenge to "Holy Land" Theology.* London: SPCK, 2010.
Burk, J. C. F. *A Memoir of the Life and Writings of John Albert Bengel.* Translated by R. F. Walker. London: Ball, 1837.

Bibliography

Calvin, J. *The Epistles of Paul the Apostle to the Romans and Thessalonians*. Translated by R. Mackenzie. 1960. Reprint. Edited by D. W. Torrance and T. F. Torrance. Calvin's Commentaries. Grand Rapids: Eerdmans, 1973.

Campbell, D. A. "Determining the Gospel through Rhetorical Analysis in Paul's Letter to the Romans Christians." In *Gospel in Paul: Studies on Corinthians, Galatians and Romans for Richard N. Longenecker*, edited by L. A. Jervis and P. Richardson, 315–36. JNTSS 108. Sheffield, UK: Sheffield Academic Press, 1994.

Carey, W. *An Enquiry into the Obligations of Christians to Use Means for the Conversion of the Heathens*. 1792. Reprint. Champaign, IL: Book Jungle, 2011.

Carson, D. A., et al. *Justification and Variegated Nomism: Volume 1—The Complexities of Second Temple Judaism*. Tübingen: Mohr, 2001.

———. *Justification and Variegated Nomism: Volume 2—The Paradoxes of Paul*. Tübingen: Mohr, 2004.

Childs, B. S. *Isaiah*. 1st ed. Louisville, KY: Westminster John Knox, 2001.

Clarke, A. *Romans*. HBCCN, vol. 5. London: Tegg, 1857.

Clouse, R. G. "The Rebirth of Millenarianism." In *Puritans, the Millenium and the Future of Israel: Puritan Eschatology, 1600 to 1660*, edited by P. Toon, 42–65. London: James Clarke, 1970.

Clouse, R. G., et al. *The Meaning of the Millennium: Four Views*. Downers Grove, IL: InterVarsity, 1977.

Coffey, D. *Romans*. CBG. Leicester, UK: Crossway, 2000.

Cohen, G. "To the Jew First: Session II." No pages. Online: http://gatewaypeople.com/videos/124440 (accessed March 2011).

Cohen, S. "Testimony." No pages. Online: http://jewsforjesus.org/resources/ebooks/archive/cohen/cohen.pdf (accessed September 2010).

Cohn-Sherbok, D. "Israel." In *A Dictionary of Judaism and Christianity*, edited by D. Cohn-Sherbok, 79–80. London: SPCK, 1991.

———. *Understanding the Holocaust: An Introduction*. London: Cassell, 1999.

Cooper, D. L. *Is the Jew Still First on God's Prophetic Program? Vital Questions Answered*. Jewish Evangelization Series 3. Los Angeles: Biblical Research Society, 1935.

Cooper, W. R., and D. Daniell. *The New Testament Translated by William Tyndale: The Text of the Worms Edition of 1526 in Original Spelling*. London: BL, 2000.

Corporation for Promoting the Gospel among the Indians in New England and H. Whitefield. *Strength out of Weakness, or a Glorious Manifestation of the Further Progress of the Gospel among the Indians in New-England. Held forth in sundry letters from divers ministers and others to the Corporation established by Parliament for promoting the Gospel among the heathen in New England*. 1652. Reprint. New York: Savin's Reprints, 1865.

Cottier, G., and A. M. Henry. *Nostra Aetate: Les Relations de l'Eglise avec les Religions non Chrétiennes*. Vatican: Holy See, 1966.

Cottrell, J. *Romans*. The College Press NIV Commentary, vol. 1. Joplin, MO: College Press, 1996.

Couch, M. O. *To The Jew First . . . : Salvation . . . To the Jew First and Also to the Gentile*. Clifton, TX: Scofield Ministries, 2009.

COWE. "Christian Witness to the Jewish People." In *LOP 7*, 4–6. Pattaya, Thailand: Lausanne Committee for World Evangelization, 1980.

Cox, W. E. *Amillennialism Today*. Phillipsburg, NJ: Presbyterian and Reformed, 1966.

Bibliography

Cranfield, C. E. B. *A Critical and Exegetical Commentary on The Epistle to the Romans*. ICC, vol. 1. Edinburgh: T. & T. Clark, 1975.

———. *A Critical and Exegetical Commentary on The Epistle to the Romans*. ICC, vol. 2. Edinburgh: T. & T. Clark, 1979.

Crombie, K. *For the Love of Zion: Christian Witness and the Restoration of Israel*. 1991. Reprint. Bradford, UK: Terra Nova, 2008.

Cullmann, O. *Heil als Geschichte: Heilsgeschichtliche Existenz im Neuen Testament*. 2nd ed. Tübingen: Mohr, 1965.

Daniell, D. *Tyndale's New Testament: Translated from the Greek by Tyndale in 1534*. 1989. Reprint. New Haven: Yale University Press, 1995.

Darby, J. N. "Lecture 4: Romans 11." In *The Collected Writings of J. N. Darby: Prophetic No 4*, vol. 11, edited by W. Kelly, 65–78. Kingston-on-Thames, UK: Stow Hill Bible and Tract Depot, n.d.

———. "Progress of Evil on the Earth." In *The Collected Writings of J. N. Darby: Prophetic*, vol. 1, edited by W. Kelly, 470–86. London: Morrish, 1840.

———. *Synopsis of the Book of the Bible: Acts–Philippians*, vol. 4. London: Morish, n.d.

Das, A. A. *Solving the Romans Debate*. Minneapolis: Fortress, 2007.

Dauermann, S. "To the Jew, of Course!" Paper given at the 9th LCJE International Conference at High Leigh. Hoddesdon, UK, August 2011.

Davids, P. H. *The Letters of 2 Peter and Jude*. PNTC. Leicester, UK: Apollos, 2006.

Davies, G. N. *Faith and Obedience in Romans: A Study in Romans 1–4*. Sheffield, UK: Sheffield Academic Press, 1990.

Davies, W. D. *The Gospel and the Land: Early Christianity and Jewish Territorial Doctrine*. Berkeley: University of California Press, 1974.

De Bruyn, T. *Pelagius's Commentary on St Paul's Epistle to the Romans*. Translated by T. D. Bruyn. Oxford: Clarendon, 1993.

De Le Roi, J. F. A. *Die evangelische Christenheit und die Juden unter dem Gesichtspunkte der Mission geschichtlich betrachtet*, vol. 1. Leipzig-Karlsruhe: Reuther, 1884.

———. *Judentaufen im 19. Jahrhundert. Ein statistischer Versuch*. Schriften des Institutum Judaicum in Berlin, vol. 27. Leipzig: Hinrichs, 1899.

Demarest, B. A. "Revelation, General." In *EDT*, edited by W. A. Elwell, 944–45. Grand Rapids: Baker, 1995.

Dickson, B. *Romains. Commentaire biblique, une lecture pastorale*. IBG. Lyon: Clé, 2005.

Dio, C. *Dio's Roman History: On the Basis of the Version of Herbert Baldwin Foster*. Translated by E. Cary, edited by E. Capps, T. E. Page, et al. 9 vols. The Loeb Classical Library, vol. 7. London: Heinemann, 1924.

DNI, "To the Jew First: Statement about Christian Ministry to Jewish People from the National Board of Directors, the Norwegian Mission to Israel." *Mishkan* 4 (1986) 53–63.

Dodd, B. J. "Universalism." In *Dictionary of the Later New Testament & Its Developments*, edited by R. P. Martin and P. H. Davids, 1188–89. Downers Grove, IL: InterVarsity, 1997.

Dodd, C. H. *The Epistle of Paul to the Romans*. MNTC. 1932. Reprint. London: Hodder and Stoughton, 1949.

Donfried, K. P. "False Presuppositions in the Study of Romans." 1974. In *The Romans Debate*, rev. ed., edited by K. P. Donfried, 102–25. Peabody, MA: Hendrickson, 2009.

———. *The Romans Debate*. Rev. ed. Peabody, MA: Hendrickson, 2009.

Bibliography

―――. "A Short Note on Romans 16." 1970. In *The Romans Debate*, rev. ed., edited by K. P. Donfried, 44–52. Peabody, MA: Hendrickson, 2009.

Downey, A. K. "Theological Impressions." *LCJE Bulletin* 105 (Sep 2011) 16–17.

Dunn, J. D. G. *The New Perspective on Paul*. 2nd ed. Grand Rapids: Eerdmans, 2007.

―――. *The Partings of the Ways: Between Christianity and Judaism and their Significance for the Character of Christianity*. 2nd ed. London: SCM, 2006.

―――. *Romans 1–8*. WBC, 38A. Dallas: Word, 1988.

―――. *Romans 9–16*. WBC, 38B. Dallas: Word, 1988.

Edwards, J. *The Jews in Christian Europe 1400–1700*. London: Routledge, 1988.

Edwards, J. R. *The Gospel according to Mark*. PNTC. Leicester, UK: Apollos, 2002.

―――. *Romans*. NIBC. Peabody: Hendrickson, 1992.

Ehrman, B. D. *The Apostolic Fathers*. The Loeb Classical Library 25, vol. 2. Cambridge: Harvard University Press, 2005.

Elliger, K., et al. *Biblia Hebraica Stuttgartensia*. 4th ed. Stuttgart: Deutsche Bibelgesellschaft, 1990.

Ellison, H. L. *The Mystery of Israel: An Exposition of Romans 9–11*. Exeter, UK: Paternoster, 1976.

Erasmus, D. *New Testament Scholarship: Paraphrases on Romans and Galatians*. 1517, 1532. Translated by J. B. Payne, A. Rabil Jr., et al. Edited by R. D. Sider. *Collected Works of Erasmus*, vol. 42, Toronto: University of Toronto, 1984.

Erdman, C. R. *The Epistle of Paul to the Romans: An Exposition*. Philadelphia: Westminster, 1925.

Eusebius. *The Proof of the Gospel*, vol. 1. Translated by W. J. Ferrar. Grand Rapids: Baker, 1981.

Fahet, D. *The Kingship of Christ and The Conversion of the Jewish Nation*. MR, 1. Dublin: HGMC-Regina, 1953.

Feuillet, A. "La situation privilégiée des Juifs d'après Rm 3,9. Comparaison avec Rm 1, 16 et 3, 1–2." *NRT* 105.1 (1983) 33–46.

Fielding, C. *Preach and Heal: A Biblical Model for Missions*. Richmond, VA: International Mission Board, 2008.

Fitzmyer, J. A. *Romans: A New Translation with Introduction and Commentary*. AB. New York: Doubleday, 1993.

Foreman, K. J. *Romans*. LBC. Atlanta: John Knox, 1961.

France, R. T. *Matthew: Evangelist and Teacher*. Grand Rapids: Academie-Zondervan, 1989.

Friberg, B., et al. *Analytical Lexicon of the New Testament*. Grand Rapids: Baker, 2000.

Fritz, A. X. J. "L'expression 'Au Juif premièrement' selon les Pères de l'Église, jusqu'à l'Empereur Constantin." Unublished research manuscript (Diplôme d'Études Approfondies), FLTE, 2006.

―――. "Le poids d'un mot dans une théologie: Le second vūv de Romains 11.31." Masters thesis, FLTE, 2002.

―――. "To the Jew First or to the Jew at Last? Romans 1:16c and Jewish Missional Priority in Dialogue with Jews for Jesus." PhD diss., London School of Theology, 2012.

Fruchtenbaum, A. "Eschatology and Jewish Evangelism—From My Perspective." *LCJE* Sixth International Conference booklet (Aug 1999) 251–64.

―――. "Romans 1:16—To the Jew First." *LCJE Bulletin* 85 (Sept 2006) 6–11.

Bibliography

Fruchtenbaum, A. G. "To the Jew First in the New Millennium: A Dispensational Perspective." In *To the Jew First: The Case for Jewish Evangelism in Scripture and History*, edited by D. L. Bock and M. Glaser, 189–216. Grand Rapids: Kregel, 2008.

Frymer-Kensky, T. S. *Christianity in Jewish Terms*. Boulder, CO: Westview, 2000.

Gadamer, H.-G. *Truth and Method*. Translated by G. Barden and J. Cumming. 2nd ed. London: Sheed & Ward, 1975.

Gager, J. G. *The Origins of Anti-Semitism: Attitudes towards Judaism in Pagan and Christian Antiquity*. Oxford: Oxford University Press, 1983.

Gaston, L. *Paul and the Torah*. Vancouver: University of British Columbia Press, 1987.

Gates, H. L., et al. "Mark the Evangelist." In *Dictionary of African Christian Biography*. Oxford: Oxford University Press, 2011. No pages. Online: http://www.dacb.org/stories/egypt/markthe_evang.html (accessed April 2012).

Gathercole, S. J. "The Gospel of Paul and the Gospel of the Kingdom." In *God's Power to Save: One Gospel for a Complex World? Oak Hill Annual School of Theology*, edited by C. Green, 138–54. Leicester, UK: Apollos, 2006.

Gaventa, B. R. "The Mission of God in Paul's Letter to the Romans." In *Paul as Missionary: Identity, Activity, Theology, and Practice*, edited by T. J. Burke and B. S. Rosner, 65–75. London: T. & T. Clark, 2011.

Gifford, E. H. *The Epistle of St. Paul to the Romans*. London: Murray, 1886.

Glaser, M. *Biblical Basis of Jewish Evangelism*. Unpublished Jews for Jesus Training Lesson, San Francisco, 1985.

———. "His Power Changed My Life." *President's Prayer Letter* (Jan 2011) 1–4.

———. "Lessons in Jewish Evangelism from the Past Century." In *To the Jew First: The Case for Jewish Evangelism in Scripture and History*, edited by D. L. Bock and M. Glaser, 220–40. Grand Rapids: Kregel, 2008.

Glasser, A. F. *Fuller Theological Seminary News Release, 12th May 1976*. Pasadena, CA: Fuller Theological Seminary, May 1976.

———. "Jakób Jocz 1906–1983: 'To the Jew First': First Principle in Mission." In *Mission Legacies: Biographical Studies of Leaders of the Modern Missionary Movement*, edited by G. H. Anderson, R. T. Coote, et al., 523–31. Maryknoll, NY: Orbis, 1994.

———. "Jesus Changed Nothing?" *JFJNL* 1:5756 (1995) 3–7.

Godet, F. L. *Commentary on St. Paul's Epistle to the Romans*, vol. 1. French ed. 1879–1880. Translated by A. Cusin. Reprint. Edinburgh: T. & T. Clark, n.d.

Goldsmith, M. *Get a Grip on Mission: The Challenge of a Changing World*. Leicester, UK: InterVarsity, 2006.

———. *Good News for All Nations: Mission at the Heart of the New Testament*. London: Hodder & Stoughton, 2002.

———. *Matthew & Mission: The Gospel through Jewish Eyes*. Carlisle, UK: Paternoster, 2001.

———. "'To the Jew, of Course!': Response to Stuart Dauermann." Paper given at the 9th LCJE International Conference at High Leigh, Hoddesdon, UK, August 2011.

González, R. D. "To the Jew First and Also to the Gentile: Capturing the Fullness of Matthew's Commission. Part I." *Mishkan* 62 (2010) 52–68.

———. "To the Jew First and Also to the Gentile: Capturing the Fullness of Matthew's Commission. Part II." *Mishkan* 63 (2010) 20–29.

Goold, W. H. *The Works of John Owen*. 1850–3, vol. 9. 2nd ed. London: Banner of Truth, 1976.

Bibliography

Grady, L. "Jews, Christians and the Stumbling Block." 16th Sep 2006 *Realtime*. No pages. Online: http://www.jewsforjesus.org/publications/realtime/39/stumbling_block (accessed January 2011).

Grayston, K. *The Epistle to the Romans*. Epworth Commentaries, Peterborough, UK: Epworth, 1997.

Grayzel, S. *The Church and the Jews in the XIIIth century: A Study of their Relations during the Years 1198-1254, Based on the Papal Letters and the Conciliar Decrees of the Period*. Rev. ed. 1933. Reprint. New York: Hermon, 1966.

Grenz, S. J. *The Millennial Maze: Sorting Out Evangelical Options*. Downers Grove, IL: InterVarsity, 1992.

Grier, W. J. *The Momentous Event: A Discussion of Scripture Teaching on the Second Advent and Questions Related Thereto*. Belfast: Evangelical Book Shop, 1945.

Grimm, C. L. W., and C. G. Wilke. *A Greek-English Lexicon of the New Testament: Being Grimm's Wilke's Clavis Testamenti*. Translated by J. H. Thayer. 1889. Reprint. No loc: International Bible Translators, 1998-2000.

Gudel, J. P. "'To the Jew First': A Biblical Analysis of the 'Two Covenant' Theory of Atonement." *CRJ* 20 (Jul-Sep 1998) 36-42.

Guthrie, S. "Why Evangelize the Jews? God's Chosen People need Jesus as Much as We Do." *CT* 52.3, March 2008, 76.

Haacker, K. "Den Juden zuerst!: Apostelgeschichte 13,14-52." *WdW* (1984) 87-93.

———. *Der Brief des Paulus an die Römer*. THKNT. Leipzig: Evangelische Verlagsanstalt, 1999.

Haenchen, E. *The Acts of the Apostles: A Commentary*. Translated by H. Anderson, B. Noble, et al. Oxford: Blackwell, 1965.

Hagner, D. A. *Matthew 1-13*. WBC, 33A. Dallas: Word, 1993.

———. *Matthew 14-28*. WBC, 33B. Dallas: Word, 1995.

Haldane, R. *Exposition of the Epistle to the Romans*. 1839. Reprint. London: Banner of Truth, 1958.

Hall, E. *Inventing the Barbarian: Greek Self-Definition through Tragedy*. Oxford: Clarendon, 1989.

Harink, D. *Paul among the Postliberals: Pauline Theology beyond Christendom and Modernity*. Grand Rapids: Brazos, 2003.

Harkins, P. W. *Saint John Chrysostom: Discourses against Judaizing Christians*. Washington, DC: Catholic University of America, 1979.

Harnack, A. von. *Marcion: The Gospel of the Alien God*. Translated by J. E. Steely and L. D. Bierma. 1924. Reprint. Durham, NC: Labyrinth, 1990.

Harris, H. *The Tübingen School: A Historical and Theological Investigation of the School of F. C. Baur*. 2nd ed. Leicester, UK: Apollos, 1990.

Harrison, E. F. *Romans*. TEBC, 10. Grand Rapids: Zondervan, 1976.

Harvey, R. "An Introduction to World Jewish Mission." *LCJE Bulletin* 36 (May 94) 23-31.

———. *Mapping Messianic Jewish Theology: A Constructive Approach*. SIMJT. Milton Keynes, UK: Paternoster, 2009.

Heil, J. P. *Romans: Paul's Letter of Hope*. Rome: Biblical Institute, 1987.

Heliso, D. *Pistis and the Righteous One: A Study of Romans 1:17 against the Background of Scripture and Second Temple Jewish Literature*. WUNT 2nd series [2. Reihe]. Tübingen: Mohr, 2007.

Bibliography

Hendriksen, W. *Exposition of Paul's Epistle to the Romans, I: 1–8*. Edinburgh: Banner of Truth, 1980.

Henry, C. F. H. "Revelation, Special." In *EDT*, edited by W. A. Elwell, 945–48. Grand Rapids: Baker, 1995.

Hertzberg, A. "Jewish Identity." In *The Oxford Dictionary of the Jewish Religion*, edited by R. J. Z. Werblowsky and G. Wigoder, 370–72. Oxford: Oxford University Press, 1997.

Heward, S. A. *Messages about 'The Jew First.' Addressed to Young People*. London: no publisher (the only copy owned by the British Library was destroyed during the bombing of the 2nd World War), 1907.

Hicks, R. H. "Romans 1:16 and the Priority of Jewish Evangelism." *Mishkan* 10 (1989) 9–13.

Hidalgo, E. E. "Why to the Jew First?" Shalom Scripture Studies website. No pages. Online: http://www.shalom-peace.com/whytoJ1st.html (accessed December 2008).

Hiebert, T. *Habakkuk*. NIB, vol. 7. Nashville: Abingdon, 1999.

Hiers, R. H. "'Not the Season for Figs.'" *JBL* 87.4 (1968) 394–400.

Hillerbrand, H. J. "Martin Luther and the Jews." In *Jews and Christians: Exploring the Past, Present, and Future*, edited by J. H. Charlesworth, 127–50. New York: Crossroad, 1990.

Hinson, K. "To the Jew First? Southern Baptists Defend New Outreach Effort." *CT* 43.13, November 1999, 18.

Hodge, C. *Romans*. 1835. Reprint. Wheaton: Crossway, 1993.

Hoehner, H. W. *Ephesians: An Exegetical Commentary*. Grand Rapids: Baker, 2002.

Hoffman Cohn, J. *Beginning at Jerusalem: Anthology on To the Jew First, Compiled from the files of The Chosen People*. New York: ABMJ, 1948.

Holmes, M. W., editor and translator. *The Apostolic Fathers in English, after the earlier version of J. B. Lightfoot and J. R. Harmer*. 3rd ed. Grand Rapids: Baker, 2006.

Holwerda, D. E. *Jesus and Israel: One Covenant or Two?* Grand Rapids: Eerdmans, 1995.

Homer. *The Iliad*. Translated by A. T. Murray. 1925. Reprint. Cambridge: Harvard University Press, 1976.

Horner, B. E. *Future Israel: Why Christian Anti-Judaism Must be Challenged*. NAC Studies in Bible & Theology, vol. 3. Nashville: B & H, 2008.

Hultgren, A. J. *The Parables of Jesus: A Commentary*. Grand Rapids: Eerdmans, 2000.

———. *Paul's Letter to the Romans: A Commentary*. Grand Rapids: Eerdmans, 2011.

Hume, C. R. *Reading through Romans*. London: SCM, 1999.

Hvalvik, R. "'To The Jew First and Also to the Greek': The Meaning of Romans 1:16b." *Mishkan* 10 (1989) 1–8.

Jeremias, J. *Jesus' Promise to the Nations: The Franz Delitzsch Lectures for 1953*. Translated by S. H. Hooke. SBT, 24. 1958. Reprint. London: SCM, 1981.

———. *The Parables of Jesus*. Translated by S. H. Hooke. 6th rev. ed. London: SCM, 1963.

Jervell, J. "The Letter to Jerusalem." 1971. In *The Romans Debate*, 2nd ed., edited by K. P. Donfried, 53–64. Peabody, MA: Hendrickson, 2009.

———. *The Theology of the Acts of the Apostles*. New Testament Theology. Cambridge: Cambridge University Press, 1996.

Jewett, R. "Following the Argument of Romans." 1986. In *The Romans Debate*, 2nd ed., edited by K. P. Donfried, 265–77. Peabody, MA: Hendrickson, 2009.

———. *Romans: A Commentary*. Hermeneia. Minneapolis: Fortress, 2007.
Jews for Jesus. *What Christians Should Know about Jews for Jesus*. San Fransisco: JFJ, n.d.
Jocz, J. *The Jewish People and Jesus Christ: The Relationship between Church and Synagogue*. 3rd ed. 1949. Reprint. Grand Rapids: Baker, 1979.
John Paul II, P. "Redemptoris Missio." No pages. Online: http://www.vatican.va/edocs/ENG0219/_INDEX.HTM (accessed January 2011).
Johnson, A. F. *Romans: The Freedom Letter*, 2 vols. EBC, 1–2. Chicago: Moody, 1984–85.
Johnson Jr., S. L. "The Gospel That Paul Preached." *BiblSac* 128 (1971) 327–40.
Kaiser Jr, W. C. "Jewish Evangelism in the New Millennium in Light of Israel's Future (Romans 9–11)." In *To the Jew First: The Case for Jewish Evangelism in Scripture and History*, edited by D. L. Bock and M. Glaser, 40–52. Grand Rapids: Kregel, 2008.
Käsemann, E. *Commentary on Romans*. German ed. 1973. Translated by G. W. Bromiley. London: SCM, 1980.
Käsemann, E., and W. F. Bunge. "Paul and Early Catholicism." In *New Testament Questions Of Today*, edited by E. Käsemann, 236–51. London: SCM, 1960.
Käser, A. "Den Juden zuerst, aber auch den Heiden: 'Mission' im Markusevangelium. Beobachtungen einer kompositionellen Lesung von Mk 4,35—8,26." *TBeitr* 35 (2004) 69–80.
Katz, S. T., et al. *Wrestling with God: Jewish Theological Responses during and after the Holocaust*. Oxford: Oxford University Press, 2007.
Keck, L. E. *Romans*. ANTC. Nashville: Abingdon, 2005.
Keener, C. S. *Romans*. A New Covenant Commentary. Eugene, OR: Cascade, 2009.
Keith, G. A. *Hatred without a Cause: A Survey of Anti-Semitism*. Carlisle, UK: Paternoster, 1997.
Kendall, R. T. *The Parables of Jesus: A Guide to Understanding and Applying the Stories of Jesus*. Tonbridge, UK: Sovereign World, 2004.
Keown, M. J. *Congregational Evangelism in Philippians: The Centrality of an Appeal for Gospel Proclamation to the Fabric of Philippians*. PBM. Milton Keynes, UK: Paternoster, 2008.
Kessler, E. *An Introduction to Jewish-Christian Relations*. Cambridge: Cambridge University Press, 2010.
Kim, S. *The Origin of Paul's Gospel*. 1977. Reprint. Tübingen: Mohr, 1981.
Kinzer, M. S. *Postmissionary Messianic Judaism: Redefining Christian Engagement with the Jewish People*. Grand Rapids: Brazos, 2005.
Kjær-Hansen, K. "One Way for Jews and Gentiles in the New Millennium." In *To the Jew First: The Case for Jewish Evangelism in Scripture and History*, edited by D. L. Bock and M. Glaser, 292–311. Grand Rapids: Kregel, 2008.
Kjær-Hansen, K., et al. "The Uniqueness of Christ and the Jewish People." *Mishkan* 56 (2008) 1–88.
Klappert, B. "Dialog mit Israel und Mission unter den Völkern." In *Miterben der Verheissung : Beiträge zum jüdisch-christlichen Dialog*, edited by B. Klappert, 407–30. Neukirchener Beiträge zur systematischen Theologie 25. Neukirchen-Vluyn: Neukirchener, 2000.
Knight, M. "*Wirkungsgeschichte*, Reception History, Reception Theory." *JSNT* 33.2 (2010) 137–46.

Bibliography

Kreider, A. "Worship and Evangelism in Pre-Christendom: The Laing Lecture for 1994." *VE* 24 (1994) 7–38.
Krey, A. C. *The First Crusade: The Accounts of Eyewitnesses and Participants.* Princeton: Princeton University Press, 1921.
Küng, H. *The Church.* Translated by R. Ockenden. London: Search, 1968.
Kuss, O. *Der Römerbrief,* vol. 1. Regensburg: Pustet, 1957.
Lagrange, M. J. *Évangile selon Saint Marc.* Études Bibliques. 1911. Reprint. Paris: Gabalda, 1966.
Landau, R. S. *Studying the Holocaust: Issues, Readings and Documents.* London: Routledge, 1998.
LBH. *Hillingdon First Directory.* Hillingdon, UK: LBH, 2009.
LCJE. "To All Concerned with Jewish Evangelism." *LCJE Bulletin* 105 (Sep 2011) 5.
LCWE. "Jewish Evangelism: A Call to the Church." *LOP 60.* Pattaya, Thailand: LCWE, 2004.
———. "The Lausanne Covenant." 1974. Reprint. *LCJE* Fifth International Conference (June 1995) 8–12.
———. "Manila Manifesto." The Lausanne Movement website. No pages. Online: http://www.lausanne.org/manila-1989/manila-manifesto.html (accessed April 2011).
Leenhardt, F. J. *The Epistle to the Romans.* Translated by H. Knight. London: Lutterworth, 1961.
Lenski, R. C. H. *The Interpretation of St. Paul's Epistle to the Romans.* 1936. Reprint. Minneapolis: Augsburg, 1961.
Leventhal, B. R. "Christian Anti-Semitism?" *Issues: A Messianic Jewish Perspective* 1.5 (1981) 1–4.
———. "The Holocaust and the Sacred Romance: A Return to the Divine Reality (Implications for Jewish Evangelism)." In *To the Jew First: The Case for Jewish Evangelism in Scripture and History,* edited by D. L. Bock and M. Glaser, 122–54. Grand Rapids: Kregel, 2008.
Liddell, H. G., et al. *A Greek-English Lexicon.* 9th ed. 1843. Reprint. Oxford: Clarendon, 1958.
Lietzmann, D. H. *An die Römer.* HNT. 1933. Reprint. Tübingen: Mohr, 1971.
Lindsay, H., and C. C. Carlson. *The Late Great Planet Earth.* Grand Rapids: Zondervan, 1970.
Llyod-Jones, D. M. *Romans: An Exposition of Chapter I. The Gospel of God.* Edinburgh: Banner of Truth, 1985.
Lohse, E. *Der Brief an die Römer.* Göttingen: Vandenhoeck & Ruprecht, 2003.
———. "Die Juden zuerst und ebenso die Griechen." In *Eschatologie und Schöpfung,* 201–12. Berlin: De Gruyter, 1997.
Louw, J. E., et al. *Greek-English Lexicon of the New Testament Based on Semantic Domains,* vol. 1: *Introduction and Domains.* New York: UBS, 1988.
Luther, M. *Lectures on Romans.* Translated by W. Pauck. Edited by W. Pauck. The Library of Christian Classics, vol. 15. London: SCM, 1961.
———. *Lectures on Romans: Glosses and Scholia.* LW 25. St. Louis: Concordia, 1972.
MacDonald, W. *Believer's Bible Commentary.* Edited by A. Farstad. Nashville, TN: Thomas Nelson, 1989.
MacLachlan, H. *Notes on the Unfulfilled Prophecies of Isaiah. Addressed to 'the Jew First, and Also to the Gentile'.* London: Nisbet, 1868.
Madden, S. *To the Jew first.* London: BSPGAJ, 1942.

Bibliography

Manson, T. W. "St. Paul's Letter to the Romans-and Others." 1962. In *The Romans Debate*, 2nd ed., edited by K. P. Donfried, 3-15. Peabody, MA: Hendrickson, 2009.

Marcus, J. R., and M. Saperstein. *The Jew in the Medieval World: A Source Book, 315-1791*. Rev. ed. 1938. Reprint. Cincinnati, OH: Hebrew Union College Press, 1999.

Martin, D. S. *The Jew First*. Auckland, NZ: Wentworth, 1955.

Martyn, J. L. *Galatians: A New Translation with Introduction and Commentary*. The Anchor Bible. New York: Doubleday, 1997.

Matera, F. J. *Romans*. PCNT. Grand Rapids: Baker, 2010.

Melanchthon, P. *Commentary on Romans*. 1532. Translated by F. Kramer. St. Louis: Concordia, 1992.

Metzger, B. M. *A Textual Commentary on the Greek New Testament*. 2nd ed. Stuttgart: Deutsche Bibelgesellschaft-UBS, 1994.

Meyer, S. "Testimony." Jews for Jesus website. No pages. Online: http://www.jewsforjesus.org/about/losangeles/stan/005-Stans_Testimony.pdf (accessed September 2010).

Michel, O. *Der Brief an die Römer*. KEK, 4. rev. ed. Göttingen: Vandenhoeck & Ruprecht, 1966.

Minear, P. S. *The Obedience of Faith: The Purposes of Paul in the Epistle to the Romans*. SBT, 2. London: SCM, 1971.

Mitchell, C. W., et al. S. *Ephraim's Refutations of Mani, Marcion, and Bardaisan.* vol. 2: *The Discourse called "of Domnus" and six other writings*. Oxford: Williams & Norgate, 1921.

Mohrlang, R. *Romans*. CornBC. Carol Stream, IL: Tyndale House, 2007.

Moo, D. *The Epistle to the Romans*. NICNT. Grand Rapids: Eerdmans, 1996.

Moreau, A. S., et al. *Introducing World Missions: A Biblical, Historical, and Practical Survey*. Grand Rapids: Baker, 2004.

Morgan, R. *Romans*. Sheffield, UK: Sheffield Academic Press, 1995.

Morris, L. *The Epistle to the Romans*. PNTC. Leicester, UK: InterVarsity, 1988.

Mosher, S. *God's Power, Jesus' Faith, and World Mission: A Study in Romans*. Scottdale-Waterloo, PA: Herald, 1996.

Motyer, S. *Israel in the Plan of God: Light on Today's Debate*. Leicester, UK: InterVarsity, 1989.

Moulton, J. H., and G. Milligan. *The Vocabulary of the Greek Testament: Illustrated from the Papyri and Other Non-Literary Sources*. 1930. Reprint. Grand Rapids: Eerdmans, 1982.

Mouw, R. J. "To the Jew First: Witnessing to the Jews is Nonnegotiable." CT 41.10, August 1997, 12-13.

Murray, I. H. *The Puritan Hope*. London: Banner of Truth, 1971.

Murray, J. *The Epistle to the Romans: The English Text with Introduction, Exposition and Notes*. 1959-65. Reprint. London: Marshall, Morgan, & Scott, 1980.

Murray, J. A. H., et al. *The Compact Edition of the Oxford English Dictionary. Complete Text Reproduced Micrographically*, vol. 2: P-Z. Oxford: Oxford University Press, 1971.

Mussen, Z. R. *The Jew First*. Los Angeles: First Hebrew Christian Synagogue, 1935.

Nadge, H. *Dem Juden zuerst!: Eine engagierte Schrift gegen die Ausgrenzung der Juden vom Evangelium*. Berlin-Neukölln: Lehmann, 2000.

Nanos, M. D. *The Mystery of Romans: The Jewish Context of Paul's Letter*. Minneapolis: Fortress, 1996.

Neill, S. *A History of Christian Missions*. London: Penguin, 1964.

Bibliography

Nessim, D. "Director's Letter." *The Chosen People* (Sep 2011) 1–4.

Nestle, E., et al. *Novum Testamentum Graece n°27.* Stuttgart: Deutsche Bibelstiftung, 1993.

Nygren, A. *Commentary on Romans.* Translated by C. Rasmussen. London: SCM, 1952.

O'Brien, P. T. *Gospel and Mission in the Writings of Paul: An Exegetical and Theological Analysis.* Grand Rapids: Baker, 1993.

———. *The Letter to the Ephesians.* Leicester, UK: Apollos, 1999.

O'Neill, J. C. *Paul's Letter to the Romans.* PelicanNTC. Baltimore: Penguin, 1975.

Oduor, R. M. J. *To the Jew First: The Believer's Responsibility towards Israel.* Nairobi: Berean, 1996.

Onions, C. T., et al. *The Shorter Oxford English Dictionary on Historical Principles. vol. 1 A–M.* 3rd ed. 1933. Reprint. Oxford: Clarendon, 1972.

Osborne, G. R. *Romans.* InterVarsityNTC. Downers Grove, IL: InterVarsity, 2004.

Packer, J. I. "Letter from J. I. Packer." No pages. Online: http://jewsforjesus.org/about/forjewsforjesus/christian/packer (accessed February 2011).

Pakula, M. *First for the Jews: The Urgency of Jewish Mission Today.* Leonard Buck Missiology Lecture at Bible College of Victoria, Melbourne: Bible College of Victoria, 2007.

Parker, D., editor. *Jesus, Salvation and the Jewish People: The Uniqueness of Jesus and Jewish Evangelism.* Milton Keynes, UK: Paternoster, 2011.

Pascal, B., and T. S. Eliot. *Pensées.* Translated by W. F. Trotter. Edited by E. Rhys. Everyman's Library: Theology & Philosophy. New York: Dutton, 1931.

Paterson, R. *The Continuing Heartcry for China.* Tonbridge, UK: Sovereign World, 1999.

———. *What in the World is God Waiting For? The Fulfillment of the Great Commission.* 2nd ed. Tonbridge, UK: Sovereign World, 2005.

Patterson, A. *To the Jew First.* Chicago: Chicago Hebrew Mission, 1910.

Pauck, W. *Melanchthon and Bucer.* LCC, 19. London: SCM, 1969.

PCE. *Obligations of Christians to Attempt the Conversion of the Jews.* London: Justins for LSPCAJ, 1813.

Pearson, B. A. "Christians and Jews in First-Century Alexandria: Essay in Honor of Krister Stendahl." *HTR* 79.1–3 (1986) 206–13.

Perlman, S. "A Tribute to Moishe Rosen." The Lausanne Movement website. No pages. Online: http://www.lausanne.org/lausanne-connecting-point/2010-may.html#4 (accessed March 2011).

Perriman, A. *The Future of the People of God: Reading Romans before and after Christendom.* Eugene, OR: Cascade, 2010.

Peterson, D. *The Acts of the Apostles.* PNTC. Nottingham, UK: Apollos, 2009.

Philo. *Quod Omnis Probus Liber Sit.* Translated by F. H. Colson. Philo in ten volumes, vol. 9. 1941. Reprint. London: Heinemann, 1968.

———. *The Works of Philo Judaeus, the Contemporary of Josephus, Translated from the Greek.* Translated by C. D. Yonge. 4 vols. London: Bohn, 1854–55.

Pilch, J. J. *Galatians and Romans.* NT 6. Collegeville, MN: Liturgical, 1982.

Piper, J. *The Future of Justification: A Response to N. T. Wright.* Nottingham, UK: InterVarsity, 2007.

———. *Let the Nations Be Glad!: The Supremacy of God in Missions.* 3rd ed. Grand Rapids: Baker, 2010.

———. "To the Jew First, and Also to the Greeks." Sermon from 5th July 1998, Desiring God website. No pages. Online: www.desiringgod.org/resource-library/sermons/to-the-jew-first-and-also-to-the-greek (accessed May 2010).
Poole, M. *A Commentary on the Holy Bible, vol. 3: Matthew-Revelation*. 1685. Reprint. London: Banner of Truth, 1963.
Poupko, Y. E., and S. Guthrie. "Christian Evangelism and Judaism: An exchange of Views between a Rabbi and a Columnist." *Christianity Today* website. No pages. Online: http://www.christianitytoday.com/ct/2008/aprilweb-only/114-33.0.html?start=1 (accessed March 2012).
Poythress, V. S. "A Biblical View of Mathematics." In *Foundations of Christian Scholarship: Essays in the Van Til Perspective*, edited by G. North, 159–88. Part two: Academic Disciplines. Vallecito, CA: Ross House, 1976.
Pratt Jr, R. L. "To the Jew First: A Reformed Perspective." In *To the Jew First: The Case for Jewish Evangelism in Scripture and History*, edited by D. L. Bock and M. Glaser, 168–88. Grand Rapids: Kregel, 2008.
Pritz, R. "Jewish Evangelism and the Gentile World. Morning Session: Acts 17:1–34." *LCJE* Fifth International Conference (Jun-1995) 207–11.
Puddifoot, R. "Hillingdon Leads the Way." *Intouch with Hillingdon Conservatives* (Apr 2011) 1.
Räisänen, H. *Paul and the Law*. WUNT 29. Tübingen: Mohr, 1983.
Reasoner, M. *Romans in Full Circle: A History of Interpretation*. Louisville: Westminster John Knox, 2005.
Reese, A. *The Approaching Advent of Christ: An Examination of the Teaching of J. N. Darby and his Followers*. London: Marshall, Morgan, & Scott, 1937.
Refoulé, F. *Et ainsi tout Israël sera sauvé: Romains 11.25–32*. Lectio Divina, 117. Paris: Cerf, 1984.
Richmond, L. *Report of The Committee to the First Half Yearly Meeting of The London Society for Promoting Christianity amongst the Jews: May 23, 1809*. London: LSPCAJ, 1809.
Rittner, C. A., et al. *The Holocaust and the Christian World: Reflections on the Past, Challenges for the Future*. London: Kuperard, 2000.
Robertson, A. T. *A Grammar of the Greek New Testament in the Light of Historical Research*. 3rd ed. Cambridge: Cambridge University Press, 1914.
Robertson, J. *"To the Jew First." Why?* Leaflet 1 (New Series). Edinburgh: Church of Scotland Mission to the Jews, 1912.
Robinson, C. H. *History of Christian Missions*. Edinburgh: T. & T. Clark, 1915.
Robinson, J. A. T. *Wrestling with Romans*. London: SCM, 1979.
Robinson, R. "Jewish Mission." In *Dictionary of Mission Theology: Evangelical Foundations*, edited by J. P. Corrie, S. Escobar, et al., 190–2. Downers Grove, IL: InterVarsity, 2007.
Rosen, M. "The Holocaust, Forgiveness and Evangelism." *JFJNL* 8.5746 (1986) 1–3.
———. "Jewish Evangelism: The Touchstone of Theology and Missiology." *EMQ* 26.4 (1990) 380–84.
———. "Moishe's Musings on Nuclear Christianity." *JFJNL* 11.5769 (2009) 7.
———. "We're Glad You Asked." *JFJNL* 7.5756 (1996) 6.
———. "Why First?" *JFJNL* 5754.3 (1994) 1–2.
Rosen, M., and B. Massie. *Beyond the Gulf War: Overture to Armageddon?* San Bernardino, CA: Here's Life, 1991.

Bibliography

Rosen, M., and W. Proctor. *Jews for Jesus*. Old Tappan, NJ: Revel, 1974.
Rosen, R. "Provoking to Jealousy." *JFJNL* 10.5764 (2004) 7.
Rosenzweig, F. *The Star of Redemption*. Translated by B. E. Galli. Madison, WI: University of Wisconsin, 2005.
Rubenstein, R. L., and J. K. Roth. *Approaches to Auschwitz: The Legacy of the Holocaust*. Atlanta: John Knox, 1987.
Ruether, R. R. *Faith and Fratricide: The Theological Roots of Anti-Semitism*. New York: Seabury, 1974.
Rydelnik, M. "The Ongoing Importance of Messianic Prophecy for Jewish Evangelism in the New Millennium." In *To the Jew First: The Case for Jewish Evangelism in Scripture and History*, edited by D. L. Bock and M. Glaser, 261–91. Grand Rapids: Kregel, 2008.
Ryrie, C. C. *Dispensationalism*. Rev. & exp. ed. (Originally called *Dispensationalism Today*, 1966). Chicago: Moody, 2007.
Sanday, W., and A. C. Headlam. *A Critical and Exegetical Commentary on the Epistle to the Romans*. ICC. Edinburgh: T. & T. Clark, 1895.
Sanders, E. P. *Paul, the Law, and the Jewish People*. London: SCM, 1983.
Sartre, J.-P., et al. "Reflection on the Jewish Question: A Lecture." 1947. *October* 67 (1999) 33–46.
Schaeffer, F. A. *The Finished Work of Christ: The Truth of Romans 1–8*. Reprint. Wheaton: Crossway, 1998.
Schaff, P. *Saint Chrysostom: Homilies on the Acts of the Apostles and the Epistle to the Romans*. SLNPNFCC, XI. Grand Rapids: Eerdmans, 1979.
Schlatter, A. *Romans: The Righteousness of God*. Translated by S. Schatzmann. 1935. Reprint. Peabody, MA: Hendrickson, 1995.
Schlier, H. *Der Römerbrief*. HTKNT. Freiburg: Herder, 1977.
Schmidt, H. W. *Der Brief des Paulus an die Römer*. ThKNT. Berlin: Evangelische Verlagsanstalt, 1962.
Schnabel, E. J. *Early Christian Mission: Jesus and the Twelve*, vol. 1. Downers Grove, IL: InterVarsity, 2002.
Schoeman, R. H. *"Salvation is from the Jews" (John 4:22): The Role of Judaism in Salvation History from Abraham to the Second Coming*. San Francisco: Ignatius, 2003.
Schonfield, H. J. *The History of Jewish Christianity: From the First to the Twentieth Century*. 2nd ed. 1936. Reprint. London: Duckworth, 2009.
Schreiner, T. R. *Romans*. BECNT. Grand Rapids: Baker, 1998.
Shenk, D. W. *God's Call to Mission*. Scottdale, PA: Herald, 1994.
Shulam, J., and H. Le Cornu. *A Commentary on the Jewish Roots of Romans*. Baltimore: Lederer, 1997.
Sibley, J. R. "'To the Jew, of Course!': A Response." Paper given at the 9th LCJE International Conference at High Leigh, Hoddesdon, UK, August 2011.
Siefried, M. A. "'For the Jew First': Paul's *Nota Bene* for His Gentile Readers." In *To the Jew First: The Case for Jewish Evangelism in Scripture and History*, edited by D. L. Bock and M. Glaser, 24–39. Grand Rapids: Kregel, 2008.
Sim, D. C. "How Many Jews became Christians in the First Century? The Failure of the Christian Mission to the Jews." *HervormdeTS* 61.1&2 (2005) 417–40.
Simon, M. *Verus Israel: A Study of the Relations between Christians and Jews in the Roman Empire (AD 135–425)*. Translated by H. McKeating. Oxford: Oxford University Press, 1996.

Sims, D. E. *The Jew First Principle*. Powder Springs, GA: The Hope for Israel, 2006.

———. "The Jew First Principle." Jew First website. No pages. Online: www.jewfirst.org/ (accessed June 2010).

Skarsaune, O. "The Mission to the Jews—A Closed Chapter?" In *The Mission of the Early Church to Jews and Gentiles*, edited by J. Ådna and H. Kvalbein, 69–83. WUNT 127. Tübingen: Mohr, 2000.

Smalley, S. S. *The Revelation to John: A Commentary on the Greek Text of the Apocalypse*. London: SPCK, 2005.

Snodgrass, K. "The Gospel in Romans: A Theology of Revelation." In *Gospel in Paul: Studies on Corinthians, Galatians and Romans for Richard N. Longenecker*, edited by L. A. Jervis and P. Richardson, 288–314. JNTSS 108. Sheffield, UK: Sheffield Academic, 1994.

———. *The Parable of the Wicked Tenants: An Inquiry into Parable Interpretation*. WUNT 27. Tübingen: Mohr, 1983.

———. *Stories with Intent: A Comprehensive Guide to the Parables of Jesus*. Grand Rapids: Eerdmans, 2008.

Snyder, A. "Created to Proclaim." Unpublished lecture for *JFJ* staff, 2007.

———. *Was Paul the Founder of Christianity?* Issues 3.4. San Francisco: JFJ, 1981.

Sokolow, N., and A. Hertzberg. *History of Zionism 1600–1918*. 2 vols in 1. New York: KTAV, 1969.

Solomon, L. "The Apostle Paul and Operation Behold Your God." *JFJNL* 5763.4 (2002) 8.

Sorko-Ram, A. *To The Jew First*. Grand Prairie, TX: Maoz Israel, 2008.

Soulen, R. K. *The God of Israel and Christian Theology*. Minneapolis: Fortress, 1996.

Spector, S. *Evangelicals and Israel: The Story of American Christian Zionism*. Oxford: Oxford University Press, 2009.

Spener, P. J. *Pia Desideria*. Translated by T. G. Tappert. 1964. Reprint. Philadelphia: Fortress, 1982.

Spurgeon, C. H. *The Restoration and Conversion of the Jews (1864)*. MTP, 56 vols. 1862–1917. Reprint. Pasadena, TX: Pilgrim, 1973.

———. *St. Luke XV.8 to Romans III.25*. TNT, 2. London: Marshall, Morgan, & Scott, 1933.

Steel, D. N., and C. C. Thomas. *Romans: An Interpretative Outline*. 1963. Reprint. Phillipsburg, NJ: Presbyterian and Reformed, 1982.

Stek, J. H. "To the Jew First." *CTJ* 7 (1972) 15–52.

———. *To The Jew First: An Exegetical Examination of a New Testament Theme*. Grand Rapids: Christian Reformed Church, 1968.

Stern, D. H. *Jewish New Testament Commentary*. 6th ed. Clarksville, MD: Jewish New Testament, 1996.

Stern, S. *Josel of Rosheim: Commander of Jewry in the Holy Roman Empire of the German Nation*. Philadelphia: Jewish Publication Society, 1965.

Stock, E. *A Short Handbook of Missions*. London: Longmans, 1904.

Stolle, V. "Die Juden zuerst: Das Anliegen des Römerbriefs." *LuThK* Jg. 14 (1990) 154–65.

Stott, J. *The Message of Romans*. BST. Leicester, UK: InterVarsity, 1994.

Stowers, S. K. *A Rereading of Romans: Justice, Jews, and Gentiles*. New Haven: Yale University Press, 1994.

Bibliography

Stuhlmacher, P. *Paul's Letter to the Romans. A Commentary*. Translated by S. J. Hafemann. Edinburgh: T. & T. Clark, 1994.

———. "The Purpose of Romans." 1986. In *The Romans Debate*, 2nd ed., edited by K. P. Donfried, 231–42. Peabody, MA: Hendrickson, 2009.

———. *Revisiting Paul's Doctrine of Justification: A Challenge to the New Perspective. With an Essay by Donald A. Hagner*. Downers Grove, IL: InterVarsity, 2001.

———. "The Theme of Romans." 1988. In *The Romans Debate*, 2nd ed., edited by K. P. Donfried, 333–45. Peabody, MA: Hendrickson, 2009.

Suetonius. "The Deified Claudius." In *Suetonius Vol II. The Lives of the Caesars (continued), Book V.—The Deified Claudius*, edited by G. P. Goold. The Loeb Classical Library. Cambridge: Harvard University Press, 1979.

Swanson, R. J. *New Testament Greek Manuscripts: Variant Readings Arranged in Horizontal Lines Against Codex Vaticanus. Matthieu*. Pasadena: William Carey International University Press, 2001.

———. *New Testament Greek Manuscripts: Variant Readings Arranged in Horizontal Lines Against Codex Vaticanus. Romans*. Pasadena: William Carey International University Press, 2001.

Tafjord, A. "Testimony." No pages. Online: http://jewsforjesus.org/about/odessa/arne (accessed September 2010).

Tatum, G. "'To the Jew first' (Romans 1:16): Paul's Defense of Jewish Privilege in Romans." In *Celebrating Paul: Festschrift in Honor of Jerome Murphy-O'Connor, O.P., and Joseph A. Fitzmyer, S.J.*, edited by P. Spitaler, 275–86. Washington, DC: Catholic University of America, 2011.

Tertullian. *Adversus Marcionem*. Translated by E. Evans. vols. 4–5. Oxford: Oxford University Press, 1972.

Thielmann, F. *Ephesians*. BECNT. Grand Rapids: Baker, 2010.

Thompson, A. E. *A Century of Jewish Missions*. Chicago: Revell, 1902.

Tidiman, B. *Nahoum, Habaquq, Sophonie*. CEB. Vaux-sur-Seine: Edifac, 2009.

Titterton, C. H. *To the Jew First: Today, Armageddon and After*. Blackburn, UK: Durham & Sons, 1950.

TLM. *The Cape Town Commitment: A Confession of Faith and a Call to Action*. Edited by J. Cameron. The Didasko Files. Peabody, MA: Hendrickson, 2011.

Torrance, D. W., and G. Taylor. *Israel, God's Servant: God's key to the Redemption of the World*. Milton Keynes, UK: Paternoster, 2007.

Triestman, M. *To the Jew First: A Textbook on Jewish Evangelism*. Levittown, PA: Lifeline, 1997.

Trocmé, É. "L'Épître aux Romains et la Méthode Missionnaire de l'Apôtre Paul." *NTS* 7 (1960–61) 148–53.

Tuchman, B. W. *Bible and Sword: How the British Came to Palestine*. London: Papermac, 1956.

Tucker, R. A. *Not Ashamed: The Story of Jews for Jesus*. Sisters, OR: Multnomah, 1999.

Turner, D. L. "Matthew 21:43 and the Future of Israel." *BiblSac* 159 (Jan-Mar 2002) 46–61.

Vermes, G. *The Complete Dead Sea Scrolls in English*. 4th ed. 1962. Reprint. London: Penguin, 1997.

Viard, A. *Saint Paul: Epître aux Romains*. SB. Paris: Gabalda, 1975.

Vogt, P. T. *Deuteronomic Theology and the Significance of Torah: A Reappraisal*. Winona Lake, IN: Eisenbrauns, 2006.

Bibliography

Vorster, J. N. "Strategies of Persuasion in Romans 1.16-17." *JSNTS* 90 (1993) 152-70.

Wallace, D. B. *Greek Grammar beyond the Basics*. Grand Rapids: Zondervan, 1996.

———. "To the Jew First: The New Testament and Anti-Semitism." Bible website. No pages. Online: http://www.bible.org/ page.php?page_id=3406accessed (accessed May 2010).

Warnke, G. *Gadamer: Hermeneutics, Tradition and Reason*. Cambridge: Polity, 1987.

Watson, F. *Paul and the Hermeneutics of Faith*. London: T. & T. Clark, 2004.

———. *Paul, Judaism, and the Gentiles: Beyond the New Perspective*. 2nd ed. Grand Rapids: Eerdmans, 2007.

———. "The Two Roman Congregations: Romans 14:1—15:13." 1986. In *The Romans Debate*, 2nd ed., edited by K. P. Donfried, 203-15. Peabody, MA: Hendrickson, 2009.

WEA. "The Berlin Declaration on the Uniqueness of Christ and Jewish Evangelism in Europe Today." *LCJE Bulletin* 94 (November 2008) 4-5.

Weber, R., and R. Gryson. *Biblia Sacra Iuxta Vulgatam Versionem*. 5th ed. 1969. Reprint. Stuttgart: Deutsche Bibelgesellschaft, 2007.

Wedderburn, A. J. M. *The Reasons for Romans*. Edited by J. Riches. SNTW. Edinburgh: T. & T. Clark, 1988.

Wengst, K. "'Den Juden zuerst und auch den Griechen.' Eine Schneise durch den Römerbrief." Jewish-Christian relations website. No pages. Online: http://jcrelations.net/de/?item=2893 (accessed February 2011).

Wertheim, S. "Sermon on Romans 1:16." unpublished sermon, n.d.

Wilckens, U. *Der Brief an die Römer*. EKKNT, vol. 1. Neukirchen/Vluyn-Zürich: Neukirchener-Benziger, 1978.

Wilkinson, B., and D. Kopp. *The Prayer of Jabez: Breaking through to the Blessed Life*. Sisters, OR: Multnomah, 2000.

Wilks Jr, W. "To the Jew First." Toward Jerusalem Council II website. No pages. Online: http://www.tjcii.org/userfiles/File/To_the_Jew_First.pdf (accessed December 1998).

William of Thierry. *Exposition on the Epistle to the Romans*. Translated by J. B. Hasbrouck. CFS 27. Kalamazoo, MI: Cistercian, 1980.

Williams, A. L. *Adversus Judaeos: A Bird's Eye View of Christian Apologiae until the Renaissance*. New York: Cambridge, 1935.

———. *Justin Martyr: The Dialogue with Trypho*. London: SPCK, 1930.

Williams, S. K. "The "Righteousness of God" in Romans." *JBL* 99.2 (1980) 241-90.

Williamson, P. R. "Covenant." In *New Dictionary of Biblical Theology*, edited by T. D. Alexander and B. S. Rosner, 419-29. Leicester, UK: InterVarsity, 2000.

Wilson, J. L., and J. M. Wilson. *The Tabernacle: To the Jew First and also to the Greek*. Absarokee, MT: Tabernacle, 1975.

Winter, B. W. *Philo and Paul among the Sophists: Alexandrian and Corinthian Responses to a Julio-Claudian Movement*. 2nd ed. Grand Rapids: Eerdmans, 2002.

Wright, C. J. H. *The Mission of God: Unlocking the Bible's Grand Narrative*. Nottingham, UK: InterVarsity, 2006.

Wright, N. T. *The Climax of the Covenant: Christ and the Law in Pauline Theology*. Minneapolis: Fortress, 1991.

———. *Jesus and the Victory of God*. COQG. London: SPCK, 1996.

———. *The Letter to the Romans*. NIB, vol. 10. Nashville: Abingdon, 2002.

———. *The New Testament and the People of God*. COQG, London: SPCK, 1992.

———. *The Resurrection of the Son of God*. COQG. London: SPCK, 2003.

Bibliography

Wright, T. *Justification: God's Plan and Paul's Vision*. London: SPCK, 2009.
———. *Paul for Everyone : Romans. Part 1: Chapters 1–8*. London: SPCK, 2004.
———. *Paul for Everyone : Romans. Part 2: Chapters 9–16*. London: SPCK, 2004.
———. *Paul: Fresh Perspectives*. London: SPCK, 2005.
———. *Revelation for Everyone*. London: SPCK, 2011.
———. *Surprised by Hope*. London: SPCK, 2007.
———. *What St Paul Really Said*. Oxford: Lion, 1997.
Wuellner, W. "Paul's Rhetoric of Argumentation in Romans: An Alternative to the Donfried-Karris Debate over Romans." 1976. In *The Romans Debate*, 2nd ed., edited by K. P. Donfried, 128–46. Peabody, MA: Hendrickson, 2009.
Wyschogrod, M. "Why is the Theology of Karl Barth of Interest." 1974. In *Abraham's Promise: Judaism and Jewish-Christian Relations*, edited by R. K. Soulen, 211–24. London: SCM, 2006.
Yeats, J. M. "To the Jew First: Conversion of the Jews as the Foundation for Global Missions and Expansion in Nineteenth-Century British Evangelicalism." *SouthwesternJT* 47.2 (2005) 207–23.
Yohannan, K. P. *Come, Let's Reach the World. Why the World Waits*. 1991 Reprint. Carrollton, TX: Gospel For Asia, 2004.
———. *Revolution in World Missions*. 1986. Reprint. Carrollton, TX: Gospel for Asia, 2009.
Zadok, D. "Mission Priority from the Gospel of John." *LCJE Bulletin* 90 (Nov 2007) 3.
Zeller, D. *Der Brief an die Römer*. RNT. Regensburg: Pustet, 1985.
———. *Juden und Heiden in der Mission des Paulus: Studien zum Römerbrief*. FB. 2nd ed. Stuttgart: Katholisches Bibelwerk, 1973.
Ziesler, J. *Paul's Letter to the Romans*. TPINTC. London: SCM, 1989.
Zwingli, U. *Early Writings*. 1912. Reprint. Durham, NC: Labyrinth, 1987.

Author Index

Abbott-Smith, G., 124n159
Abelard, P., 14
Aland, B., 59n90, 111n72, 112n81, 162n63
Alexander, M. S., 30n119
Alsted, J. H., 24n93
Althaus, P., 35
Ambrosiaster, 9–10, 162
Anderson, G. H., xxxvin60, 91n284
Apollinaris of Laodicea, 10
Aquinas, T., 17
Ariel, Y., 82n235, 178
Arndt, W. F., 72, 75n195
Augustine, 11–12, 16, 18, 24, 42
Aune, D. E., 83n242
Austin, J. L., xxxixn69

Bailey, K. E., 171n109, 177
Balz, H., 67n134, 118–24
Barclay, W., 39n160
Barnett, P. W., 69n153
Barrett, C. K., 39, 60, 73, 125n162
Barrett D. B., 196n14
Barron, A., 46n19, 50–52, 56n71, 61n97, 63, 72, 75
Barth, K., 33, 54n56, 72n172, 118, 131n213, 164
Bauckham, R., 60n92
Bauer, W., 72, 118–20, 124n155, 133
Baum, G., 37–38
Baur, F. C., 33–34, 100n11
Beasley-Murray, G. R., 94n296

Beker, J. C., 120, 137
Bell, R. H., 136n240, 150n9, 152–54, 163
Bénétreau, S., 129, 172n113
Bengel, J. A., 27
Berry, G. R., 156n36
Bietz, K. H., xxxn28
Bjoraker, B., 55–56, 72–73, 85
Black, M., 126
Blaising, C. A., 179n146
Blass, F., 76n205, 117n102, 123n150, 134n226
Blocher, H., xxxiv, 79n222, 136, 157n42, 161n55, 165n85, 173n114, 183–85
Blomberg, C. L., 170–71, 177n137
Bock, D. L., xxx, 50n41, 75n200, 90n277, 166n86, 179n146
Bohak, G., xxxiiin44
Bonar, A. A., 52n51, 68n148, 78n216, 82n237, 88n259, 90–91
Bonar H., 88, 91
Borgen, P., 123n152, 135n228
Bornkamm, G., 100–101, 154n28
Boston, T., 26
Bowen, R., 126
Bray, G., 9–11
Brickner, D., xxviiin24, xxxii, xxxiiin38, 32n127, 44–46, 48, 50, 52, 59, 61, 71n170, 81n231, 83–84, 89n271, 95, 154–55, 178–83

Author Index

Brindle, W. A., 52n51, 70n158, 70n160, 76–77, 141n263
Briscoe, D. S., 125n163
Broughton, H., 24
Bruce, F. F., xxxin31, 39n160, 102n26, 103n36, 125–26
Brunner, E., 35n145
Bucer, M., 21, 23
Bultmann, R. C., 34n140, 104n37, 148
Bunge, W. F., 164n79
Burchartz, A., 50n39
Burge, G. M., 68, 95n302, 95n307
Burk, J. C. F., 27n105

Callenberg, H., 27
Calvin, J., 22–23, 73, 135, 160n53
Campbell, D. A., 131n213, 134
Carey, W., xxivn12
Carlson, C. C., 83n239, 83n241, 95n306, 179n147, 181n160
Carson, D. A., xxxviiin68
Childs, B. S., 67
Christiani, P., 16
Chrysostom, 10
Clarke, A. 33
Clement of Alexandria, 111n76
Clouse, R. G., 24n93, 179n145
Coffey, D., 127
Cohen, G., 79, 91–92, 182n166
Cohen, S., 45n11
Cohn-Sherbok, D., xxxiii–xxxiv, 37n153
Cooper, D. L., 56n71, 65n121, 67, 80n225, 89n266, 116n97
Cooper, W. R., 22n83
Corporation for Promoting the Gospel among the Indians in New England, 25n98
Cottier, G., 40n167
Cottrell, J., 127, 131n214
Couch, M. O., 31n126
COWE, xxxvn53, 50n40, 74n189, 97n313
Cox, W. E., 183n171
Cranfield, C. E. B., xxvn13, 99n4, 112, 117, 122n145, 125n162, 129, 131n211, 143n273, 161–62
Crombie, K., 29–30, 40n168
Cullmann, O., 148–49

Dalman of Leipsic, G., 80n222
Daniell, D., 22n83
Darby, J. N., 31–32, 178
Das, A. A., 100–101, 103, 106n53
Dauermann, S., xxvin14, xxxv–xxxvi, 48–49, 58
Davids, P. H., 53n55
Davies, G. N., 128
Davies, W. D., 148n2
De Bruyn, T., 11n41
Debrunner, A., 76n205, 117n102, 123n150, 134n226
De Le Roi, J. F. A., 27n106, 36n151, 80n222
Demarest, B. A., 153n24
Dickson, B., 127
Dietzfelbinger, C., 148
Dio, C., 101n20
DNI, xxiin5, 57n79
Dodd, B. J., 73n177
Dodd, C. H., xxvi–xxvii, 35, 99n4
Donfried, K. P., 99–105
Donin, N., 16–18
Downey, A. K., xxxvn54
Dunn, J. D. G., xxxiiin41, xxxviin68, 5–6, 34n140, 70n157, 122n139, 127–28, 131n211, 142n270

Edwards, J., 14n54, 17, 36
Edwards, J. R., 127, 175n128
Ehrman, B. D., 8n26
Elliger, K., 140n256
Elliot, J., 25
Ellison, H. L., 150n9
Ephraem, 110
Erasmus, D., 19
Erdman, C. R., 35
Eusebius, 9, 134

Feuillet, A., 126, 131n213
Fielding, C., 196n16
Fitzmyer, J. A., 108, 125n162, 127

Author Index

Foreman, K. J., 39n160
France, R. T., 57n78
Frere, H., 31
Frey, J. S. C. F., 28
Friberg, B., 124
Fritz, A. X. J., xxin1, xxin2, xxiii, 12, 158n47, 162n64, 179n152, 184n175
Fruchtenbaum, A., xxxn27, 62, 74–75, 78, 81–82, 88n263, 92, 96–97

Gadamer, H.-G., 2–3
Gager, J. G., 34n141
Gaston, L., 133n218
Gates, H. L., 68n147
Gathercole, S. J., 117
Gaventa, B. R., 149n7
Gifford, E. H., 73
Gingrich, F. W., 72, 75n195
Glaser, M., xxvin14, xxx, xxxiv–xxxv, 36n150, 38, 46n19, 48n29, 50–52, 54–56, 58, 60–61, 63, 72–75, 80–82, 90n272
Glasser, A. F., xxxn27, 45n7, 55, 91
Godet, F. L., 33–34, 111, 123n148, 135n236
Goforth, J., 91
Goldsmith, M., xxvin14, 58n80, 74, 133n217, 146n283
González, R. D., 57–59, 61–62, 64, 82, 194n7
Goold, W. H., 26n101
Grady, L., 45n13
Gray, J. M., 91
Grayston, K., 127
Grayzel, S., 13n52
Gregory IX, 13, 16
Gregory the Great, 13
Grenz, S. J., 38n158, 41n175
Grier, W. J., 183n171
Grimm, C. L. W., 124n158
Gryson, R., 110n66, 165n81
Gudel, J. P., 58, 60, 63–64
Guibert of Nogent, 15
Guthrie, S., 1–2, 38n156, 42n177

Haacker, K., 47n24, 64n116, 64n119, 119, 127, 131n211, 141n263
Haenchen, E., 66n129
Hagner, D. A., 75n196, 167n94, 167n95, 175n125
Haldane, R., 30–31, 135n236
Hall, E., 121n138
Harkins, P. W., 10n39
Harnack, A. von., 34n140, 110–11
Harris, H., 33n139
Harvey, R., xxxvi–xxxvii, 23n87, 38n159, 79n221, 151n16, 178n142
Headlam, A. C., 34n143, 73, 131n213
Heil, J. P., 125n163
Heliso, D., 137n244
Hendriksen, W., 126, 141n263
Henry, A. M., 40n167
Henry, C. F. H., 153n24
Herschell, R., 28n109
Hertzberg, A., 34n144
Heward, S. A., xxxn26
Hicks, R. H., 3n9, 52n51, 68–69, 79
Hidalgo, E. E., 54, 69n150
Hiebert, T., 139n253
Hiers, R. H., 176
Hillerbrand, H. J., 21
Hinson, K., xxiin5, 1n2
Hodge, C., 31, 52n51, 72–73, 90
Hoehner, H. W., 144n277
Holmes, M. W., 7
Holwerda, D. E., xxxin30
Homer, 156–57
Horner, B. E., 40n168
Hultgren, A. J., 99n4, 107n56, 125n162, 128, 131, 134–35, 152n18, 167n94, 170–71
Hume, C. R., 127, 143
Hvalvik, R., 64, 66, 72n171, 75–77, 79

Innocent III, 13
Irving E., 31

Author Index

Jeremias, J., xxvin16, 54n57, 55n64, 57n79, 63n111, 65, 168n96, 168n99
Jervell, J., 65n126, 102n25, 168n100
Jewett, R., 99n5, 102n26, 104, 108, 127
Jocz, J., 23, 52n51, 91
Johnson, A. F., 73
Johnson, T. M., 196n14
Johnson Jr., S. L, 123n149

Kaiser Jr, W. C., 58n81
Käsemann, E., 73, 103n32, 111n74, 125n162, 126, 137, 148, 164
Kaser, A., 47n24
Katz, S. T., 37n153
Keck, L. E., 127
Keener, C. S., 127
Keith, G. A., 3, 13n50, 14n53, 14n54, 14n55, 16n62, 17n66, 18n70, 21n80, 22n84, 23n88, 24, 25n95
Kendall, R. T., 176n132
Keown, M. J., 146n283, 150n14
Kessler, E., 47n26
Kim, S., 116n97
Kinzer, M. S., 52n51
Kjær-Hansen, K., xxxvi, 51n47, 91n284
Klappert, B., xxiv
Klein G., 148
Knight, M., 2n6
Kopp, D., 90n275
Kreider, A., 146n283
Krey, A. C., 15n59, 16n61
Küng, H., 3n9
Kuss, O., 39n163, 99n4, 122n140

Lacunza, M., 31
Lagrange, M. J., 175n128
Landau, R. S., 37n153
LBH, 98n2
LCJE, xxvin14, xxxv–xxxvii, 48
LCWE, xxxivn49, xxxvi, 38n157, 87n253
Le Cornu, H., 125n163

Leenhardt, F. J., 39n163, 118, 145n282
Lenski, R. C. H., 35, 123, 131n211
Leventhal, B. R., 45n12, 87n257
Levison, Sir L., 36n151
Liddell, H. G., 125n159
Lietzmann, D. H., 35n145, 123n151, 131n214
Lightfoot, J. B., 34n140
Lindsay, H., 83n239, 83n241, 95n306, 179n147, 181n160
Llyod-Jones, D., 126
Lohse, E., 47n24, 127, 131n213, 143n272
Louw, J. E., 104n40, 122, 124n159
Lull, R., 16
Luther, M., 19–23, 34n141, 118, 188
Luz, U., 148

MacLachlan, H., xxxn28, 94, 176n133
Madden, S., 85
Manson, T. W., 100n16
Marcus, J. R., 13n51
Martin, D. S., 90n276
Martyn, J. L., xxxivn46
Martyr, P., 24
Massie, B., 179n150, 183n169
Matera, F. J., 127, 140n259
McCaul, A., 30
M'Cheyne, R. M., 30, 52n51, 68n148, 78, 82n237, 88n259, 90
Mede, J., 24n93
Melanchthon, P., 21n79, 100
Metzger, B. M., 110n69
Meyer, S., 45n11
Michel, O., 113–14, 116n98, 118
Milligan, G., 125n159
Minear, P. S., 102n27
Mitchell, C. W., 110n67
Mohrlang, R., 129
Moo, D., xxvn13, 76n203, 86, 99n4, 99n7, 100n15, 117n104, 123, 125n162, 129, 131n213, 140n259, 141n260, 143n275,

Author Index

144n279, 152n21, 158n44, 161, 163n66
Moody, D. L., 31
Moreau, A. S., 195n12
Morgan, R., 125n163
Morris, L., 126
Mosher, S., 57n74, 127-28
Motyer, S., xxiv, 107n58, 125n162, 150n9, 152n19, 153n25
Moulton, J. H., 125n159
Mouw, R. J., 1, 87, 91n285
Müller, C., 148
Munck, J., 148
Murray, A., 91
Murray, I. H., 24n89, 25n96, 25n98, 27n105, 31n125, 32n133
Murray, J., 39-40, 52n51, 73, 76n202, 90, 99n4
Murray, J. A. H., xxxvn56
Mussen, Z. R., xxx

Nadge, H., 47n24, 50n39, 94n299, 95n305
Nanos, M. D., 58n81, 128
Neill, S., 4n11, 16n64
Nessim, D., 90n273
Nestle, E., 110n68, 134n225
Nicholas III, 16
Nygren, A., 39, 99n4, 100, 107n56, 108n64, 115n90, 129n201

O'Brien, P. T., 146n283
O'Neill, J. C., 99n7
Oduor, R. M. J., 64n116, 87n255, 88n262, 89, 94
Origen, 8-9, 73, 134
Osborne, G. R., 129
Osiander, A., 21
Owen, J. 26

Packer, J. I., 46
Pakula, M., xxvn13, 28n109, 69n154, 125n162, 162
Parker, D., xxxvii
Pascal, B., 11n45
Paterson, R., 60n92, 63, 69n152, 192, 195

Patterson, A., 82n237, 85-88, 91, 93
Pauck, W., 100n12
Paul of Burgos, 17
PCE, 29n116
Pearson, B. A., 68n145
Pelagius, 10-11, 22
Perlman, S., xxxiiin37, xxxvi-xxxvii
Perriman, A., 107-8, 142n264, 142n265, 194n7
Peterson, D., 58n83, 60n94, 61, 65n123, 66n129, 66n131, 67n134, 67n139, 67n141
Philo, 123, 135, 156
Pilch, J. J., 125n163
Piper, J., 74, 93n292, 138, 195n11, 197
Poole, M., 25-26
Poupko, Y. E., 1-2, 38n156, 42n177
Poythress, V. S., xxxixn71
Pratt Jr, R. L., 39n165
Pritz, R., 55
Proctor, W., xxviiin20, 40n169
Puddifoot, R., 98n1

Reasoner, M., 9, 11, 14
Reese, A., 32n129
Refoulé, F., 158n46
Richmond, L., 28
Ritschl, A., 34n140
Rittner, C. A., 37n153
Robertson, A. T., 130
Robertson, J., 88n264
Robinson, C. H., 80n222
Robinson, J. A. T., 125n163
Robinson, R., xxxivn50, 46
Rosen, M., xxii, xxviiin20, xxxvi, 30, 40, 45n7, 46, 50n39, 59n91, 61n102, 71-72, 74, 90n277, 92, 95, 179, 183n169
Rosen, R., 155, 179
Rosenzweig, F., 73
Roth, J. K., 37n153
Rubenstein, R. L., 37n153
Ruether, R. R., 5, 37
Rydelnik, M., 18n69

Author Index

Ryrie, C. C., 84, 178n141, 179, 180n157

Sanday, W., 34n143, 73, 131n213
Sanders, E. P., 68
Saperstein, M., 13n51
Sartre, J.-P., xxxii
Schaeffer, F. A., 198n19
Schlatter, A., 35
Schlier, H., 122–24, 126, 131n213
Schmidt, H. W., 39, 121, 129n201, 131n211
Schnabel, E. J., 70n157
Schneider, G. E., 67n134, 118–24
Schoeman, R. H., 47, 55, 79n221
Schonfield, H. J., 28n109, 79n222, 161n55
Schreiner, T. R., 120n127, 129, 131n211
Shenk, D. W., 195n10
Shulam, J., 125n163
Sibley, J. R., xxvin14
Simon, M., 6n20, 8n28, 12
Sims, D. E., 31n123, 33, 54, 56–58, 62–64, 66–67, 70, 75–78, 82, 88, 91n278, 92–93, 98n3, 112n80
Snodgrass, K., 108n61, 163n73, 167n91, 168n100, 170n102, 174, 177
Snyder, A., 45n12, 52, 61
Sokolow, N., 34n144
Solomon, L., 48, 68
Sorko-Ram, A., 96, 158
Soulen, R. K., 49, 52n51
Spener, P. J., 26–27, 29n113
Spurgeon, C. H., 24n89, 33, 52n51, 90
Steel, D. N., 39n160
Stek, J. H., xxxi, 5, 56–57, 64, 66n134, 70n161, 172
Stern, D. H., 93n291
Stern, S., 21n80
Stock, E., 80n222
Stolle, V., 47n24
Stott, J., 127n193

Stowers, S. K., xxxix, 103n35, 104n37, 121, 133n221, 136n242, 155–56
Stuhlmacher, P., xxxviiin68, 102n30, 103, 116–17, 125n162, 128, 131n214, 133n219, 148
Swanson, R. J., 111n76, 134, 162n63, 170n104

Tafjord, A., 45n11
Tatum, G., 47n25
Taylor, G., 88n264, 94–95
Tertullian, 110
Thielmann, F., 70n155
Thomas, C. C., 39n160
Thompson, A. E., 27n107, 91n281
Tidiman, B., 139n250, 139n251
Titterton, C. H., 54–55
TLM, 193n2
Torrance, D. W., 88n264, 94–95
Tremellius, E., 23n87
Triestman, M., 57, 69
Trocmé, E., 105n49
Tuchman, B. W., 24–25
Tucker, R. A., 36n151, 46
Turner, D. L., 175n125
Tyndale, W., 22

Urban II, 13–15

Vermes, G., 172n111
Viard, A., 126, 131n213
Vogt, P. T., 157n42
Vorster, J. N., 105, 107n57, 110n65, 115n89, 117n105, 120

Wallace, D. B., 93n291, 114, 130
Warnke, G., 3n7
Watson, F., 103, 106
WEA, xxxvii–xxxix
Weber, R., 110n66, 165n81
Wedderburn, A. J. M., 100n11
Weiss, J., 34n140, 111n74
Wengst, K., 47n24
Wertheim, S., 46n20, 50, 72n174, 72n176
Whitefield, H., 25n98

Author Index

Wilckens, U., 107n56, 122n144, 126, 131n213
Wilke, C. G., 124n158
Wilkinson, B., 90n275
Wilks Jr, W., xxxvn52, 73n186
William of Thierry, 15–16
Williams, S. K., 134n223
Williamson, P. R., xxxviii
Wilson, J. L. and J. M., xxxn28
Winter, B. W., 156n38
Wrede, W., 34n140
Wright, C. J. H., xxiii, xxxivn51, xxxv, 148
Wright, N. T., xxxin32, 6n17, 52n49, 55n62, 80n224, 81n227, 81n230, 83, 99, 101n21, 102n28, 103, 106n52, 113–15, 118n112, 119–20, 127, 137–42, 156, 170–71, 176
Wuellner, W., 104n40
Wyschogrod, M., 164n75

Yeats, J. M., 29–30
Yohannan, K. P., 78n217, 196n15

Zadok, D., 93–94
Zeller, D., 103n32, 122n139, 123n151, 124, 126, 131n213, 131n214, 135n237, 136n239, 143n271, 148–50
Ziesler, J., 126, 131n213
Zwemer, S. M., 94
Zwingli, U., 21

Biblical Reference Index

Genesis

	157
3:15	55
12:1–3	49n33, 52, 56n71, 88, 189
12:3	45, 53, 55, 90, 94, 148
15:6	138
15:18	180
21:12	88n259
22:2	xxiiin8
28:14–15	88n259
37	21n77

Exodus

4:22b	96
19:6	54

Numbers

15:17–21	158

Deuteronomy

	157
4:5–8	54
4:7–8	136n238
4:30–31	20n77, 80
6:4	54
7:6	54
7:6–7	52n48
11:26–28	90n276
18	152–53
30	136, 151
30:1–10	80
30:11	151
30:11–14	138
31:16	154
32	154
32:21	152–54
33:26–29	54

Joshua

2	54

Judges

2:1–3	55
Ruth	54, 120n131

1 Samuel

15:22	171

2 Samuel

6:6–7	xi
7:12–16	55

1 Kings

5	54
8:41–43	54
10–11	55
17	54
17:13	89

Biblical Reference Index

2 Kings

17	54

1 Chronicles

4:10	90n275
17:20	54

Psalms

	137
19:4	152
20:2	118
28:8	140n255
59:12	12
62:12–13	142n266
80:9–17	174n120
98:1–3	145n282
98:8–9	145n282
139:8	118
144:15	54
147:19–20	136n238

Ecclesiastes

10:1	144n280

Isaiah

	67n139, 165, 176
2:3	30
3:14	174n120
5:1–7	174n120
6	67
6:9–10	64, 66–67, 141n261
6:13	67
7:14	55
9:6	55
10:20	67
25:6–9	172
27:2–3	174n120
40:1–2	87n255
40:9	115n91, 173
41:4–6	165
42:6	53
45:17	176
48:12	165
49:5–6	61
49:6	54
52:7	152, 173
52:13—53:12	165n84
53	173
53:1–2	152
64:6	144n280
65:1	152
65:2	153
66:8	82n237

Jeremiah

2:21	174n120
5:10	174n120
6:9	174n120
8:13	174n120, 175n127
12:10	174n120
17:10	142n266
24:1–10	175
25:29	77, 141n263
31	28
31:31–33	56n70
31:31	49n34

Ezekiel

9:6–7	77
15:1–8	174n120
17:6–10	174n120
19:10–14	174n120
38:1–2	180
38:8–9	180
40:1—43:27	181

Daniel

	95n306
9	84
9:24–27	182
9:27	32, 180, 183

Hosea

3:4–5	21n77
5:12	21n77
5:15	21n77, 80n225
9:10	174n120
10:1	174n120

Amos

3:2	77n209, 141n263

Biblical Reference Index

Obadiah

54

Jonah

54

Micah

7:1 175n127

Nahum

54
2:1 152

Habakkuk

1:4 139n253
1:5-11 139
1:5 140
2:4 139
3:17 175n127

Zechariah

83n238
2:12 54
8:23 82n237
12:10 80, 180

Matthew

1:1 55
1:21 145, 173n115
2:2 138
3:2 81
4:17 81
5-7 102n28
5:21-48 143
5:45 148
5:47 122n141
6:7 122n141
6:24 167n93
6:33 75, 130
7:13-14 166
8 57
8:10-12 163n71
8:11-12 166
8:11 57n73

8:38 118n108
9:22 119n123
10 57-58
10:5-6 xxvi, 4, 56
11:28 8
13:2 138n249, 174n121
13:10-17 67n138
13:13-15 141n261
14:14 138n249
15:21-28 166n87
15:24 xxvi, 4, 34, 56
15:28 163n71
16:27 141
18:17 122n141
19:13—22:14 175
19:13-26 167n92
19:16-30 150n10
19:27—20:16 167-69
19:27-30 162n61, 167n90
19:28 168
19:30 134n227, 165
20:1-16 150n10, 167
20:8 168
20:10 18, 134n227
20:16 vi, 134n227, 165
20:20-28 167n92
20:27 166n89
21:1-9 174n121
21:12-17 142n267
21:18-22 163n74, 175n126
21:18-19 142n267
21:19 176
21:28-32 163n73, 170
21:31-32 172
21:33-46 142, 175n125
21:33-44 163n70, 174n117
21:31 167
21:33 81n228
21:43 74n193, 174
22:1-14 35, 163n69, 171n107
22:29 118n112
23:15 55
23:37-39 21n77, 81, 169
23:39 180
24 176n129
24:1-44 142n267
24:4-8 180
24:9 57n78

229

Biblical Reference Index

Matthew (cont.)

24:13	140n258
24:14	57n78, 184
24:32–33	176
25:1–13	166
25:14–30	142n267
25:32	57n78
27:22–23	174
27:25	5, 173
28:18–20	57, xxivn12
28:19–20	50, 57–58
28:19	xxvi, 4, 57, 194

Mark

4:12	141n261
4:28	74
5:34	119n123
6:21	174n119
6:35	167
7:27	4, 35, 56, 124
8:38	117
9:35	166
10:13—12:12	175
10:13–27	167n92
10:17–31	150n10
10:28–31	162n61, 167n90
10:31	134n227, 164–65
10:35–45	167n92
10:44	166n89
10:45	65
10:52	119n123
11:12–14	163n74, 175n126
11:13	175
11:14	176
11:20–25	163n74, 175n126
12:1–12	81n228, 163, 174n117
12:23–24	118n112
13	176n129
13:10	85
13:28–31	176n132
14:24	65
22–23	176n129

Luke

2:32	52n50
7:50	119n123
8:10	141n261
8:48	119n123
9:26	117
10:33–37	163n71
11:47–51	141n263
12:31	75n195, 75n196
12:48	10, 78n214
13	168
13:1–5	177
13:6–9	163n74, 175n126, 176–77
13:10–17	177
13:22–30	150n10, 166–67
13:28–30	162n61, 164
13:29	166
13:30	134n227, 165–66
14:7–11	166
14:11	166n89
14:16–24	163n69, 171n107
15:11–32	163n73, 170–71
16:13	167n93
16:31	144n278
17:19	119n123
17:21	81
18:15–27	167n92
18:18–30	150n10, 167n90
18:42	119n123
19:47	172, 174n119
20:9–19	81n228, 163n70, 174n117
21:23–24	20n77
21:24	40, 41n176, 81, 95, 164, 180, 185n176
21:29–33	176n132
22:20	49n34
22:24–27	167n92
22:24–30	168n100
24:25	168n97
24:46–48	59, 145n282
24:47	26, 59
24:49	39

John

3:3	51n46
3:16	94, 148n3
3:36	142n266
4:22	18, 31, 160
4:54	119n124
8:56	136n241
9:22	6
11:48	122n142

Biblical Reference Index

11:50	173n115
12:31	49n37
12:28–43	152n23
12:37–43	67n138
12:40	141n262
12:42	6n16
14:6	51n46
16:2	6n16
16:11	49n37
19:37	80

Acts

xxvi–xxvii, xxix, 5, 26, 58–70, 69, 96, 124n154, 126, 129n203

1:4	39
1:6	81
1:8	xxvii, 26, 39, 59, 66, 75, 94
1:22	55
2:17	179n151
2:32	55
2:5–22	60
3:17–26	81
3:17–18	173
3:19–21	169
3:25	65
3:26	58, 60–61, 124, 131
4:5–22	60n96
4:12	51n46
5:17	154n30
5:27–42	60n96
6:5	63n111
7:1–53	60n96
7:12	58
7:25	119
7:38	48n31
7:51–53	159n49
8	60
9:15–20	61–62
9:15–16	67n139
9:19b–20	66
9:23–30	154n30
10–11	60
10	63, 65
10:34	92n288
11:1–3	62–63
11:19	63
12:12	68n146
12:18	117n107
12:25	68n146
13:5	35
13:5–6	62
13:13–15	62
13:26	67
13:41	140
13:45	154n30
13:46—14:1	63–64
13:46	xxvii, 5, 26, 34, 39, 58, 63–64, 70, 97, 124, 127, 173, 189
13:47	52n50
13:50	174n119
14:1–7	154n30
14:1	63, 65n128
14:5	65n128
14:8–18	58
14:16	183
14:19	154n30
14:28	117n107
15:7	65
15:14	58, 65
15:16–18	65
15:37–39	68n146
16:11–13	62
17:1–2	64n115
17:4	117n107, 174n119
17:5	154n30
17:10	64n115
17:12	117n107
17:13–14	154n30
17:16–17	64n115
17:30	183
18:2	62n106, 101n19
18:6	63n113, 154n30
18:12–17	154n30
19:1–8	64n115
19:6	63n113
19:8–10	67
19:9	154n30
19:10	65n128
19:11	117n107
19:17	65n128
19:23–24	117n107
20:12	117n107
20:18	123n150
20:21	65–66
21:39	117n107
25:2	174n119

Acts (cont.)

26:19–20	65–66
26:20	58, 66, 123
27:20	117n107
28:1–10	58
28:2	117n107
28:7	174n119
28:16–17	64n115, 174n119
28:25b–28	64, 66–67, 159n49
28:26–27	67

Romans

	99–110
1:1–17	115
1:2	128
1:3	55
1:4	118n112
1:5–6	103
1:15	117n103
1:16–17	110–46
1:16	xxix, 1, 46, 57n74, 64n119, 71–76, 87, 89, 91n280, 110–37, 164
1:17	137–40
1:18–32	152n22
1:18	108
2:1–11	124
2:6–10	7
2:7–12	93n291
2:7	142n266
2:9–10	xxix, 7, 9, 11, 22n83, 76–78, 140–44, 190
2:9	9–10, 64n119, 77, 99, 131n212
2:10	12n47, 20
2:11	92n288, 93, 189
2:14–16	50n39
2:17–24	102n28, 143
2:17	122n143
2:28	xxxiv, 122n143
2:29	122n143
3–8	135
3	54, 99, 132, 134n223
3:1–4	122n139
3:1–2	77–78
3:1	34, 105n47, 122n143
3:2	9, 128n197, 131–37, 189
3:3	105n47
3:5	105n47
3:9–31	93n291
3:9	105n47, 129n201
3:27	105n47
4:1	105n47
4:3	136, 138
4:9–12	93n291
5:12	93n291
5:17–19	93n291
6:1	105n47
6:15	105n47
6:21	105n47
7:7	105n47
8:31	105n47
9–11	12, 36, 42, 76, 78–85, 96–97, 105, 146, 147–64, 183–86, 190
9	134n223
9:1–5	34
9:3	xxi, 148n4
9:4	xxxviii, 9, 136n238
9:4–5	51, 85, 128n197, 157
9:14	105n47
9:20	105n47
9:24	11, 12n47, 93n291
9:27	51n43
9:33	157
10:1	51, 61n101
10:4	120n126
10:5–21	151–53
10:5–13	151–52
10:9–21	79
10:12–13	93n291
10:14–21	152–53
10:14	150n14
10:15	115n91
10:18	79
10:19	154
11	xxxi, 11n45, 20, 49, 162, 169, 172–76, 179, 185n176
11:1	54, 151, 153
11:5	136, 157, 190
11:7–11	141
11:11–15	153–55, 163
11:11	79, 154–55, 168
11:12	25, 82, 96
11:13–14	61n99

Biblical Reference Index

11:14	27, 79, 154
11:15	51n43, 82
11:16	158, 157n40
11:17–24	168
11:18	122n139
11:23–32	158–61
11:23	172
11:24	85, 157
11:25–27	26, 42, 79
11:28–29	52
11:25–32	97, 161–63, 184
11:25	25, 79–80, 82, 157, 190
11:26	24, 164
11:28–29	56n70, 122n139
11:30–32	54, 93n291, 172
11:31	ix, xxi, 157n41, 160n51, 162
11:32	120
12–15	120
14	102n29
14:12	142n266
15:8	xxvii, 65, 69
15:8–9	143n276, 189
15:9–11	189
15:19	59n89
15:27	85–86
16	103
16:1–2	100
16:5	158
16:23	100

1 Corinthians

	33, 146n283
1:18	114, 118
1:21	51
1:22–24	122
1:23	20
1:24	122n147
3:4	116n96
4:5	144n281
6:14	118
9:20	128n199
10:18	xxxiii
11:18	132
10:32	76
12:28	135n235
14:11	118
15:1–9	116n95
15:15	165
16:15	158n45

2 Corinthians

3:14–15	159n49
3:15	141n262
5:10	144n281
8:5	75, 123n151
11:15	142n266
13:4	118

Galatians

	33
1:16b–17	66n131
2:7–9	xxvii, 61n99
2:9	68
2:14–15	122n139
2:15	172
3	139n253
3:8–9	94, 53, 90
3:8	136n240
3:28	92n288, 122n139, 129n201
6:16	xxxiv, 49n32, 160

Ephesians

1:11–12	143, 144n277
1:12	70n155
2:14–15	129n201
3:6	70
4:1–13	53n55
6:8	144n281

Philippians

	146n283
2:1–11	165
2:13	xiv
4:5	117n103

Colossians

1:21–23	116n95
3:11	122n139

1 Thessalonians

2:14–15	86
2:16	141

233

Biblical Reference Index

2 Thessalonians
1:6	141n260
1:11–12	53n55
2:3–11	184
2:13	158

1 Timothy
1:15	116n97
5:24–25	144n281

2 Timothy
1:8–9	53n55
1:8	117, 118n108
3:14–15	136n240
4:8	144n281
4:14	142n266

Hebrew
1:2	57n74
2:3	57n74
4:1–7	136n240
9:15–17	173n115
10:37–38	139n254
11:40	160n50

James
1:18	158n45

1 Peter
1:5	118
4:6	136n240
4:17	77, 141n263

2 Peter
1:10	53n55
3:9	85n247

3 John
7	122

Revelation
	82, 95n306
1:7	80
1:17	165
2:8	165
2:9	xxxiv
3:9	xxxiv
7:4–8	83–84
7:9–14	83
11:1–14	83
11:3–13	83
20	36, 179
20:1–10	183
20:1	184n174
21	49, 181
22:13	165

Subject Index

Abrahamic Covenant, cf. Covenant Advantage, 33n139, 39, 77–78, 121, 132–36, 143, 145–46, 174, 185, 190
American Board of Missions to the Jews, cf. CPM
Amillennialism, 183–85
Anti-Judaism, 5, 7, 13, 34n141, 40n168
Anti-Semitism, 3, 5, 7, 13, 17, 19, 21–23, 25n95, 38, 41–42, 50, 114n84, 155, 197
Arabs, xxviii, xxxvii, 66n132, 69n152, 72, 74, 92–95, 193

Barbican Mission to the Jews, cf. CWI
Barbarian, 8, 15–16, 103, 121–22

Call, xxxv, 22, 28n109, 35, 51–54, 61–62, 65, 73n187, 128n199, 139, 173, 194–95
Cape Town Commitment, 192–93
Catholicism, 2–3, 16–17, 37, 40, 47
China, 69, 90–91, 195
Chosen People Ministries or CPM, 46n19, 59n91, 89–90, 196, 198n18
Christian Witness to Israel or CWI, 89
Church Fathers, xxii, 4, 8–13, 111n76
Church-planting, 70

Circumcision, 63, 77, 80, 102, 122n143, 132, 134
Council of Javneh, 6
Covenant, xxviii–xxix, xxxviii, 6–9, 17, 23, 28, 42, 49, 51–54, 60, 65, 70, 73, 80, 127, 136, 137–39, 144, 148, 150–51, 154, 157n42, 162–63, 168, 170, 173, 180, 182–86, 188–90, 192
Crusades, 3, 14, 19

Debt of Christians to the Jewish People, 85–86, 188
Deicide and other accusations against Jews (child ritual murder, cannibalism, etc.), 3, 14, 40, 86
Destruction of Jerusalem, 6–7, 140–42, 176, 183
Diaspora, 22, 68–69
Direct Evangelism, xxviii
Dispensationalism, 23, 31–33, 35–36, 38, 81, 178–80, 190
Dual-Covenant Theology, cf. Two-Covenant Theology

Election, xxviii, 5, 35–36, 39, 50, 52–53, 56, 94, 125, 128n197, 141, 149, 161, 164, 192
Epistle of Barnabas, 7, 165
Eschatology, xxi, xxiii, xxix, 23, 36, 38, 48–49, 78–85, 95n306, 97, 137, 150–51, 162–63, 166, 170, 177–85, 190, 192

235

Subject Index

Essenes, 6
Evangelical(s), x, xxxi, xxxvii–xxxix, 2–3, 26, 38, 40–41, 44, 47–48, 51, 87, 191–92, 194
Evangelism Explosion mission, 71
Evangelization of the world by the Jewish People, 82–85, 150

Faith / Faithfulness, 110, 137–40, 144, 150
Fullness / Full number, 25–26, 42, 79, 80, 82, 160–61, 169, 183–85, 186, 190

God-fearer, xxxiii, 55, 67, 102–3, 148
Gospel / Good News, xxvi, xxxiv, 1–2, 45, 57, 59n89, 63, 65, 85, 91n284, 98, 115–18, 126, 136, 138, 144–46, 152–53, 168, 184, 190
Great Commission, xxiv, 50, 57n76, 57n77, 57n78

Holocaust, cf. Shoah

Impartiality of God, 92–93, 104
Inquisition, 14, 16–17
Israel / New Israel, xxxii–xxxiv
Israel's Need, 78, 150
Israel's Restoration or Revival or Conversion, 13–14, 17, 20, 24–29, 41–42, 49, 79–80, 82–84, 94, 150, 160–61, 163, 168–69, 171, 175–77, 182, 184, 186
Israel's Unbelief or Blindness or Hardening, xxiv, 25, 42, 67, 80, 97, 102, 157, 159–61, 163, 176, 184–85, 186

Jealousy, 27, 64, 79, 153–55, 157, 163, 197
Jesus Movement, 38, 40–41
Jewish People / Jewishness / Jews, xxxii–xxxiv
Judaism, xxxii–xxxiv, 5–6, 8, 12, 16, 23, 34, 85–86, 111n71, 128, 141

Judgment, 6–8, 34, 67, 77–78, 107, 133, 140–43, 165, 170, 176–77, 181, 185, 190
Justice, cf. Righteousness

Kosher laws, 102n28

Land of Israel, xxxn28, 29, 32, 41, 52, 68, 80, 94–95, 148n2, 161n55, 175–76, 180–82
Lausanne Congress on World Evangelism, xxxvi, 38n157, 44, 87n253
Lausanne Consultation on Jewish Evangelism, xxviin14, xxxv–xxxvii, 48
Lausanne Movement, xxxiv, xxxvi–xxxvii, 49
Law, xxxiii, 5, 8–9, 12–13, 16–17, 35, 51n46, 77, 90, 101–2, 106, 117n101, 136n238, 136n240, 139, 142–46, 148, 153, 171, 173, 189
London Society for Promoting Christianity amongst the Jews, x, 27–31, 36, 178

Marcion, 4, 7n25, 34n141, 110–12
Messianic Jews, xxi, xxxvii, 41, 45n12, 56, 69, 79, 82, 86, 89n265, 151, 178, 182
Millennium, 49, 180–85
Missiology, x, xxii–xxiii, xxix, xxxivn51, 72, 151, 192–98
Mission statement, xxviii, 48, 189
(Post-)Modernity, 23, 39, 41
Money, 29, 86, 89–90, 194, 196
Monotheism, 5
Moody Bible Institute, 31n127, 46n19, 91, 179

Nations, xxvi, xxxiii, xxxvii, 4, 11, 19, 25, 29, 38, 41, 45, 49–54, 57–60, 64, 74n193, 77–80, 85, 90, 103, 122–23, 136, 139–40, 142, 145, 160, 169, 181–82, 184–86, 189, 194, 196–97

236

Subject Index

New and Old Perspectives, xxxviii, 102n28, 191

One issue mission, xxviii–xxix

Parting of the ways, 5–8, 42
Pentecost, 5, 58–60
Persecution, 1, 6, 13, 16–17, 19, 23–25, 42, 63, 86–87, 93, 102, 188
Prayer, x, 6, 26, 69n150, 89–90, 101, 129n203, 129n205, 155, 194, 196
Presuppositions, xxxix
Proselyte, xxxiii, 55, 60, 63n111, 102, 120n131, 128, 148
Prosperity Gospel, 90
Philo-Semitism, 3, 50n39, 88
Pietism, 23, 26–28, 36, 188
Postmillennialism, 81
Power of God, 108, 112–19
Premillennialism, 32, 41, 81, 178–79, 190
Puritanism, 23–26, 36

Reformation, xxxiii, xxxix, 19–23, 42, 191
Remnant, 50n39, 51, 54, 56, 67, 79, 136, 157–61, 164, 169, 175, 182, 184, 190

Replacement theology, cf. Supersessionism
Reverse Eschatological Priority, 166, 190, 192
Righteousness of God, 8–9, 19, 75, 104–5, 110, 113, 130, 132–33, 137–38

Sabbath, 17, 62, 85, 102n28
Sadducees, 6
Shoah, xxiii–xxiv, 3, 23, 36–41, 45n7, 73, 79, 87, 192, 195
Speech-Act Theory, xxxviii, xxxixn69
Supersessionism, 49, 56, 72, 101n21

Talmud, 13–14, 16–18
Temple, xxxiv, 5–7, 51n46, 54, 77, 121, 141–42, 176–77, 180–81, 183
Time of the Gentiles, 180, 184, 186
Tübingen School, 23, 33–34
Two-Covenant Theology, xxxix, 51, 72–73, 161n57, 192

Universalism, xxxix, 37, 51–52, 72–73, 126
Unreached peoples, 169, 192–95
Wrath of God, 107, 110, 138, 141–44

Zealots, 6
Zionism, 3, 23, 34–36, 40–41

237

www.ingramcontent.com/pod-product-compliance
Lightning Source LLC
Chambersburg PA
CBHW071246230426
43668CB00011B/1614